Democracy Rising

D1715893

Civil Rights and the Struggle for Black Equality
in the Twentieth Century

SERIES EDITORS

Steven F. Lawson, Rutgers University
Cynthia Griggs Fleming, University of Tennessee

Democracy Rising

South Carolina and the Fight for Black Equality Since 1865

PETER F. LAU

THE UNIVERSITY PRESS OF KENTUCKY

Publication of this volume was made possible in part by a grant
from the National Endowment for the Humanities.

Editorial and Sales Offices: The University Press of Kentucky
663 South Limestone Street, Lexington, Kentucky 40508-4008
www.kentuckypress.com

10 09 08 07 06   5 4 3 2 1

Portions of the essay "From the Periphery to the Center: Clarendon County, South Carolina,
Brown, and the Struggle for Democracy and Equality in America," in *From the Grassroots to the
Supreme Court:* Brown v. Board of Education *and American Democracy*, edited by Peter F. Lau
(Durham: Duke University Press, 2004), are reprinted courtesy of Duke University Press.

Library of Congress Cataloging-in-Publication Data

Lau, Peter F., 1971-
  Democracy rising : South Carolina and the fight for Black equality since
1865 / by Peter F. Lau.
     p. cm. — (Civil rights and the struggle for Black equality in the twentieth century)
  Includes bibliographical references and index.
  ISBN-13: 978-0-8131-2393-6 (hardcover : alk. paper)
  ISBN-10: 0-8131-2393-3 (hardcover : alk. paper)
    1. African Americans—Civil rights—South Carolina—History—20th century. 2. South
Carolina—Race relations—History—20th century. 3. Civil rights movements—South
Carolina—History—20th century. 4. South Carolina—Politics and government—1865-1950.
5. South Carolina—Politics and government—1951- I. Title. II. Series.
  E185.93.S7L38 2006
  323.1196'073009757--dc22   2005031051

This book is printed on acid-free recycled paper meeting the requirements of the American
National Standard for Permanence in Paper for Printed Library Materials.

Manufactured in the United States of America.

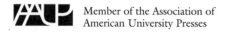   Member of the Association of
American University Presses

For Sophie

Contents

Acknowledgments   ix

Introduction:
   The Politics of Civil Rights Struggle   1

1 Segregation and Self-Determination:
   The Making of the NAACP   15

2 Riot and Reaction:
   The Lineaments of Reinvention   49

3 Radicalism and Liberal Reform:
   The NAACP during the New Deal   71

4 Civil Rights and Collective Action:
   The Battle for Black Empowerment   107

5 Popular Fronts:
   From New Deal Coalition to Black Rights Revolution   145

6 Cold War Civil Rights:
   Brown v. Board of Education and the Emerging Power
   of the Periphery   187

Conclusion:
   Movement, Memory, and American Democracy   215

Notes   233

Bibliography   283

Index   317

Illustrations follow page 144

Acknowledgments

The intellectual, personal, and financial debts accumulated during the production of this book are deep and can never be repaid adequately. Nevertheless, I would be remiss not to take this opportunity to give thanks to all those who helped make this book possible and who helped me tell a better story about a human struggle that has shaped the American democratic experiment so profoundly.

My hope is that *Democracy Rising* stands as a living testament to the men and women who gave much of their lives in the struggle for a more democratic world. The willingness of movement participants and their families to donate personal papers to libraries and to share their stories with scholars never ceases to amaze me, even though I am convinced that the generous spirit of the movement continues to reside in our present-day world in ways both large and small. James E. Jackson Jr. and Esther Cooper Jackson graciously contributed oral histories, personal papers, and photographs to this project. Alfred D. Byrd, the son of Levi G. Byrd (a key movement leader in the story to follow), not only invited me to his home in Hampton, Virginia, but also provided me with recollections, papers, and rare family photographs that allowed me to provide a more full accounting of the South Carolina movement and its relationship to the National Association for the Advancement of Colored People (NAACP). J.A. DeLaine Jr. and B.B. DeLaine shared their memories, family papers, and expert knowledge of Clarendon County and their father's role in South Carolina's contribution to *Brown v. Board of Education*. Dorothy Burnham, Bernice S. Robinson, and A.J. Whittenberg also supported my research efforts and helped ensure the fullness of the human dimension of the history I tell. The treasure trove of oral histories compiled in Duke University's "Behind the Veil" documentary collection furthered my efforts to make movement participants a central part of this historical narrative. Blair L.M. Kelley, a good friend and scholar, personally recorded a number of the oral histories I drew upon and guided me through the Behind the Veil collection.

Cecil J. Williams of Orangeburg, South Carolina, and his photographs of the struggle for black equality in South Carolina during the 1950s and 1960s proved an inspiration to me. A number of his photos are included in this book, and one of my favorite images from his collection graces the cover. Williams was one of a handful of black photographers covering the civil movement before the nation recognized it as a movement, and for years he has argued that South Carolina should be considered at the center of the movement's history. During my research I was fortunate enough to collect a number of movement photographs from the 1940s, many of them taken by another black South Carolinian, E.C. Jones. Jones, I later learned, was Cecil Williams's mentor and the two men worked together to publicize movement activities across the Palmetto State, often at the request of NAACP officials. Their photographs included in *Democracy Rising* bridge the years 1940–1970 and demonstrate the generational links so crucial to the ongoing nature of the movement.

Without the support of numerous librarians, archivists, universities, and institutes, this book could not have been written. Thanks are owed to the staffs at the Avery Research Center at the College of Charleston, the South Caroliniana Library and Modern Political Collections at the University of South Carolina, especially Beth Bilderback and Henry Fulmer, who each went above and beyond the call of duty to facilitate my research efforts, the James B. Duke Library at Furman University, the Schomburg Center for Research and Black Culture in New York City, the Manuscript Division at the Library of Congress, the Moorland-Spingarn Research Center at Howard University, the National Archives, the Rockefeller Archives in Sleepy Hollow, New York, the Rare Book, Manuscript, and Special Collections Library at Duke University, and the Miller F. Whittaker Library at South Carolina State University. Institutional and financial assistance were provided by Rutgers University, the Institute for Southern Studies at the University of South Carolina, where Walter Edgar and Tom Brown proved generous supporters, the John Hope Franklin Center for African and African American Documentation at Duke University, and the Avery Research Center for African American History and Culture at the College of Charleston.

Personally and intellectually I have benefited from a remarkable group of scholars dating back to my undergraduate years at the University of Virginia. Julian Bond and Patricia Sullivan piqued my interest in the southern civil rights movement. During the fall of 1994, I began working with Pat and Waldo E. Martin Jr. on a National Endowment for the Humanities-funded "Teaching the History of the Southern Civil Rights Movement" institute at Harvard University's W.E.B. Du Bois Institute. Pat and Waldo's friendship and scholarship have shaped my thinking and scholarship ever since. Before scholars started writing about a "long civil rights movement," Pat and Waldo were teaching scholars how to teach the movement as an ongoing and ceaseless campaign to reshape notions of freedom and the practice of democracy. At the University of Massachusetts, Amherst, Kevin Boyle, John Bracey, John Higginson, Carl Nightengale, and Manisha Sinha supported my efforts and guided my scholarly course. Chapter Five of *Democracy Rising* began in Kevin's seminar and his questions about the relationship of African American history to the history of American liberalism have continued to guide my thoughts and inquiries.

At Rutgers University I was fortunate to be surrounded by a wonderful group of graduate students and colleagues. William Jelani Cobb, Gary Darden, Sara Dubow, Justin Hart, Tiffany Gill, Sarah Gordon, Matthew Guterl, Dan Katz, Amrita Meyers, Khalil Muhammad, Rob Nelson, Jennifer Pettit, Kelena Reid, and Stephanie Simms Wright proved good friends and welcome critics. Sara, Justin, Gary, and I met regularly during the fall of 1999 with our colleague and dissertation committee member James Livingston to explore historical philosophy and the relationship between narrative form and historical knowledge. Our kitchen-table seminars in Jim's home prodded deep thinking and influenced the writing of this book in ways not always perceptible in the notes. In meetings of the Black Atlantic fellows program, in the classroom, and in numerous conversations, I benefited immensely from the thoughts and work of Mia Bay, Herman Bennett, Carolyn Brown, Will Jones, and Jennifer Morgan.

It goes without saying that my dissertation committee at Rutgers, Steven Lawson, David Levering Lewis, James Livingston, Mark Naison, and Deborah Gray White, shaped the contents of this book from beginning to end. Collectively, I am indebted to their pioneering scholarship and their laserlike critiques of my work. Their generous advice made turning my dissertation into a book a painless and enjoyable endeavor. David Levering Lewis and Steven Lawson continued to play major roles in the revision process beyond my time at Rutgers. As friends and mentors, both men have provided me with insight, advice, criticism, and support well in excess of any that could be reasonably expected from graduate school advisors. Not only has Steven read and reread every chapter of *Democracy Rising*, but his call to write a truly interactive history of the civil rights movement and the depth of his work in the field of civil rights studies inspire my work in the field. I continue to be awed by the scope and elegance of David's scholarship and the graciousness with which he has taken on my scholarly and professional pursuits. His exhaustive research and erudite prose are the standard by which all scholarship must be measured and a substantial source of my own scholarly humility.

In addition to shaping my scholarship, Steven guided me to The University Press of Kentucky under the able direction of Steve Wrinn. My experience working with Steve and his staff has been wonderful. Anonymous readers provided me with insightful critiques that helped give final shape to the book. Nichole Lainhart, Robin Roenker, and Anne Dean Watkins kept the publication process moving and saved me from numerous errors of form and content. While any errors that remain are my responsibility alone, Steve and his staff share credit for the look, feel, and substance of this book, which has been a pleasure for me to create with their guidance and expertise.

To friends and family I owe a debt of gratitude as well. Lara Smith and Blair L.M. Kelley were sounding boards for my work as we began our scholarly careers. Jack McKenzie, Brian Clark, and Jennie and Marc Carruth provided me with friendship and places to stay during my research trips. At Lincoln School, Rich Canedo provided me with valued library resources and Amy Jenson helped me preserve photographs on digital files. My sister, Kristen Lau Gest, took time from her legal career to track down contact information of potential interviewees, as well as crucial legal documents. My in-laws, Richard and Mary Glenn, have proved steadfast supporters of me, and more importantly my family. My own parents, Stephen and Bonnie Lau, deserve their own chapter full of thanks. They instilled in me a love of learning and sense of justice and fair play that inform all that I am and do. Their love and support anchor all my life's endeavors. Although I will never be able to thank them fully, this book is a small token of my boundless appreciation.

Lastly, this book is the product of the life I live together with my spouse, Sophie Glenn Lau. We met in graduate school and now share two beautiful children, Emmie and Thompson. This book is inconceivable in her absence and the creation of it involves her labor as well as mine. When I began graduate school, I had a very different sense of time and love than I do today. I have grown to revel in the twists and turns and complexity of each, in large measure because I have shared the last decade with a woman of great intellect, strength, and grace. Sophie has filled my life with immeasurable love and joy. For that reason and many more, I dedicate this book to her.

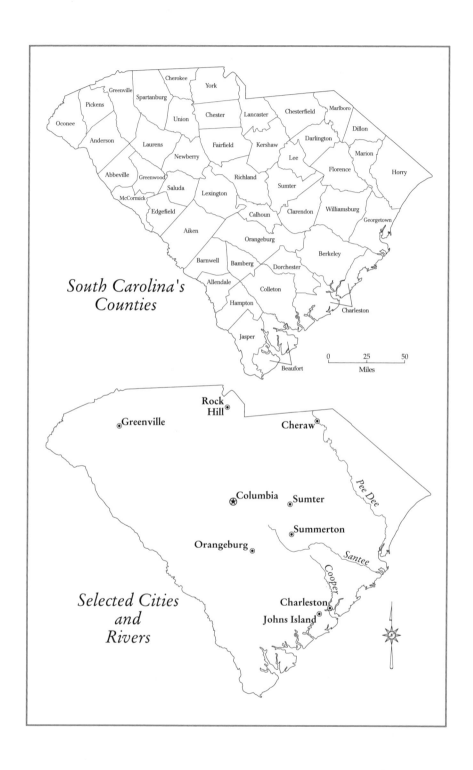

South Carolina's
Counties

Cherokee
York
Greenville
Spartanburg
Pickens
Union
Chester
Lancaster
Chesterfield
Marlboro
Oconee
Anderson
Laurens
Fairfield
Kershaw
Darlington
Dillon
Newberry
Lee
Marion
Abbeville
Greenwood
Richland
Sumter
Florence
Horry
Saluda
Lexington
McCormick
Edgefield
Calhoun
Clarendon
Williamsburg
Georgetown
Aiken
Orangeburg
Berkeley
Barnwell
Bamberg
Dorchester
Allendale
Colleton
Charleston
Hampton
Jasper
Beaufort

0   25   50
Miles

Selected Cities
and
Rivers

Rock Hill
Greenville
Cheraw
Pee Dee
Columbia
Sumter
Summerton
Orangeburg
Santee
Cooper
Charleston
Johns Island

Introduction

The Politics of Civil Rights Struggle

This book is a history of the African American struggle for civil rights in South Carolina and the United States from Reconstruction through the decade following *Brown v. Board of Education* (1954), the landmark U.S. Supreme Court ruling that smashed the legal underpinnings of Jim Crow segregation. As the scholarship concerned with the origins and impact of the civil rights revolution of the 1950s and 1960s has amply shown, the African American struggle for civil rights was and continues to be one of the most important reform movements in the history of the United States.[1] However, the search for the movement's precise origins and its impact on American life continues to be elusive. The problem is that the search for the origins of the movement and its broader significance coexist in uneasy tension; the search for the former keeps obscuring the latter. Although *Democracy Rising* explores institutional beginnings and utilizes key legal victories as signposts to guide its narrative course, it dispenses with the quest to locate the origins of the African American struggle for civil rights in a particular moment in the historical past. Its central insight is that the African American struggle for civil rights cannot be adequately comprehended as an event with a discrete beginning and ending. It was and continues to be a movement in the fullest sense of the term—a movement of people, institutions, and ideas bending and stretching the meaning and practice of democracy in America. From Edmund Morgan's notion that the idea of American freedom was a product of racial slavery, to David Roediger's insistence that the white working class and industrial capitalism were constituted through an embrace and rejection of blackness, historians have powerfully argued that American

1

democracy, and the very idea of America, have been the products, in part, of the tension borne of the nation's history of racial slavery, exclusion, and discrimination. As this book demonstrates, the African American civil rights movement was about many things. But its broadest significance rests in its relationship to a much larger and ongoing struggle on the part of African Americans and their allies to redefine the contours and meaning of democracy in America—that is, to make the realization of self-determination and equality the acid test of the nation's democratic promise.[2]

By emphasizing the ongoing nature of the black struggle for civil rights and the centrality of black demands for self-determination and a refashioning of American democracy to that struggle, this book joins a growing body of civil rights scholarship, much of it concerned with the urban North. More typically associated with the Black Power movement of the late 1960s, self-determination—the capacity to shape one's life and community in accordance with one's sense of its possibilities—has animated the struggles of black people in America across time and space. By necessity, the achievement of a greater measure of self-determination in the face of racial enslavement, Jim Crow, and urban isolation has required the vigilant and simultaneous pursuit of social, political, and economic justice. Civil rights, defined as the rights guaranteed by the U.S. Constitution, especially those articulated in the Thirteenth, Fourteenth, and Fifteenth Amendments, have been a central demand among African Americans, precisely because the possession of civil rights has been understood as a crucial means to full participation in the shaping of their individual lives and communities, as well as the nation and larger world. Seldom have African Americans waged a struggle for civil rights in the absence of broader calls for social and economic justice. To the contrary, African Americans have consistently linked the possession of civil rights to a transformation of American democratic theory and practice, including the distribution of economic opportunity and resources.[3]

There are few better venues for exploring the full meaning of the African American struggle for civil rights and its relationship to democracy in America than South Carolina. Well-developed historiographies of slavery and Reconstruction in the Palmetto State attest to the ways in which racial slavery, exclusion, and discrimination have subjected black people to unthinkable horrors and simultaneously inspired some of the nation's grandest visions of and battles for an expansive conception of freedom and democracy. During the antebellum era South Carolina slaveholders and political officials were key leaders of a transatlantic backlash to the full implications of the Age of Revolution. From the Nullification Crisis of 1828–1834, to efforts to reopen the African slave trade in the 1850s, to the movement for southern secession in 1860, South Carolina's planter politicians rebelled against the rise of the modern world and questioned the very "ideals of universal liberty, equality, and democracy." On the other hand, virtually from the moment Confederate forces fired on Fort Sumter in April 1861, black South Carolinians seized upon the opportunity presented by the Civil War and the onset of Reconstruction to express and agitate for an expansive vision of freedom rooted in the experience of slavery, but altered to meet the new circumstances brought on by its institutional destruction. Formerly enslaved black people insisted on the right to control their own bodies and those of their offspring. They wanted protection against arbitrary violence and the right to just compensation for their labor, if not the entire fruits of it. More than merely a vision of slavery's negation, the former slaves sought to institutionalize or preserve those aspects of their lives that they had worked so hard in slavery to develop, including marriages, networks of family and friends, and slavery's "invisible institution," the black church. To achieve this vision of freedom, black South Carolinians sought political rights, education, and the redistribution of their former masters' land. Taken together, political rights, education, and land redistribution were part of a larger quest for what Julie Saville has called a "redistribution of social power." Above all, what the former slaves wanted was the right and the tools necessary to be self-determining, to be full agents in the making of their own and the broader community's collective future.[4]

Reconstruction was, as Eric Foner has definitively argued, a world-revolutionary event. The Thirteenth, Fourteenth, and Fifteenth Amendments to the U.S. Constitution abolished the institution of slavery, mandated national birthright citizenship, guaranteed the right of due process to all persons, and established the right of suffrage without regard to race, in effect, repudiating the notion of America as a white nation and launching a unique experiment in interracial democracy.[5] With black people as full participants, the state of South Carolina experienced the lengthiest and one of the most thoroughgoing Reconstruction experiments. Between 1867 and 1876 more than half of the 487 elected state and federal officials from the Palmetto State were African American. Through Union Leagues, black churches, informal community gatherings, and the Republican Party, African Americans formed a cross-class coalition of former slaves, black and white men from the North, and members of South Carolina's freeborn elite, many with familial ties to the state's planter aristocracy. Although black women were formally excluded from voting they remained crucial participants in the political process itself. To be sure, South Carolina's black Republican majority was internally variegated and, as Thomas Holt has argued, social and class cleavages among black South Carolinians would play a key role in the undoing of the Republican Party's hold on political power by the mid-1870s. But for a period of ten years, faced with the daunting task of remaking the state of South Carolina in the aftermath of slavery's destruction and the devastation of war, black South Carolinians pieced together a potent political coalition and presided over a democratization of the state's political process. In doing so, they helped establish the state's first state-funded public school system, legalized divorce, passed laws requiring equal treatment in all places of public accommodation, created publicly funded healthcare for the poor, and worked to write contract laws in favor of agricultural laborers. Indeed, only a sustained decades-long campaign of political and violent extra-legal opposition from the overlapping forces of the white Democratic Party and the Ku Klux Klan finally smashed the state's black-led Republican majority, began the process of securing white male domination of the state's political decision-making process, and created the political climate necessary for the legalization of white supremacy in the form of Jim Crow segregation.[6]

In turning back the revolutionary implications of Reconstruction and fighting to restore white supremacy as a legal and social fact of life in South Carolina, the state's white supremacist leadership, along with its counterpart in Mississippi, was unsurpassed. Although violence had been a featured component of everyday life during Reconstruction, by 1874 white rifle clubs had begun stepping up what amounted to an organized campaign of violence intended to destabilize the Republican Party and restore white domination of the state's political process. On July 8, 1876, members of various white rifle clubs, many of them under the command of former Confederate Gen. Matthew Butler, seized on events surrounding a seemingly minor racial skirmish in the town of Hamburg to seal the fate of the Reconstruction experiment that hung in the balance of that fall's statewide and national elections. Located just over the Savannah River from Augusta, Georgia, in the westernmost stretch of South Carolina, the small town of Hamburg was a black Republican Party stronghold. On July 4 the recently reorganized black-led militia had been marching in celebration of the nation's centennial when a buggy driven by two white men on a public road near the plantation of a prominent white family approached. Although the militia ultimately allowed the buggy to pass, its initial refusal to do so set off a chain of events that led to what became known as the Hamburg Massacre. In response to the Independence Day confrontation, white rifle clubs from throughout the area, including a young Benjamin Tillman's Sweetwater Sabre Club, descended on Hamburg on the eighth, donned red shirts, besieged the black militia men in a local armory, captured as many as forty men, proceeded to execute at least five, and then ransacked black homes and businesses. The event, historian Stephen Kantrowitz has noted, "became one of Tillman's proudest memories." Its short-term effect was to rally white South Carolinians under the banner of the Democratic Party, the party of white supremacy, to destabilize an already fragile Republican Party, and to virtually ensure that a coalition of white and black moderates could not form a "fusion" ticket that might thwart the efforts of white Democrats to seize power in the impending elections. Indeed, under the leadership of Confederate war hero Gen. Wade Hampton, the Democratic Party was restored to power in that fall's hotly contested and wholly corrupt elections. At noon on April 10, 1877, as part of the Faustian bargain brokered by national Republican Party leadership to secure the presidency for Rutherford B. Hayes, U.S. soldiers marched out of the South Carolina State House in Columbia. Following behind them was the moderate Republican governor, Daniel Chamberlain. And with that, Reconstruction was no more.[7]

The formal end of Reconstruction did not, however, simply usher in the era of Jim Crow and near total white domination of life in the state. But the withdrawal of federal troops and an embattled and increasingly fractured Republican Party more than opened enough room for South Carolina's white political leadership to begin crafting the law, article by article, bill by bill, to secure the formal exclusion of African Americans from participation in the political process and to ensure black subordination in the broader life of the state and nation. The road to black disfranchisement and Jim Crow segregation would take better than twenty years to accomplish, but the state legislature commenced a concerted legislative campaign to disfranchise the state's African American population beginning in 1882. That year the legislature moved to tighten voter registration regulations and pioneered the "Eight Box Law" designed to confuse and intimidate black voters by requiring them to match individual ballots with appropriately labeled boxes. By allowing governor-appointed election officials to assist any voter who requested assistance, the law effectively targeted black voters and the Republican vote was cut by more than half by 1884. As black votes continued to decline under the crush of new suffrage restriction, fraud, and intimidation, the state's white political officials called for a constitutional convention to finish the job already underway. In November 1895, convention delegates met in Columbia and rewrote the state constitution to disfranchise the state's African American population. Strict residency requirements, the poll tax, and the literacy test were written into law. To ensure the effectiveness of the measures, delegates placed the power to determine who qualified for the right to vote in the hands of local registrars, who were empowered by a provision of the literacy test, known as the "understanding clause," to determine who was fit to vote and who was not. Within a year, the state Democratic Party restricted participation in its primary to whites only, a move that combined with the new registration restrictions effectively eliminated African Americans from meaningful participation in the political life of the state.[8]

Aided by black disfranchisement, legalized white supremacy in the form of Jim Crow segregation began to emerge in force after 1896, the year that the U.S. Supreme Court gave legal sanction to the doctrine of "separate but equal" in *Plessy v. Ferguson*. In 1897 Charleston's new electric streetcars were segregated, and the state legislature passed laws segregating railroad coaches, trolleys, and finally textile mills in the years that followed. Soon, a combination of state and local ordinances gave shape to a world in which everyday life was marked indelibly with visible reminders of black subordination and white supremacy. From streetcars, to water fountains, to stairways, to public parks, to schools, segregation became more than ritualized custom; it became the law. For black and white South Carolinians, however, legalized segregation proved only one measure of the pattern of racial separation and black subordination that was emerging in full force at the turn of the century. Indeed, twenty-two years after the Hamburg Massacre, the Phoenix Riot of 1898 announced that the unfolding terms of legalized white supremacy would be maintained by any means necessary. Two days before white Democrats overthrew the "fusion" government in Wilmington, North Carolina, in a bloody race riot, white vigilantes in Greenwood County, South Carolina, forcefully challenged the efforts of the white Republican Tolbert family to encourage the region's black residents to vote in that fall's election. What began as an altercation at a polling place in the town of Phoenix rapidly devolved into widespread gunfire and bloodshed. For a period of several days, some three hundred armed white men from nearby Edgefield, Newberry, and Abbeville joined with men from Greenwood and roamed the countryside, seeking out, torturing, and then murdering those they deemed Republican activists. At least twelve black people lost their lives at the hands of their white pursuers and at least one black church was ransacked. Although black people resisted the vigilante assault with all means at their disposal, in the wake of the "riot" hundreds of black people boarded trains and took to the roads in a hurried effort to escape the violence-torn region.[9]

The system of racial subordination that emerged in South Carolina at the turn of the twentieth century was exceptional only to the extent that it represented the cutting edge of a violent system of racial subordination that would vary from town to town, county to county, and state to state, across the South. To be sure, in the same way that South Carolina's white political officials once led the antebellum South in the politics of reaction and white supremacy, the Palmetto State would prove a leader of racist reaction in the twentieth century as well. And in much the same way that black South Carolinians found ways to withstand the crushing force of racial enslavement and lead the state of South Carolina in one of the world's first experiments with interracial democracy, so too would black South Carolinians lead the battle against white supremacy and for an expansive conception of democracy in the twentieth century. Indeed, as this book demonstrates, the struggles of these two centuries were very much of a piece. While white supremacy was never something fixed in time, as scholars have argued so effectively in recent years, black South Carolinians continually fought to challenge each and every manifestation of it. If white supremacy was less than a continuous force in the life of the South, if its peaks and valleys may be carefully historicized, it was the ongoing struggle of African Americans to resist its most deleterious effects and to destabilize its hold on the life of the South and the nation that kept white supremacy on the run.[10]

But the struggles of black South Carolinians were never merely about resistance to white supremacy and cannot be reduced to a battle against the institution of slavery, or against Jim Crow, or against the institution of white supremacy itself. Over the past twenty years, the growth of local and state studies in the field of civil rights history, along with the sometimes parallel and sometimes overlapping fields of African American women's history and black migration, have powerfully suggested the impossibility of understanding the battles waged by African Americans against white oppression in the absence of a thorough knowledge of the internal dynamics and continually shifting boundaries of black communities. This book takes this insight seriously and represents an effort to demonstrate the inseparability of African American social history from the study of civil rights and democracy in the United States. Put another way, a critical engagement with African American social history is crucial for understanding American political history. *Democracy Rising* is, in part, a collection of local studies that explore the ways in which African Americans struggled for survival, built and sustained local institutions, negotiated the terms of community, and battled for self-determination. From the South Carolina piedmont and the sandhills of the Pee Dee region, to the black belt and the low country, to the urban centers of Columbia and Charleston, this book examines the ways in which the individual and social identities of African Americans, including race, gender, class, and region, gave shape to local communities and, in turn, gave shape to a broader trans-local and finally national black movement for civil rights. Its central argument is that the local, the national, and international are inseparable from one another, the one unintelligible without the other. Indeed, the struggle for civil rights in South Carolina is incomprehensible in the absence of an analysis of the *movement* of people, institutions, and ideas across real and imagined boundaries of geography and social identity.[11]

At the center of the argument for the inseparability of the local and the national, of the social and the political, is a history of the National Association for the Advancement of Colored People (NAACP). The association was formally organized in 1910 in the wake of the 1908 Springfield, Illinois, race riot by a band of progressive white

men and women and a handful of African Americans, including the
Harvard-trained intellectual and outspoken critic of Booker T. Washington, W.E.B. Du Bois; the founder of the National Association of
Colored Women (NACW), Mary Church Terrell; and the antilynching crusader Ida B. Wells-Barnett. Some of its leading white members,
such as Mary White Ovington and William English Walling, were Socialists; others like Oswald Garrison Villard were direct descendents
of nineteenth-century abolitionists; others such as Lillian Wald and
Jane Addams hailed from the ranks of the trade union and settlement house movements; still others, such as Florence Kelley and John
Dewey, were leading lights of feminism and pragmatism. Created as
the modern large-scale corporation was fast becoming a central fea-
ture of American life, as the size and scope of the federal government
rapidly expanded to meet the growing needs of a modern society,
as Jim Crow tightened its grip in the South, and as racial violence
increasingly knew no regional boundary, the NAACP was organized
with the single-minded goal, as John Bracey and August Meier have
explained, of securing the rights of citizenship for African Americans
as guaranteed by the Fourteenth and Fifteenth Amendments of the
U.S. Constitution. Top-down, legalistic, and bureaucratic (i.e., corporate) by design, the NAACP was formed to win civil rights *for* African
Americans by waging battle within and through the very institutions
it sought to transform. If large-scale corporations, expanding federal
government bureaucracies, and the wholesale denial of African Ameri
cans' rights to participate in the growing array of public and private institutions governing their lives set the terms of the battle to be waged,
then the NAACP sought to meet the challenge head on. The problem
that the white leaders of the association confronted, however, virtually from the moment of the organization's creation, was that winning
civil rights *for* black people was practically a contradiction in terms.
For African Americans within the organization and for the many who
would later join its branches, the struggle for civil rights was very
much about a struggle for self-determination, for the right to possess the necessary tools to craft their own lives and the world around
them in a manner commensurate with their imagined capacities for
both. Although this struggle never precluded interracial alliances,
and over the long run it required them, black people would have to
become leaders in their own right, leaders of their own quest for liberation, for civil rights to have meaning. Civil rights, in other words,

had to be achieved in a way that was consistent with their intended purposes.[12]

The pages that follow are in substantial measure a history of the ways in which the NAACP was transformed from a top-down, bureaucratic, largely white, and board-dominated organization to a mass organization funded by, led by, and responsive to the needs of African Americans across lines of class, gender, and region between 1917 and 1955. In those years the NAACP became the most important organization representing the interests of African Americans in South Carolina and the United States. And with black South Carolinians in the lead, the NAACP led a region-wide and national campaign to smash the white primary, secure quality education for black children, and challenge the legal and cultural moorings of Jim Crow segregation. Although the association is much maligned by contemporaries and present-day historians for its hierarchical, bureaucratic, and legalistic approach to winning full citizenship for African Americans, its story is far more complicated. Most significantly this study argues that there was never a single NAACP. Rather, as Charles Houston, the architect of the NAACP's legal strategy, put it in 1933, there were many NAACPs. There was the NAACP of the national office that concerned itself "with matters of national and state importance" and then there was the NAACP of the branches with "as many local programs as there are local branches." The key, then, to understanding the organization is to begin understanding the relationship *between* the national and the local. Over the course of a forty-year period the lines of power and influence ran both ways, from the national to the local, and the local to the national; the national office shaped the lives and struggles of black South Carolinians and black South Carolinians, in turn, shaped the tenor and agenda of the national organization. When branches grew in number and strength, the national organization proved flexible and accommodating to local concerns. When branches dwindled in size and local leadership failed to sustain grassroots support, often in the face of economic turmoil and racist violence, the national office proved more autocratic and rigid. The logic of the organization was, in other words, democratic to its core. Power, of course, was never even. As individuals, leaders from James Weldon Johnson, to Walter White, to Thurgood Marshall, to Roy Wilkins, by virtue of their national platform and their ability to direct human and financial resources, wielded disproportionate power within the organization.

But as its national leaders would learn, and in some cases refuse to learn, the organization could succeed only to the extent to which its branches wielded power and influence in the organization. Its central mission, securing the full citizenship rights of African Americans, could not succeed without a strong base of support in African American communities.

But this book is more than a history of the NAACP. It is every bit as importantly a history of the ways in which African Americans struggled for civil rights and how they invested meaning in that struggle. In recent years it has become a virtual truism that while the civil rights movement of the 1950s and 1960s defeated the legal edifice of Jim Crow it failed to address the seemingly more intractable economic problems faced by African Americans and the nation at large. "As Martin Luther King pointed out," the historian Numan Bartley has written, "the civil rights movement had dealt largely with surface issues—the right to drink a cup of coffee, to vote, to compete with whites for jobs. As important as such civil rights were, they did not address basic questions of poverty and power, and they did not question national practices and institutions." Following this essential logic, scholars have traced the roots of the movement's shortcomings to the 1940s. They argue that under the auspices of Franklin Delano Roosevelt's New Deal, liberal policymakers, Congress of Industrial Organizaiton (CIO) affiliated unions, members of the Communist Party, and black civil rights advocates pieced together a powerful, essentially class-based, coalition of progressive reformers, dedicated to the structural reform of the American economy. Only as the winds of the cold war made talk of structural economic reform seem all too statist, even totalitarian, and liberals ducked for cover as anticommunist hysteria emerged in full-force, did a left-liberal agenda narrow and the struggle for black civil rights, especially, though not exclusively, under the auspices of the NAACP, emerge without a thoroughgoing critique of the American capitalist economy. In this rendering of the story, the 1940s appear as the decade of "Opportunities Found and Lost," *The Rise and Fall of the New Deal Order*, and the *End of Reform*. It is, by and large, a tragic history constructed around the search for lost opportunities, around a search for a moment in the past when history might have gone another way. But, as this book will make plain, this narrative of post–World War II American reform has exaggerated the possibilities of one era at the cost of misunderstanding and minimizing the revolutionary advances of another. It has invested the cold war with far more explanatory power than is warranted by a close examination of black activism at the grassroots level. Moreover, it has imposed a lengthy narrative of decline on the history of postwar American reform that stands at odds with the histories of many of the nation's most revolutionary reform movements, most notably the African American struggle for civil rights.[13]

As a movement, the African American struggle for civil rights cannot be captured by a tragic narrative, and certainly cannot be comprehended by a narrative that reduces it to a battle for the mere possession of abstract constitutional rights. A central assumption of this work is that ordinary men and women have a tremendous capacity to observe the world around them and utilize the means available to them to shape it in accordance with their imagined sense of its possibilities, while understanding, to be sure, that their actions are constrained by historical circumstances seldom of their own choosing. During World War I and the 1920s, the Great Depression and the advent of the New Deal, and from World War II to the cold war and beyond, ordinary African Americans seized onto the opportunities presented them to remake their world. Black South Carolinians experienced more horrors, more violence, and more tragedies than most Americans for their efforts, but never did they stop struggling and rarely, if ever, did they view the possession of formal civil rights as an end in itself. Indeed, understood as an integral part of a larger struggle for self-determination and equality, the African American civil rights movement did not represent a turn away from the economic concerns of the New Deal era. Rather, the movement brought to the surface the limits of the New Deal era's ostensibly universal reform efforts and forced a larger and long-delayed confrontation with the nation's history of racial exclusion and discrimination. In doing so, the movement for African American civil rights raised serious questions about the relationship between racial discrimination *and* economic justice and between self-determination *and* democracy that continue to pose problems and concerns for historians, union leaders, politicians, and the larger world at the dawn of the twenty-first century.

A central task of this book is to write a history of the African American struggle for civil rights that reflects the open-ended quality of the movement and that keeps the tension between rights possession and rights application a constant theme. In a related sense, its purpose is to suggest that current debates among scholars and politicians about the relationship between civil rights and economic reform represent a continuation of America's ongoing struggle to come to terms with the problem of race in American history and life. In its broadest application this book is an experiment in narrative history. It seeks to tell the story of the civil rights movement in South Carolina and the United States without ending in utter tragedy (as if nothing ever changes for the good) or in a flight into fantasy (as if progress is automatic and American democracy is tirelessly triumphant). The African American civil rights movement does not fit neatly within either a tragic or Whig-like narrative. Both narratives are too rigid, too flat, too closed to express the broad significance of a movement that has sought not only to secure access to the formal rights guaranteed by the U.S. Constitution, but has simultaneously sought to make the possession of these rights a means to the creation of a more equal and democratic America. Only by creating an open-ended narrative, one without an ending, this book argues, can we begin to see how the tension borne of the nation's history of racial exclusion and discrimination continues to shape the problems and promises of our own time.[14]

As an experiment in historical writing, this book is also an attempt to provide a human face to the theoretical notion that those on the margins of history and the periphery of power shape history and power in the most profound ways. More than fifty years ago, the noted scholar of southern politics V.O. Key argued that local friend and neighbor networks formed the nuclei of South Carolina's white political establishment and, in turn, informed the larger political affairs of the state and the nation. Although Key argued that race played a central role in southern politics, his work focused largely on the actions and institutions of the region's white political officials. In his analysis of southern politics, black people were not actors in the main drama; rather, they were the objects of white political affairs, present by their absence, not by their actions. *Democracy Rising* takes Key's concern with race and his insight to the connections between the local and national seriously, but it moves African Americans into the center of its history of South Carolina, the South, the nation, and the larger world. Disfranchised, Jim-Crowed, and relegated to the periphery of the social, political, and economic life of South Carolina and the United States, African Americans actively pursued ways to make their voices and concerns a central part of each. In the century following the Civil War, black South Carolinians not only found ways to make their voices and concerns heard. Through their individual and collective actions they fundamentally shaped the course of southern, U.S., and world history. What follows is their story . . . and ours.[15]

1 Segregation and Self-Determination: The Making of the NAACP

The NAACP from the beginning faced this bogey. It was not, never had been, and never could be an organization that took an absolute stand against race segregation of any sort under all circumstances. This would be a stupid stand in the face of clear and incontrovertible facts. When the NAACP was formed, the great mass of Negro children were being trained in Negro schools; the great mass of Negro churchgoers were members of Negro churches; the great mass of Negro voters voted with the same political party; and the mass of Negroes joined with Negroes and co-operated with Negroes in order to fight the extension of this segregation and to move toward better conditions. . . . So long as we were fighting a color line, we must strive by color organization. We have no choice.

—W.E.B. Du Bois, *Dusk of Dawn*

By all accounts, Anthony Crawford embodied the Booker T. Washington philosophy of self-help and racial uplift. He was born in Abbeville County, South Carolina, in 1865 not far up the road from the site of the 1898 Phoenix race riot and only a county north of the 1876 Hamburg Massacre that helped secure Ben Tillman's reputation as a steadfast champion of white male supremacy. Upon the death of his formerly enslaved father, Crawford inherited a small plot of land seven miles northwest of the town of Abbeville. For a time, Crawford managed to navigate the state's precarious racial terrain on his way to accumulating some 427 acres of prime cotton land and a net worth of an estimated twenty thousand dollars. But on Saturday morning, October 21, 1916, Crawford violated an unwritten code of racial etiquette that cost him his life: he quarreled with a white storeowner, W.D. Barksdale, over the price of cottonseed. In the events that followed the argument, Crawford was arrested, released to a gathering mob, and chased into a boiler room basement at a nearby cotton gin.

After managing to strike one of his would-be assailants with a hammer blow to the head, Crawford was carried by the mob to a road outside, stabbed repeatedly with a knife, and kicked and beaten until almost dead. After forty-five minutes, Abbeville's sheriff put a stop to the assault and removed Crawford to the local jail. Later that day, when a rumor spread that Crawford might be spirited out of town by train, the mob stormed the jail and finished the job they had earlier begun. Once again pulling Crawford to the street, the mob kicked him to death, tied a rope around his neck, dragged his body through the streets of Abbeville's black neighborhood, hung the corpse from a pine tree near the gates of the county fairgrounds, and fired a couple hundred rounds of ammunition into it for good measure. Although "cooler heads" thwarted efforts to force Crawford's family to flee the county, in March 1917 a grand jury refused to indict a single member of the lynch mob.[1]

Just one year before the Crawford lynching, Richard I. Manning replaced South Carolina's most notorious defender of lynch mob justice, Coleman Livingston Blease, as the state's governor. Manning was touted as a "Progressive" reformer and is often credited with bringing South Carolina into the modern world of the twentieth century.[2] For black South Carolinians, however, the advent of progressivism looked a lot like Jim Crow and lynch mob terror. In 1915 a coalition of "Progressive" and "Bleasite" South Carolina state legislators passed a law formally segregating the textile industry, the largest industrial enterprise in the state and a driving force of New South development. Although the law did not substantially alter existing racial practices in the textile industry, it did, in effect, secure the subordination of black South Carolinians within the state's most important industrial enterprise.[3] Of course, by the time of the law's passage, state law and municipal ordinances already provided legal authority for Jim Crow segregation, while the state constitution of 1895 and the advent of the white primary in 1896 provided the legal basis for white male supremacy in the state's political decision-making process. But what black South Carolinians understood all too well, and what Anthony Crawford's lynching demonstrated yet again, was that violence proved the ultimate arbiter of racial interaction and black opportunity in South Carolina. Between 1904 and 1918 forty-two black South Carolinians lost their lives at the hands of parties unknown, a figure that represented better than one-fourth of the 161 lynchings that occurred in the state between 1882 and 1923.[4] Under the regime of Jim Crow, violations of everyday codes of racial conduct could provoke extreme violence, making the prospects for sustained challenges to the status quo seem virtually unthinkable.

At least since the publication of C. Vann Woodward's *Origins of the New South* in 1951, the lost promise of Populism and the recovery of past moments of interracial political activity have served as animating themes of southern history. For a brief period of time before Jim Crow and before the reign of lynch mob terror, Woodward maintained, an era of racial fluidity, of "flexibility and tolerance," defined the outer horizons of progressive possibilities in the South. But in the wake of a concerted campaign of racial violence, disfranchisement, and codification of Jim Crow, he argued, racial lines hardened, African Americans turned inward, and the interracial and egalitarian promise of the era, no matter how limited, was soon extinguished. Although there can be no doubting the horror of Jim Crow's bloody assent and its cost to southern politics as a whole, and to interracial politics in particular, the search for the "forgotten alternatives" or past moments of interracial cooperation has served to focus historical attention on what was not (or what historians believed should have been), rather than on what was. This focus has certainly contributed to the recovery of praiseworthy moments in southern history, both before and after the rise of Jim Crow. But it has done so with a price paid to understandings of larger patterns, power arrangements, and the South's most vibrant political reform tradition—the African American struggle for civil rights, self-determination, and equality.[5]

In perhaps the most important recent book in the Woodwardian tradition, Glenda Gilmore maintains, with North Carolina providing her primary evidence, that amid the wreckage of Jim Crow's bloody assent, middle-class white and black women found a way to resurrect the Populist tradition and offer the South its best source of hope for social and political deliverance. By the opening years of the twentieth century, she argues, black men had been "forced from the political," "expelled," and banished from politics. In an ironic twist, however, the removal of black men from the formal political arena opened new room for white and black women to forge ties, first through the work of social uplift associated with organizations such as the Young Women's Christian Association (YWCA) and the National Association of Colored Women (NACW), but most significantly through the common quest for suffrage. "Women suffragists were the first group since the Populists to formulate a political critique," she writes, "that pushed aside race in the South to focus on a substantive issue." In doing so, female suffragists not only created new room for women in the political arena, but they also "cleared a narrow path for black men to return to electoral politics." "Interracial cooperation," she concludes, "led straight into politics." For Gilmore, the recovery of the Populist tradition by middle-class white and black women provided the crucial first step toward passage beyond a particularly brutal, violent, and masculine form of white supremacy and political culture that characterized the nadir of African American life at century's turn. Although this argument may hold for North Carolina, its application to South Carolina and the larger South is more dubious. In South Carolina, in particular, it was the collective organization of black women *and* men by the onset of World War I, largely through the NAACP, that issued the sharpest challenge to white supremacy, to the highly masculine political culture of the nineteenth century, as well as to the class-bound dynamics and paternalistic ethos of racial uplift work. This is not to discount the importance of interracial work and alliances across the divide of race forged around common concerns. It is, rather, to suggest that the larger patterns and developments of the era flowed principally from the collective actions of African Americans who explicitly challenged white supremacy through efforts to secure civil rights and achieve a greater measure of self-determination.[6]

Confronted by Jim Crow segregation, disfranchisement, and the pervasive threat of physical violence, by design and necessity black South Carolinians looked to their own neighborhoods, social networks, and institutions to meet their economic and social needs in the early twentieth century. Black churches, private and religious-based schools, fraternal and benevolent associations, literary and social welfare clubs, and a range of black business enterprises provided the institutional basis of black communities. Lacking access to the formal political process in the state, the masses of black South Carolinians relied on individual ingenuity and a select group of black men and women to represent their needs and interests in the larger public arena from health and education, to jobs and government services. In South Carolina, this select group of black men and women, most of whom hailed from the ranks of the black community's educated and professional classes, served as de facto "ambassadors" to the white

community. But without the capacity to threaten local and state officials with political retribution, these "diplomats to the white community," as Gilmore aptly describes them, negotiated with white officials
at a decided disadvantage. Often separated from the masses of black
South Carolinians by education, profession, economic security, social
connections, and at times by geography, color, even language, these
ambassadors remained junior partners in a Jim Crow system that left
black opportunities and many basic needs dependent on the goodwill
of white South Carolinians. In the context of the era, the efforts of
these diplomats to the white community to uplift the race, through
a combination of self-reliance and carefully negotiated white beneficence, were truly heroic. But as Deborah Gray White has explained,
the ideology and practice of racial uplift "was as heartening as it was
crippling." It represented an implicit capitulation to racism, a seeming
abdication of the civil and political rights necessary for black people
to represent their own interests in a broader public arena, even as it
served as a means to meet their most basic needs.

Between 1915 and 1920, however, growing numbers of black
South Carolinians looked to a new organization, the National Association for the Advancement of Colored People (NAACP), to represent
their interests and to serve as a vehicle for individual and collective
empowerment. The year 1917 marked a critical moment in the self-
transformation of the black struggle for civil rights and equality in
South Carolina and for the less-than-eight-year-old NAACP. It was a
moment in which black South Carolinians looked for alternatives to
the limited ideology and program of racial uplift. And it was a time
when the NAACP began to make a transition from an explicitly interracial organization led and funded by its white-dominated board of
directors, to an organization led by its black executive secretariat and
funded by its newly organized branches comprised almost exclusively
of black men and women. Indeed, the NAACP's own transition was
both cause and effect of mounting demands among African Americans
for the right and means to be the leaders of their own fight for civil
rights and equality.

Less than two years after the death of Booker T. Washington, in
the spring of 1917, Columbia and Charleston formed the first two
branches of the NAACP in South Carolina, helping to launch a new
stage in the black struggle for civil rights in the state and the nation.
Founded in 1786 to serve as the seat of state government, Columbia

served as the nerve center of state commerce and the mediator of conflict between the regional interests of the low country and piedmont sections of the state. The port city of Charleston had long served as a gateway to the Atlantic world and was an important locus of political, economic, and cultural power in the state. On the eve of World War I, Columbia and Charleston were the two largest urban centers in the state and home to a well-developed class of black professionals and an organized network of racial uplift institutions.[7] For the black men and women living in Columbia and Charleston, the relative strength of black institutional life, the existence of a substantial class of educated, black professionals, and the proximity to white seats of power afforded certain opportunities for political organization virtually unimaginable in the relatively isolated rural countryside. The circumstances in Columbia and Charleston did not, however, offer only possibilities, they also offered constraints. Just as the relatively advantaged position of black people living in the two urban settings could serve as a means to political mobilization, the same class, institutional, and geographic advantages that helped make such mobilization possible also placed distinct limits on the scope and trajectory of that mobilization and that politics. Between 1917 and 1920, black South Carolinians fought against white supremacy, Jim Crow, and economic hardship, but they also battled among themselves. In those battles, the NAACP became a critical site of conflict and mediation. And while the association entered the state on the class, gender, institutional, and geographic terrain forged in the era of racial uplift, in the process of struggle, black South Carolinians helped turn the attention of the NAACP southward and the NAACP, in turn, provided a vehicle for challenging the paternalistic and class-bound dynamics of uplift work, as well as nineteenth-century constructions of male and female civic participation.

The "Dixie District" and the Remaking of the NAACP

If the lynching of Anthony Crawford provided Jim Crow in South Carolina with the appearance of invincibility, the lineaments of legalized white supremacy's undoing began to emerge at the same moment. The year 1915 marked the death of Booker T. Washington and the symbolic passing of his accommodationist philosophy. Twenty years after Washington's infamous "Atlanta Compromise" speech, racial violence, disfranchisement, and mounting Jim Crow laws had exposed the limits of self-help, petit capital accumulation, and racial uplift in the absence of political power and access to the institutions of civil society free of racial restrictions. Although the NAACP (initially called the National Negro Committee) had begun in 1909–1910 as a board-dominated organization, whose policies and direction were determined by a handful of northern white progressives and W.E.B. Du Bois—the editor of the association's magazine, *The Crisis*—local branches began to emerge around the United States by 1915. When first organized in New York City, largely through the efforts of the white Socialist Mary White Ovington, the NAACP had no formulated plan to organize branches. "We were a group primarily of white people," Ovington explained, "who felt that while the Negro would aid in the Committee's work the whites, who were largely responsible for conditions and who controlled the bulk of the nation's wealth, ought to finance the movement." Almost immediately, however, branches formed in Boston, Washington, D.C., and Chicago.[8]

In 1913 the NAACP expanded from three to ten branches located (with the exception of branches in Baltimore and Washington) in the urban North and Midwest. There were twenty-four branches by the end of 1914 and two years later the NAACP could claim seventy branches with a total membership of 8,785. Across the country, individuals and organizations inquired about joining the organization and forming branches of their own. "I would like to know from you," Butler W. Nance, a black attorney living in Columbia, South Carolina, wrote W.E.B. Du Bois at *The Crisis*, "if there is any chance to attach our organization [Capital Civic League] to the Natl Ass'n for Advancement of Colored People—There are several things that could be done if you would not be afraid to operate in the South."[9]

In April 1917, the United States formally entered World War I. For African Americans, the war to make the world safe for democracy led to social upheaval at home and provided the NAACP with an opportunity to appeal to a broad constituency of African Americans. Wartime mobilization helped spur a mass migration from the rural countryside to southern cities and northern industrial centers. Between 1916 and 1920 approximately five hundred thousand black southerners left the South, exposing cracks in the racial order of the region and unleashing a wave of antiblack violence from East St. Louis to Chicago, Illinois. By the end of 1919 national membership in the NAACP reached almost one hundred thousand and half of the organization's revenue derived from funds raised by its branches. For the first time in the association's history, the majority of its members lived in the South. In a 1918 memo, the association's white secretary, John R. Shillady, explained:

> There are many evidences that the thoughtful colored people of the country regard the Association as especially their spokesman and representative in the large field of civic and political affairs, not the least of which is to be found in the recent substantial increase in the number of new branches of the Association which have sprung up all over the country, the great majority of which have come into being without the immediate stimulus of the presence of a field officer to organize them, but impelled to affiliate with the Association by an apparent realization of the vital necessity of the organization to their welfare and to their fuller participation in the common citizenship of the country.

As August Meier and Elliott Rudwick have argued, by the opening of the 1920s, the NAACP had passed a critical threshold in a transition from a predominantly white, board-dominated organization, to one funded, led by—and increasingly responsive to the needs of—black people.[10]

Although World War I provided an important context for the NAACP's membership growth, changing racial composition, and new funding base, its development was driven in large part by the appointment of James Weldon Johnson to the position of field secretary in December 1916. The NAACP's white chairman, Joel E. Spingarn, recognized the void left by the death of Washington and the shifting currents of black thought and action. In August 1916, he organized a conference at his estate near Amenia, New York, to discuss the current situation and plan future action. As Du Bois recalled:

> By the middle of the year 1916, it was evident to thinking people that the American Negroes were achieving a unity in thought and action, partly caused by the removal of Mr. Washington's powerful personality and partly because of pressure of outward circumstances. This realization was not entirely voluntary on our part; it was forced upon us by the concentration of effort and unity of thought which rising race segregation, discrimination and mob murder were compelling us to follow.[11]

Organized as a "get-together" rather than as an official NAACP gathering, the hope was to bring together many of the nation's key black and white leaders interested in furthering the cause of equal rights for black people. At what became known as the Amenia Conference, Du Bois was the tentmate of James Weldon Johnson, the association's recently appointed field secretary. Johnson was a Bookerite who had written for the New York *Age*, served in the U.S. Foreign Service as a consular official in Venezuela and Nicaragua, and published *The Autobiography of an Ex-Colored Man* in 1912. Although well connected among the followers of Washington, Johnson had joined the New York NAACP in 1915. In countless ways, he embodied the transition from the era of racial uplift to the emerging era of the New Negro. Born in 1871 in Jacksonville, Florida, and a graduate of Atlanta University, Johnson was smooth and cosmopolitan, a literatus and a politico. He combined a philosophical commitment to black institution building and to ceaseless agitation for political rights. And when he and Du Bois spent the Amenia Conference together, he expressed an interest in forming a "secret organization" to energize the black struggle for civil rights. Indeed, it would be Johnson's ties to the Washington machine that offered the NAACP a way to tap into the organizations and institutions that sustained black Americans during the era of racial uplift. For an organization that had just begun to make inroads into the hostile racial climate of the American South, Johnson promised to provide the NAACP with the kind of legitimacy that, perhaps, only an ostensibly cool-headed Bookerite could offer in the violent racial climate of 1916.[12]

The Amenia Conference, Du Bois later wrote, "marked the beginning of the new era," for the NAACP and for the black struggle for equality. But it was the addition of Johnson to the NAACP's national office staff that proved instrumental in turning the organization's attention southward. "It was my deep conviction," Johnson wrote, "that the aims of the Association could never be realized by only hammering at white people. . . . I realized that, regardless of what might be done *for* black America, the ultimate and vital part of the work would have to be done by black America itself." On January 16, 1917, only a few months before the United States formally entered the First World War, Johnson personally launched the NAACP's first full-fledged organizing campaign in the Deep South. Johnson was well aware of the terrain of struggle he entered as NAACP field secretary in the early

months of 1917. Between January 16 and March 15 he toured the
southeast region of the United States, organizing branches in Richmond and Norfolk, Virginia; in Durham, Greensboro, and Raleigh,
North Carolina; in Atlanta, Athens, Savannah, and Augusta, Georgia;
in Tampa and Jacksonville, Florida; and in Columbia and Charleston, South Carolina. The organization of the "Dixie District" or the
"Southern Empire," as it became known, established the NAACP's
first substantial foothold in the South. It represented, Du Bois reported in *The Crisis*, the creation of "a real first line defense facing
the enemy at proper range." "There is no doubt that a new spirit is
awakening in the South," Johnson exclaimed:

> and that the National Association for the Advancement of Colored
> People offers the precise medium for the exercise of that spirit. When
> the Association has spread over the entire South, as it is certain to
> do, and the thinking men and women of the race feel and know that
> they are leagued together with thinking men and women of both races
> all over the country for one and the same purpose, when each group
> feels and knows that it has the co-operation and support of all other
> groups, many are the changes that are going to be brought about.[13]

For Johnson, the southern tour was significant because it established the institutional presence of the NAACP in the South, but he
also believed that its broader significance lay in its role of facilitating a
shift in thinking—of consciousness. The tour, in effect, began a process of revealing to Johnson, the NAACP, and black people—North
and South—the possibility and necessity of mass-based collective black
action. "It is not so much the concrete thing we are doing," he later
explained. "The great job before this organization is to awaken the
American Negro, to work him up. That is the job." In the 1910s,
the NAACP worked to publicize racial discrimination and violence
and the association battled peonage, police brutality, mob violence,
residential segregation, and disfranchisement in America's court-
rooms and legislatures. Johnson's appointment, however, signaled a
recognition that the NAACP's legal or rights-based program was connected inherently and necessarily to a broader social struggle. Johnson envisioned the NAACP as a vehicle for connecting black people
together across the nation in the pursuit of racial justice, a project he
understood to be critical to the future of democracy in America. "If

you do not free the Negro in Mississippi," he argued, "you will very soon find the Negro in Massachusetts in slavery." "We must get over the idea," he stated, "that this is an individual problem . . . it takes mass action. You can educate individuals, you can give them money, they can live cultured lives, but they will find they run up against this thing until we have mass power competent to wake the majority in this country to a realization of our fitness when we are fit and to give us those privileges that correspond to that fitness." "Power is the key," he came to believe, and he sought to use the NAACP as a way to promote an understanding of the importance of collective organization and the need to utilize group-based power in a manner he compared to Jewish and Irish Americans.[14]

If Johnson retained a dose of a Bookerite ethos and abided a new faith in Du Bois's "Talented-tenthism" that allowed "fitness" to remain a qualification for the "privileges" of citizenship, he put both to work in what he clearly understood as the building of a mass movement. Johnson's organizing style was geared toward mobilizing already existing institutions in black communities in an effort to leverage their human and financial resources and to inculcate a new way of thinking about the "race problem"—an NAACP way. In other words, he sought to connect black uplift institutions to the NAACP and to push them to embrace an agenda of ceaseless agitation and protest politics. Early during his tenure as field secretary he compiled a list of black churches, lodges, and fraternal orders. He created a directory of black ministers, heads of schools, and other black organizations. And he made a point of creating an NAACP presence at the national conventions of groups like the Knights of the Pythias, the Elks, the Baptist Church, and the National Negro Business League.[15]

As a strategy, Johnson's organizing method reflected the realities of southern black communities living under the regime of Jim Crow, communities that were only beginning to emerge from the era of Booker T. Washington. In the nineteen-teens, black southerners survived in abysmal conditions. In 1920, for example, 85 percent of South Carolina's 2,144 public schools for black children employed only one teacher in single, ungraded classrooms, for an average school term of eighty-four days. The state ran five public high schools for black children, but none had four-year programs and the state tagged each with the lowest possible "third-class" rating. Jim Crow violence remained pervasive and the vast majority of black South Carolinians remained impoverished in agricultural employment. Between 1900 and 1920, South Carolina lost as many as 175,000 black people to out-migration.[16] Those men and women who remained and were interested in and able to confront the deeply entrenched problems faced by black people were already working in and through black churches, private schools and colleges, benevolent associations, women's clubs, and fraternal orders. Johnson's strategy, then, of tapping into critical sources of human and economic power in black communities, represented a necessary concession to existing circumstances. And while the strategy had the potential of reproducing (even reinforcing) already existing power arrangements and class tensions, it also held out the possibility of transforming them. Johnson placed a premium on collective action and proposed to make the NAACP an organization that represented the interests of *all* black people. This approach represented an important break from the era of racial uplift that had emphasized the individual over the collective, and in which the dominant model of citizenship and selfhood was symbolized by the self-made (white) man. It is important, here, to emphasize that Johnson helped introduce a new era of possibilities. The introduction of the NAACP hastened an ongoing process of change that built upon existing historical circumstances and required continuous human struggle.[17]

The Past Meets the Present in Columbia

As already noted, Butler W. Nance, a black attorney in Columbia, South Carolina, wrote W.E.B. Du Bois in June 1915 to announce his interest in "attaching" the Columbia-based Capital Civic League to the NAACP. As a reader of *The Crisis* "for sometime," Nance viewed the work of the NAACP as similar to the work being carried out in Columbia under the auspices of the Civic League. In an enclosed "Address to the People of South Carolina," Nance provided Du Bois with an explanation of the Civic League's objectives and organizational rationale. "The Capital Civic League," the Address explained:

> is an organization composed of qualified electors of the City of Columbia, S.C. and adjacent territory, who are banded together for the sole purpose of contesting and contending for our every Constitutional right, privileges and immunity, in a quiet, legal and peaceful manner. . . . What we need in this sore hour of oppression, this cru-

cial period in the history of our radical development, is the siege gun of intelligence, the acquisition of property, stability of character, fortitude, bravery, patience, courage, forbearance, long-suffering and that registered Christian manhood that will nerve us to continue to hammer at the forts of citizenship until we conquer [*sic*].

"About 40 years have been lost," the Address continued, "that could have been spent in agitation and organization looking forward to the restoration of our civil and political rights. . . . Next to Christianity, this is the most fundamental principle in the well-being of the American Negro."[18]

In 1915, "qualified electors" meant men, and the Civic League was, de facto, a men's organization designed to spur interest in voting and agitation for full citizenship rights. It was comprised of some of Columbia's most prominent black citizens who would become early leaders in the NAACP, including Nance, I.S. Leevy, a mortician and influential Republican Party leader, and N.J. Frederick, an educator, lawyer, newspaper editor, and Republican Party stalwart. Although Frederick's wide-ranging participation in and commitment to the cause of black civil rights could be matched by few of his contemporaries, his social background reflected that of the Civic League's leadership. His life and activism were forged in and traversed many of the uplift era's key institutions, and his involvement with the Civic League and the NAACP embodied the confluence of three overlapping moments in the history of black struggle for self-determination and equality: Reconstruction, racial uplift, and the twentieth-century battle for civil rights.

Frederick was born in Orangeburg, South Carolina, in November 1877. In April of that year, U.S. soldiers marched out of the State House in Columbia, marking the formal end of Reconstruction and the final withdrawal of federal support for Republican government in South Carolina. By the elections of 1878, the Republican Party was, in effect, defeated and soon ceased to represent a significant political force in the state. Despite the decline of the party's influence, Frederick maintained a substantial role in the Republican Party into the 1930s, serving as the Richland County commissioner and as a delegate to the National Convention in 1920, 1924, and again in 1932. His connections to the Republican Party and the Reconstruction era were deep and familial. He was married to Corrine R. Frederick, the daughter of Capt. J. Carroll, a prominent figure in the state Republican Party who served as commissioner of Richland County's public schools during Reconstruction. Frederick earned degrees from the state's black private schools created during the Reconstruction era, including Claflin College and Benedict College. Frederick began his career as the principal of the Howard School, at the time Columbia's only school for black children. Later he was admitted to the South Carolina bar, became an attorney, and represented a number of black fraternal orders, including the Knights of the Pythias, the Masons, and the Good Samaritans, as well as Columbia's only black bank, Victory Savings. In the 1920s and 1930s he served as the NAACP's principal attorney in the state and was responsible for litigating its critical cases. A newspaper editor as well, in the 1910s he edited the black-owned *Southern Indicator*, and he founded *The Palmetto Leader* in 1925.[19]

The Capital Civic League brought together a number of black men, like Frederick, under the banner of "Christian manhood," "courage," "character," "property," and the "restoration" of civil and political rights. Its members sought compulsory education, better schools, better teachers, better pay, and the prohibition of alcohol, that "fearful octopus that has done so much to impoverish our people." The Civic League asked for the assistance of "wives and mothers" to "rear up a generation of citizens and voters" and to instill in the "souls of their sons" the "valor and courage" to fight for their citizenship rights and a better world. In one sense, the league reflected an orientation to the nineteenth century, to a time when manhood was defined by Victorian ideals of self-restraint, property ownership, and one's role in the public world of work and politics, and a time when the ideal of womanhood was defined solely by a woman's capacity as mother, daughter, wife, and keeper of the home.[20] But laying claim to nineteenth-century ideals of manhood and womanhood has never been an easy or uncomplicated endeavor for black men and women. The legacy of slavery, the persistence of racism, and economic inequality made the ideal of Victorian manhood and womanhood an untenable one for most black people. Indeed, white supremacy endowed the very struggle for Victorian "respectability"—the struggle to be "real men" and "true women"—with a double meaning: it represented *both* an accommodation to nineteenth-century patriarchal norms *and* resistance to the ideology and practice of white supremacy that denied black people the *choice* to work and participate in the public world or to tend to the duties of and life in the home. For black South Carolinian men, then, the apparent adherence to the norms and values of nineteenth-century Victorianism could represent at once a badge of manliness and class distinction *and* a subversion of racially proscribed—even traditional—roles.[21]

In another and perhaps more important sense, in its call for collective organization, the Capital Civic League helped to create the institutional and discursive space for a movement that challenged the norms and values of the nineteenth century. The Civic League took as its central task "increased agitation" and the creation of an "organized movement" for full civil and political rights—a direct challenge to white supremacy and the real and symbolic authority of white men. It took to task "weak-kneed ministers who claim that the Church is no place to talk civil rights" and demanded that the church, "all conventions, conferences, associations, assemblies, lodges, grand lodges, and all other gatherings of whatever nature," be mobilized to serve the interests of black people. The Civic League looked to Jewish Americans as an example of how collective power could be effectively organized around nationality and race. Similarly, the organization held up the white women's suffrage movement as "an example to Negro men." "We may learn another lesson," the Civic League announced, "from the activity of the white women of America in regard to equal suffrage." Like the emerging feminist movement, the Civic League sought the elaboration of individual rights through collective activity. In doing so, they challenged, as Nancy Cott writes of white feminists, "the individualistic premises of the political theory of individualism," even as its members expressed their grievances in the very idiom of liberal individualism. Black men wanted individual rights, to be sure, but they recognized that power in American society flowed from organized groups.[22]

Members of the Civic League looked to the NAACP as a means of expanding their organizational strength and political power and connecting their local battles to a national arena of struggle. In early 1917, during James Weldon Johnson's southern organizing tour, Columbia finally chartered a branch of the NAACP.[23] Columbia's first branch president, Butler W. Nance, explained to a crowd at the NAACP's tenth annual conference: "Our biggest trouble in South Carolina is, and the one thing I would like the Northern Branches to help us do, is to bring sufficient pressure through Representatives and Senators in Congress to alleviate us a little bit along that line. We can get a respectable audience with any Congressman in the State, but after we leave it is just like water falling off a duck's back. . . . We suffer from want of the ballot in Richland County."

Nance recognized and announced that black South Carolinians could no longer rely on white benevolence to meet their needs and represent their interests. Without the right to the vote, that is, to self-representation, the needs and interests of black people would continue to go unmet or be ignored. Indeed, by July 1918, the Columbia NAACP had helped increase the number of registered black men in Richland County to some 2,200. The branch set up a registration committee to instruct black men on how to register to vote. For those who lacked the education and skills necessary to pass the state literacy requirements or lacked the adequate property qualifications necessary to register, the committee took steps to provide instruction. "Any man who can't read well," Nance explained, "we teach them; we put the Constitution in their hands, and when they come by the office we teach them."[24]

The Civic League became, in effect, the NAACP, rooting the organization in the institutional and cultural life of black men. But, by the time black Columbians officially chartered an NAACP branch, black women had become active in the organization and began to reshape it and move it in directions that black men may not have imagined or even desired. Rebecca Hull Walton and her sister, Rachel Hull Monteith, the mother of future NAACP stalwart Modjeska Monteith Simkins, were both active in the founding of the Columbia NAACP branch. Rachel Hull, like N.J. Frederick, was born in the 1870s. Her mother was a light-skinned woman, born into slavery and likely the daughter of the man who owned her mother. In 1898, Hull married Henry Monteith, a bricklayer and member of Columbia's Bricklayers and Plasterer's Union #5. Henry Monteith was born in 1870 and could trace his lineage to the Wade Hampton family plantation. Henry was the son of Mary Dobbins and Walter Monteith, a prominent white lawyer in Columbia for whom Dobbins worked as a nursemaid. Although Henry forbade his daughters from working in the homes of white families, fearing that they would be exposed to circumstances similar to those confronted by his mother, Rachel worked as a teacher before they married and again after the children were old enough to attend school. She was a supporter of the Niagara movement that preceded the founding of the NAACP, and she was a regular subscriber to *The Crisis*. In addition to her involvement and early interest in the NAACP, she was also active in the Second Cavalry Baptist Church, as well as the Bethlehem Baptist Church and Stover's Chapel A.M.E. (African Methodist Episcopal).[25]

While men initially seized the initiative to become registered voters, with the close of World War I and the passage of the Nineteenth Amendment, black women in Columbia laid claim to the vote and full citizenship rights. When the registration books opened in September 1920, a group of black women took the city's white male registrars by surprise when they reported to the registrar's office and demanded to be registered. Without a formal organization, a number of black women had worked by word of mouth to build sentiment for a collective voter registration effort. Many appeared at the registrar's office armed with the necessary tax receipts and ready to read passages from the state or federal Constitution. On the first day of the registration drive, the registrars had no apparent plan to block the registration of the black women. Instead, they resorted to delay, forcing black women to stand in line as the registrars insisted on allowing white people to register first. Despite the delays, black women waited in line from 11:30 in the morning until 8:00 at night, and on the first day, at least, a number of women managed to place their names on the voter registration rolls. "Who stirred up all these colored women to come up here and register?" was evidently the only comment one registrar could muster in disbelief.

While a number of black women managed to register on the first day of the campaign, the registrars were ready to put a stop to the enrollment campaign by the second. In addition to long lines and stalling tactics, black women were greeted "with scowls, rough voices, and insulting demeanor." Registrars were prepared to subject the women to the state's literacy requirement, and, with the assistance of a lawyer, required the women to read long passages from various state and criminal codes rather than from the state or federal Constitution as required by law. Although state law required only that registrants be capable of reading to the satisfaction of a registrar, the women were asked to explain passages and were subjected to questioning and cross-examination. Women, many of whom were college graduates and teachers, were disqualified for "mispronouncing" words, for being unable to explain legal terms such as *mandamus*, and for refusing to read sections of the criminal code that defined the crimes of miscegenation, sodomy, and incest.[26]

During the registration campaign, the women formed their own temporary organization and were soon working in conjunction with the Columbia NAACP. South Carolina native and NAACP field secretary, William Pickens, came to Columbia to report on the registration effort and to investigate the discriminatory practices of the state registrars. During his stay, Pickens visited registration locations and attended a mass meeting where he encouraged people to join the NAACP and helped raise money for the registration drive. "The recent registration of voters in South Carolina may be taken as an example, as this state has been ever representative of the South," he wrote in *The Nation*. "The black race slightly outnumbers the white in South Carolina, and colored women outnumber colored men. The colored woman is accordingly the largest class in the State, and her right to vote gives a new concern to the maintainers of 'white supremacy.'"[27]

Butler Nance and the NAACP branch responded in kind by filing a lawsuit against Richland County's Board of Registration "for refusing to register the Negro women based on the EDUCATIONAL test." "I have always admired the courage and nerve of the Negro woman," he wrote to Walter White, "and I want to tell you that they are exhibiting a wonderful amount of it at this time. Though treated in every way, save humane, they continue to present themselves to be registered only to be refused. So you see what a fight we have on our hands here, and we mean to stay in the fight until every woman who possesses the qualification is registered or fight the case through the Supreme Court of the U.S."[28]

Later that fall, the NAACP presented evidence of widespread discrimination against black women voters to the U.S. Congress and lobbied in a failed effort for the passage of the Tinkham Bill that proposed to reduce congressional representation from states that discriminated against female voters, placing the organization on the front lines of modern feminism.[29]

Despite the NAACP's legislative defeat and the successful efforts of white officials in South Carolina to put a stop to the registration of black women voters, the black struggle for civil rights and self-determination in Columbia had reached a new point of departure by the fall of 1920. Although black men would continue to occupy the formal leadership roles of the NAACP, the passage of the Nineteenth

Amendment, the grassroots efforts of black women to demand their full rights of citizenship, and the growth of female membership in the NAACP represented a not so subtle shift from the gendered norms of the nineteenth century and the bifurcation of male and female roles and organizational affiliations that marked the uplift era. Black Columbians now had an organization dedicated to achieving full citizenship rights for black men *and* women. True, the new organization and the rise of the New Negro threatened to subordinate the cause of the New Woman to a rhetoric and agenda dedicated to a struggle for "manhood rights." But, in emphasizing the need for the collective organization of black people, the new organization opened the possibility for challenges to more rigidly male understandings of struggle, citizenship, and civic participation. In effect, the NAACP emerged as a new arena of contest and struggle, a struggle that had no clear (or predetermined) direction in 1920.[30]

The Past Meets the Present in Charleston

While Columbia rests at the center of the Palmetto State where the Congaree and Saluda rivers converge, the city of Charleston lies on the coastline where the Ashley and Cooper rivers empty into the Atlantic Ocean. "There is a subtle flavor of Old World things, a little hush in the whirl of American doing," W.E.B. Du Bois wrote of Charleston following his visit there in March 1917. "Between her guardian rivers looking across the sea toward Africa sits this little Old Lady (her cheek teasingly tinged to every tantalizing shade of the darker blood) with her shoulder ever toward the street and her little laced and rusty fan beside her cheek, while long verandas of her soul stretch down backward into slavery."[31] Less than a month before Du Bois's visit, twenty-nine black men and women had met and formed a Charleston branch of the NAACP. Much like the Columbia branch, the branch in Charleston represented a mixing of old and new, the coming together of individuals, institutions, and ideas in an effort to demand equal rights for black people.[32] Since the days of slavery, the black community of Charleston had been known for its high degree of internal differentiation: urban and rural, free and slave, skilled and unskilled, light-skinned and dark-skinned. In the antebellum era, Charleston was home to a sizeable population of "free people of color," a group of men and women (three-fourths of whom were of "mixed-race" ancestry in 1860) whose access to education and jobs skills and familial and economic ties to elite white Charlestonians set them apart from the masses of black South Carolinians. While a number of these "aristocrats of color" translated their prewar advantages into postwar political and economic power, the fall of Reconstruction era Republican government, disfranchisement, the rise of Jim Crow, and the gradual growth of residential segregation had begun to erode, though not erase, the internal divisions among black Charlestonians. Organized as the United States made preparations for World War I and as black out-migration posed new challenges and new opportunities for southern black communities, the Charleston NAACP became a crucial site that reflected and gave shape to the shifting currents of black life in the low country.[33]

Eighteen black men and eleven black women came together on February 27, 1917, to organize a branch of the NAACP in Charleston. The initial members of the association were tied together by a number of factors, including family, neighborhood, profession, education, club or associational activity, and a shared interest in addressing the twin problems of racial discrimination and political powerlessness. The group was comprised of some of Charleston's leading black professionals, business owners, and skilled tradesmen. There was John McFall of McFall's Pharmacy and Richard and Edward Mickey of Mickey's Funeral Home. The branch included four doctors, one dentist, two carpenters, an electrician, three dressmakers, a hairdresser, a school principal, a teacher, two real estate salesmen, one insurance salesman, and a lawyer. There was also its principal leader and first president, Edwin (Teddy) A. Harleston.[34] Harleston was born in 1882. He graduated from Charleston's Avery Normal Institute in 1900 and then received his B.A. from Atlanta University, where he was a student and friend of Du Bois. After graduating from Atlanta University, Harleston attended Boston's Museum of Fine Arts School. Although he earned a reputation as a fine artist, he returned to Charleston in 1913 to help with the family undertaking business. His father, "Captain" Edwin Gaillard Harleston, was a prominent member of the black Charleston community and owned a funeral home on Calhoun Street across from the Emanuel A.M.E. Church. "Captain" Harleston was the son of an enslaved woman and a white planter. He worked his way into the ranks of Charleston's black elite through the shipping business as the owner of a schooner that transported rice along the Carolina and Georgia coastline. "Captain's" sister, Hannah Mickey, was the mother of Richard and Edward Mickey. He got his start in the undertaking business when, following the death of his sister's husband, he helped oversee the Mickey family business until the Mickey boys were old enough to run the business on their own. "Captain" Harleston's daughter, Eloise, was also a charter member of the NAACP. She was married to Daniel J. Jenkins, a Baptist minister who founded Charleston's Jenkins Orphanage for black children in 1893.[35]

Many of the Charleston NAACP's early members, like Harleston, had attended the Avery Normal Institute, including William H. Johnson, the association's first vice president; Richard Mickey, its first secretary; and Susan "Susie" Dart Butler, who served as the organization's first treasurer. Established in 1865 by the American Missionary Association (AMA) as the Tappan School, in honor of the abolitionist Lewis Tappan, in 1868 the school relocated and was renamed the Avery Normal Institute, after the northern philanthropist Charles Avery. Francis L. Cardozo, a member of Charleston's antebellum free black community, led the effort to establish Avery at the site of its permanent home on Bull Street. He then left the school to become South Carolina's secretary of state. Between 1868 and 1913, white school principals appointed by the AMA presided over Avery. The school took as its central mission the training of black teachers, although Charleston city officials permitted only two black women (both Avery graduates) to teach in the city's black public schools. Nevertheless, Avery trained many of the state's black teachers, future college graduates, and business leaders. The school embodied and inculcated an ethos of service and racial uplift in an era marked by few opportunities for advanced education for black South Carolinians.[36]

In 1915, Benjamin F. Cox was appointed principal of Avery. Cox was a graduate of Fisk University and the previous head of AMA schools in Georgia and Alabama. When he began his tenure as principal of Avery, he was the first black man to hold that position since Francis Cardozo had done so in 1868. Principal Cox and his wife, Jeannette Keeble Cox, also a graduate of Fisk, oversaw critical changes to the school during their tenure at the institution. They worked to strengthen the school's commitment to teaching black history, infusing the school with the work and teachings of Du Bois and Carter G. Woodson; they sought to encourage Avery students to concern themselves not just with the world of education, but also with politics and international affairs. Principal Cox set a personal example. He served on the Charleston NAACP's Executive Committee from its inception. Both he and his wife remained active in and supporters of the organization. Principal Cox also sought to combat Avery's reputation for classism and color prejudice.

Avery had long reflected and given shape to the divisions and biases woven into the fabric of life in black Charleston. "I never wanted to go to Avery Institute," recalled the darker-hued Mamie Garvin Fields, "because the colored people there discriminated against dark-skinned children." Although many of Avery's students hailed from the ranks of Charleston's black (and often light-skinned) elite, as the school's leading historian, Edmund Drago, has documented, many of its students came from families of modest means that struggled to get the best education possible for their children. Once at Avery, according to Drago, Cox worked tirelessly to hire black teachers such as Septima Poinsette Clark and J. Andrew Simmons (both Avery graduates and future civil rights activists), who detested caste and class prejudice and discrimination. In short, with the arrival of Benjamin and Jeannette Cox, Avery rapidly became a critical institution in the making of a more unified and activist oriented black community in Charleston. It became, along with the NAACP, an important institutional site where conflict was mediated and a program for racial advancement formulated.[37]

In addition to her work at Avery, Jeannette Cox also became active among Charleston's black clubwomen. In December 1916 she helped organize the Phyllis Wheatley Literary and Social Club, which became affiliated with the South Carolina Federation of Colored Women's Clubs (SCFCWC) and the National Association of Colored Women (NACW). In 1909, Marion Birnie Wilkinson, an Avery graduate and wife of State College president Robert Shaw Wilkinson, had spearheaded the organization of the SCFCWC. The SCFCWC was the statewide affiliate of the NACW, which had been formally organized in Washington, D.C., in the summer of 1896. The SCFCWC and the NACW were organizations that linked black women together under the guiding principle of racial uplift through self-help. In the era of Jim Crow, such organizations became, according to Deborah Gray White, "black women's primary vehicle for race leadership."[38] "If one knows the officers and leaders of the South Carolina Federation of Colored Women's Clubs," wrote South Carolina State College professor, Asa Gordon, in 1929, "he knows most of the women in the state who are doing most of the uplift work of the Negroes so far as the colored women are concerned." Throughout South Carolina, black women's clubs mobilized black women through social networks to become active in educating less-privileged young people, sponsoring cultural events, finding homes for orphans, tending to the health-care needs of black communities, as well as lobbying white authorities for much-needed services such as garbage collection, street drainage, and tuberculosis control. Clubwomen, like Wilkinson, were also active in interracial organizations, including the YWCA and local Interracial Committees that were created in the aftermath of the widespread racial conflicts that marked the bloody year 1919.[39]

Susan Dart Butler was a founding member of the SCFCWC, but Charleston did not create a city organization until the spring of 1916. At that time, the NACW's first president, Mary Church Terrell, spoke at Charleston's Mt. Zion A.M.E. Church. "Oh, my," recalled Mamie Garvin Fields, "when I saw her walk onto that podium in her pink evening dress and long white gloves, with her beautifully done hair, she *was* the Modern Woman. . . . No one wanted to miss a word." As Fields remembered, Terrell counseled the women in the audience, "to do more than other women." "We must go into our communities and improve them; we must go out into the nation and change it," Terrell implored the audience. "Above all, we must organize ourselves as Negro women and work together." Terrell asked the women in attendance to look to the examples of Harriet Tubman and Sojourner Truth. "WHO OF YOU KNOW HOW TO CARRY YOUR BURDEN IN THE HEAT OF THE DAY?" she demanded to know. Capitalizing on the enthusiasm generated by the gathering, Ida Green, the wife of Centenary Church pastor Nathaniel Green, led the organization of the City Federation. Jeannette Cox was subsequently chosen as a delegate to the annual meeting of the State Federation later that year.[40]

On December 5, Cox organized the Phyllis Wheatley Literary and Social Club in the Avery Teachers' Home on Bull Street. "The Phyllis Wheatley," Cox wrote, "was to be a sort of social crucible in which we might begin a mixture of a perfect social compound. For at that time all of Charleston's ills were laid to the lack of unity among its social groups." At the core of the Phyllis Wheatley's mission was the goal of "self improvement" through "literary and community work." Over the history of the organization, its members supported the Jenkins Orphanage, raised money for the NAACP's Anti-Lynching Crusade, worked with the State Interracial Committee, sponsored speaking events for Du Bois and Langston Hughes, and organized cultural events, including a Marion Anderson recital. From the beginning, the club was closely tied to the NAACP and Avery. Susan Dart Butler and Pauline Seba both became charter members of the Charleston NAACP as did the husbands of Cox and Lula W. DeMond. Half of the Phyllis Wheatley's initial members, which the club limited to twenty, were Avery teachers.[41]

Cox and the early members of the Phyllis Wheatley envisioned the creation of the club "as a splendid little way of beginning that united, homogenous Negro society." Although Cox assumed that a "homogenous Negro society" was both desirable and achievable, she also recognized that the creation of a unified (in her words "homogenous") black community was a process, a struggle, that she later explained, she and her contemporaries would have to "look forward to others completing long after [they] had passed from the state of action." For Cox, the Phyllis Wheatley was to serve as a laboratory for the creation of a united black community. And yet, as she later noted, the club's limited membership called for a "ruthlessness of selection." Indeed, the very social divisions that Cox sought to combat arrested the club's own efforts to unify the community. "For instead of that perfect affinity and blending of certain elements," she later lamented, "in several instances we had a few explosions and in the process, some of the members escaped as uncontrollable gasses. . . . It is safe to say that all of one group withdrew and finally we were resolved into a club whose members were representative of one group and so we have remained until the present day."[42]

Born in Charleston in 1888, Mamie Garvin Fields understood the problem of Charleston's early club movement through the lens of color and class. "Charleston attitudes held back progress," she explained. "Many people in the community were not invited to join the individual clubs; regardless to your ability, your education, your readiness to serve, you were excluded." So, in 1925, along with Lem Lewis and Viola Turner, two nurses at Charleston's McClennan Hospital, Fields organized her own club, the Modern Priscilla. "We didn't look for women of any particular description, and we didn't just call together people we already knew," she remembered. "We wanted to find energetic people who wanted to do more than meet and socialize." The largest group of members, according to Fields, was teachers, but the Modern Priscilla also counted several housewives, a domestic worker, businesswomen, and beauticians among its membership. Susan Dart Butler was a member of both the Phyllis Wheatley and the Modern Priscilla. Fields and other members of the Modern Priscilla worked tirelessly in a range of uplift activities. They raised money for school scholarships, lobbied for recreational facilities for black children, worked to remedy dismal housing conditions in Charleston's black waterfront neighborhoods, and helped to deliver much-needed healthcare to workers and sharecroppers in the Charleston countryside and surrounding sea islands.[43]

Although black Charlestonians were, to be sure, divided by class, color, and organization on the eve of World War I, it would be a mistake to understand those divisions and differences as either immutable or somehow transhistorical. Intra-racial class and color distinctions, like interracial ones, mark relationships of power—they are products of history and, therefore, subject to contest and revision. Put another way, class identities, like race and gender identities, are historically produced; there is nothing natural or automatic about class. "Power can only be *realized* at the level of everyday practice," Thomas C. Holt explains, "and it is dependent—ultimately and inherently—on the production of the relations, idioms, and the world-views that are its means of action. In short, the everyday is where the macro-level phenomena— politics, economics, ideologies—are lived." Indeed, despite the elite social and economic backgrounds of its founding members, almost from its inception, the Charleston NAACP demonstrated that its initial class biases were subject to change and even transformation.[44]

In the midst of wartime mobilization, and as black Charlestonians migrated North in growing numbers, Charleston's NAACP played a critical role in encouraging *intra*-racial cooperation across lines of class, organization, and geography. Between 1910 and 1920, the number of black people living in the city of Charleston declined from 52.8 percent to 47.6 percent of the total population.[45] In May 1917, Charleston's first NAACP secretary, Richard Mickey, explained the pressures of war mobilization and black out-migration this way:

> During the past few months several hundred colored people have left Charleston for various points in the North and West to fill po-

sitions [in wartime industry]. This means that the very best labor among the colored people is leaving because of lack of work.

This also means a decrease, not only in the gross earnings of the colored people, but also in the gross earnings of whites. It is not now a question of sentiment, but one of economic moment for this City. At present, the majority of those who have left for other points are not from the home owning class. The EXODUS from Charleston is only beginning. In all probability, it will reach two thousand by June 30th.[46]

For Mickey and the NAACP, the rising tide of black migration provided the impetus and rationale to demand that Charleston's Navy Yard begin to employ black workers—specifically black women. In the spring of 1917, Charleston's local civil service secretary refused to hire black women in the Navy Yard's Clothing Factory. With the assistance of Francis Grimké, a former Charlestonian and, at the time, the Washington, D.C., NAACP branch president, the Charleston NAACP carried out a letter-writing and lobbying campaign that secured 250 jobs for black women in the Navy Yard Clothing Factory. The jobs secured for the women paid an aggregate salary of "no less than $150,000.00 a year," a substantial sum for the women and for the local economy that stood to benefit from the new source of revenue.[47]

The motives of Charleston's NAACP leaders were mixed. Its early members were worried as much (perhaps) about the cost of black out-migration to local black businesses as they were about the livelihoods of potential black migrants. "Can the Landlords, Real Estate Agents, Grocers, Butchers, Dry Goods and all other classes of Merchants afford the loss which will ensue?" Mickey asked. Yet, in this particular moment, the interests of Charleston's black business community converged with the interests of the city's black female workers, who, under less unusual circumstances, typically found little employment outside of domestic service. Regardless of motive, the Charleston NAACP achieved a growing level of respect and prestige among black Charlestonians in the aftermath of the Navy Yard victory. By the spring of 1918, membership in the organization had begun to push beyond its original social and professional boundaries. Women employed by the Navy Yard joined the local branch, as did "housekeepers," employees of the U.S. Mail Service, and common laborers. These new members did not displace the association's existing leadership, but they represented a new dues-paying constituency within the organization that could exert new pressures and make new demands on the branch.[48]

In 1918 and 1919, the Charleston NAACP continued to expand its membership base and its influence. In large part it did so through its efforts to force city officials to employ black teachers in the city's black public schools. Following his visit to Charleston in March 1919, Du Bois wrote in *The Crisis*, "Of all the cities in the South, Charleston is guilty of the meanest act toward colored folks. It keeps in their schools white teachers, teachers who do not want to be there; teachers who do despise their work and who work mainly for the money which it brings them. . . . The colored people of Charleston have stood this long enough," he stated incredulously. "They should awake and stop it."[49]

For black Charlestonians, the issue of securing quality education for their children had long been of great concern, and the exclusion of black teachers from black schools proved a constant reminder of the state of black public education and black political powerlessness. "Is it fair to our sons and daughters," one black Charlestonian wanted to know in 1886, "that after graduation from the city schools and other high schools, they are not allowed even to teach their own race?" From a practical standpoint, the city's anomalous practice of reserving all but two teaching jobs in its black public schools for white teachers meant a loss of jobs for educated black Charlestonians, and it left the education of black children in the hands of teachers who were often as racist as the city officials who reserved teaching jobs for whites only. Symbolically, the exclusion of black teachers from the public school system was a visible reminder of black powerlessness—of black Charlestonians' continued reliance on the goodwill of white people to meet their basic needs.[50]

Charleston had three public schools for black children in 1917. Black children attended either the Simonton School or the Shaw Memorial School through the fifth grade. The latter school was named after Col. Robert Gould Shaw, the commander of the Fifty-fourth Massachusetts Colored Regiment and founded, in part, by black Union soldiers. The Burke Industrial School, which opened in 1911 as the Charleston Colored Industrial School, originally educated children through only the eighth grade, but included a program through grade eleven by 1925.[51] Mamie Garvin Fields entered the Shaw Memorial School in the third grade and later remembered how first and second graders were crammed into classrooms and seated on bleachers to accommodate the overcrowding. She also recalled her experience with one of her white teachers, Miss Dessisseaux. She was "a Rebel, a pure Rebel," Fields recounted. "Her job was to teach little children, but it seemed that she couldn't stand the little black children that she had to teach. She always walked with an old-time parasol, rain or shine, and she used that parasol to make sure you didn't come too near her."[52]

The practice of excluding black teachers from the public school system proved "very irksome to the colored people in Charleston," NAACP branch president "Teddy" Harleston explained. "[T]hey have tried to have it changed three times; they tried it thirty-five years ago and they tried it twenty years ago, but failed."[53] Understanding the broad appeal of the issue, by late 1917, the Charleston NAACP contemplated a campaign to secure employment of black teachers in the black public school system. NAACP officials spent much of 1918 rallying the city's black male and female residents for a campaign that they understood correctly would require broad-based community support. "We conducted 16 public meetings throughout the city," Harleston later told an NAACP convention audience. "I spoke at every one of them, and on every occasion I took the pains to put them on notice that if there were any traitors among us we should read them out."[54]

Harleston and other members of the branch Executive Committee addressed audiences at twelve of Charleston's largest churches. In doing so, they built support not only for the campaign to employ black teachers, but also for the NAACP. In the summer of 1918, the Charleston NAACP lobbied successfully to move local law enforcement officials to arrest and prosecute (albeit unsuccessfully) a white streetcar conductor who had murdered a black passenger and a white man accused of attempting to rape a ten-year-old black girl. By November, more than one thousand black Charlestonians had become members of the NAACP. "We find that the thousands of people addressed have enthusiastically hailed the establishment of this Branch as a blessing," Harleston wrote, "and we feel that they will back us in any undertaking in their behalf."[55]

In the fall and early winter, local NAACP officials lobbied the Charleston Board of Commissioners, sending a petition requesting that the city employ black teachers in black schools. The city responded with vague promises that it would employ black teachers just as soon as new schools were constructed in the future. After hearing the city's response, Harleston began making plans to petition the state legislature. "We had that talk before," he explained. "I told them I could not go back to our people and give them any such promise, that we had to have something definite and tangible." To make his case before the state legislature, Harleston relied on the aging black Reconstruction era leader Thomas E. Miller to chair the campaign committee.[56] The fair-skinned Miller had been born to free parents in 1849. In 1874 he served as the Beaufort County school commissioner. He went on to serve four terms in the lower house of the state legislature, one term in the state senate, and two terms in the U.S. Congress. Miller became the chairman of the state Republican Party in 1882. He was a delegate to the 1895 state constitutional convention and served as the first president of the Colored Normal, Industrial, Agricultural and Mechanical College (later South Carolina State College) in Orangeburg, from 1896 until Governor Coleman Blease removed him from the position in 1911. Harleston's choice of Miller was likely intended to draw on the spirit of Reconstruction era black Republican Party politics and to capitalize on Miller's old legislative connections. With Miller on board, the NAACP-sponsored committee drafted a petition requesting that the state legislature amend existing state law to make it "unlawful for a person of the white race to teach in the free public schools of South Carolina provided and set aside for the children of the Negro race."[57]

With the assistance of Butler Nance and the Columbia NAACP the petition was submitted to the state legislature as a bill. The petitioners were themselves wary of a legal prohibition of white teachers in black schools, but they also understood the Jim Crow realities of the world in which they lived. Indeed, by invoking the full logic of segregation law and practice, the Charleston and Columbia NAACP were able to muster enough support in the legislature for their bill to outmaneuver strident opposition and force Charleston officials to accept their demand for black teachers in black public schools. On February 3, the Charleston board of public commissioners voted that beginning September 1, 1920, "no white teachers shall be employed in the public schools in the city of Charleston to teach Negro pupils, but that Negro teachers will be employed to teach Negro pupils." In effect, the resolution avoided legislative action at the state level and, by the fall of 1920, all of the teachers employed in Charleston's black public schools were black. It was a triumph for black teachers, the black community in Charleston, and also for the NAACP.[58]

The victory represented, in many ways, the dawning of a new stage in the black struggle for civil rights and self-determination in Charleston and in South Carolina, revealing both the limits of inter-racial diplomacy and the effectiveness of independent black political organization. The cooperation of the Columbia branch revealed the possibilities of new intra-racial alliances and future coordinated political activity on a statewide level. Just as significant, however, were key developments at the local level. The struggle to secure the employment of black teachers involved heightened levels of participation and interaction among black Charlestonians. Large public meetings and the NAACP's effort to obtain the signatures of black city residents in favor of the petition campaign connected black Charlestonians together in new ways. "In 1919 the NAACP raised up an army to collect signatures from door to door," Fields recounted. "I joined. In fact, so many joined until you almost wonder who was left at home just to sign. The whole community joined hands." By the spring of 1919, black Charlestonians were increasingly conscious of their rights and of their collective capacity to demand and secure them. Membership in the Charleston NAACP reached 1,300 and, as the organization grew in size, it incorporated members who would play important roles in the future movement in the state.[59]

One of the new movement participants was Septima Poinsette Clark. Clark was born in Charleston in 1898. Her father had been enslaved on a low country plantation and her mother, although born in Charleston, grew up in Haiti. Clark began her education in the Charleston public schools, but she graduated from Avery and passed the state teacher's exam in 1916. Unable to teach in the city's public schools, she—as did countless educated black women in Charleston, including Mamie Garvin Fields—found a teaching job on Johns Island, one of the many sea islands off the coast of Charleston. "Today over great bridges and rolling concrete highways one may travel in a few minutes," Clark later recalled, "to the place I would reach only after what seemed an interminable pushing along wide rivers and intercoastal waterways into a strange land that might have been, for all I knew about it, on the other side of the Atlantic."[60]

For Clark and women like Fields, the experience on Johns Island opened their eyes to the conditions of black people in the most isolated rural areas of South Carolina. In 1919 the men and women who lived on Johns Island made their livings as sharecroppers, tenant farmers, small landowners, and day laborers. Many spoke in an African and Caribbean inflected, regional dialect known as Gullah, believed in "hag" or witchcraft, and practiced a style of folk Christianity. Illiteracy was pervasive and healthcare sorely lacking. For the children of Johns Island, the school year followed the rhythms of the cotton planting and harvesting seasons. Visiting teachers were often individually responsible for educating as many as one hundred students in rundown, one-room schools with few supplies. Island parents were, in turn, responsible for providing teachers with food, housing, and sometimes pay, which could take the form of locally produced goods. Transportation to and from the island was still done by boat when Clark taught there, leaving island inhabitants geographically separated from the city of Charleston. The separation was, however, not simply one of geography. "The Johns Island folk, like those on other sea islands," Clark explained, "were suspicious of the mainland folk, even the Charleston Negroes, and the Charleston people in turn looked down on the islanders." Even well-intentioned teachers such as Clark and Fields viewed the people of Johns Island with a mixture of pejorative intrigue, mild disdain, sincere empathy, and genuine admiration. But, despite their prejudices, the struggle of teaching on Johns Island armed Fields and Clark with experiences that tied them (however tenuously) to the men and women of the island and (for Clark in particular) laid a foundation for future cooperation and struggle.[61]

After two years of teaching on Johns Island, Clark took a teaching position at Avery in the fall of 1918. "I realize now," she would later write, "that the experience at Avery was one of the most important and formative experiences of my life. It was then that I first became actively concerned in an organized effort to improve the lot of my fellow Negroes." Once at Avery, Clark became active in the NAACP's mounting campaign to employ black teachers in Charleston's black public schools. According to Clark, Thomas Miller approached Principal Cox to ask the assistance of Avery teachers in the NAACP's door-to-door petition drive. "That's when I got into the fight," Clark wrote. "I volunteered to seek signatures and started visiting the grass roots people. I worked Cannon Street, a very long street, from Rutledge all the way to King." Clark brought her experiences and concerns from Johns Island to the rapidly growing NAACP. In turn, she was politicized by her work with the civil rights organization. Not even twenty-one when she canvassed door-to-door collecting signatures for the NAACP's petition drive, Clark would draw from this early political and organizing experience in her future work for the association, the Highlander Folk School, and the Southern Christian Leadership Conference.[62]

The changes of early 1919 were immediately palpable in Charleston. During the NAACP's petition drive, white Charleston officials resorted to old political tactics to defeat the nascent social movement. Attempting to divide black Charlestonians by class and color, Clark recalled, some white Charlestonians "shouted for all to hear that mulattoes were the only ones who wanted Negro teachers for their children. The cooks and laundresses, they declared, didn't want their children taught by Negro teachers."[63] While such a strategy might have worked in an earlier era, it failed to do so in early 1919. When questions were raised about the "true" representative nature of the campaign's "highbrow and mulatto" leadership, Thomas Miller and Edwin Harleston were able to produce the signatures of twenty-five thousand black men and women, stamping their leadership with a symbol of legitimacy. Moreover, what had started as a campaign to employ black teachers had begun to transform into a more expansive and multi-issued movement for black empowerment.[64]

The issue of the franchise and black political power had emerged as pressing topics of concern by the spring of 1919. The campaign for black teachers revealed, ever so clearly, that access to the ballot was critical if past gains were to be secured and future ones made possible. "At every one of the meetings which we addressed during a part of last year and this," Harleston informed an audience at the NAACP's 1919 annual meeting, "I urged my people to register and vote." During the campaign for black teachers, Harleston organized, "for the sake of saving expense to the Charleston branch," an "imaginary" association, the Cosmopolitan Club, to help register black voters under the direction of the Charleston NAACP. In April, Harleston claimed that one thousand black men had registered to vote in Charleston, even though local registrars refused to register more than forty to fifty men a day. "It has been a most interesting sight to see men extending halfway around the block heading in to the registration office," Harleston proudly noted. For Harleston, the spirit and activity in Charleston were hopeful signs of things to come, but he recognized that recent victories would prove fleeting in the absence of formal political power. The Navy Yard and black teacher campaigns had been important first steps in an emergent movement, but a campaign to secure employment for black men in the Navy Yard loomed in the future. Moreover, black Charlestonians never simply wanted black teachers in black schools; they also wanted more schools, and better ones at that.

Harleston believed that the future of the movement and the fate of black Charlestonians depended on the ability of black people in South Carolina and around the nation to fight for and win the right to vote. "If we register 3,000 Negroes in Charleston," he surmised, "we shall be holding over the heads of the white voter the possibility of a black primary." "I want the National Association branches all over the country to be thinking more of the extension of the franchise." Because, he explained, "After all methods have been tried, and after all the plans that we have devised have been used—it all reverts back to the ballot for our salvation."[65] On this point, Harleston was not alone. On February 4, black leaders from across the state gathered in Columbia to formulate a "magna carta of rights and aspirations of the race to blend with the new freedom and spirit of the reconstruction era." While Harleston envisioned the possibility of a "black primary," an all-black alternative to the white primary, Allen University president Bishop W.D. Chappelle envisioned black South Carolinians wielding the "balance of power" between competing factions in the state Democratic Party. "What I want to see," Chappelle expounded at the meeting, "is the Democratic party divided. . . . I would be willing to follow anyone, even the old devil himself part of the way, who could split the Democratic party." Those in attendance were urged to awaken interest in the franchise, to form voting clubs, and to work to register voters. Participants passed resolutions demanding better schools and equal rights for black people. "No people can hope to continue long to exist, and wield any influence in the body politic," they resolved, "unless it, not only represents high and lofty principle, but has the power to enforce and sustain those principles."[66]

By the early months of 1919 the black struggle for civil rights, self-determination, and equality in South Carolina had found new life, and the NAACP emerged as a central institution in that struggle. Following the lead of Columbia and Charleston, six additional NAACP branches were organized in South Carolina between April 1918 and June 1919. The branches traversed the state, from Aiken and Anderson in the state's western piedmont region, to Darlington and Florence in the northeast along the Pee Dee River, to the university town of Orangeburg situated in the heart of the state's cotton-producing black belt, to the low country town of Beaufort just north of Savannah, Georgia. The NAACP promised to tie black South Carolinians together in new ways and connect them to a national black community that was only beginning to take shape at the close of the First World War. Despite and because of Jim Crow, racial violence, war mobilization, the upheaval of mass migration, and the limits of uplift work, black South Carolinians turned to the NAACP as a vehicle for leveraging their collective power to lay claim to full citizenship rights and a greater measure of self-determination. In the process of struggle, the initial gender, class, and regional biases of the organization and the movement were subtly (if only temporarily) transformed, and the paternalistic ethos of racial uplift and backroom interracial diplomacy was issued a sharp challenge. To be sure, the struggle was far from over by the close of World War I. In a sense, it had only just begun.[67]

2 Riot and Reaction: The Lineaments of Reinvention

Every step of progress realized by the black man seems to be an occasion for the South to renew its assault upon him.

—Bishop John Hurst

This is the day of racial activity, when each and every group of this great human family must exercise its own initiative and influence in its own protection, therefore, Negroes should be more determined today than they have ever been, because the mighty forces of the world are operating against non-organized groups of peoples, who are not ambitious enough to protect their own interests.

—Marcus Garvey

In the early months of 1919 the black struggle for self-determination and equality in South Carolina continued to grow in size and power. The NAACP began to expand beyond its initial base of operations in Columbia and Charleston and its original gender and class biases became subject to challenge and revision. By the fall, black teachers were teaching in Charleston's black public schools and within a year black women were organizing to secure voting rights. Edwin "Teddy" Harleston and W.D. Chappelle even imagined the potential of an organized black populace capable of splitting the all-white state Democratic Party and holding the balance of power in statewide elections. In the May 1919 issue of *The Crisis*, W.E.B. Du Bois captured the spirit of the times and announced a new stage in the black struggle for freedom. "Make way for Democracy!" he exclaimed. "We saved it in France, and by the Great Jehovah, we will save it in the United States of America, or know the reason why."[1] At the end of June, the NAACP held its first national conference since the gathering in Amenia three years earlier. A predominantly black audience representing thirty-four states attended the meeting in Cleveland, Ohio. The strong presence of branches from the Deep South, including Columbia and Charleston, was a testament to James Weldon Johnson's wartime organizing efforts and offered great promise for the future of an escalating black social movement confined to no single region of the United States.[2] But if circumstances, in part created by the war to make the world safe for democracy, provided black South Carolinians with an opportunity to organize, to raise questions about inequality, and to demand citizenship rights, the war and growing levels of black assertiveness simultaneously produced countervailing forces. There was nothing natural or automatic about seizing the opportunity presented by the tumult of war and out-migration to secure a greater measure of political and economic justice. Indeed, at the same moment that President Woodrow Wilson linked international democracy to the issue of national self-determination in efforts to galvanize support for the Treaty of Versailles, as Du Bois called for a new era of black militancy and American democracy, and as the NAACP teetered on the edge of newfound power, an era of reaction was inaugurated in a race riot on the streets of Charleston. Over the course of the 1920s, the winds of progress forged during the war were slowly strangled and, yet, apparent disaster simultaneously laid the groundwork for the remaking of the black struggle for civil rights and American democracy.

Riot and Reaction

During the early Saturday evening of May 10, 1919, on the corner of Beaufain and Charles streets just outside Harry Police's pool hall in downtown Charleston, a group of white Navy sailors, known as "blue jackets," stationed at the Sixth Navy District's headquarters in North Charleston, clashed with a group of local black men. What likely began as verbal altercation or mild jostling inside the pool hall, turned into a clash of fists and pool hall sticks on the streets outside. In the ensuing melee, two white sailors, George Holloday and Jacob Cohen, shot and killed Isaac Doctor, an unarmed black man who was likely involved in the initial scuffle inside. Whatever the origin of the fight, soon thereafter the brawl escalated into a full-scale race riot when white civilians joined the blue jackets and chased the crowd of black men through the city streets south toward Charleston's "segregated district."[3]

As the mob gave chase down King and Meeting streets, two of

Charleston's main north-south thoroughfares, sailors broke into two local shooting galleries and armed themselves with small caliber rifles and ammunition. Once fully armed, members of the mob fired indiscriminately into crowds of black people ducking into alleyways and scurrying for cover. Peter Irving, Edward Campbell, and James Wilson took bullets in the back, while others took shots to the head and legs. The shot that hit the thirteen-year-old Irving paralyzed him from the hips down. At the corner of King and Market streets, members of the mob pulled a black man from a streetcar and murdered him in full sight of horrified diners in a nearby restaurant. Further to the south on Broad Street, another black man was yanked from a streetcar, beaten, and shot. On King Street, the mob broke into Fredie's Central Shaving Parlor, a black-owned barbershop that catered to a white clientele, and ransacked it. Reported to be "several thousand" strong, by midnight the mob virtually controlled the downtown area. By then, rumors spread that black Charlestonians had armed themselves to fight back, and it was reported that black snipers fired on servicemen as they attempted to make their way back to their base in North Charleston.

Initially the city police and on-duty naval provost officers could do or did little to control the rioters. Although the riot began at approximately 9:30 P.M., Charleston's chief of police did not request additional assistance from military commanders in North Charleston until near midnight. By the time a few truckloads of marines arrived downtown at approximately 1:30 A.M. the riot was largely over. Marines patrolled the streets through the night, but the streets were clear and city officials began the task of assessing the damage by morning. In all, three black men were murdered—two died the night of the riot and another passed away within the week. The number of injured black civilians remains difficult to assess, in large part because friends and family treated many of the injured who stayed clear of Charleston's Roper Hospital. However, reports of the riot indicate that, in addition to those murdered, as many as forty black Charlestonians were shot or beaten by the mob.[4] In the days following the riot, a coroner's jury refused to determine the identity of the sailors involved in the murder of two of the victims, Doctor and James Talbert. Although the city's police chief identified Holloday and Cohen as the killers, the jury concluded only that the deaths of the two men "came from wounds inflicted with a rifle or pistol . . . in the hands of enlisted men while engaged in a riot on May 10."[5]

The riot and its aftermath left black Charlestonians battered and enraged. Harleston and the local NAACP immediately began their own investigation of what they understood as a clear-cut case of lynching—a murder at the hands of parties unknown.[6] But despite attempts to spur federal action, black Charlestonians were left to make the best of circumstances marked by a rising level of racial animus. Harleston and other layman leaders joined forces with the Interdenominational Ministers' Union (IMU) to "deplore the action of the mob and the conditions which made its action possible." In a statement published in the *News and Courier*, the group demanded that the mayor and city officials use their influence to bring all members of the mob to justice, and they demanded that the city take proactive steps to prevent future violence. In addition to requesting an official acknowledgement and condemnation of the "spirit of mob rule," the IMU called for an enlargement of the city police force and the inclusion of black officers on it. They also sought overall improvements in the living conditions of black Charlestonians, from housing, to sanitation, to education.[7] Ultimately the city reimbursed the owners of Fredie's Central Shaving Parlor for damages sustained during the riot and the Navy finally convicted and punished six of the sailors involved in the May 10 rampage.[8] For black Charlestonians these remedies were small consolation for a problem they deemed to run much deeper.

The riot did not on its own signal the collapse of the growing movement for social justice in South Carolina. It did, however, prove to be a sign of a perceptible shift in the climate of reform in the state and the nation. The riot in Charleston marked the beginning of the long and bloody Red Summer of 1919, a summer that witnessed a nationwide wave of antiradical and antiblack violence, and opened a decade of rising racist and nativist sentiment.[9] In the weeks following the Charleston riot, Harleston's life was threatened for his ongoing protest activities. Although he refused to scale back his efforts, he also recognized the overwhelming challenges ahead. "We are continuing this work," he explained at the NAACP's June convention. "We have the right to live in Charleston in pursuit of happiness. We keep it up [but] if we go down we want you, The National Association to know we go down fighting."[10]

During the 1920s, fighting just not to "go down" is what the NAACP had to do simply to remain a presence in South Carolina. The riot in Charleston demonstrated that South Carolina's urban centers were no havens from racial violence. Even in the state's most cosmopolitan and self-consciously gentile city, the smallest challenge to the racial status quo could provoke massive violence and pierce the city's veneer of racial civility. But despite the ever-present possibility of such violence, the urban centers of Charleston and Columbia offered black South Carolinians a certain degree of political maneuverability virtually unimaginable in other areas of the state. In Charleston and Columbia, at least the NAACP could organize publicly—a luxury that most other black South Carolinians could ill afford without devastating consequences.

Outside of Charleston and Columbia, NAACP activity could and did bring swift white racist reaction. In March, black residents in the piedmont town of Anderson assumed the risk to their lives and careers and chartered their own NAACP branch. Located in the heart of South Carolina's bustling textile industry and surrounded by fertile cotton land, the town of Anderson sat just twenty miles to the north of Abbeville where Anthony Crawford had been brutally lynched three years earlier. The branch chose as its leader M.H. Gassaway, a well-respected member of Anderson's black community. Thirty years earlier he had begun a small school for black children, which by 1919 had split into a grammar school and a high school with a total enrollment of twelve hundred students and twenty-three teachers, and was administered by the county. At the time Gassaway was elected president of the Anderson NAACP branch, the county employed him as principal of the high school. Reflecting the interests of Anderson's black residents and his own professional predilections, Gassaway immediately turned the NAACP branch's efforts to a campaign to secure additional funds to hire better teachers and extend the length of the school year. At the same time, the branch worked to protect black soldiers returning to Anderson from military service in France and elsewhere. Gassaway fought Anderson officials who turned work or fight laws into a postwar means to force returning soldiers back into the cotton fields. "I got that stopped," Gassaway explained, "by talking to the Mayor and stating the facts regarding our soldiers and that if this were not stopped, they would leave Anderson."[11]

Almost from the branch's inception, Gassaway came under attack for his work on behalf of the NAACP. The editor of the *Anderson Tribune* carried on a two-month-long newspaper campaign in an attempt to discredit Gassaway and force him to cease his NAACP activities.

He accused Gassaway of "preaching social equality" and called for Anderson officials to fire him from his job as principal. When the editor's written efforts failed to persuade Anderson officials to fire Gassaway, he resorted to other means. Soon Gassaway learned that his life was in jeopardy if he remained in Anderson. According to one report, Gassaway sought the assistance of Anderson's chief of police, but when he did so, the *Tribune* editor confronted him at the police station. "Gassaway, if you are not out of town by sundown and no one has killed you," he warned, "I will do the job for you." On the advice of friends, Gassaway made the painful decision to leave Anderson and head for the North where he settled in Cleveland, Ohio. He did not leave alone. Two other men who had attended the NAACP's annual meeting in Cleveland, including the Reverend S.B.B. Simmons, were forced to leave town as well.[12]

The forced departure of the three NAACP leaders led to the rapid decline of Anderson's NAACP branch, which remained dormant until the 1940s. It also signaled a crisis for the national office of the NAACP. On the one hand, the national office was exuberant; by the end of 1919 its membership reached nearly one hundred thousand and the majority of its members lived in the South where four out of five African Americans still resided in 1920. Hope ran so high that the association made the decision to hold its 1920 convention in Atlanta, the first such NAACP convention to be held in the South and a sign of the growing power of black southerners in the organization.[13] On the other hand, the NAACP's new presence in the South and its growing national power made the organization a target of rising racial animus and inspired a wave of reaction to the organization in the region. "I believe that as the Negro gains in education and power," Mary White Ovington explained, "discrimination will increase and conditions in the South will grow worse."[14] In an important sense, Ovington was right. In the South, progress was revealed as much by growing levels of violence and mayhem as it was by quantifiable statistics indicating rising levels of education, income, and registered voters. While Gassaway's forced departure from South Carolina provided a visible symbol to black South Carolinians of the dangers and costs of organizing a chapter of the NAACP, events in Texas contributed to a region-wide climate of intimidation, with serious ramifications for the NAACP in the Deep South and the nation.[15]

During the war years, black Texans organized the most vibrant group of NAACP branches in the South and perhaps in the nation. By September 1919 thirty-three NAACP branches operated across the state with a total membership of nearly 7,700. Black Texans chartered branches in rural and urban areas and membership transgressed lines of class and gender. But from the beginning the NAACP in Texas faced heavy opposition from state officials and vigilance committees that blurred distinctions between state and private authority.[16] In August 1919, the governor's office took measures to force the NAACP to halt operations in the state. Utilizing laws that required corporations doing business in Texas to register with the state, the state attorney general subpoenaed the records of the recently formed Austin branch. Shortly thereafter, John Shillady, the NAACP's secretary, traveled to Texas to investigate and attempt to make clear to state officials that the NAACP was a nonprofit organization and did not need to register as a corporation. After meeting with an acting attorney general, state officials served Shillady with a subpoena and required him to answer questions before a "secret session" of a Court of Inquiry. The morning following the state interrogation, as he stepped outside of his hotel room to make a phone call, Shillady was assaulted and beaten unconscious by a mob that included members of the previous day's Court of Inquiry. After receiving medical treatment and belatedly recognizing the danger posed to his life, Shillady quickly boarded a train and headed north. At year's end, Shillady resigned from the staff of the NAACP.[17]

Shillady's exit was only one of many indications of the NAACP's growing troubles. By the end of 1921, only seven of Texas's thirty-three branches remained and membership hovered at barely 1,100.[18] In Mississippi, leaders of a newly formed branch in Vicksburg were forced to flee the state. In 1920, the Mississippi state legislature took steps to outlaw the distribution and possession of literature deemed likely "to disturb relations between the races," leading to the arrest, beating, and imprisonment of a *Crisis* agent. Even with repeated efforts to organize branches in the state, by 1929 only a single officially chartered branch remained in operation.[19] In Thomasville, Georgia, the local branch disbanded in 1920 after the life of its president was threatened and he was fired from his job as a mail carrier.[20] In Louisiana the NAACP could not establish a substantive foothold in the state. "The NAACP is thoroughly hated in this section," explained Shreveport's branch president in 1923. "The great trouble here is that they do not want the southern Negro to have much dealings with his northern brother."[21] Across the region, as established branches struggled to survive amid mounting opposition, the dramatic growth of new branches experienced by the NAACP between 1916 and 1920 came to a careening halt by the first years of the 1920s.[22]

Although opposition to the NAACP proved most daunting at the local level, it also registered at the national level in a speech delivered on the floor of the U.S. House of Representatives in late August 1919 by James F. Byrnes, a fifth-term congressman from South Carolina. "I have become convinced," he exclaimed, "that the race antagonism manifesting itself throughout the country is due to the incendiary utterances of the would-be leaders of the race now being circulated through negro [*sic*] newspapers and magazines." Singling out Du Bois and his May 1919 *Crisis* editorial, "Returning Soldiers," Byrnes linked the NAACP to the radical International Workers of the World (IWW) and placed the blame for the nation's summer-long spasm of violence squarely on the shoulders of both. He called for the federal government to prosecute leaders like Du Bois under provisions of wartime espionage law. "If . . . charging the Government with lynching, disfranchising its citizens, encouraging ignorance, and stealing from its citizens, does not constitute a violation of the espionage law," he argued, "it is difficult to conceive language sufficiently abusive to constitute a violation." For Byrnes, the upsurge of black activism during the war years represented a clear challenge to the structure of a world he understood to be regulated inherently by the principal of white male supremacy. "It may as well be understood," he counseled, "that the war has in no way changed the attitude of the white man toward the social and political equality of the negro [*sic*] . . . because this is a white man's country, and will always remain a white man's country."[23]

Byrnes's speech on the House floor came just a little over a year after the death of South Carolina's most notorious white supremacist, Ben Tillman. In 1913 as a second-term congressman representing South Carolina's Second District, Byrnes had linked his political fortunes to the ailing Tillman, who had just begun serving his fourth term in the U.S. Senate. "I came to love him," Byrnes recalled, "and in return he treated me as one of his sons." Edgefield County was Tillman's home and he lorded over the state's Second District that included the town and county of Aiken, where Byrnes had relocated from Charleston in 1900 and where he established his base of political operations. Tillman's own political career had been dedicated to the preservation of white male supremacy until his death in 1918. At that time, Byrnes was positioned to expand his own political influence and vie for a greater share of South Carolina's white political leadership.[24] In his speech before the House of Representatives, Byrnes took steps to assure his South Carolina constituency that the legacy of Ben Tillman—that is, of white supremacy and racial segregation—was in good hands. "I know the Negroes of my district do not seek to participate in politics," he informed the Congress and reassured his South Carolina constituency. "I know that left alone they will continue contented, and I do not want these radical negro [sic] publications, whether supported by the I.W.W., the Bolsheviki of Russia, or the misguided theorist of the North, to be circulated among them, arousing the passions of the criminal class of Negroes, and resulting in injury to the law-abiding negro [sic] as well as to the white people of the South."[25]

Perhaps Byrnes was ill-informed about the racial dynamics at work in his home state and district, or perhaps he turned a blind eye to signs of racial unrest, confident that white supremacy would be maintained in South Carolina if "outside agitators" could be kept at bay. In his hometown of Aiken, black residents had formed a branch of the NAACP in the spring of 1918, but by 1923 the branch was inoperative. "We have not been able to get our members together," the branch president wrote the national office. "If we can get to work again I will let you know." The branch would, however, not become active again until the late 1930s.[26] In the meantime, Aiken's black residents witnessed the horror of a wave of lynch terror that swept the state in the 1920s, a wave of terror that provided yet another reminder of the lawless circumstances in which they lived and of the lengths some white people would go to preserve a world ordered by white supremacy.

Between 1919 and 1927 fourteen black South Carolinians died at the hands of lynch mobs. In 1921 alone, mobs took the lives of five black people.[27] In South Carolina, the Ku Klux Klan, as it had elsewhere in the nation, made a steady resurgence in the early 1920s. Through fraternal orders, churches, and other civic organizations, the reborn Klan recruited new members from a broad cross section of the white South. In a powerful national movement bent on preserving traditional hierarchies rooted in white male supremacy, the Klan employed a host of tactics from political organization, to cross burnings, to beatings and murder in an effort to arrest the forward march of the modern world.[28] In South Carolina the Klan policed the permissible limits of black progress with the ever-present threat of brutal violence. On a Saturday evening in May 1923, with the assistance of the town's mayor, 280 hooded and robed Klansmen paraded down Main Street in the piedmont industrial town of Union displaying their "Fiery Cross."[29] In Florence, the Klan ordered the local NAACP branch to disband in 1924.[30] And in Horry County, the Klan issued a warning to black laborers working for the Conway Lumber Company who had encroached on land reserved for whites only. "To you colored folks," read the warning, "we have got to carry out our line of business and you all no where you are and we have a dose for you and it these dont move your bowels i think the next will [*sic*]."[31]

In the early part of April 1925, robed and hooded Klansmen made a visit to the home of Sam Lowman, a sharecropper working the land of William Hartley some thirteen miles from the town of Aiken. They called Lowman's son, Demon, outside and whipped him severely. The reason for the beating is not known, but within two weeks, Aiken's sheriff, H.H. Howard, received an allegedly anonymous tip that the Lowmans were selling whiskey. On April 25, accompanied by three deputies, the sheriff made his way to the Lowman home armed, supposedly, with a legal search warrant to investigate. As the four plainly dressed men approached the home, Sam Lowman was away having cornmeal ground at the local mill. His wife, Annie, and daughter, Bertha, were at work either inside the house or in the yard nearby. Although the order of events is unclear, as the sheriff and his men entered the Lowman home, Lowman's son, Demon, and nephew, Clarence, who had been plowing a field some one hundred yards away, ran to the house to assist the family members inside. In the brief moments that followed, gunshots were exchanged. In the volley of gunfire, Demon, Bertha, and Clarence were shot, and Sheriff Howard and Annie Lowman lay dead. Demon, Clarence, and Bertha, and two other family members were arrested and all five were promptly tried on charges of murder. Demon, Clarence, and Bertha were each convicted. The fourteen-year-old Clarence and his cousin Demon were sentenced to die and Bertha was sentenced to life in prison. For good measure, Sam Lowman received a two-year sentence on the chain gang.[32]

In Columbia, N.J. Frederick kept abreast of the proceedings through local press reports. Appalled at the trial in which court appointed attorneys "did nothing but see that the forms of the law were observed," Frederick decided to take up the case and appeal it to the South Carolina Supreme Court. "I saw as a lawyer that justice was far from that Court house during the trial of those people," he explained. "Being so convinced, I, at my own expense, made an appeal to the Supreme Court of South Carolina setting up seven exceptions to the proceedings." In April, Frederick convinced the state supreme court to uphold six of the seven exceptions and to order a new trial for the Lowman family.[33]

On October 5, 1926, a second trial began in Aiken in a special session of the Court of General Sessions presided over by Judge S.L. Lanham of Spartanburg. With the assistance of a white attorney, also from Spartanburg, Frederick argued the case before Judge Lanham. After poking gaping holes in the prosecution's case, Frederick won a directed verdict of "not guilty" for Demon Lowman on October 7, and the case against Clarence and Bertha appeared in jeopardy as well. Immediately following the judge's verdict, Demon was rearrested on new charges and the three defendants were returned to the Aiken jail. "That, it seems, was the deciding point for mob violence," Frederick recalled, "though from an outward indication everything was serene."[34]

In the early morning hours of October 8 prisoners in the Aiken jail heard a number of cars pull up to the jail and the laughs and chatter of a mob outside. Amid screams and scuffling, a group of men removed Bertha, Clarence, and Demon from the jail with the likely assistance of the jailor.[35] The three were then driven to an old tourist camp outside of Aiken where a large crowd of onlookers awaited. After being ordered to line up and run, they were shot down by members of the mob. Demon and Clarence each died from the first round of gunfire, but Bertha's life took repeated shots to extinguish. With the killings completed, a grand jury investigated and ruled that there was no evidence to indict members of the lynch mob. Although a region-wide outcry and national publicity followed, the killers were never brought to trial.[36]

Despite the chilling capacity of mob violence to curb black dissent and a southern judicial system that refused to protect the lives of black citizens, the decline of NAACP and black political activity during the 1920s cannot be attributed to those two factors alone. The decade of the 1920s was an economic disaster for most black South Carolinians that unleashed a virtual revolution in social relations as waves of black people voted with their feet and migrated to the North.[37] Nearly three-fourths of all black South Carolinians lived in rural areas and farmed for a living in 1920. A small portion owned their land. Others paid cash to landlords and worked their plot of land as tenants. Most traded their family's labor for a share of the landlord's crop at the end of the harvesting season. Still others hired their labor out to landlords or tenants in return for cash wages.[38] Largely locked out of the textile industry, where rural white South Carolinians often made the transition from the farm to town living, better wages, and educational opportunities, black South Carolinians possessed few options for employment within the state. During World War I, many seized the opportunity to earn higher wages in the industrial centers of the urban North, while others took advantage of a very brief upturn in the cotton economy to earn higher wages or work their way out of debt at home. But the end of the war brought with it a collapse of the cotton boom and signaled the beginning of the end of cotton tenancy in the state and region.[39]

The boll weevil, a grayish-brown, quarter-inch-long bug with a cotton-eating snout half its length, crossed Georgia's eastern border and began its invasion of South Carolina in 1917. Within two years, the boll weevil made its way to the South Carolina low country and began to feast on its world-renowned sea island cotton.[40] By the fall 1922 harvest, the production of cotton bales in the state had fallen to 493,000 from 1,623,000 two years earlier. And while production rebounded slightly in the years that followed, the overall trend was a downward spiral, a spiral accompanied by a precipitous decline in farm wage rates.[41] Most South Carolinians felt the effects of the sharp decline of cotton production, but black South Carolinians already occupying the lowest rungs of the state's economic ladder felt its effects with particular acuteness. "It was so bad we didn't have no food or nothing then," remembered one man from Greenwood County in the western region of the state. "The only crop we made that year [1919] was some peas," recalled Lizzie Wims Nash. "We ate pea bread, pea soup, peas boiled up. Farming was dead then."[42]

Migration, the UNIA, and the Unmaking of the NAACP

Between the fall 1922 harvest and the opening of the 1923 spring planting season, black South Carolinians left the state of South Carolina in droves. An estimated 50,000 exited the state between November 1, 1922, and March 31, 1923. Forty-one counties reported substantial losses of black residents. In violence-ridden Anderson, black South Carolinians abandoned a reported 700 farms. In Laurens, the site of a lynching in April 1920, some 2,000 black people packed their bags and left 1,000 farms behind. The black population dropped by 2,000 in Aiken, while in McCormick County a reported 3,600 black residents took to the road and left 2,520 farms without families to farm them.[43] For the first time since the colonial era, South Carolina passed from a majority black to a majority white state.[44] By decade's end, as many as 240,300 black South Carolinians had migrated out of the state.[45] "Folks has to mov' w'en boll weevil come," explained one sea island man. "Yes, suh. In Savannah people say, 'Yo' goin' home?' 'No, suh, I 'ent goin' home. 'Ent nothin' there but boll weevil!'"[46]

While economic hardship certainly inspired many black people to leave the state, hard economic times were not new to those who toiled in the fields of South Carolina. Nor was mob violence. Nor were Jim Crow, police brutality, and lawless courts. Black people had long deployed migration as a strategy for survival and as a means to seek out a better life, to escape racial oppression, to break free from the constraints and violence of rural households, to obtain an education, and to secure better wages. To be sure, many continued to migrate for many of these reasons.[47] But what was new about the 1920s was that a critical mass of black southerners had established themselves in the urban North by the close of World War I, connecting black people to the world outside of the South in a way they had not been connected before. "The people had been livin' in the dark," explained one South Carolina migrant. "They didn't know they was in reach of any place other that the cotton field. Then the war broke out and soldiers were carried away. . . . Their eyes were opened. They tasted something better. They wrote to their friends after they came to New York, and *opened their* eyes so people began coming."[48]

From as early as 1915, new communities of transplanted black South Carolinians began to emerge in northern urban centers such as Philadelphia and Harlem, slowly carving out spaces for themselves in cramped urban quarters already occupied by earlier generations of migrants, longtime black residents, and white ethnic workers.[49] By 1930, black people born in Virginia, South Carolina, and North Carolina accounted for better than two-thirds of black Philadelphia's population.

And one in ten of those migrants made their way to the city from South Carolina. Between 1917 and 1923 nearly one of every two African Americans leaving South Carolina found their way to the City of Brotherly Love.[50] Through letter writing, visits home, and the hosting of southern guests, transplanted black South Carolinians connected friends and family in the South to these new northern communities.[51] In the urban North, black South Carolinians established churches and businesses that functioned as community centers and helped to create a community of black South Carolinians "up North." Once in Philadelphia, George Bailey Sr., a native of Greenwood, started his own grocery store after working for a time at the Campbell's Soup Company. The store served as a communication center for arriving migrants and was a critical site in the making of a new northern black community. Another group of black South Carolinians established the Morris Baptist Chapel Church, which held its first service in a horse stable in 1917. The creation of the church was an explicit attempt to re-create the Morris Baptist Chapel Church that the migrants left behind in Greenwood. By 1927 the church had relocated and served as an important institution that brought transplanted black southerners together in a new northern context.[52]

Life in the urban North was hardly easy. Migrants often left the South for overcrowded, unhealthy living conditions, low-wage unskilled service jobs, chronic unemployment, as well as white hatred and racist violence. Beulah Nelson left the regiment and obligations of sharecropping in South Carolina for domestic work in Washington, D.C. Life in the District of Columbia, she explained, "was not good like home. Crowded smelly streets, noise, and confusion was all I saw. And people talked about it like it was somethin' near 'bout heaven!"[53] "Down South, they'll give a nigger a job, but they don't want him to spend his money 'long side them," explained another migrant in search of work as a skilled artisan. "Here in Boston, he can spend with the whites, but he can't work with them. Of course, they'll tell him there is no openin' or somethin' like that. They'll tell him in a nice way."[54] But for many migrants the very idea, if not also the experience, of moving north represented a profound break from the world they knew before. "You can buy more things you want up here. Get things for the house and buy clothes up here that you couldn't think about having down South," explained a woman who left St. Helena Island in 1925 at the age of twenty.[55] "Got tired of living on Island," another female migrant said. "Too lonesome. . . . No dances, no moving picture show, nothing to go to. Cos' every once in a while they would have a dance, but here you could go to 'em every Saturday night."[56] For young black women, in particular, despite the dangers and hardships of city life, the move north offered new opportunities to earn wages and for self-expression and pleasure; it represented a potential path beyond the drudgery and hardships of rural southern life. "Nothing for a colored girl down there," recounted the same woman who left St. Helena Island in 1925. "Only thing a girl could do is work in the oyster factories, and that's considered men's work. Too nasty for a girl, too. Of course, I had a teaching job there one year, but you know there are not many teaching jobs on the island for girls."[57]

The experience of the migration varied among the migrants themselves, but the overall impact of the migration in the 1920s was potentially revolutionary and inextricably linked to the development of the black struggle for self-determination and equality. The black migration, James Grossman writes, "represented a new strategy in the struggle for the full rights of American citizenship, including the right to equality of opportunity."[58] In effect, the migration was a social movement that hastened the erosion of the political, economic, and cultural divide between the North and South and it set into play, however provisionally, a bold challenge to longstanding hierarchies of race and gender.[59] During the World War I years, the emergence of the NAACP in South Carolina inspired a shift in social relations and an interrelated change in consciousness among a growing number of black South Carolinians. The NAACP helped to link black South Carolinians together in new ways, helped to create an awareness of the possibilities of collective action, and tied communities in South Carolina to a broader national community of struggle. During the decade of the 1920s the migration picked up where the NAACP left off, and it broadened the scope of the black struggle in a way no single organization could.

At the same moment that black South Carolinians packed their "freedom bags" and headed north in growing numbers, Marcus Garvey's Universal Negro Improvement Association (UNIA) made substantial inroads in South Carolina and across the South. Although oftentimes understood in terms of its mass appeal in the context of the urban North, more than half of the UNIA's branches in the United States were located in the South by the mid-1920s. As Winston James has explained, "It was in the Southern states that the organization, with its loyal Afro-American base, operated most smoothly, if clandestinely, during the turbulent years of UNIA in-fighting after the indictment of Garvey in 1922."[60] At a celebration of emancipation day, black South Carolinians held their first public UNIA rally on January 22, 1922. Marching through the streets of Charleston, members of the UNIA waved the organization's signature Red, Black, and Green flag, despite orders from city officials that it could not be flown. Later that week the UNIA held a mass meeting "in order to allow all who were interested to hear, and more freely understand the plan and object of the U.N.I.A." Responding to the call to redeem Africa and liberate the world's four hundred million black people, black South Carolinians formed at least twenty-five UNIA branches throughout the state during the 1920s. Located disproportionately in the small towns and incorporated villages of the low country, UNIA branches were also formed in Rock Hill in the north-central portion of the state and in the violence-torn town of Anderson in the west.[61] As economic hardship spread, as Jim Crow and racial violence pressed in on black communities, and as out-migration appeared to be an increasingly attractive liberation strategy, Garvey's brand of black nationalism contributed to the changing shape of the movement in South Carolina and beyond.

Although it would be foolish to discount the significance of the UNIA's call for black self-organization and spiritual revitalization, and the connections the organization encouraged nationally and internationally among black people, there is little evidence to suggest that the UNIA served as a vehicle for mass-based collective organization and action. A UNIA branch could consist of a mere handful of Garvey loyalists; in Charleston, where the organization held its most public events, membership in one of its two branches, Division 113, only claimed numbers in the hundreds. The lack of mass participation in the UNIA in South Carolina should come as little surprise, especially if it is understood in the broad context of the repressive conditions of the 1920s. Indeed, as an organizational force the NAACP faired no better than the UNIA during the decade.[62]

The NAACP was a moribund institution in South Carolina by the end of the 1920s. It maintained a presence in Charleston and Columbia, where a relatively well-established, urban, black middle class kept the organization afloat, but the association's growing capacity to represent the interests of the state's black people in a coordinated and sustainable way expired under the crushing pressures of the 1920s. Despite the efforts of individual members and occasional membership drives prompting old members to rejoin, the NAACP in Charleston and Columbia virtually disappeared from the scene. "I have tried very hard to make or have Charleston folks realize the value of the N.A.A.C.P," the branch president, Dr. E.B. Burroughs, wrote the national office in early 1929. "My meetings have been sparsely attended and seemingly interest [is] at a very low ebb. I hate failure—but we seem to be doing very little. Unfortunately we are 'very much dormant.'"[63]

In Columbia, N.J. Frederick worked to fill the void left by the death of Butler Nance in 1923. In the aftermath of the Lowman lynching, membership in the organization temporarily reached five hundred, and, following the lead of the national office, black women in Columbia formed an NAACP Women's Auxiliary to spur further interest in the organization. But by October 1928 Frederick was despondent over the lack of interest in and funds available for the work of the association. "Oh, if only we could get Negroes here and elsewhere to realize just what the N.A.A.C.P. means to them, and the work it is really doing! [N]ever would there be a day when the Association would need money, for it would be on hand." One member of the Columbia branch pinned the blame for inaction on the organization's new branch president, Dr. J.G. Stuart. "Our blunder began with the election of Dr. Stuart as president," Sam Wallace explained. "He is a delightful fellow . . . but he has no more N.A.A.C.P. spirit than has Tom Heflin or Cole Blease, and the entire Executive Committee . . . has taken the ground that there is nothing to be done or even attempted in local affairs. This is the rock upon which Rev. Brown and I were wrecked."[64]

If branches in Charleston and Columbia were barely able to hang on in the difficult conditions of the 1920s, branches beyond the relatively well-off environs of South Carolina's two largest urban centers fared even worse. Between 1917 and 1929, twelve South Carolina communities chartered NAACP branches and as many as nine others attempted to do so, but only Charleston and Columbia maintained officially chartered NAACP branches by the dawn of the depression decade; the rest fell dormant.[65] Branches in Anderson and Florence, as has been noted, were crushed under the weight of white resistance. In 1921 black residents of Colleton County, a county known for its fertile soil and large lumber mills, chartered an NAACP branch that included carpenters, porters, lumbermen, common laborers, teachers, a merchant, and a laundress. By 1923 the branch reported that its activities were "at a standstill" and after attempts to revive it failed, it fell inactive until the 1940s. "We is Doing all We can to carry on this Good movement for advancement of Colored people," explained J.H. Holmes. "We had Gone in the hole But We is trying to Bill it up again I think we will make successful. You know it is a job [*sic*]."[66] In Beaufort County a coalition of merchants, laundresses, carpenters, doctors, housewives, housekeepers, and fifty-seven farmers chartered an NAACP branch in 1919. Although the branch drew support from across the county, including many of its sea island communities, the branch was inoperative by 1927 and would remain so until the 1940s. "Some years ago, we had here in our town, a strong Branch of the N.A.A.C.P.," wrote the Beaufort branch secretary, "but because of a lack of interest, I presume, we allowed this branch to become inactive."[67]

In rural, cotton-producing Calhoun County, bordered by the Congaree and Santee rivers to the north and east, Orangeburg County to the south, and the state's sandhill region to the west, black residents chartered an NAACP branch in 1925. Defying any notion that the NAACP appealed only or even primarily to an urban, professional, black middle-class constituency, the Calhoun County NAACP was chartered by forty-four farmers, a clerk, four merchants, one teacher, four students, and a minister. Nearly half of its fifty-four members were women. Organized in the small town of Lone Star, the home to the Calisco Hardwood Lumber plant and one of the county's principal shipping points for cotton and lumber, the formation of an NAACP branch there signified the extent to which the association had won the hearts and minds of black southerners across lines of class, gender, and region. But the organization was short-lived. In September 1928 a major hurricane hit the coast of South Carolina and destroyed Calhoun County's cotton crop, crushing the nascent NAACP branch. "We are very sorry that [the] Calhoun County Branch has not been able to pay her full quota," wrote the branch's secretary in early 1929. "We very much desired to pay our quota but as the September hurricane and floods destroyed all the crops raised in the community it could not be done, but we are planning to send to you all the money that we can get our hands on. Just give us a little time. We are deeply interested in the great work you are doing." One year later the organization's vice president wrote the national office detailing the branch's continued difficulties. "Very Sorry, Sorry, that conditions here are such that make it impossible for us . . . to pay our full apportionment," he explained. "Many of our members have moved away to parts unknown, but we are doing everything possible to keep alive."[68] Faced with the choice between short-term economic survival and long-term social and political transformation, black residents of Calhoun County necessarily opted to earn a living and put food on the table. By year's end the NAACP, as it had in so many other towns and counties, ceased operations in Calhoun County, leaving black residents to search for a way to survive as cotton production continued to decline, as real farm wages plummeted to levels no higher than they had been in 1890, and as the nation sank deeper into an economic depression in the wake of the October 1929 stock market crash.[69]

John Birks "Dizzy" Gillespie and the Lineaments of Reinvention

The end of the 1920s was, once again, a time for black South Carolinians to assess their options, and, as so many had before, many chose to leave the South with hopes of creating life anew in the precarious surroundings of the urban North. Between 1930 and 1940, 113,700 more black South Carolinians migrated from the state in search of a better life.[70] One of those migrants was a seventeen-year-old trumpet player named John Birks Gillespie. Born in Cheraw, South Carolina, in 1917, Gillespie was the seventh and youngest child of James and Lottie Gillespie.[71] Cheraw was a small town where shady elm trees lined the streets and where many black and white residents traced their oftentimes intertwined family roots to Chesterfield County's cotton plantations during the era of slavery. Gillespie would later learn, in fact, that he was related through his mother's family to one of the town's most prominent white families. In many ways, Cheraw, population 3,500, resembled the South of the nineteenth century, steeped as it was in a low wage cotton economy. But the town was hardly a sleepy backwater. Situated along the western banks of the Pee Dee River, a short distance from the North Carolina border, it served as a hub of the region's agricultural commerce. On Saturdays Cheraw's Market Street hosted visitors from throughout the region who arrived in town to purchase goods and to socialize. And on Sundays black people gathered in the town's many black churches, including the Second Presbyterian Church, Wesley United Methodist Church, Pee Dee Baptist, the A.M.E. Zion, as well as the Sanctified Church, where Gillespie "learned the meaning of rhythm . . . and all about how music could transport people spiritually."[72]

Life for the Gillespie family was better than it was for most of the region's black families, but it was by no means easy. James Gillespie was a brick mason during the week and on the weekend he played piano and led a local band. He loved music and filled his home with musical instruments purchased with extra cash he managed to save. He was also a brutal patriarch, a "real man, who roared when he talked" and who turned the hardships of rural southern life inward on the family members he loved and supported. "Every Sunday morning, Papa would whip us," the youngest Gillespie recalled. "Papa was big and bad waving that strap." He beat me "for anything and everything that I'd done during the week because Papa was sure that I must have done something wrong in that span of time." "He treated us that way," Gillespie supposed, "because he wanted us all to be tough . . . with so many kids around he had to be strong."[73]

The financial support and the beatings did not, however, last beyond Gillespie's tenth year. In June 1927, James Gillespie died from a sudden asthma attack and thereafter the family's essentially middle-class life rapidly declined. "A great depression, sudden and devastating," Gillespie remembered, "overwhelmed my family two years earlier than the one that closed all the banks and left people out of work and hungry in 1929. Our family was struggling hopefully at the time . . . thinking we might beat poverty, but this thing knocked the wind out of us."[74]

To make matters worse, whatever money James Gillespie had saved for his family was lost in a rash of bank closings in the fall of 1928. Following torrential rains in the late summer that decimated the county's cotton crop, in a span of six weeks, seven of Chesterfield County's eight banks closed their doors, as did five of eight banks in neighboring Darlington County. Chesterfield County's economy followed the rest of South Carolina's into full-blown depression. By 1930 the state's farmlands and buildings had lost more than half their value and by 1932 cotton sold for 4.6 cents per pound, the lowest price since 1894.[75] "Poverty hit us right in the face," Gillespie explained. "We were so poor Mama didn't have enough money to buy food, much less clothes, and we started to feel ashamed about not having anything."[76] While James Gillespie had managed to earn enough money to keep his wife out of the paid workforce, his death and the family's economic decline forced her to begin taking in laundry for some of Cheraw's wealthiest white families. By 1934, she and the future trumpet-great had had enough and joined extended family members in Philadelphia.

Once in Philadelphia, the now seventeen-year-old Gillespie acquired a trumpet from his oldest sister's husband and joined a small jazz trio. By late 1935 he was a member of Frankie Fairfax's band. Fairfax was one of Philadelphia's best-connected musicians and provided Gillespie with an entrée into the city's black jazz scene. It was as part of the Fairfax band that John Birks Gillespie became "Dizzy" Gillespie, although he was often referred to as the "Cheraw Flash" for the remainder of the 1930s.[77] As his most recent biographer notes, his time in Philadelphia provided him with "the chance he had never had before to try out new ideas, discuss technique, experiment and then put the ideas to test for real every night on the band stand."[78] Philadelphia was where Gillespie absorbed the music of Roy Eldridge, the great swing era trumpeter, and began the process of transforming his southern-style inflected trumpet playing into the sound and style that would be dubbed "bebop" in the 1940s. In 1937 he joined his older brother James in Harlem at 142nd Street, between Seventh and Eighth avenues, and started playing the New York City jazz scene, from George's in Greenwich Village, to Harlem's Savoy Ballroom, to Monroe's Uptown House, to Minton's Playhouse at 210 West 118th Street. It was in New York City that Gillespie played in Cab Calloway's big band, and corroborated with musicians like Thelonious Monk, Charlie Parker, and Kenny Clarke to revolutionize jazz and American pop culture.[79] In the 1940s Gillespie became synonymous with bebop; his tilted black beret, heavy-frame glasses, and dazzling trumpet playing represented the cutting edge of modernism and the essence of progress.[80]

For Gillespie, the migration north opened new avenues for self-expression and offered a new means to earn a living. Much as the music he helped create revolutionized jazz and American culture in the 1940s, the continued migration of African Americans from the South to the urban North laid the groundwork for a transformation of American race relations. After 1930, no longer could America's race problem be conceived in terms of the South alone. Rooted in the changes of the World War I era, the black struggle for civil rights increasingly took on the characteristics of a national movement. Migration, the NAACP, as well as the UNIA, each played roles in enlarging the scope of the black struggle for self-determination and equality. Once in the North, despite the persistence of racial discrimination and economic hardship, black people constituted a new political constituency with the capacity to articulate the needs and interests of black Americans in a way their southern counterparts could not. In the years ahead, this newfound power would prove an important source of strength, but it would also prove a ready source of conflict. There was no ready-made understanding about the relationship between the struggle in the South and the struggle in the urban North. Indeed, this relationship would become the subject of much debate in the opening years of the 1930s.

3   Radicalism and Liberal Reform: The NAACP during the New Deal

We want an equal chance to contribute to the world the best that is in us whatever may be our social standing. We aim to make opportunity democratic. . . . In a democracy liberty requires self mastery; it calls for a condition in which men respect themselves and respect each other. That is an ideal well worth struggling for because in my judgment it is the very essence of civilization.

—Robert F. Wagner

Doubtless, and in the long run, the greatest human development is going to take place under experiences of widest individual contact. Nevertheless, today such individual contact is made difficult and almost impossible by petty prejudice, deliberate and almost criminal propaganda and various survivals from prehistoric heathenism. It is impossible, therefore, to wait for the millennium of free and normal intercourse before we unite, to cooperate among themselves in groups of like-minded people and in groups of people suffering from the same disadvantages and the same hatreds.

—W.E.B. Du Bois

With declining prospects for movement expansion in the violence-torn South and the ongoing migration of black people to the urban North, African Americans searched for new directions in their ongoing struggle for civil rights and self-determination, and the NAACP remained at the center of the search. Through the pages of *The Crisis* magazine, W.E.B. Du Bois helped the association publicize racial violence and discrimination and provided black people with a forum to share thoughts, articulate their needs, and debate the future course of struggle. Along with the National Urban League, the association sponsored an outpouring of black literary and artistic production, known as the Harlem Renaissance, as part of what David Levering

Lewis has termed a self-conscious effort to achieve "civil rights by copyright." Meanwhile, the NAACP waged a protracted legal and legislative battle to protect black people from lynch mob terror and to secure full citizenship rights. In *Moore v. Dempsey* (1923), *Nixon v. Herndon* (1927), *Harmon v. Taylor* (1927) and *City of Richmond v. Deans* (1930) the NAACP won important U.S. Supreme Court victories, striking respective blows against the denial of due process law in criminal trials, against the state-sponsored exclusion of black people from participation in primary elections, and against residential segregation ordinances.[1]

In an important sense, the NAACP established itself as a national force dedicated to securing and protecting the rights of African Americans. But despite its legal, legislative, and cultural successes, the organization faced a series of related crises by decade's end that called its institutional strength and future direction into question.[2] By the time the Great Depression engulfed the nation, the NAACP's membership rolls dipped to little more than twenty thousand. As branches struggled to survive the turmoil of the 1920s, subscriptions to the NAACP's propaganda engine, *The Crisis*, declined precipitously, seriously undermining the financial solvency of the magazine and subjecting the role of its editor, W.E.B. Du Bois, to scrutiny within the organization. "The mass of Negroes, even the intelligent and educated, progressively being thrown out of work" Du Bois recalled, "did not have money for food, much less for magazines."[3] Under James Weldon Johnson's tenure, the association made the transition from an organization funded by wealthy white benefactors to one funded predominantly by its branches and black members. This provided the association with a substantial degree of independence and helped ensure its black constituency that it truly represented their interests. By decade's end, however, the collapse of its branches and declining membership rolls exposed the highly contingent circumstances that made this independence possible at the very moment that Walter White officially replaced Johnson as the organization's secretary in 1931.

As assistant secretary under Johnson in the 1920s, White earned the respect of many black Americans through his often covert and dangerous investigation and reporting of lynchings in the Deep South. He also made himself indispensable to the NAACP through his close working relationship with Arthur Spingarn, the association's legal committee chairman, and through his mastery of the legal matters that played a growing role in the NAACP's fight for black equality.[4] Like Johnson, White recognized the importance of an independent political force to represent the needs of black people in what he termed "the most acute period" in Negro history. "It seems inevitable," he explained in early 1931, "that there will be major political realignments in both major political parties within the next few years. The Negro must be ready, through political independence, to take advantage of these changes and thus better his lot." "Only by intelligent organization, such as represented by the National Association for the Advancement of Colored People," he added, "and only through biracial movements can white and colored people" face down the social and economic forces that exacerbate race hatred.[5] While White recognized the need for black political independence, an independence he deemed not to be exclusive of white alliances and support, he inherited the reigns of the NAACP at a moment in which the erosion of the organization's black membership base militated against such independence. "We have been handicapped sorely," he explained, by "the great unemployment among Negroes, which has materially cut our income." Without ample funds derived from a base in black communities, White acknowledged, the association would be more dependent on the contributions of "a few individuals or organizations which would control its policies."[6]

To be sure, White came to power in the NAACP at a time of economic turmoil. With *The Crisis* running deficits and without recourse to the branches, White and the NAACP looked elsewhere for financing to keep the organization in operation. In the 1920s the organization had derived the lion's share of its financial resources from its black membership, even as it counted on a number of prominent white and Jewish attorneys to litigate its most important cases and upon periodic donations from wealthy philanthropists to supplement its financial coffers. But as the long-term decline of branch strength continued and the Depression tightened its grip on already financially strapped black communities, that balance began to shift as White and the NAACP increasingly sought contributions from the organization's Jewish allies and other philanthropic sources, who were themselves stung by depression conditions. In 1930, Jacob Billikopf, the director of the Federation of Jewish Charities in Philadelphia and the son-in-law of Louis Marshall, one of the NAACP's key volunteer legal councils in the 1920s, introduced William Rosenwald, the youngest son of Sears, Roebuck president Julius Rosenwald, to the NAACP. The youngest Rosenwald helped initiate a series of financial pledges from Jewish benefactors, such as Herbert H. Lehman, Samuel Fels, and Felix and Frieda Schiff Warburg, as well as non-Jews such as Edsel Ford, that saved the NAACP from financial ruin and possible collapse. In June of the same year, the American Fund for Public Service (also known as the Garland Fund, a left-wing organization founded by Charles Garland) provided the NAACP with a $100,000 grant to be parceled out in installments to support the association's campaign to fight racial discrimination in the courts. Although the NAACP utilized a portion of the grant to launch its campaign against segregated education, the Garland Fund soon succumbed to financial difficulties and the NAACP received only $20,000 from the fund.[7]

Financial assistance notwithstanding, budget problems persisted. In 1932 the NAACP took defensive measures to preserve the organization by cutting the salaries of executive officers and staff members on two separate occasions. Already low salaries had been cut by a total of 31 percent by the end of 1933. Robert Bagnall, the NAACP's longtime director of branches, had been let go. Roy Wilkins, the recently hired assistant secretary, had been assigned to part-time status at half salary, and additional reductions in national office personnel had been made.[8] In a perverse, if unavoidable logic, the NAACP's budget decisions further undercut the organization's capacity to deal with its most fundamental problem, the collapse of its branches and its funding base in black communities. The short-term effect of the NAACP's financial crisis and White's skillful solicitation of donations from wealthy philanthropists was, then, to consolidate a disproportionate share of the organization's power in the hands of the new secretary.[9] As branch strength continued to decline, particularly in the South, money problems and the trend toward White's growing power within the organization, in turn, set the stage for a rancorous debate over the NAACP's program and future direction. In South Carolina, however, theoretical debates gave way to the harsh realities of everyday struggle. And black South Carolinians found a way to turn the NAACP into a vehicle for their own advancement by the last years of the 1930s, helping to set the course for the transformation of the NAACP into a mass-based organization in the state and the nation.

The NAACP's Second Amenia Conference
and the Radical Challenge

In his March 4, 1933, inaugural address to the nation, President Franklin Delano Roosevelt sought to allay the fears of the American people and instill a sense of hope that they would survive and conquer the economic disaster that plagued them. The following day Roosevelt issued a presidential edict that called for a special session of Congress to launch the legislative program for economic recovery that became known as the Hundred Days. By the time the special session closed on June 16, an unprecedented flurry of legislation had been passed into law in an attempt to resuscitate the ailing American economy. From the creation of the Agricultural Adjustment Administration (AAA), the Civilian Conservation Corps (CCC), the Tennessee Valley Authority (TVA), and the Federal Emergency Relief Administration (FERA), to the passage of the National Industrial Recovery Act (NIRA)—which sanctioned the right of industrial workers to organize unions and allowed industries to set wages, prices, and production levels under the supervision of the National Recovery Administration (NRA)—the Roosevelt administration ushered in a new era of expanded federal government involvement in the economic life of the nation.[10]

The 1930s had not begun well for the embattled NAACP. Despite defeating the nomination of the conservative southern jurist John J. Parker to the U.S. Supreme Court, the NAACP's ambivalent, if not indifferent, response to the plight of nine black youths wrongly accused and convicted of raping two white women on a train near Scottsboro, Alabama, in the spring of 1931 had cost the organization mightily in the court of public opinion. The Communist Party's well-publicized defense of the youths and its denunciations of the NAACP as an organization of "bourgeois reformists" and "betrayers of the Negro liberation struggle" so committed to "the paraphernalia of capitalist class government that . . . they will kiss the rope that hangs their brothers, if only the rope is blessed by a ruling class judge," pushed the association to admit that its problems were more than financial.[11] In May 1932 the NAACP's Board of Directors acknowledged that the association seemed "to be losing ground with the average man in the street," that it did not "attract and hold the minds of young people," and that because of branch inactivity it had failed to publicize adequately its ongoing legal work to "the masses." At the same meeting, Joel Spingarn, the NAACP's chairman, suggested that the organization sponsor a second Amenia Conference to once again assess the circumstances facing black people and the NAACP and chart a direction forward. In March 1933, after some degree of internal wrangling, the board approved a resolution calling for a conference at the Spingarn family estate at Amenia, New York, "in order to obtain a new vision of the future of the American Negro."[12]

As the legislation passed during the Hundred Days was transformed from law into practice, thirty-three men and women answered an invitation from Joel Spingarn to attend the second Amenia Conference held August 18–21, 1933. Like the first conference, the second was convened through the efforts of the NAACP, but was intended to be more than a meeting of NAACP leadership. Rather, the conference was conceived as a means to bring a wide range of philosophies and opinions together to debate and help set the future course of the black struggle for civil rights and equality.[13] "It was an attempt," Du Bois wrote, "to bring together and into sympathetic understanding, Youth and Age interested in the Negro problem." The average age of the participants was thirty-two. "Eliminating four admittedly among the elders," Du Bois reported, "the others ranged in age between twenty-five and thirty-five, with a median age of thirty." Each, he noted, "were well out of college and started on their life work, and yet . . . they were still with inquiring minds and still unsettled as to their main life work."[14]

The gathering was, as David Lewis suggests, a showcase of "Talented Tenth exemplars" and tinged with undertones of elitism and paternalism, even as its objectives were "intended to be socially progressive at the least and even economically radical."[15] To be certain, the Talented Tenth had no monopoly on vanguard politics in the 1930s as Roosevelt's "Brain Trust" planned an overhaul of the nation's political economy and the Communist Party espoused a Leninist-inflected brand of revolutionary Marxism. For their own part, a group of young black intellectuals trained in some of the nation's most prestigious universities and just beginning careers as academics and social activists had become intrigued by the writings and philosophy of Karl Marx and sought to redirect the trajectory of black protest thought and activity. As members of the Howard University faculty, the economist Abram L. Harris and the Harvard-trained political scientist Ralph J. Bunche engaged in extensive discussions of Marx and the economics of social struggle with fellow colleagues, including the sociologist E. Franklin Frazier, the poet Sterling Brown, as well as Charles Houston, the dean of the law school.[16] In 1931 *The Black Worker: The Negro and the Labor Movement*, coauthored by Harris and Sterling Spero, was published and helped establish the terms of the evolving debate. Its authors chronicled the rise of black workers in American industry and detailed their contentious relationship with labor unions, notably the American Federation of Labor (AFL). Harris and Spero spared no criticism of the AFL and took it to task for its history of racism and its policies of racial segregation and exclusion. Although the authors took note of the NAACP's efforts to fight the exclusionary practices of unions, they criticized the association for waging battle on behalf of black workers on "the ground of civil liberty rather than upon the principle of labor solidarity." "Negro leadership for the past generation," they argued, "has put its stress on the element of race" and turned "a deaf ear to those who say that the Negro's plight is the plight of the working class in general merely aggravated by certain special features."[17]

The message of their book and the one Harris and his cohorts, most notably, Ralph Bunche, brought to the 1933 upstate retreat was clear: despite the persistence of racism and its myriad manifestations, the NAACP's traditional emphasis on race and civil rights was in need of substantive revision. What was needed, they argued, was a new focus on class solidarity and what they understood as the economic roots of racial oppression. Buoyed by the latest social scientific data proving that race had no basis in biological fact, that racial characteristics were products of culture and the environment, not biology, Harris and Bunche moved to radically reorient the program and agenda of the NAACP and the black struggle for civil rights.[18] Race, Bunche would write, was "a ruse," "a myth," a "smoke-screen," a "compelling sort of social voodoo" that mystified more "fundamental conflicts and issues confronting society."[19] For Bunche and Harris the race problem was a derivative of more fundamental problems of economic inequality and ought to be considered "as merely one aspect of the class struggle," "as an incidental and aggravating factor in the fundamental problems of all workers."[20] Both men were convinced that "race prejudice and conflict" would subside in direct relationship to a radical restructuring of the American economy. "So long as the society endures an economy which demands and thrives on human exploitation," Bunche wrote, "race will be employed as an effective device in the promotion of the process of group exploitation—economic, political, and cultural."[21]

As Du Bois recalled, economic questions "and the influence of education and politics" on economic conditions dominated the discussion at the weekend-long conference. In the midst of depression conditions, virtually all in attendance could agree that the primary problem facing black people in 1933 was economic. The conferees passed resolutions reflecting the concerns of the young radical intellectuals, who became known collectively as the Young Turks. "It is the opinion of the conference," read one resolution, "that the welfare of white and black labor are one and inseparable and that the existing social agencies working among and for Negroes have conspicuously failed in facing a necessary alignment between black and white labor." Conferees asserted that the collapse of the American economy called into question "the whole system of private property and private profit" and resolved that only a "new labor movement" could advance the collective interests of white and black workers. By design the conference was, however, intended only as a venue "to make a critical appraisal of the Negro's existing situation in American Society and to consider underlying principles for future action." As a result, it provided no concrete proposals for a reorientation of the NAACP or the black civil rights struggle. Instead, the specifics became the responsibility of a continuing committee that became the Committee on the Future Plan and Program of the NAACP in the summer of 1934.[22]

Chaired by Harris, the Committee on the Future Plan and Program also included Mary White Ovington, James Weldon Johnson, Rachel Davis Du Bois, Sterling Brown, and Louis T. Wright, the soon-to-be chairman of the NAACP Board of Directors and the first African American to hold the position, although its findings bore the unmistakable imprimatur of Harris.[23] Formally presented at the NAACP's 1935 annual conference, the Future Plan and Program of the NAACP, which became known as the Harris Report, provided a clear encapsulation of the Young Turks' critique of the NAACP and their thoughts about the future of the association and the black civil rights struggle. Much as Harris's earlier work acknowledged the NAACP's important support for black workers, the Harris Report acknowledged the NAACP's past efforts to protect black workers from racial discrimination, violence, and intimidation. It also applauded the association's more recent battles to ensure fair treatment and just wages for African Americans working on federally funded projects such as the Mississippi Flood Control Project and the construction of the Hoover Dam and to secure fair representation within the various federal agencies and programs created as part of New Deal relief efforts. For Harris, the problem was not, though, one of effort. Rather, it was one of objective and philosophy. The NAACP's accomplishments, he argued, revealed that the association's "primary objective" was to secure "for the Negro his rights as an American citizen under prevailing economic and social conditions." Its philosophy, he added, "grew out of the faith in the founders of the Association in the principles of 18th century liberalism," a philosophy that "guaranteed freedom in the use of property once it was acquired," but that had failed to "create the conditions which made the acquisition of property open to all members of society." For years the NAACP had "conducted a militant fight under this illusory banner," Bunche would write. Its "extreme faith" in the ballot and the courts resulted, he expounded, "in the failure to appreciate the fact that the instruments of the state are merely reflections of the political and economic ideology of the dominant group, that the political arm of the state cannot be divorced from its prevailing economic structure, whose servant it must inevitably be."[24]

Although the Harris Report lacked the polemical punch of Bunche's published writings, its central message was unmistakable: the NAACP must radically transform its traditional civil rights agenda and become a vehicle dedicated to the creation of a black-white labor alliance. In the report, Harris did not suggest that the NAACP abandon its legal and legislative work on behalf of black people, but he argued that the association must "attempt to get the Negroes to view their special grievances as a natural part of the larger issues of American labor as a whole." Without a discussion of the specific conditions and difficulties faced by black people who organized or attempted to organize branches during the previous fifteen-odd years and without addressing the association's ongoing financial difficulties, Harris offered an agenda for the remaking of the NAACP. At the core of his proposal was an economic program. He proposed that the NAACP "conduct classes in worker education to create among Negro working men . . . a realization of their identity of interests with white labor";

"foster the building of a labor movement"; "lay the intellectual basis for united action between white and black workers in local, state and national politics"; and fight "every manifestation and form of racial chauvinism in the labor movement and among workers everywhere." He envisioned, indeed, found it "imperative that the local branches become transformed from centers of sporadic agitation to permanent centers of economic and political agitation."[25]

To facilitate the reorientation of the NAACP along economic lines, Harris also suggested a restructuring of the association's administrative hierarchy. Whether he was unaware of the trying conditions facing local branches, most notably in the Deep South, or whether he chose to ignore evidence of their ongoing troubles, Harris nevertheless called for the association to "decentralize" its administrative structure and become "a more closely knit but democratic type of organization." For Harris, it seemed, the association's difficulties stemmed principally from problems at the national level. He chafed at the disproportionate power wielded by the board and Walter White, without addressing the particular circumstances that had made the centralization of authority possible, perhaps necessary in the early 1930s. He called for the office of secretary to become, in essence, a central coordinating agency that would oversee five independent committees within the organization: Economic, Legal and Political, Educational, Publicity, Research and Investigations, and Financial. He then suggested that the association divide itself into no less than five regional districts to be supervised by permanent regional secretaries. And he suggested that the method by which members of the Board of Directors were selected be altered to provide branches with more power in the selection process. Although rank-and-file members had always had the power to nominate board members and vote for the candidates of their choice at the NAACP's annual business meetings, in practice a board-appointed nominating committee had for years selected board candidates and sparsely attended annual business meetings simply ratified the selections. Harris sought to provide a more direct means for electing board members by allowing four members of the board's nominating committee to be elected directly by members attending the larger annual conferences, while allowing the board to select three.[26]

In the early 1930s, Harris and the Young Turks were not alone in criticizing the top-heavy administrative structure of the association.

In his own battles with Walter White and members of the Board of Directors over the financing and control of *The Crisis*, Du Bois confronted the severe limitations of the top-down lines of authority emerging in the troubled years of the early 1930s, and he called for a restructuring of the organization to provide branches with more power in the organization.[27] Like the Young Turks, Du Bois believed that the NAACP ought to concern itself more explicitly with the economic aspects of black liberation. Du Bois had long considered himself a socialist and in the early 1930s he also immersed himself in the writings of Karl Marx. Unlike the Young Turks, who zealously sought to break free from all philosophies and practices they deemed to be tainted by vestiges of racial determination, Du Bois was unwilling to abandon race as either a category of analysis or a description of lived social realities. Put another way, he was unwilling to replace racial determinism with a new doctrine of economic determinism.[28] Writing at the turn of the century amid the codification of Jim Crow, the rise of disfranchisement, and the emergence of the modern corporation, Du Bois had sought to come to terms with the particular circumstances faced by black Americans and chart a way forward. He sought to do so without effacing the history of black people or by demanding that black people adjourn their sense of self as black people. Rather he sought a double strategy, one in which it would be "possible for a man to be both a Negro and an American, without being cursed and spit upon by his fellows, without having the doors of Opportunity closed roughly in his face." For Du Bois, the question posed at the turn of the century was not how to resolve the tension between the desire to be both Negro and American; it was how to transform the world to allow for the peaceful and dynamic coexistence of both identities.[29] In the early 1930s as black Americans, once again, faced daunting circumstances and as the Young Turks sought to allow class, not race, to define the legitimate horizon of struggle, Du Bois worked to articulate a means to legitimate struggle on both fronts.

Throughout the early 1930s Du Bois published a series of articles in *The Crisis* exploring the applicability of Marxism to the particular circumstances faced by African Americans, an exploration that culminated in the publication of *Black Reconstruction* in 1935. Although Du Bois would be roundly criticized by the Young Turks for his attempts to revise Marx, dismissed as a "black chauvinist" and accused by Harris of being a "racialist whose discovery of Marxism as a critical instrument has been too recent and sudden for it to discipline his mental processes or basically to change his social philosophy," he sought to theorize a battle plan for black liberation that refused the racial determinism of old and maintained a critical stance toward theories of class struggle that resorted to essentialized conceptions of class politics or subscribed to economic determinism. "It was a great loss to American Negroes," he wrote, "that the great mind of Marx . . . could not have been brought to bear at first hand upon the history of the American Negro between 1876 and the World War." Still, he maintained, Marxist analysis had much to contribute to contemporary circumstances, although it must "be modified so far as Negroes are concerned by the fact that he had not studied at first hand their peculiar race problem here in America."[30]

In an argument that he would develop over the course of the decade, Du Bois sought to situate the black struggle for civil rights in the context of rapidly changing economic circumstances. "New techniques, new enterprises, mass production, impersonal ownership and control," he wrote in 1935, "have been largely displacing the skilled white and Negro worker in tobacco manufacturing, in iron and steel, in lumbering and mining, and in transportation . . . [while the] world-wide decline in agriculture has moreover carried the mass of black farmers . . . down to the level of landless tenants and peons." Largely excluded from manufacturing jobs in the textile and chemical industries, he explained, and stung by the technological displacement that had begun in the 1920s, black Americans were struck by the Great Depression with particular acuteness.[31] In an important sense, Du Bois had identified the economic lineaments of what future scholars would call postindustrial society, that is, the development of the technological and managerial means to increase productivity levels in industrial production without additional inputs or direct capital investment out of savings, thus allowing, indeed requiring, the reallocation of labor and capital investment into other sectors of the economy, most notably the service sectors.[32] To be sure, in the early 1930s, the changes Du Bois identified were understood as the collapse of capitalism, not as the coming of postindustrial society. But what Du Bois did recognize, nevertheless, was that the process of economic recovery underway under the auspices of the New Deal involved the creation of new forms of economic organization. "Either the industry of the nation in the future is to be conducted by the private trusts (read corporations) or by government control," he wrote. In either case, the persistence of race prejudice was sure to leave black people on the outside looking in. "There seems no hope that America in our day will yield in its color or race hatred any substantial ground," he conjectured, "and we have no physical nor economic power, nor any alliance with other social or economic classes that will force compliance with decent civilized ideals in Church, State, industry or art."[33]

For Du Bois the circumstances confronting black people required self-conscious "group action." Echoing James Weldon Johnson's call for collective action in the World War I era, Marcus Garvey's demand for self-organization, and his own writings on the global dimensions of black subordination, Du Bois wrote, "American Negroes will be beaten into submission and degradation if they merely wait unorganized to find some place voluntarily given them in the new reconstruction of the economic world." "They must," he argued, "force their race into the new economic set-up and bring with them the millions of West Indians and Africans by peaceful organization for normative action or else drift into greater poverty, greater crime, greater helplessness, until there is no resort but the last red alternative of revolt, revenge and war."[34] Du Bois's internationalist vision ran against the tide of the New Deal's America-first plan of economic recovery, but he also recognized the very pressing need for the collective organization of black people in the U.S. context. "In the recent endeavor of the United States government to redistribute capital so that some of the disadvantaged groups may get a chance for development," he wrote, "the American Negro should voluntarily and insistently demand his share." In terms that sparked debate throughout the NAACP, Du Bois called for black people to turn the segregated realities of their lives into a powerful force for collective empowerment. His plan called for the creation of black cooperatives designed to pool financial resources and to harness mass purchasing power in support of black liberation.[35] "We must make our segregated institutions so fine and outstanding and put so much of belief and thought and loyalty in them," he explained to one critic, "that the separation upon which they are based, and the doctrine of inferiority which led to them, will be confounded and contradicted by its inherent and evident foolishness."[36]

Responses to Du Bois's discussion of segregation ranged, David Levering Lewis writes, from "bafflement to apoplexy," but whether critics accused Du Bois of supporting race chauvinism, petit bourgeois economics, or of lending tacit if not outright ideological support for racial segregation and thus discrimination, most refused to grapple with the crux of his argument.[37] Du Bois insisted that without acknowledging the social fact of racial segregation and the continued significance of race—and without a conscious effort to mobilize already existing black institutions in pursuit of social justice—neither integration nor economic justice were possible. "Doubtless, and in the long run," he explained, "the greatest human development is going to take place under experiences of widest individual contact. Nevertheless, today such individual contact is made difficult and almost impossible by petty prejudice, deliberate and almost criminal propaganda and various survivals from prehistoric heathenism. It is impossible, therefore, to wait for the millennium of free and normal intercourse before we unite, to cooperate among themselves in groups of like-minded people and in groups of people suffering from the same disadvantages and the same hatreds."[38] For Du Bois, the collective organization of black people was not antithetical to a long-range vision of economic justice across lines of race; it was, rather, its necessary but insufficient precondition. The task at hand in the 1930s, he informed the Young Turks at the "National Conference on the Economic Crisis and the Negro," held at Howard University in the spring of 1935, is not revolution, but the creation of "class consciousness." This, he argued, is the historic burden of Socialism, and "the first proof of conversion is the abolition of race prejudice."[39]

Du Bois's argument, however, did not win many converts in the mid-1930s. He certainly did not convince the Young Turks to abandon their class-first agenda and he did not convince the NAACP to adopt a self-conscious program of organized segregation. In April 1934 the national Board of Directors sidestepped the heart of Du Bois's proposal and passed a resolution on segregation to clarify its official position. "The National Association for the Advancement of Colored People is opposed to the principle and practice of enforced segregation of human beings on the basis of race and color," it resolved. "Enforced segregation by its very implication carries with it the implication of a superior and inferior group and invariably results in the imposition of a lower status on the group deemed inferior. Thus both principle and practice necessitate unyielding opposition to any and every form of enforced segregation."[40] But while Du Bois's segregation proposal did not substantially alter official NAACP policy, neither did the Harris Report. Indeed, by the time Harris's revised report was formally circulated and approved at the NAACP's annual conference in June 1935, both he and Du Bois had resigned from the organization. Du Bois resigned in June 1934 for reasons that were personal and philosophical. That May, as criticism of Du Bois's writings on segregation mounted and as his personal battles with Walter White continued, the Board of Directors passed a resolution that, in effect, censored Du Bois's freedom to criticize the organization or its policies in the pages of *The Crisis.* Shortly thereafter, Du Bois made his exit.[41] Harris resigned from his position on the Board of Directors in March 1935, three months in advance of the annual conference where his revised report was to be debated. By that time, amid substantial criticism of the Future Plan and Program, he had become convinced that the organization was not committed to his economic program and he too made his exit.[42]

The resignations of Du Bois and Harris and the apparent defeat of their challenges to the NAACP's form and function notwithstanding, the organization was in the process of a substantial transformation in the mid-1930s. The driving force for change was not, however, emanating principally from the national office, but rather from its branches. At the NAACP's 1933 annual conference, Charles Houston had informed the radical insurgents in attendance that they ought to remember that the NAACP had two programs. "The Association," he explained, "has a national program sponsored and made effective by the National Office [and] is concerned with matters of national and state importance. It [also] has a local program, or local programs, as many local programs as there are local branches; and upon the local branches rests the responsibility of carrying out these programs, calling on the National Office for support when they face conditions with which they are unable to cope."[43] At the time of the 1933 conference, Houston was the dean of Howard University's law school and working to transform it into a laboratory for civil rights activism. To that end he sought to articulate the relationship of the NAACP's legal agenda to the daily struggles of black people in their respective communities. The legal struggle, he surmised, was part and parcel of the development of a broader social insurgency.[44] The central problem facing the organization in the early 1930s, he told the gathering, was how to energize and mobilize local branches. "Our difficulty has been not that the National Association has not fostered or promoted national programs for Negro welfare," he argued. "The difficulty is, in too many instances, that the national program has been hamstrung by weak-kneed, yellow-backed support on the part of local Negro leaders." Confronting circumstances not unlike those faced by James Weldon Johnson in 1917, Houston argued that the NAACP must be an organization that draws from all classes of black Americans. "This Association for its greatest effectiveness," he said, "must be of the Negroes, by the Negroes, and once and for all for all the Negroes." To that end, Houston believed that black professionals had to be encouraged to work in concert with the black masses and the NAACP's branch membership had to expand to include more than black professionals.[45]

As a colleague and friend of Harris and Bunche, Houston agreed that the association must concern itself more with the economic circumstances faced by black people, but he also believed that black communities had to play the principal role in charting their own course for freedom. "Radicalism," he extolled the Young Turks, "just like everything else, should begin at home." He urged those espousing radical ideas to move from theory to practice. "While the parlor radical who sits in Illinois and New York and attempts to tell people in Georgia and Mississippi how radical they should be," he counseled, "may be as good as the man who has gone down there and risked his skin, on the streets, in the courts, and has investigated conditions at the risk of his safety, I say the suggestions from such a parlor radical should be made with becoming modesty." The point, Houston attempted to impress upon his audience, was that change had to come from the branches. "I ask again," he exclaimed, "how far have you attempted to introduce radical movements in your own local branch?"[46]

The Greenville County Council for Community Development and Liberal Reform

As debate raged within the NAACP over its future plan and program, racial realities pressed in on the lives of black South Carolinians. On the night of November 16, 1933, a seventy-three-year-old African

American tenant farmer was lynched by a mob of Ku Klux Klansmen, becoming the third victim of lynch mob violence in the state that year. Despite the assistance of a local white attorney, "Tireless" Joe Tolbert, a former federal district attorney and Republican Party leader whose family's open courting of black voters sparked the Phoenix race riot in 1898, and the testimony of four mob members turned state's witnesses, all members of the mob went free. That same month, another African American man, Roy Hudson, was brutally beaten to death by four prison guards while serving a sentence on the Greenville County chain gang. After Tolbert succeeded in winning a hung jury in the first trial, a second ended with a not guilty verdict and the four defendants went free. In both cases, apparently with some reservations about Tolbert's ability to win convictions, the NAACP's national office scrounged together enough money to retain his services as special prosecutor, but without a substantial foothold in South Carolina, the association could do little but watch events unfold from New York City. "For twenty years we have been railing against the chain gang system and gnashing our teeth because we could get no effective action out of the county governments and because the federal government has always refused to intervene," Roy Wilkins lamented, "and here we have presented to us on a platter the opportunity to assist in the prosecution *after* the county itself has taken the necessary steps, and we haven't the money to retain the best possible prosecutor under the circumstances."[47]

Located in South Carolina's violent northwest piedmont region, Greenville County would become, despite and because of the violence endemic to the region, an epicenter of black political activism that would help resuscitate an ailing black struggle for civil rights in the state and the nation in the late 1930s. On the eve of the Great Depression, Greenville County was at the center of South Carolina's booming and segregated textile industry, an industry whose very success in the 1920s placed it on course for violent conflict in the 1930s. Between 1930 and 1940 the population of the county grew from 117,009 to 139,580, a growth that represented only about half that experienced by the county in the 1920s. In those same years, the African American population grew from 27,855 to 30,432, but decreased as an overall percentage of the population, dropping from 24 to 22 percent. In Greenville County many of the textile mills and all-white mill villages that housed their workforce formed an extended circle around the county seat of Greenville, forming what was known as the "belt line." Technically the city limits of Greenville were home to approximately 35,000 people in the 1930s, making it the third-largest city in the state, although, including the belt line, the population ballooned to about 75,000. Black South Carolinians comprised approximately 37 to 40 percent of the population within Greenville's city limits, where they lived largely segregated east of South Main Street. Virtually no black people lived within the belt line, though some lived in a number of suburban regions and scattered throughout the county's rural sections and various small towns.[48]

If life in the county's rural area proved precarious and violent for many, life in metropolitan Greenville proved no haven for African Americans either. In the 1930s Greenville was home to a small class of black professionals, mostly teachers and ministers, small business owners, a few doctors, dentists, funeral directors, and tailors. Most black city-dwellers worked as domestic or personal servants and rented and lived in substandard, overcrowded housing. Many had access to city water, but most lacked indoor plumbing. In one study, more than half of those surveyed did not have electricity, and two-thirds of the households studied used outside toilets that they shared with one or more families. In the same study, which admitted to not having included "some of the worst living conditions among Negroes to be found in the city," researchers found that two-fifths of black homes lacked a front yard and only one in five was located on a paved street. Few black residents had regular access to open space. Black residents attended twenty-five black churches, but that represented only one church for every 425 black residents and, as late as 1938, there were no public parks open to black people. Although Greenville had a number of schools for black children, there was still no accredited black high school at mid-decade.[49] Moreover, matters were compounded by an oppressive police force. John Bolt Culbertson, a white labor attorney who also handled many court cases for black city residents in the 1930s, explained that the Ku Klux Klan worked "hand in glove" with the city police force, establishing a climate of fear and intimidation within the city limits. "Most of the patrolmen," he told an interviewer, "are members themselves."[50] Recounting the large number of black residents with police records, Culbertson noted that for years black residents were simply conscripted for city roadwork. "You see," he said, "it's decided how many Nigroes [*sic*] they need, then that many are arrested. For 13 years, we had a police judge here who, for 13 years fixed things so that this city didn't have to hire Negro laborers."[51]

Much as in Charleston and Columbia, the burden of addressing Greenville's dismal urban and rural living conditions faced by its black residents was assumed by members of a small black middle class and a handful of beneficent white residents with the financial resources and interest. In the 1930s the focal point of black Greenville's associated life and uplift work was the Phillis Wheatley Center, organized and run by Hattie Logan Duckett. As the daughter of a Methodist minister, a graduate of Claflin College, a former schoolteacher, a social worker, and a recent widow, Duckett founded the Phillis Wheatley Association in 1919 after traveling to Cleveland, Ohio, to visit a friend and native South Carolinian, Jane Edna Hunter. In Cleveland Hunter had struggled for some years to convince the Young Women's Christian Association (YWCA) to open its doors to black women. Finally, with the YWCA's assistance, she established the first Phillis Wheatley Association in Cleveland, essentially a black YWCA, which began serving the employment, housing, and health needs of black girls and women in 1913. Hunter's Phillis Wheatley Home soon became a model for black women's club work across the nation, and Hunter fast became a major figure in the NACW. During Duckett's visit to Cleveland, Hunter offered her employment in the Cleveland Home. "No, no," Duckett is said to have replied, "I'm going home and organize a Phillis Wheatley Home for Girls."[52]

Back in Greenville, Duckett secured the aid of prominent white and black men and women to establish the Phillis Wheatley Home for Girls. In 1924 the Home for Girls moved to its permanent location at 121 East Broad Street in the city's black business district and became known as the Phillis Wheatley Center. In addition to serving as a de facto employment agency for domestic workers, the Center provided much-needed health and education services to the city's black residents and was the principal meeting place for black organizations outside of churches and private homes. In the 1930s some nineteen men's and boy's clubs met there regularly, including the Plasterer's Union, the Ministerial Union, the Elks, the Boy Scouts, and the Veterans of Foreign Wars. Countless girl's and women's clubs met at the Wheatley Center, including the NACW affiliated Lend-A-Hand Club, the Girl Scouts, and the Professional Women's Club. And the

Center, not insignificantly, served as a place for general recreation and socializing.[53]

In an era in which racial separation and violence structured the day-to-day lives of Greenville's white and black residents, Hattie Logan Duckett and the Phillis Wheatley Association also served as a critical connection between Greenville's black and white communities. Prominent white and black residents served together on the Phillis Wheatley Center's Board of Trustees and Duckett served on the South Carolina Committee of the Commission on Interracial Cooperation that helped provide state and region-wide connections to other liberal-minded white and black men and women. Under the leadership of a white Methodist minister and YMCA activist, Will W. Alexander, the Commission on Interracial Cooperation (CIC) emerged out of the Red Summer of 1919 as a region-wide organization, based out of Atlanta, dedicated to promoting racial understanding and the amelioration of the South's climate of racial violence. Intent on providing an alternative to existing racial practices in the South without confronting segregation or advocating racial equality, the founding members of the CIC, as Jacquelyn Dowd Hall explains, sought "to resurrect a tradition of *noblesse oblige*." In South Carolina white men and women, such as Charleston's Celia McGowan and Columbia's Rev. F. Clyde Helms, played key leadership roles in the organization. In cooperation with prominent black South Carolinians, such as Duckett and Charlestonian Marion Birnie Wilkinson, they met to discuss the myriad problems faced by black communities and attempted to remedy them without challenging the fundamental tenets of white supremacy. Elite and hierarchical by design and practice, the CIC nevertheless helped provide Duckett with important interracial contacts upon which the work of the Phillis Wheatley depended in the 1930s.[54]

But if the decade of the 1930s began on the paternalistic terms set in the crucible of the Progressive Era and the brutal ascent of Jim Crow, the onset of the New Deal began to transform the very context for reform in the piedmont county. Emboldened by the passage of the NRA, notably section 7(a), which provided workers with the theoretical right to organize unions of their own choosing for purposes of collective bargaining, white textile mill workers struck textile mills across the region beginning in the fall of 1933. During the strike-wave of 1933–1934 conflict between textile workers, mill owners, police,

the Ku Klux Klan, and national guardsman erupted in bloody violence. The American Federation of Labor's United Textile Workers
(UTW) union led carloads of striking workers—union shock troops
armed with guns and clubs known as "flying squadrons"—from mill
to mill in an attempt to persuade workers to join them and shut
down the mills. Although the mill workers in Greenville participated
in the strikes through the summer of 1934, most of the county's
mill workers refrained from union and strike activity by the onset
of a nationwide general strike in September. On September 4 flying
squadrons arrived at area mills only to be repulsed by armed troops.
With the assistance of Governor Ibra Blackwood and the Ku Klux
Klan, Greenville's mills remained in operation and the county managed to avoid the same level of violence that cost six strikers their
lives in Honea Path, some forty miles southeast of Greenville in Anderson County.[55]

In 1933, Eugene Bennette Geer, a former English professor and
a leading light of Greenville's thriving textile industry, was tapped
to serve as president of Greenville's Furman University, a small Baptist men's school, and to represent the textile industry on the NRA's
Cotton Textiles Industrial Relations Board, also known as the Bruere
Board. Geer combined the New South industrial spirit of men such
as Atlanta's Henry W. Grady and the tobacco giant James B. Duke,
with the progressive vision of education exemplified by the University
of North Carolina's president, Frank Porter Graham. Geer was dis-
heartened by the violence that plagued the piedmont in 1933 and
1934. In the aftermath of the 1934 strike-wave and the subsequent
disbanding of the Bruere Board, Geer began efforts to pacify labor
unrest in the belt line and launched a campaign to foster the creation of "an enlightened and happy community life" in Greenville.
In 1936 he received an $80,000 grant from the Rockefeller Foun-
dation's General Education Board (GEB) to turn Furman University and Greenville County into a living laboratory for a project in
community development. Based "squarely upon the principle that
a community should educate itself," Geer sought to harness "the
latent possibilities of the individuals of the community—teachers,
social workers, business men, housewives, socially minded citizens,
doctors, et al.," in order to bring Greenville into the modern world
being ushered in by the New Deal. With the support of Edmund de
S. Brunner of Columbia University's Teachers' College, the Chapel

Hill social scientist Howard W. Odum, and Lawrence Peter Hollis, the superintendent of Greenville's Parker School District, former YMCA activist, and champion of adult literacy, Geer created the Greenville County Council for Community Development (GCCCD). The GCCCD was designed to serve as an umbrella organization charged with coordinating the various organizations and programs contributing to the social welfare of Greenville, from the public schools and library, to social welfare and government agencies at the local, state, and federal levels. Furman was to become the organization's base of operations and its faculty, including the sociology professors Laura Smith Ebaugh and Gordon Blackwell, respectively trained at the University of Chicago and Harvard University, were to retool Furman's curriculum to educate its students to become leaders in this "enlightened" community in the making.[56]

During its first years, the GCCCD focused its efforts on the Parker School District that serviced the needs of Greenville's white textile mill workers. Meanwhile, Furman's Sociology Department began offering an array of new courses in community organization, community and recreation leadership, social problems, and government and vital statistics.[57] The GCCCD's initial grant proposal had made no mention of plans to work with Greenville's black community, although Geer had been one of the Phillis Wheatley Center's earliest financial supporters. However, at the suggestion of the GEB's Leo Favrot, the GCCCD began efforts to work with Greenville's black residents from its inception. In its first year the GCCCD hired Cora Chapman, an African American registered nurse, to help provide health services to Greenville's many black neighborhoods and communities. Through the first three years of the GCCCD's existence, Chapman personally visited over two hundred black homes across Greenville County to administer much-needed healthcare. She set up impromptu health clinics and aided the South Carolina Tuberculosis Association's efforts to provide TB tests; she canvassed black neighborhoods providing advice on diet and sanitation; she established three health clubs, addressed Sterling High School, conducted a clothing drive, and helped find homes for orphaned children. Very much in the tradition of black women's uplift work, Chapman's labors helped address many of black Greenville's critical needs while her community canvassing also helped establish lines of awareness and communication between Greenville's city residents and those black people living in communities scattered outside the city limits. "Her work held the community together," noted the GCCCD's third annual report, "and furnished impetus to work in other fields." Although Chapman's work might not have appeared political in any formal sense, her work in community health and education addressed the needs of black Greenville's bodies and minds in ways large and small, undoubtedly helping to raise expectations and collective consciousness to critical levels at a key moment of the county's history.[58]

In the first year of the program, members of the GCCCD helped create a local Committee on Interracial Cooperation and began coordinating social welfare work in Greenville with Hattie Duckett and the Phillis Wheatley Center, as well as with the Negro Division of the National Youth Administration (NYA).[59] In 1938, Blackwell directed a survey of black housing conditions in metropolitan Greenville in conjunction with black students from the city's Sterling High School and Furman sociology students. It documented the state of black housing, family structure, income level, community organizations, and public space, to be used, in part, to make appeals for local and federal aid to address the manifold problems faced by black city residents.[60]

Although the GCCCD made substantive efforts to include Greenville's black residents in its early reform efforts, white supremacy, Jim Crow segregation, and the organization's elite social composition structured its program in subtle and not so subtle ways. In 1938 the GCCCD hired an experienced African American educator, R.O. Johnson, to coordinate the organization's "Negro work." Johnson, a native Tennessean and graduate of the University of Iowa, became the first black member of the GCCCD's Executive Committee and was charged with the authority to create a separate Negro Council to oversee the GCCCD's activities among the county's black population. Under Johnson's leadership the Negro Council was formed with a carefully selected group of forty-five black men and women. Members of the Negro Council hailed solely from the ranks of black Greenville's professional classes, including Cora Chapman and Hattie Duckett, ten school administrators, three physicians, seven ministers, a teacher, two insurance directors, two farmers, a number of small business owners, and a few other selected professionals. Decidedly elite in its social composition, the council's members nevertheless sought to use their relationship to the GCCCD and Greenville's white power structure to address the needs of the county's black population.

Soon after its creation, the Negro Council turned its attention to an effort to secure recreational facilities and funding for a federally supported housing project for the city's black residents. Citing the need for black mothers to work outside the home, the council argued that recreational facilities and supervised play were critical for the development of black youth, and they strategically linked questions of access to public recreational space to problems of juvenile delinquency and black crime. "Organized playgrounds," the council explained, "are becoming more and more necessary. Many working mothers are away from home all day. Small yards and crowded conditions generally make play around the house not only difficult but unsafe and destructive to property. Organized play develops good citizens." Very much in the tradition of middle-class racial uplift, the council managed to secure much-needed funds for its limited agenda, yet it remained ever so dependent on the beneficence of Greenville's white community to carry out its work.[61]

Such dependence quickly revealed its limitations. Virtually from the moment Geer took the presidential reigns at Furman, he had come under sustained opposition from the school's conservative board members, local Baptist clergy, and city government officials. Criticized for the "progressive social tendencies" of his educational program and his "unsound" fiscal policies, Geer was forced to resign in the fall of 1938, although he maintained the chairmanship of the GCCCD. In the midst of Geer's conflict with Furman, Greenville's city council rebuffed the GCCCD's and Negro Council's efforts to secure funding for a park for black city residents. Soon thereafter the city council rejected a GCCCD- and Negro Council-sponsored proposal for a black housing project to be funded with a portion of federal government funds that had been earmarked for the construction of a white and black housing project in the city. Despite the GCCCD's study of black housing conditions, lobbying efforts, and the signatures of six hundred black city residents, Greenville's interracial liberal coalition proved incapable of gaining access to the fruits of New Deal largesse for the city's African Americans.[62]

While white liberal reformers were unable to help Greenville's black residents push the federally funded housing project through the city council, and secure the Works Progress Administration

(WPA) jobs that might have come with it, Greenville's struggling labor movement proved to be of little help either. In the wake of the bloody strike-wave of 1934, white textile mill workers, who comprised one in five Democratic Party voters, had been the deciding factor in that fall's election of the pro–New Deal governor, Olin D. Johnston. In the hard-fought election, Johnston defeated the vitriolic racist and strongly antistatist former governor, Cole Blease, for whom textile mill workers had long been staunch supporters. Throwing their weight behind Johnston, a man who had been reared in a textile mill town and supported the positive state action of the New Deal, textile mill workers, according to their most recent historian, placed their class interests ahead of their race interests and hoped that Johnston and the New Deal would usher in "the dawn of a new day" in South Carolina. However, neither Johnston's election nor the New Deal made the task of organizing textile mill workers substantially easier. The passage of the National Labor Relations Act, also known as the Wagner Act, finally provided workers with the right to organize labor unions of their own choosing and the federal government authority to enforce that right in 1935. And in July 1937, the Textile Worker's Organizing Committee (TWOC), an alliance of the UTW and a number of other unions that had broken away from the AFL to join the recently formed Congress of Industrial Organizations (CIO), moved into South Carolina. Although Johnston lent public support to the CIO, the Ku Klux Klan opposed the TWOC organizing drive in Greenville and within weeks of the union's arrival in South Carolina, nearly all of the state's two hundred mills had increased wages between 5 and 10 percent and reduced weekly hours, blunting the CIO's bread and butter appeal.[63] As they battled just to gain a foothold in Greenville, TWOC organizers proved unwilling to lend support to the black struggle for a federally funded housing project. According to a local organizer, Ralph Simmerson, the housing project was "a ready made political issue for labor" and one that concerned its own welfare. But other labor leaders did not view the fight for the housing project as "labor's fight particularly," and believed that any talk of the "Negro issue" threatened to split union membership "wide open."[64] For white textile mill workers, class interests, it seems, did not extend beyond the workplace or across the color line.

Segregated, disfranchised, and relegated to the status of junior-

partner to the state's timid and politically weak white liberal establishment, African Americans in Greenville remained on the outside
of New Deal era reform efforts looking in. While the insipient labor movement struggled for its own survival, it neither would nor
could serve as a vehicle for black empowerment. In Greenville, New
Deal-inspired liberal reform efforts failed to address the most pressing needs of African Americans and class alliances looked a lot like
the race-based alliance of white textile mill workers. Although most
recent historians of the New Deal argue that Roosevelt's "universal" mid-1930s economic reform agenda empowered a class-based
social movement dedicated to expanding the parameters of American economic and political democracy, those reform efforts took on
a distinctly white racial cast in the South Carolina piedmont; class
politics, in other words, appeared in practice as race-based interest-
group politics. To be sure, New Deal legislation certainly helped
to empower American workers, but it did so in uneven and discriminatory ways. Indeed, the location of African Americans in the
piedmont's economic structure and their near total exclusion from
the nation's political decision-making process, virtually ensured their
subordination in the emerging New Deal order.[65]

The NAACP in Greenville: Black Voting Rights and Gendered Strife

For black South Carolinians, the flow of New Deal dollars into Greenville, the GCCCD's efforts to modernize Greenville's social welfare
system, and the CIO's presence ostensibly sanctioned by the federal
government, must have suggested what Du Bois had sought to impress upon the readers of *The Crisis* in 1934: that is, that collective,
group-based organization represented the precondition for access to
and full participation in the new social order being ushered in by the
New Deal. Between 1929 and 1934 a number of dedicated African
Americans had worked to create a branch of the NAACP in Greenville. But despite the creation of a fledgling paper organization, members had been unable to garner enough support to officially charter
a fifty-member branch.[66] However, as New Deal–inspired reform efforts began subtly shifting the context of reform in the region, an
aging African American schoolteacher and dedicated activist, named
James A. Briar, managed to jumpstart the organization of a branch

in 1936. After two years of organizing he finally established an officially chartered branch with seventy members on July 24, 1938. The branch represented a cross-class coalition of African Americans. It included six ministers (one described his occupation as "huckster" and another doubled as a barber), three morticians, three teachers, a physician, two janitors, two bricklayers, three carpenters, a painter, a mechanic, two insurance salesmen, two barbers, a few small business owners, five farmers, seven employees at Greenville's Poinsette Hotel, five "skilled laborers," and ten "laborers," a number of whom worked for C.F. Sauer Company, a mayonnaise manufacturer. Six of the charter members were also members of the Negro Council. Although R.O. Johnson was not a charter member, he would surreptitiously join the branch in March 1939.

Notably, the branch included no women. Echoing the language employed by white and black men in the nineteenth century to assert claims to manhood suffrage and political power on the basis on their status as "Best Men," Briar wrote proudly to the national office to announce the successful organization of the branch. "We have seventy of the best men in South Carolina and expect to make it no less than one hundred in the near future," he explained. "We have not given the women an invitation to join us yet, but I understand many of them wish to join. . . . [P]lease give us instructions as to how to organize a women's auxiliary to operate in connection with our branch."[67]

In his letter to the national office, Briar provided insight to his and many of his fellow compatriots' understanding of the struggle they were committing to wage. Born before federal troops withdrew from the state capital in 1877, the nearly seventy-year-old schoolteacher shared a generational kinship with the men who had played key roles in the organization of the state's first NAACP branches during World War I. His father, Tom Briar, had chaired Greenville's Republican Party during Reconstruction and had been active in the short-lived, interracial offshoot of the Knights of Labor, known as the Cooperative Worker's of America in the 1880s. "I've always been active in politics," Briar explained, "because my father before me was active in politics."[68] For Briar, the creation of the Greenville NAACP and the tumultuous moment in which he brought it into being must have recalled the era of Reconstruction, a time when black men forcefully organized Union Leagues and Republican Party clubs and waged battle for political power in the streets, the countryside, and at the ballot box. The battle for full citizenship rights and representation in the civic arena, as he conceived it, was about claiming rights as an African American *and* a man; for him, the experience of racial discrimination was understood as a denial of his manhood. The battle against it, then, was a battle for his manhood rights.[69]

But if Briar's conception of black liberation required that men play leading public roles and women work alongside them in an auxiliary capacity, his choice to pursue that vision of liberation through the vehicle of the NAACP quickly led to a reorientation of his practices, if not his views. The omission of women did not escape the notice of the national office. "There is one little mistake I wish to call to your attention: Your taking for granted that women are not to be admitted to the general membership of the branch," the NAACP's outgoing field secretary, William Pickens, politely explained to Briar after receiving his August letter. "In all our branches and in every field of activity, women are on equal fo[o]ting with men." "Therefore," he counseled, "I am advising that you get as many women members as possible. . . . Women do not serve only in auxiliaries in the NAACP but are regular members and officers of our branches as are men." "We do not have any all male branches in the Association," Pickens wrote in a more sternly worded letter to another leader of the new branch. "Women members must be admitted on equal terms with men in the branch membership and they have the privilege of joining all branch activities and of holding office. In fact, the women members of our branches have in many cases been the source of our greatest strength." Pickens's longtime fieldwork had most certainly demonstrated to him the important work of black women in the NAACP and he, no doubt, recalled the leading roles black women had played in voter registration efforts in South Carolina in 1920. Indeed, William Pickens was soon to be replaced as NAACP field secretary by Daisy Elizabeth Adams Lampkin, whom the NAACP had hired in 1930 as regional field secretary to help resuscitate its declining branch support. Lampkin had begun her political career in 1915 as president of the Negro Women's Franchise League, and she served as the national organizer and chair of the executive board of the NACW in the 1920s, providing her with extensive connections among the nation's black women activists. When the NAACP hired her in 1930 it had signaled in practice that the organization acknowledged the crucial role that black women played in black communities and within the NAACP itself.[70]

Whether or not the national office's scolding of Briar altered his fundamental understanding of the roles of men and women cannot be known for sure, but it certainly altered the practices of the branch. Available membership records indicate that at least by the beginning of 1939 women had not only become members of the branch, but also were elected to its Executive Committee. Hattie Duckett's name appeared on branch membership rolls as early as the fall of 1939 and, for a time at least, the NAACP held meetings in the Phillis Wheatley Center. Much as the NAACP functioned in other towns and cities as a site of conflict and mediation, by the beginning of 1939 the NAACP had become a critical organization in black Greenville, bringing black men and women together in a collective effort to raise issues of concern to the city's black residents and to formulate a means to address them. Just as importantly, if not more so, the creation of a local NAACP branch connected black people in Greenville to a national organization and a broader community of struggle. In doing so, it opened up local issues and relationships to national scrutiny and in this case it subjected patriarchal constructions of race struggle to criticism and revision.[71]

Significantly, the NAACP began establishing itself as a key engine of racial organization during the GCCCD- and the Negro Council-sponsored petition drive to secure access to federal funds for a black and white housing project in the fall of 1938. At the same time, a division of the short-lived government relief worker's union, the Workers' Alliance, worked to organize local WPA workers. Its separate Negro Division, dubbed by its principal leader, J.C. Williams, the "Baby NAACP," took an active role in the fight for the construction of a public park and housing project for black city residents. Indeed, the fight for the park and housing project began to animate a cross-class community-wide movement by highlighting the issues of access to public space, the need for adequate housing, and the desire for a fair distribution of New Deal largesse, including jobs. The park and housing project were, of course, not to be. But the failure itself—the limits of New Deal reform—proved to be a crucial impetus for future reform efforts.[72]

Indeed, shortly after Greenville's city council blocked funds for the park and housing project, talk began to circulate within NAACP circles about the need to secure the right to vote and about the possibility of sponsoring a mass registration of black voters. "We had the idea," R.O. Johnson explained, "of flooding [the] general election and sponsoring an independent candidate." With the city elections pending that fall, Briar recalled, "There was much talk about an independent ticket for Mayor with colored people running."[73] It would not be until May, however, that talk turned to action. In the meantime, the GCCCD made plans to host a weekend-long conference on consumer cooperatives to be held in Greenville in cooperation with the University of North Carolina. The conference, chaired by Howard Odum, was entitled, "Educating People to Help Themselves," and was intended to help "southern people gain a fuller realization of the possibilities of adult education and cooperative action."[74]

Held on the weekend of May 18, the conference at once highlighted the limits of southern white liberal reform and helped launch a summerlong battle for black voting rights. In the preparation for the conference, the issue of segregation and black participation became an issue of conflict within the GCCCD. At a March 6 meeting of the Executive Committee Geer laid out his position. "I think any movement like this should take into consideration the development of the Negro," Geer explained. "I see no objection to having Negroes come and sit, ask questions, and get the benefit of the meeting. [But] I do not believe that at the present time it would be wise to have any Negro on the program." In the debate that followed, questions were raised about the problems faced in housing black participants from out of town and about the problems posed in finding a place to meet in the city if black people were to attend. Ultimately, the committee agreed that the conference would include black participants on a segregated basis only and only if black people were left off the official program. In private, Geer and School Superintendent Hollis expressed a desire to avoid segregated seating and to include black participants in the program, but segregation prevailed nevertheless. "The group is not enthusiastic about the conference," Hollis lamented, "but if we can segregate the Negroes in the meetings, it will be all right to have them come. The facilities for entertaining the Negroes will be limited to private homes. The number of Negroes should not exceed twenty-five. Negroes should not be on the program, and the program should be submitted to the executive committee for approval."[75]

If segregation prevailed in the preparations for the conference, the conference, as R.O. Johnson remembered it, proved to be a springboard for a sustained assault on Jim Crow. In his address to the segregated gathering, the renowned sociologist and research and field secretary of the Commission on Interracial Cooperation, Arthur Raper, pushed the logic of the cooperative movement to its logical conclusion. "We must discard the poll tax and the white primary," he boldly pronounced, "if we are to have cooperative action, for there is no such thing as cooperative action among slaves." "Responsible participation is the bedrock of the cooperative movement," he added, and he pinned many of the South's economic problems on its failure to end disfranchisement. Indeed, by the time Raper openly supported an end to the poll tax and white primary, African Americans in Greenville had begun "an extensive underground movement" to register black voters.[76]

In May a number of African Americans quietly placed their names on Greenville's registration rolls in preparation for that September's scheduled mayoral election. Meanwhile, an array of individuals and organizations worked to bolster support for a mass voter registration drive. J.C. Williams and the "Baby NAACP" held weekly meetings in a local Presbyterian church to discuss voter registration and make preparations for an impending strike of WPA workers. "Men, at [the] next meeting bring your ammunition," one man reportedly remarked. "We'll teach you how to use it. We're going on the offensive." James Briar and the NAACP held voter registration schools. "Briar was really the worker for the whole move," explained the head porter at Greenville's Poinsette Hotel, Henry Percival Sr. "He and the NAACP held schools around at peoples['] houses, teaching them simple facts about the constitution and helping them to learn to pronounce the difficult words." That June the recently formed NAACP Youth Council, led by a nineteen-year-old janitor and charter member of the adult branch, William H. Anderson, held two community forums on "Youth and Democracy." Although TWOC, which by 1939 had become the Textile Workers Union of America (TWUA), continued to keep its distance publicly from the black movement in Greenville, individual members lent their assistance to the voter registration drive in its earliest days. For a time the black Worker's Alliance worked out of the TWUA's Greenville office, and organizer Don McKee allowed leaders of the registration drive to use the TWUA's mimeograph to print leaflets. And John Bolt Culbertson, a lawyer who worked for the CIO and regularly defended black clients in court, made the rounds to black churches encouraging black people to register to vote.[77]

Until the early days of July, the black voter registration effort remained largely hidden from the broader white Greenville community. Then on July 5, J.C. Williams and William Anderson, among others, helped usher groups of African Americans, most of them women, into the county courthouse to obtain voter registration certificates and then into city hall to place their names on the city's voter registration rolls. The next day the *Greenville News* broke a front-page story announcing, "57 Negroes Register In Single Day For Coming General Election." The story, which was accompanied by a photograph of black women lined up to place their names on the registration books, broke the secrecy of the organized registration effort. According to news reports, Williams identified himself as a leader of the Worker's Alliance and claimed that the organization had some two thousand members. For his part, Anderson identified himself as president of the Youth Council, boasted that Briar and the NAACP had organized a voter's club, and that he fully anticipated the registration of between one thousand and five thousand African Americans by the end of the year. In the days ahead, newspaper headlines announced "Ku Klux Official Declares Klan Will Act in Negro Registration Here" and made it known that lawyers from the New York–based Worker's Defense League were lending aid to the registration drive. Editorials encouraged white citizens to respond to black registration efforts by realizing "the wisdom of performing their civic duty at the ballot box," and asked in horror, "What is Going on in Greenville?"[78]

In the days and months that followed, the response of Greenville's white residents to the voter registration drive suggested the degree to which the black insurgency represented a challenge to a world ordered by hierarchies of race and gender—that is, by white male supremacy. As newspaper reports fanned white fears of racial unrest across the county, a campaign of intimidation and terror unfolded that lasted well into the late fall months. During the summer, J.C. Williams was arrested on three separate occasions and was visited by Klan members while held in police custody. On July 16, Jerry Owens, a thirty-one-year-old bootblack, was arrested for attempted rape after he allegedly propositioned a white waitress in a hand-scribbled note he passed to her in a café. According to Henry Percival, Owens was illiterate and, only days before his arrest, had been kidding his white customers about how many black people were going to register to vote in Greenville. The next day, James Anderson was arrested by police for attempting to make a date with a white girl from a phone at the school where he worked as a janitor. Owens would ultimately be convicted and sentenced to fifteen years in prison. Anderson was convicted on lesser charges of breach of the peace and disorderly conduct and eventually served thirty days on the chain gang.[79]

Following the arrest of Anderson and Owens, the GCCCD called a meeting of its Executive Committee to assess recent events, "lest the movement on the part of Negroes in registering bring about a bad situation." "[I]f registration keeps up," warned Geer, "the Klan will ride and that will set Negro work in South Carolina back at least ten years." At the meeting, committee members expressed fears that any association with the NAACP and the registration drive would place the work of the GCCCD and the Negro Council in jeopardy, and they resolved to distance themselves from both. Although the members were willing to work with Greenville's black community in a slow-paced effort to ameliorate the most egregious effects of racial discrimination, its members were unwilling to lend their names or the GCCCD's voice to the efforts of African Americans to secure the franchise and play an equal role in the decision-making processes of the Greenville community. "After the registration began," Henry Percival noted that, except for "a few old faithfuls," white members of the GCCCD-sponsored Interracial Committee "stopped coming" to meetings. To be sure, the threat of Klan violence marked the outer limits of permissible black activity in Greenville, but the GCCCD and its members, for reasons of self-preservation and continued commitment to white supremacy, played their own roles in turning back black challenges to Jim Crow by failing to support them.[80]

The GCCCD was not the only organization to distance itself from the black voter registration drive or shrink from the growing terror campaign sponsored by the joint force of the Ku Klux Klan and the Greenville city police. The Phillis Wheatley Center and at least one black church, probably more, closed their doors to meetings of the NAACP and the Worker's Alliance. Despite the efforts of the Worker's Defense League to force action on the part of the U.S.

Department of Justice, the federal government also refused to intervene. And while members of the TWUA had provided assistance to the registration campaign in its earliest phases, as public opposition mounted, labor organizers similarly withdrew their support. "I think the niggers ought to have the right to vote," TWUA organizer Ralph Simmerson admitted. "I'd do almost anything I could, personally, to help them get it." Simmerson believed, however, that the benefits of supporting the rights of African Americans to vote were outweighed by the risks such support posed to the immediate exigencies of organizing a virtually all-white textile mill workforce. "Sooner or later," he explained, "we've got to get [their votes] because we're not going to have enough by ourselves." But for the time being, Simmerson surmised, "Negroes had better fight it out for themselves."[81]

With the support of liberals and labor leaders in rapid retreat, the Ku Klux Klan was free to unleash a reign of terror across Greenville and the South Carolina piedmont. Although as many as two hundred African Americans registered to vote in the September 12 election, on election day only thirty-four cast their votes at the polls. In the weeks that followed, the Klan terrorized the region as if to eliminate all vestiges of resistance to the rule of white male supremacy. On a Saturday evening, September 24, in the Greenville County village of Fountain Inn, between ten and fifteen carloads of heavily armed and robed Klansmen wreaked havoc in black neighborhoods, ransacking at least one black business and beating some twenty African Americans. In nearby Simpsonville, a number of black men were beaten by Klansmen and a black woman was stripped of her clothes. In early November, Klansmen pulled a black World War I veteran from his home, and for publicly criticizing the Klan, stripped him naked, lashed him mercilessly, and dumped his limp body on the front steps of Joe Tolbert's home. Then the Klan turned its attention to James Briar.[82]

On November 15, carloads of Klansmen raided the black neighborhood in and around South Calhoun and Dunbar streets looking for the NAACP leader. "They had gone to my house, but I wasn't home," Briar recalled. "They went to my niece's house and my neighbor's house, but they couldn't find me. I was over at Walker and Sullivan's Funeral Home." Receiving daily reports from a black man who worked at a downtown café where Klan members met to discuss their evening plans, Briar's friends, family, and other supporters shuffled him from house to house over the course of the next week, while armed guards posted watch on front porches throughout the neighborhood. "For about a week," Briar explained, "a company of Negroes, fully armed, patrolled my street. I wasn't bothered further." "My best help," he added, "came from so called bad 'niggers' and from Negro women." While the Klan was unable to administer its own brand of extralegal discipline, Briar was arrested by city police on November 30 for carrying a concealed weapon, a crime for which he was forced to pay a fine and received a suspended sentence.[83]

In a rampage of violence aimed at arresting the efforts of African Americans to become full agents in the civic life of Greenville and the nation, the Ku Klux Klan smashed the insipient black movement in Greenville. If Briar and the charter members of the NAACP believed that their struggle was necessarily a battle for manhood rights, many white South Carolinians shared their view. Indeed, the voter registration movement in Greenville was perceived by many white people as a threat to a world ordered by white male supremacy; the fears of black men assaulting white women and the sexualized symbolism of the Klan's campaign of terror demonstrated just how much hierarchies of race were intertwined with hierarchies of gender. But while the reaction to the black movement in Greenville demonstrated the ways in which the ideology and practice of white male supremacy still held a powerful grip on the lives of South Carolinians, it also signaled that the black movement was launching a new phase of challenges to it.

Across the nation, the black struggle for voting rights in Greenville and the violent efforts to suppress it served as a rallying cry. Youth Councils from Boston, Massachusetts, to Jackson, Mississippi, raised money for William Anderson's legal defense. In South Carolina the voting rights movement in Greenville helped provide a crucial impetus for the formation of a statewide NAACP that would help coordinate NAACP activities across the state and spur the massive growth of branches and membership during the 1940s. Just as importantly, the struggle in Greenville demonstrated in a dramatic way that the right to vote was fast becoming an issue with broad popular appeal. In the spring of 1940, as the NAACP's battle against the white primary in Texas wound its way through the courts, the association announced in the pages of *The Crisis* that it was moving the issue of the vote to the front of its national agenda. "The N.A.A.C.P. campaign, now out in the open," read the May edition, "is a result of the activities of many of its branches in the southern states dating back a year ago and includes the spectacular fights in Miami, Fla. and Greenville, South Carolina." Moreover, as the New Deal signaled that collective, group-based political organization was fast becoming the sine qua non of American political and economic life, events in Greenville also demonstrated that in the absence of an independent organization dedicated to extending the rights and advancing the interests of African Americans, African Americans would continue to be left behind in a rapidly changing world. By the beginning of the 1940s, then, the organization that black people in South Carolina and the nation would increasingly choose to represent their interests was the NAACP, and the issue that animated their activism was the vote.[84]

4 Civil Rights and Collective Action: The Battle for Black Empowerment

Faith of our fathers! living still
In spite of dungeon, fire and sword:
O how our hearts beat high with joy
Whene'er we hear that glorious word!
Faith of our fathers! Holy faith!
We will be true to thee till death!

Our fathers, chained in prison dark,
Were still in heart and conscience free:
How sweet would be their children's fate,
If they, like them, could die for thee!
Faith of our fathers! Holy faith!
We will be true to thee till death!
　　　　　—"Faith of Our Fathers," sung to open the annual meeting of the
　　　　　South Carolina State Conference of NAACP Branches, June 1941

For 79 years Negroes have begged,
tired themselves out holding meetings with whites,
dying and praying for political freedom.
But they have gotten nowhere.
Now they are trying the sure and certain way—
they are going to the polls and do their pleading and fighting there.
　　　　　—South Carolina Progressive Democratic Party flier, 1944

In 1919 a number of black South Carolinians imagined the possibilities of creating a statewide black political party capable of challenging the all-white, state Democratic Party's stranglehold on life in South Carolina. The 1920s were, however, years of repression and contraction, rather than expansion for the black struggle for self-determination and equality in South Carolina and yet, at the same moment that the political possibilities of the World War I years ap-

107

peared to have exhausted themselves, the seeds of future change were taking root. In 1927, the same year that John Birks Gillespie's father died of an asthma attack, Levi Grant Byrd arrived in Cheraw, South Carolina, to make a new start in life. While the death of Gillespie's father and the onset of the Great Depression led the future trumpet-great to migrate to Philadelphia and on to New York City, where he helped usher in a revolution in American popular culture and became part of an emerging African American voting bloc in the urban North, Byrd's arrival in Cheraw marked a critical juncture in the self-transformation of South Carolina's black struggle for civil rights. Although a man of little formal education, between 1933 and 1939 Byrd used his folksy, persistent, and iron-willed ways to organize an underground NAACP branch in the small town of Cheraw. From a town much like those where branches had failed to withstand the trying conditions of the 1920s, Byrd then spearheaded the organization of the South Carolina NAACP State Conference of Branches, helping to connect numerous local struggles across the state together in a collective and coordinated effort to smash Jim Crow and demand a full say in the making of their own and the nation's collective future. In the process, Byrd challenged old lines of black political authority, helped launch the expansion of the NAACP in the state, and, in doing so, paved the way for a new generation of civil rights activists to live out the imaginings of an earlier one.

Levi G. Byrd: Toward a Politics of Interdependence

Levi Byrd was the eldest of nine children born to Alfred D. Byrd and Pinkie Hancock Byrd in January 1891. Reared on a tobacco farm in Anson County, North Carolina, near the town of Lilesville, he grew up just thirty-odd miles north of Cheraw. In 1911 Byrd married and spent two years farming before he and his wife moved to Hamlet, North Carolina, where he took a job as a freight handler for the Seaboard Air Line railroad company. Following the death of his wife seven years later, Byrd continued the strenuous lifting work required by his railroad job, until, as the story is told, he noticed some writing on the inside of a boxcar. "In 1918 I was trucking in Hamlet, N.C.," Byrd remembered. "I was carrying boxes into a boxcar and on one end it was written, 'What is your life.' And on the other end it said, 'Your life is what you make of it.'" Shortly thereafter, the story continues,

Byrd resolved to do something with his life, to do something more than work all day and return home at night with little hope for a better future. After leaving behind the railroad work, he spent several years in a number of different North Carolina towns before he made the decision to move to Cheraw, where his cousin, Annie Hancock, graciously provided him a place to stay until he found work. Soon Byrd found a job as a plumber's assistant to an aging white man named C.F. Pendleton, married Mary Ann Love, a neighbor of his cousin, and became an active member of the Pee Dee Union Baptist Church.[1]

By 1931 Byrd and his wife had begun a family and Byrd made the decision to leave the employment of Pendleton and work for himself. In a situation potentially fraught with conflict, Byrd managed, despite his employer's protestations, to negotiate a separation, and soon he became the only plumber in Cheraw, servicing the plumbing needs of a largely white clientele and the few fortunate black people afforded the luxury of indoor plumbing. Had Jim Crow and white supremacy not maintained such a tight grip on life in South Carolina, the forty-year-old's newfound monopoly on the plumbing needs of the small Pee Dee River town might very well have signaled a passage to middle-class security. But in the early part of 1933, less than a year after the birth of his second son, Alfred, Byrd became a victim of racial violence that launched his activist career. From that point forward his struggle for economic security and human dignity would be waged in and through a battle for racial justice.

As the Great Depression swept South Carolina in the early 1930s, racial violence permeated the timber and cotton producing county of Chesterfield. In 1933, Bill McNeil, a trombone player in John Birks Gillespie's makeshift band, allegedly "vanished." Although the exact cause of his "disappearance" was not known, Gillespie and his cohorts understood it as a clear signal to "get the hell out of Cheraw." As he remembers it, "A rumor came out that a group of white men had caught him and put him on the railroad tracks in front of a train, because someone said Bill had been a 'Peeping Tom' and had been caught in some white person's house. No one ever found his body." "We all knew," he added, "that it could just as easily have happened to one of us."[2] On a Saturday afternoon in early June of the same year, as he attempted to investigate the mistreatment of black residents in Cheraw's small downtown business district, Byrd was severely beaten by a group of white men. For Byrd the event revealed, in no uncertain terms, the limits imposed on the life he had carved out for himself and his family. "When Daddy was hit," recalled his son Alfred D. Byrd, "that was the turning, there."[3]

Byrd's assault was only one of a series of brutal beatings meted out to black residents of Cheraw in the early part of 1933, and, thereafter, Byrd resolved to put an end to the ongoing violence and commenced efforts to organize a branch of the NAACP. Beginning in June 1933, in a series of roughly typed and handwritten letters reflecting his lack of formal schooling, Byrd began what would become a virtually continuous correspondence with the NAACP national office that would last well into the 1950s. Rare among NAACP branch file correspondence for their regularity and detailed accountings of black life and organizing efforts in a small rural town, Byrd's letters began to crack the regional isolation of a black community that lacked legal protection and political representation, and was regularly brutalized by white residents. "[T]hir has been so miny out rages cormited own our race hear in Cheraw latly," Byrd wrote directly to Walter White. "We are wishing to form a branch of the N.A.A.C.P. hear to fight the Brutal way thay doin our Race hear for the last 6 are 8 Months we Had 5 are 6 Brutal Beaten hear in town bye the whites and there has not one of them bee eaven arrested for it we have no propten [protection] hear when it comes to law." Only two weeks later Byrd wrote the national office to inform them that, "The Police Beat up A Woman of our Race hear in Cheraw Saturday June 24 and is Getting worse Each Day." "We are treated as Slaves hear in Cheraw," he explained. "[T]hey have no law hear to protect our race at all. [S]o you see how we feel about it."[4]

For Byrd, the organization of an NAACP branch represented an important first step toward the amelioration of what he described as the slavelike conditions under which black people lived in Chesterfield County. But organizing a branch of the NAACP in a small town like Cheraw and a rural county like Chesterfield was a dangerous and seemingly impossible task in the mid-1930s. Cheraw was a town where everybody knew everybody and where leading white residents prided themselves on what they perceived as their close, even familial, ties to the town's black residents. In a special 1934 edition of *The Cheraw Chronicle* designed to tout the town's progressive spirit, the paper celebrated the ties of its black residents to the town's white families and to the lands "worked by their forbears as slaves." It boasted that

Cheraw was noted for its "good class" of "negroes" [*sic*]. "Never," it explained, "have they given the least trouble. Many of them are the best house servants to be found anywhere." Whether bloodlines crossed, as they did in the case of the Gillespie family, or whether white people imagined close familial ties to black residents, life in Cheraw was regulated by a veneer of paternalism that masked underlying conflict, suppressed dissent, and justified brutal violence in response to the slightest challenge to the racial dreamworld it supported.[5]

Just as significantly, black residents of Cheraw were anything but a monolithic group. Although opportunities for economic advancement were slim for most, class identities in black Cheraw were shaped as much by religious belief, morals, manners, and social practices as they were by the hard economics of income and occupation or the demographics of street address. In black Cheraw, church affiliation and modes of religious expression were critical markers of social status. "It's very interesting," Gillespie recalled, "how the blacks became divided over religion in Cheraw." At the top of the social pyramid were those who attended the Second Presbyterian Church, which was also home to the Coulter Memorial Academy, a private school for African Americans that educated students through the tenth grade and trained most of the region's schoolteachers. Founded in 1881 by the Presbyterian National Home Mission as the Coulter School, throughout its history Coulter maintained close ties to Biddle College (now Johnson C. Smith University) in Charlotte, North Carolina, and, in 1933, under the leadership of an African American minister, Rev. George Waldo Long, it achieved state accreditation as a junior college. Next in the social order were those who attended the Wesley United Methodist Church, and they, in turn, were followed in descending order by the members of the Pee Dee Union Baptist Church and the A.M.E. Zion, where some degree of "shouting" took place, and they by members of a number of smaller churches, including the Sanctified Church, where Gillespie remembered, "everyone knew that the whole congregation shouted." "That was the lowest you could go," he explained, "because they practiced spirit possession and speaking in tongues, which was considered too much akin to African religion." Most black children attended Cheraw's Robert Small Graded and Junior High School. The ten-room, nine-teacher school provided six hundred students with an education through the ninth grade during the 1933–1934 school year. The state funded seven months of the term and the Parent-Teacher Association helped raise enough money to extend the school year an additional month.[6]

Organizing in such a context was hard work, but Byrd's somewhat ambiguous social position in black Cheraw placed him in an opportune position to organize the community. As the town's only plumber serving a largely white clientele, Byrd occupied a position of relative economic privilege in black Cheraw and represented the values of hard work and thrift required for middle-class respectability. However, his membership in the Pee Dee Union Baptist Church and lack of formal education made him neither a member of Cheraw's black elite nor a member of its lowest-ranking social classes. Byrd had also become a well-known figure among black residents of Cheraw and Chesterfield County by the early 1930s through his work as a regional agent for a number of black newspapers. Every Saturday morning, Byrd, who would never learn to drive a car, toted a small red wagon through Cheraw's black neighborhoods and hand delivered copies of *The Pittsburgh Courier*, *The* (Norfolk) *Journal and Guide*, and *The Baltimore Afro-American* to subscribers. On those same afternoons, as black people from the surrounding countryside made their way into town to shop and socialize, Byrd stood near McBride's Market and sold papers to all those interested, allowing him to become a visible presence in the town and acquainted with people from across the county. For Byrd, black newspapers served as a conduit to the world outside of Cheraw and proved a ready-made organizing tool.[7]

There was nothing natural about Byrd's capacity to organize black Cheraw. From the earliest moments of his organizing efforts, Byrd worked hard to piece together an organization that could represent the interests of a broad cross section of Chesterfield County's black population. Recognizing the importance of church leaders to the county's black residents, Byrd took on the difficult task of recruiting ministers into the organization. "Some of our Leaders hear Seem to be afred of ofindin thir good white folks," he explained to the national office. "We have Good Leaders hear when it comes to the Church. But not much own this." In the earliest days of recruiting, Byrd pushed one sympathetic minister to take the lead in recruiting new members. "I am Gonto Let Rev. J.E. Davis take the Lead in secun membis," he wrote the national office. He also used the influence of the national office as a means to persuade more reluctant members of Cheraw's professional classes to join the organization, attempting to

make civil rights activism and membership in the NAACP a qualification for respectability. At Byrd's request, the national office sent letters
to Coulter Memorial Academy's principal, Reverend Long, its leading
teacher and future principal, Henry L. Marshall, as well as the pastors
of the Pee Dee Union Baptist and A.M.E. Zion Churches. "You have
been recommended to us as one of the key persons in Cheraw," the
national office cajoled, "and we are writing to solicit your interest and
cooperation in the organization of a branch in your community. . . .
There is no question that this work demands the support of every self-
respecting Negro."[8]

Byrd did not, however, recruit solely or even predominantly from
Cheraw's traditional leadership classes. In the late 1930s the organization and its membership, by necessity, remained underground and, in
that sense, its mass appeal was limited. But Byrd labored to educate
people about the purposes of the NAACP and to encourage them to
join the organization. "Some of the People Dos not understand much
about the NAACP," he wrote. "We will have to work hard among
some of us to Give them the real meaning of the NAACP."[9] As part of
his efforts to teach people about the meaning of the NAACP, at some
point, likely during the NAACP's first antilynching button drive in
1937, Byrd began wearing an NAACP button in public, becoming the
only recognizable member of the organization in Cheraw. Much like
labor union members who wore their CIO buttons openly in the workplace, Byrd's choice to wear his NAACP button in public symbolized
a new allegiance, a connection to a national organization, a new attitude, and even a new identity.[10] For a time black people avoided Byrd
on the streets of Cheraw, crossing the street when he approached and
bypassing the corner where he sold newspapers on Saturdays. But his
public demonstration of fearlessness and his assertion of independence
made a powerful case for joining the organization. If Byrd could "step
out" and risk his own economic well-being and personal safety in the
interest of racial justice, perhaps others could do the same.[11]

Slowly, but persistently, Byrd convinced black residents of Chesterfield County to join the NAACP. Finally, after years of organizing, on
May 19, 1939, seventy men and women met and chartered the Cheraw and Chesterfield County NAACP branch. "We have been sleeping on our rights," proclaimed the newly elected branch president,
J.L. Dickson, "and we should be awake and about our business for
we have a long distance to go as to accomplishments and we need to

prepare ourselves." The organization drew members from across black Cheraw's social spectrum and reflected Byrd's vision of the NAACP. It included teachers from Coulter Memorial Academy and the pastors of the Wesley United Methodist, Pee Dee Union Baptist, A.M.E. Zion, and the Sanctified Churches. Four domestic workers added their names to the charter, as did two barbers, a hairdresser, a midwife, four brick masons, five farmers, an undertaker, two merchants, and fifteen men who listed their occupations as common laborers. Four of its members were also members of the Addie H. Pickens Club, which was an affiliate of the SCFCWC and the NACW. Teachers occupied the positions of president, vice president, and secretary, and Byrd held the formal title of treasurer and the informal position of corresponding secretary. "Because," he explained, "I have worked this part in the past and understand more about that part." As would remain his practice in the years ahead, Byrd pushed members of the more "articulate" classes to assume the organization's formal leadership roles even as he remained the key leader in the day-to-day operations of the organization. Reflecting his religious faith, his understanding of the importance of black churches in the lives of many African Americans, and the need to maintain the support of the town's ministers, the Cheraw branch would, in the future, hold its meetings in the town's various churches on a rotating basis. NAACP meetings, patterned along the lines of other church-affiliated organizations, were held on "Third Sundays" and prayers and hymns were regular components of the gatherings.[12]

The NAACP State Conference of Branches and the Struggle for Group Recognition

As Byrd and other African Americans pieced together a branch of the NAACP in Cheraw, resurrecting the promise that the organization had symbolized for residents of places such as Calhoun County in the 1920s, James Briar and African Americans in Greenville had begun their own underground movement and voter registration drive that would explode in violence that July. In organizing NAACP branches, black residents of Cheraw and Greenville began connecting their local movements to a national arena of struggle, yet in the context of South Carolina, the two movements emerged independently from one another and from the state's traditional centers of black political and economic power in Charleston and Columbia. That would begin to change, however, as Byrd commenced efforts to create a statewide NAACP and the violence in Greenville provided black South Carolinians with an issue that dramatized the need for intrastate cooperation.

During the World War I years, African Americans in Columbia and Charleston had become champions of a brand of protest politics that openly challenged white supremacy and began reshaping an older commitment to the more limited politics of racial uplift. Although a new commitment to protest politics could not be extinguished in the troubled years of the 1920s, the politics of racial uplift had, once again, become the predominant mode of black activism by the beginning of the 1930s. For the better part of the 1930s the NAACP remained largely inactive in both cities, and efforts to look beyond the immediate demands of local circumstances were met with substantial levels of skepticism and trepidation. While the two branches periodically sought to secure new members and raise funds for the national office's antilynching campaign, little could mask the organizational drift of the branches. In both cases, an aging generation of activists, those who had been born before the advent of Jim Crow and for whom the NAACP had become a forceful engine of protest during the World War I years, was rapidly fading from the scene and a new generation of black leaders had yet to assert their voices or offer a vision for the future of the black civil rights struggle. In Columbia the drift was made manifest by the death of longtime NAACP leader N.J. Frederick in August 1938. In the spring of 1932, temporarily revitalizing the dreams of the World War I years, Frederick had filed a lawsuit in state and federal court on behalf of a handful of 1920s NAACP stalwarts as part of yet another challenge to the Democratic Party's white primary. Both suits failed, and that July, in the wake of the NAACP's limited Supreme Court victory in *Nixon v. Condon*, the second case in a series of cases challenging the constitutionality of the white primary in Texas, Frederick made the decision to postpone further challenges to the white primary in South Carolina, a challenge he did not live to see. In Charleston, the NAACP's travails were magnified in 1937 when John H. McCray, a brash, twenty-five-year-old graduate of Avery and Talladega College, assumed the presidency of the branch only to embroil it in controversy. McCray was the editor of the fledgling black-owned newspaper *The Charleston Lighthouse*. He had achieved the reputation as a "radical" in 1935 for aggressively investigating a number of African Americans' deaths at the hands of Charleston police. But in an April 1937 *Charleston News and Courier* editorial, McCray broke with his earlier aggressive posture and took issue with the NAACP's campaign for federal antilynching legislation, arguing, in effect, that black South Carolinians were "content to wait" for the inevitable decline of lynching. In words befitting the most ingratiating of accommodationists, McCray eschewed the use of "caustic methods" in the service of racial justice and sought to distance southern African Americans from the actions of their northern counterparts. He reminded white readers that black Charlestonians had long sought "to promote the basic principles of friendship." "Our record over fifty years verifies this statement," he wrote. "Hence, we are not involved in the going-ons beyond the Mason and Dixon line." Lambasted by Louise Purvis Bell, a member of the Charleston NAACP's Executive Committee, for being an "uncle Tom and a traitor," McCray was forced to resign his position as branch president, no doubt learning a lesson that would shape what was soon to become a formidable career of caustic agitation for racial justice.[13]

As Levi Byrd struggled to turn the NAACP into a forceful vehicle to represent the interests of black South Carolinians in rural Chesterfield County, he viewed the dearth of NAACP activity elsewhere in the state as an impediment to the success of his own locally rooted organizing efforts, and he began to search for ways to energize the NAACP across the state. Breaking the isolation of life in Cheraw was, for him, the precondition for, rather than inhibitor of, progress. In June the Cheraw NAACP sent two members to the NAACP's annual conference in Richmond, Virginia, only to learn that the state of South Carolina was represented by only one additional branch. "One thing that did not speak well for The State of S.C.," he wrote the national office, "[is] that only 2 Brinches of the State of S.C. were thir to Reps—— thir Brinches."[14] Since 1929 the NAACP had been encouraging branches in various states to pool their collective resources and form State Conferences of NAACP Branches. Intended to serve as "connecting link[s] between the branches and the National Office," state conferences were also viewed as a means to actively encourage and facilitate the participation of small communities in the work of the association through their partnership with larger branches. They functioned, in practice, in much the same way that Abram Harris had argued regional divisions of the NAACP should, but on a state-by-state basis. Across the South, African Americans began creating state conferences during the 1930s, pooling financial resources and ideas, and opening up the possibility for coordinated statewide political and protest activity.[15] The idea of creating a state conference was an attractive one to Byrd. "We wont to Farm A State Conference so as to try to Keep all Branches alive and Keep Them are Get Them to Work," he wrote the national office. "Will you Send me the Names of Each Branch President and his Address," he asked, "so that we May get in Turch With of them so we mayget to gether own that. Would you not think that a good way to living those Dead Branche up."[16]

With a list of officers of the state's nominally active branches in hand, Byrd began a letter-writing campaign to urge the formation of a State Conference of NAACP Branches. By September Byrd had secured positive responses from branch leaders in Florence, Georgetown, Greenville, Sumter, and Charleston, but the recently elected president of the Columbia branch, the Reverend James M. Hinton, refused to lend the support of the Columbia organization. Although Hinton advocated a certain amount of aggressive activism, the ongoing repression of black voter registration efforts in Greenville gave him pause. He believed that the well-publicized battle in Greenville would ultimately aid the plight of black South Carolinians generally, but he understood the role of the Columbia branch in the broader struggle for black equality in narrow terms. It is our responsibility, he explained, "to supply the material and money" to the national office while "the folks up North have got to stick their necks out for us." In 1939 Hinton's concerns remained largely circumscribed by local circumstances. The simultaneously privileged and strained resources available to black Columbians made a strategy of independent and locally focused activism preferable to one that required a more broad-based cooperative effort. The responsibilities of the state conference, Hinton feared, would be carried disproportionately by the Columbia branch and would sap the struggle in Columbia of already scarce dollars. "Our branch was not entirely sold on the State Conference," he wrote the national office in 1940, "for we felt that it would be just another drain on our funds, which you know are limited."[17]

Byrd's efforts to create a state conference also represented a challenge to traditional lines of black power and authority in South Carolina, and to Hinton's in particular. Hinton was a newcomer to the state in 1939, having arrived in Columbia only a year earlier to expand the business operations of the black-owned Pilgrim Health and Life Insurance Company. When Byrd began organizing the state conference, Hinton was in the early stages of establishing his business and his personal authority in the state. Born in 1891 in Gates County, North Carolina, Hinton was reared by an aunt in New York City from the age of three until he was drafted into the U.S. Army in 1917. While stationed in Augusta, Georgia, he earned the rank of lieutenant, and after the war, the Augusta-based Pilgrim Health and Life hired him and sent him to Alabama to establish a base of operations in the state. By the time he arrived in South Carolina, Hinton had become a shrewd businessman and possessed a wealth of organizational skill gained during his years of business activity in Alabama. In Columbia, Hinton would also serve as a supply pastor for the Second Cavalry Baptist Church and fast acquired a reputation for fine oratory. He was a commanding presence, and from his days as a lieutenant in the Army, to his career in the insurance business and the ministry, he was accustomed to giving orders and delegating authority. He was, to be sure, unprepared to take orders from an upstart plumber from Chesterfield County.[18]

For Byrd, Hinton was just one of the men he liked to call the "ain't ready yet boys" and he immediately searched for a means either to convince him to participate in the state conference or, if need be, to circumvent his leadership.[19] As the state's geographic center, the seat of government, and stronghold of black political and economic power, Columbia was a strategically and symbolically important site for the organization of the State Conference of NAACP Branches. Without the support of its branch, Byrd could readily deduce, the state conference had little chance for success. From the earliest days of organizing the Cheraw NAACP branch, Byrd solicited the aid of prominent members of Cheraw's and the surrounding region's black population, especially those who represented the larger community's key institutions. The strategy always ran the risk of allowing relatively privileged African Americans to dominate the organization, but it also provided Byrd and the branch with access to financial resources, personal and institutional connections, and a degree of legitimacy practically impossible in their absence. By luck or by design, Byrd's organizing strategy also proved instrumental in enabling him to circumvent the intransigent Columbia branch and to hold the founding meeting of the state conference in the capital city.

In his efforts to build support for the newly formed Cheraw NAACP and expand its reach in South Carolina's Pee Dee region, Byrd managed to win the support of one minister, in particular, who provided him with a way around Hinton. The minister was the Reverend Arthur Jerome Wright, the father of the future civil rights attorney and Children's Defense Fund founder, Marian Wright Edelman. Wright lived in the town of Bennettsville located just across the Pee Dee River from Cheraw in neighboring Marlboro County. Wright had become the full-time pastor of Bennettsville's Shiloh Baptist Church in 1930 when the Reverend J.J. Starks, who at the time was the president of Morris College in Sumter, relinquished his responsibilities there to become the first African American president of Columbia's Benedict College. Starks was Wright's mentor and a close friend of the family. As the president of Benedict, he was Byrd's entrée to Columbia. By mid-October 1939 Byrd managed to convince Starks to lend his support to the state conference. Generally regarded as a racial moderate, even an accommodationist, Starks offered Byrd a way to circumvent Hinton's leadership. Starks also provided the fledgling state conference with an air of legitimacy at a critical juncture in its history, and he allowed the organization to hold its founding meeting on the Benedict campus.[20]

On the weekend of November 10, 1939, twenty-nine representatives from branches in Florence, Georgetown, Sumter, Cheraw, Greenville, Charleston, and Columbia attended the founding meeting of the South Carolina NAACP State Conference of Branches in the library of Benedict College. The state conference was not a political party in any formal sense—the NAACP was specifically a nonpartisan organization—but, for the first time since Edwin Harleston imagined the creation of a "black primary" and W.D. Chappelle imagined an organized statewide challenge to the political exclusion of black South Carolinians, the makings of an institutional challenge to Jim Crow and legalized disfranchisement were in the works on a statewide scale. In this case, however, the call for a collective challenge to Jim Crow and political exclusion emanated from a small town, in a rural county, stretching the organization well beyond the urban confines of Columbia and Charleston and setting it on a new trajectory. Indeed, it is unclear whether or not Hinton even attended the founding meeting of the state conference, and it appears from the documentary record that the participation of the Columbia branch remained in doubt until the last minute. What can be known for certain is that the Cheraw delegation took the lead at the November 10 meeting, helping to elect the pastor of Cheraw's Wesley United Methodist Church, the Reverend Alonzo W. Wright, to the position of president, and the head of the Robert Small School's Adult Education program, Maggie B. Robinson, to the position of secretary. Wasting little time, after James Briar gave a report about the ongoing repression of black civil rights activities in Greenville, the state conference pledged its support to the struggle in the piedmont city and it raised funds to send two delegates to the NAACP's annual conference that spring.[21]

Despite its great promise, it would be a mistake to understand the founding meeting of the state conference as a triumphant moment that somehow ensured the cooperation of existing NAACP branches in the state or set in motion a process that inevitably led to the expansion of the black struggle for civil rights in the 1940s. Within days of returning to Greenville, Briar became the target of the Klan's terror campaign in the region and would be arrested and convicted of weapons charges in December. The following year the Greenville branch did not send a representative to the gathering of the state conference and would remain a reluctant and only occasional participant in the activities of the state NAACP. In Georgetown, branch president and state conference Executive Committee member D.T. Prioleau returned from the November meeting and began efforts to expand branch membership in the low country county. In early February, a prominent white businessman showered Prioleau with a barrage of "vile names" and insults on the streets of Georgetown. If his NAACP activities did not cease, the man warned, it would not be long before he was lynched. Fearing for his life, Prioleau wrote the national office asking for protection. "This is similar," he warned, "to Professor James Brier [sic] in Greenville."[22]

While violence threatened the continued existence of the state's newest branches, the Columbia NAACP continued to withhold its full support from the state conference for over a year. In early 1940 the Columbia branch was itself virtually moribund. "Our plan and hopes to muster new and young blood to direct the work of our branch," explained R.W. Jackson, "did not meet with the ready response which we had anticipated." Already confronted with the demands of his business activities, Hinton only reluctantly agreed to assume the position of branch president for one additional year after "undue pressure was brought to bear" upon him. Even then, Hinton maintained a limited view of the role of the branch and its relationship to the national office and the larger black fight for civil rights.[23] Nevertheless, Byrd continued to press Hinton and the Columbia branch to support the state organization. After much prodding and negotiation, Hinton agreed to take an active role in the state conference, but not without exacting a price for his participation. "I'll go along with you," Hinton told Byrd, "but if I can't run it, I'll tear it up." For Byrd the price was worth paying. Black people in Cheraw, he had already decided, could not go it alone. Although Reverend Wright and Maggie Robinson did much to advance the cause of statewide cooperation in 1940, by 1941 Wright's ministerial responsibilities and health limited his ability to perform the duties of state president and Robinson, who also ran the National Youth Administration (NYA) Center for Negro Girls in Cheraw, cited the problems of distance and organizational training as part of her request to relinquish the responsibilities of state secretary. Thus at the June 1941 meeting of the state conference, Hinton was elected president, effectively transferring the formal reigns of power from Cheraw to Columbia. Robinson would stay on for an additional year as recording secretary, but, in the spring of 1942, her work with the NYA and NAACP landed her a sixty-day term in the state penitentiary in Lexington County. She was accused and convicted of illegally soliciting funds from NYA participants in order to make repairs and improvements to the NYA Center.[24]

Although it took Byrd two years to secure the support of the Columbia branch, support that threatened to place a disproportionate share of institutional power in the hands of a reluctant and all-too cautious advocate of protest politics and intrastate cooperation, the state conference had begun revolutionizing the black struggle for civil rights in South Carolina by the spring of 1941. If Hinton and the Columbia NAACP clung more tightly to an older individualistic ethic of racial uplift and feared that a broader cooperative movement might compromise their own locally rooted uplift efforts, the state conference provided a means to challenge and reorient this vision of struggle. In the months leading up to the 1941 election of state officers, the state conference produced a pamphlet, "Exhortation for Solid Voluntary Action," that was printed and distributed by member branches, and that launched a new phase in the black civil rights movement. "The day of rugged individualism is said to have passed," the pamphlet announced. "You can't win by yourself. The only action that has a chance in the world today is mass action." Building on the New Deal's mandate for collective, group-based organization, the pamphlet made plain the notion that "hundreds of group organizations" exist in the United States and shape the "destiny of the nation" in powerful ways. "Think of the major political parties in America," it explained, "the minor parties—Communists and Socialists; also the late, in point of birth not death, hyphenated local party built up to defeat the New Deal; the C. I. O.; A. F. of L.; Urban Leagues; Luncheon Clubs; Parent-Teacher Association; all such groups including the Interracial Commission and the National Association for the Advancement of Colored People are all pressure groups using their powers and influences to bring about conditions of life which are more to their liking and idea of living." Reflecting Du Bois's mid-1930s insight to the emerging landscape of struggle in the United States and anticipating a key argument of Harold Cruse's controversial 1967 publication, *The Crisis of the Negro Intellectual*, the pamphlet argued that black people must understand the group basis of American political culture. "All pressure groups active in American life," it noted, "are of interest to Negroes since they are active in the moulding [*sic*] of sentiment for or against them. It is to the advantage of the Negro to be acquainted with the policy and program of all pressure groups that he may know friend from foe and what should be his attitude for his own defense." "To be set aside as a subject group by social prejudice and government sanction," it further expounded, "is to be robbed of the same native rights which others demand and for which they barter their lives."[25]

Designed to launch a membership drive, the pamphlet provides important insight to how the organizers of the state conference understood and represented the meaning of the NAACP and how they conceived of the struggle they were committed to waging. For state conference organizers the NAACP was the bridge connecting local struggles to a broader arena of struggle, a means to the creation of "social solidarity—A Great American Negro Need." Battles at the branch level, the pamphlet reminded its readers, were not isolated from, but rather integral to struggles at the national level, and battles at the national level were, in turn, critical to struggles at the local level. "Without branches there can be no National," it asserted. "Powerful branches make a powerful National." Membership in the NAACP, state conference organizers insisted, supported the national organization's efforts to protect "the Negro from assaults by any of his enemies" and to establish "further the Constitutional rights of the Negro." Both efforts, as they conceived them, were not ends in themselves, but part of a larger struggle. Taking membership in the NAACP, they argued, represented "a stroke for emancipation from the present evil of social, economic and political slavery." The battle at hand, as state conference organizers understood it, was a multi-front contest for "[r]epresentation on all American fronts, in government, industry and education." Put another way, state conference organizers recognized that while their fight for an end to "social, economic, and political slavery" required a sustained assault on the legal and legislative basis of racial inequality, their needs and desires were in no way reducible to a narrowly defined struggle for constitutional rights.

In mapping their conception of the relationship between local and national activism, between battles in South Carolina and the nation at large, state conference organizers charted a path beyond the parochialisms of the ideology and practice of racial uplift, and they did so in a dramatic way. It would be three more years before a collection of essays penned by a cross section of African American leaders and edited by the Howard University historian Rayford Logan, entitled *What the Negro Wants*, announced to the nation, in no uncertain terms, that African Americans, regardless of political persuasion, desired an end to racial segregation.[26] But members of the state conference did not need to wait for an event of such national import to come to the same conclusion. In the most radical passage from "Exhortation for Solid Voluntary Action," state conference members declared:

> What the Negro needs is INTEGRATION, instead of SEGREGATION. These conditions are exact opposites. They are to each other as plus is to minus. The one affirms, the other denies. All the blessings of life, liberty and the pursuit of happiness are possible in integration, while in segregation lurk all forces destructive of these values.

For decades black South Carolinians had battled within the terms of racial segregation, bending and stretching the legal strictures and social practices of Jim Crow and the ideology of white supremacy to demand a modicum of social, political, and economic justice. In 1941, to be sure, racial segregation continued to hold sway over the lives and consciousness of black and white South Carolinians, but segregation had never before produced uniform responses. For Levi Byrd and others who created the state conference, the segregated realities of life in South Carolina encouraged them to look beyond their own local communities and to link up with others interested in the cause of racial justice. In so doing, they loosened the hold of local circumstances over their own lives and opened old practices and ideas to the possibility of revision. Although the future of the state conference was anything but determined in 1941, it had already begun to challenge the regional isolation of countless local struggles and offered a potential vehicle for large-scale cooperation and the building of a mass-based fight for self-determination and equality.

The state conference was, in many ways, the product of Levi Byrd's labors; to understand its formation in the absence of Byrd and the Chesterfield County NAACP is to miss the significance of the organization as a means toward breaking down barriers between small towns and cities, between rural counties and urban centers, between the local and the national, and between an older African American leadership class and an emerging civil rights cadre. But the state conference was not created in isolation from the broader currents of life in South Carolina, the United States, and the world; rather, the creation of the state conference was both cause *and* effect of a much larger social upheaval and transformation in the making.

The New Deal and mobilization for World War II meant that new and vast sums of federal dollars poured into South Carolina, helping to prime the pumps of the state's ailing economy.[27] For many black South Carolinians, the early 1940s were experienced as a combination of social tumult and newfound economic opportunity. Over the long term, aided in part by New Deal measures that hastened the mechanization of agricultural production, the capacity to make a living off the land continued to spiral downward. As many as 195,700 African Americans would migrate out of South Carolina by decade's end, and the state's African American population would fall below the 40 percent mark. But the war years provided new, if sometimes only temporary, reprieve from long-term trends. The possibility of finding work in defense industries and the increased region-wide demand for black labor in agricultural production led to a spike in wages for picking cotton and to a momentary increase in the number of nonwhite sharecroppers in South Carolina.[28]

Across the state, complaints about chronic labor shortages provide an indication of the ways in which black agricultural workers used the circumstances brought about by the war to negotiate better wages, working conditions, and sharecropping arrangements. "I have never encountered a more perplexing condition," wrote an exacerbated Charles J. Ravenel from St. Andrews Parish in Charleston County. "I have been using an average of 40 or 50 hands each day," but now, he explained, "I am reduced to three men, which are men by name, as they are old, sick, and incapacitated." "I had to give negroes two dollars a day to break [my land] so this was buying back my own corn," wrote the president of the Agricultural Society of South Carolina. "I heard of one farmer having to run his own tractor and his health is not good. Lots of such cases," he added. In the fall of 1942 letters and telegrams poured into the governor's office detailing the labor travails in the South Carolina countryside. "I wish to ask you if anything can be done about a man living here transporting all the farm labor to the Savannah shipyard as our farms has been depleted so that we can get no labor," wrote a man from Beaufort County. "I can speak for a ten mile radius and can certainly say that it is serious and weekly getting worse," lamented a farmer in Orangeburg County. "We have three trucks right in our own community that [are] hiring them and hauling them to Charleston daily. . . . The little labours whom we have left are kept dissatisfied by bribery." "I think most of the trouble is the fact that the labor is leaving the farm and going to the Charleston Navy Yard and other defense projects," explained another man investigating labor troubles in the low country. "The labor that has left from [here] traveled by bus or train to Fla. to work in the cane fields."[29]

African Americans scrambled to take advantage of the wartime economy to better their economic lot and order their lives in accordance with their own sense of its possibilities. In some instances, better wages available to black men allowed black women and children to withhold their labor from service to white people. "The negro houses in the County are all occupied but the men are all gone," W. McLeod Hampton observed with a great degree of consternation. "Salaries paid men induces their family not to work but to stay at home and become consumers and use the food the Army needs to win the war." In others, the war provided black women with an opportunity to negotiate with their employers for better wages and working conditions. During the fall of 1942, the state constabulary and the governor's office received reports that black female domestic workers were being urged to strike and demand higher wages in Marlboro and Cherokee Counties. In the city of Spartanburg, talk circulated that black cooks were organizing an "Eleanor Roosevelt Society" to demand better wages. In the low country, South Carolina's chief constabulary officer held the "Eleanor Roosevelt Society" responsible for demands made by black residents for better wages and time off from work. "In some instances," he wrote, "I hear that they often demanding that they be addressed as Mister and Miss [sic]." These reports coincided with a wave of wild rumors about threats of Negro insurrection and stories about black women promising to have "every white woman in her own kitchen by Christmas." Although the observations of white employers are worthy of skepticism, such reports must be taken seriously because they are consistent with a broader pattern of more readily observable and recognized conflict in the realm of agricultural and industrial production.[30]

Pervasive discrimination in Charleston and Columbia, the state's largest recipients of federal defense spending, limited wartime employment opportunities for African Americans. Nevertheless, along with their white counterparts, black migrants continued to converge on the two cities in search of opportunity. The immediate effect of this war-induced migration was to force underlying racial conflict into the open and push hitherto reluctant black leaders to assume more aggressive postures in defense of black South Carolinians across lines of class. For Reverend Hinton, the accelerated wartime changes were made manifest in the mounting conflicts between African Americans and police in Columbia's segregated business district. On the stretch of Washington Street between Assembly and Park streets, Columbia's black professional classes encountered the masses of African Americans who patronized the street's barrooms and dancehalls. As police escalated an ongoing crackdown on vice in the spring of 1941, the interests of black business owners and residents of the nearby middle-class Taylor Street neighborhood converged with the interests of the black masses who were the alleged targets of the crackdown. Not only did increased police surveillance threaten to damage black businesses; such harassment rarely discriminated by class when it came to African Americans. Still committed to a politics of local amelioration, Hinton first took the lead of a hastily pieced together organization, the Colored Citizens Committee, in an effort to investigate police misconduct and lobby local nearby Fort Jackson officials for redress.

By August, however, he had become exasperated by his inability to win concessions through tried and rarely true appeals to white benevolence. "Our Committee cannot expect anything from reporting such cases to proper authorities in Fort Jackson," he finally concluded, "and we regret this, as we had hoped, that we would not again have to resort to Washington to get relief from such occurrences, but there is no other course open to us. . . . It *appears* that facts mean nothing in an apparent white-washed case."[31]

Byrd had been working for two years to convince Hinton that local remedies were inconceivable in the absence of participation in a broad-based organization with ties to a national arena of struggle, but it took the conditions created by the war to change the way Hinton thought about and participated in the black struggle for civil rights. In the spring of 1941, A. Philip Randolph and a coalition of civil rights organizations, including the NAACP, utilized the participation of the United States in the fight against fascism in Europe to call for an end to racial discrimination at home. By organizing and threatening to hold a March on Washington to demand racial justice, Randolph and Walter White secured a meeting with President Roosevelt, who then issued Executive Order 8802. The executive order created the President's Committee on Fair Employment Practice and prohibited racial discrimination in defense industries, marking, perhaps, the most important civil rights victory for African Americans since Reconstruction to that point.[32] Black South Carolinians were well attuned to national and world events, and the state conference's "Exhortation for Solid Voluntary Action" reflected and gave shape to a shift in the ways in which a growing number of African Americans thought about their everyday efforts to earn a living, secure an education, and participate in the making of their individual and collective futures. Increasingly the black struggle for self-determination and equality was represented and understood in terms of its relationship to the American nation and to world events. "Although the pitch of battle is on the shores of Europe, the fate of America will be determined by the outcome of this war," the pamphlet explained. "The conflict in Europe is not a bit more serious to the parties actively engaged than is the conflict in America that has been going on for as long a time as America has borne its name." Although Hinton had been a reluctant participant in the state conference, he too was swept up in the tumult of the early war years. Indeed, by the third annual meeting of the state conference in

June 1942, a gathering organized by the theme of "Double Victory—Democracy at Home and Abroad," Hinton would become one of the organization's most forceful champions and would help to spearhead a dramatic expansion of the NAACP in South Carolina and a challenge to the white primary in the state.[33]

The Progressive Democratic Party and the Fight for Black Empowerment

The creation of the State Conference of NAACP Branches marked a critical point of departure for the black civil rights struggle in South Carolina and the United States, precisely because it navigated the transition from the ideology and practice of racial uplift to the ideology and practice of racial protest and because its creation represented a movement from the local to national (even international) and from the individual to the collective. It is worth reemphasizing that in no way should any of these transitions be understood as total or complete. The institutional framework of the state conference contained, in both senses of the word, the old and the new, the politics of uplift and the politics of protest, the local and the national, the individual and the collective, and all the tensions (class, gender, region) therein.[34] In doing so, the state conference became a powerful vehicle for representing the interests of a large cross section of black South Carolinians, even as it simultaneously became a vehicle through which the differences and tensions among black South Carolinians played out.

By the third annual meeting of the state conference in June 1942, the organization had begun the work, in earnest, of connecting numerous local movements and people together and facilitating an exchange of ideas, experiences, and resources that provided for, but did not guarantee, the expansion of the movement in South Carolina.[35] Since the mid-1930s the NAACP's national office had been promoting a legal campaign to challenge educational inequality in the South. The campaign was never conceived as a narrow attack on inequality in public education, but was, rather, formulated as a critical front in a multi-front battle against "discrimination and segregation in all phases of American life." By the spring of 1941 the NAACP's campaign for educational equality had made important inroads into South Carolina, first in the unsuccessful efforts of Charles B. Bailey, a graduate of Morehouse College, to sue for admission to the School of Law of

the University of South Carolina and, second, in the ultimately successful fight for the equalization of teachers' salaries. Initially taken up
by Osceola E. McKaine, a World War I veteran who had recently returned to his native Sumter, South Carolina, from Brussels, Belgium,
where he had lived and owned a cabaret, "Mac's Place," since the
early 1920s, the campaign for the equalization of black teachers' salaries proved an important vehicle for expanding the membership base
of the NAACP and publicizing its ability to win legal victories and
improve the economic lot of black South Carolinians. From his days
of active duty in France, to his membership in the radical veterans'
organization, the League for Democracy, McKaine had long-running
connections to the radical Left, and in 1941 and 1942 he utilized the
teacher salary campaign to rally support for the NAACP across the
state and to establish himself as one of the state's most forceful advocates of social justice.[36]

Beginning in the spring of 1943 the state conference took responsibility for the campaign to equalize teachers' salaries. That fall
Thurgood Marshall and Harold Boulware, the chairman of the state
conference's Committee on Legal Redress and a 1938 graduate of
Howard University Law School, argued a class-action lawsuit, filed
by Viola Louise Duvall on behalf of Charleston's black public school
teachers, before Judge J. Waties Waring in U.S. District Court for
the eastern district of South Carolina. This was Marshall's and the
NAACP's first encounter with Waring, a native Charlestonian who,
explains his biographer, "embraced southern racial traditions through
most of his adult life," but whose personal and judicial turn toward
racial liberalism paralleled and intersected with the expansion of the
black struggle for civil rights in South Carolina between 1944 and
1951. The result of the Duvall case proved a surprising legal victory
for the NAACP. It was "the only case I ever tried with my mouth
hanging open half the time," Marshall later recalled. During the trial,
Waring demonstrated clear support for the plaintiff's claim that the
discrepancy between white and black teachers' salaries constituted a
violation of the Fourteenth Amendment's equal protection clause,
and, in February 1944, the Charleston school board agreed to a con-
sent decree that provided for the equalization of salaries for teachers
and principals to be phased in by September 1946. Following the apparent victory in Charleston, the state's general assembly responded
by passing legislation designed to channel challenges to discriminatory

pay scales through the all-white county and state school boards and the state court system and, in 1945, it established a teacher certification plan to be administered by the National Education Board. But, in May 1945, Waring ruled in favor of Albert N. Thompson, a teacher at Columbia's Booker T. Washington High School, who claimed that Richland County failed to provide him with a salary equal to white teachers with similar qualifications. While Waring left the state's ostensibly race-neutral certification plan intact, he found that Thompson had the right to bring suit in federal court and he ordered the county to establish a plan to equalize teachers' salaries by April 1946 that was to be retroactive for the 1945–1946 school year.[37]

Much as the drive to employ black teachers in Charleston's public school system had helped spur mass support for the NAACP and encouraged an expansion of grassroots black political activity during the First World War, so too did the teacher salary campaign during the Second. For Septima Clark, the teacher salary campaign was her reintroduction to grassroots political mobilization and protest activity. Following the death of her husband of barely five years and another brief teaching sojourn on Johns Island, Clark made her way to Columbia to take a teaching job at Booker T. Washington High School in 1929. Long committed to the uplift of black people, in Columbia she became involved in an adult literacy program directed by Wil Lou Gray, was active in club work, and participated in her first interracial meetings. But it was the teacher salary campaign, she later recalled, that represented her "first effort in a social action challenging the status quo, the first time I had worked *against* people directing a system for which I was working." "[T]his fight," she explained, "was what might be described by some, no doubt, as my first 'radical' job." As Clark understood it, the teacher salary campaign represented a departure from her earlier uplift work because of its "social" or group-based character, because it signaled that black people would no longer accept the "status quo," and because it marked the passing of the idea that justice could be achieved through peaceful negotiation within the existing Jim Crow system. In the same way that the state conference provided an institutional means for its reformulation, the teacher salary campaign allowed for the transformation of the ideology and practice of racial uplift. Through the issue of educating black people and through a battle to raise the salaries of black teachers, the black struggle for civil rights began to assume the form and adopt the ideological posture of a collective and forceful protest movement.[38]

The teacher salary campaign was also the struggle through which Modjeska Monteith Simkins navigated the transition from uplift to protest politics, contributing to her personal radicalization and, in turn, the remaking of the movement in South Carolina. Simkins was a prominent member of black Columbia's elite professional and business class. Born in 1899, she was reared by a business-minded father who worked as a brick mason and stressed the importance black financial independence and a mother who worked as a teacher and was a founding member of the Columbia NAACP. During the 1920s Modjeska Monteith worked as a teacher in the elementary division of the Booker T. Washington School until she was required to resign after marrying Andrew W. Simkins, a well-to-do real estate holder who owned a gasoline station and later acquired a state licensed liquor store. In 1931 Simkins plunged into the work of racial uplift as the first Director of Negro Work for the South Carolina Tuberculosis Association (SCTBA), a position that, her biographer writes, "proved important in the development of her political consciousness, for she was exposed to the dire poverty and utter deprivation in the rural areas of the state." In addition to her work with the SCTBA, Simkins played an active role in the Civic Welfare League, a black organization dedicated to improving the economic and civic needs of black Columbians, from securing adequate playgrounds and housing, to addressing issues such as police brutality and crime.[39]

By 1939 Simkins was serving on the Executive Committee of the Columbia NAACP. Although, like Hinton, Simkins does not appear to have been a participant, at least not an active one, in the founding of the state conference, she became the organization's corresponding secretary and assumed the duties of publicity chairman in 1941. As the state conference became increasingly visible in 1942, the SCTBA began pressuring her to choose between her work with the SCTBA and her work with the NAACP. "I couldn't divorce my interest in civil rights from my dedication to trying to solve these health problems," she later recalled. "I'd rather all Negroes die and go to hell with tuberculosis than go through some of the things they're suffering right now, and that the NAACP is trying to stop them." For Simkins the work of addressing the basic health needs of black people was inseparable from her activism on the civil rights front; basic health and civil rights were both deeply human needs. As she immersed herself in civil rights work, the latter increasingly appeared as a precondition for the former, and she parted ways with the SCTBA.[40]

As Barbara Woods explains, the SCTBA served as a "training ground" for Simkins, enabling her to hone her skills as a publicist, public speaker, and organizer, and her work with the SCTBA provided her with extensive contacts among white and black South Carolinians across the state.[41] But it was her work with the NAACP on the teacher salary issue that marked her move from uplift to protest politics. In the early stages of the teacher salary campaign, the leaders of the black teachers' organization, the Palmetto State Teachers' Association (PSTA), refused to support the NAACP's efforts and submitted their own petition for salary equalization to the state board of education. By 1943 Simkins had befriended Osceola McKaine and hired him to manage a family-owned liquor store. Together the two lobbied black teachers to support the NAACP's campaign. In a stinging newspaper editorial she lambasted the leaders of the PSTA and demanded that black teachers, "hundreds of whom are my personal friends and co-workers," leave old practices of racial deference behind. "Resolve NOW," she wrote, "that you will acquit yourselves as American citizens and not as sniveling, crawling nonentities that the petition of your Executive Committee would intimate that you are. . . . Believe me, that BEGGING will not improve your economic condition, or any other condition, for that matter." In the editorial, Simkins gave notice that the racial deference of the uplift era was no longer an acceptable political posture in the emerging era of civil rights protest. As her words suggest, forceful, self-assertive political action was fast becoming the new prerequisite for legitimate race leadership. They also reveal that the *transition* from uplift to protest politics was anything but an easy, natural, or complete progression, that it involved bitter and often divisive struggle. "Swear vengeance against your 'misleaders,'" she encouraged black teachers. "Single out your delegates from your county and demand proof of how each stood on an issue that is of fundamental economic importance to you."[42]

Hardly lacking in conflict, the teacher salary issue ultimately helped legitimate the NAACP's work in South Carolina, but it was the issue of the vote that most animated the concerns of the state conference and provided the crucial impetus for the mobilization of a grassroots social movement during the 1940s. At their 1942 annual meeting, members of the state conference pledged to focus their efforts on breaking into the white primary and formed the Negro Citizens Committee of South Carolina (NCC) to raise money and rally support for the campaign. Created in part to avoid the charge that the NAACP was encouraging lawsuits, the NCC served as the voting rights arm of the organization. Fully aware of the NAACP's legal battle already underway in Texas challenging the constitutionality of the white primary, the NCC plunged the South Carolina NAACP back into the work that had inspired and bedeviled an earlier generation of activists. The Reverend E.A. Adams, an A.M.E. minister who had been a litigant in Frederick's 1932 legal challenge to the white primary, chaired the NCC. With Hinton's assent to the position of state conference president, Adams also assumed the presidential duties of Columbia's NAACP branch. He was, according to Thurgood Marshall, "the power behind the throne," and he was the direct link to an earlier era of activism on the voting rights front.[43]

The creation of the NCC revived the hopes of an earlier era of black activism at the same time that it suggested a passage beyond an earlier generation's parochial predilections. If earlier battles for the vote had been couched too often in a rhetoric that emphasized injury to a particular class of "qualified" black voters, the NCC represented the denial of the franchise and exclusion from the Democratic white primary as an injury to all black people. The organization urged "every citizen—male and female—register to VOTE." "A man, a woman without the ballot is as bound as a SLAVE," it argued. "In South Carolina—as in every Southern state—'nomination' in the 'primary' is the same as the LEGAL ELECTION of an official. Since that is true," it explained, "every citizen should have a part in making the choice." For the state conference and its voting rights arm, the right to vote was a universal right and the battle to secure the franchise required the broad support and sacrifice of black South Carolinians across class, gender, and regional lines. "Decide now," the NCC demanded, "to 'strike the blow' by giving until it hurts, by assuring the committee your moral support, by urging others to cooperate."[44]

Far more than a fight for abstract constitutional rights, the NCC made it clear that its fight was for meaningful representation, for the right to be active agents in the political decision-making processes that governed the lives of black people. Invoking the rhetoric of the American Revolution, the NCC compared the plight of black South

Carolinians to the plight of American colonial subjects under English rule. "Taxation without representation is tyranny," it declared. While the NCC appealed to the one indigenous revolutionary tradition acknowledged by white Americans, it worked to distinguish its democratic hopes from the "American Way of Life." In a promotional pamphlet it explained that "as Americans—THE NEGRO CITIZENS' COMMITTEE OF SOUTH CAROLINA believes that DEMOCRACY—equal rights and privileges for all—and not the so-called 'American Way of Life' which so often compromises, discriminates, or even denies where Negroes are concerned, should come into full play for all Americans. We want to live for the very same things here in America for which we are willing to die anywhere in order that all men may know the sweetness of Democracy." Put another way, members of the NCC did not represent their project as one of simple inclusion under the existing terms of the "American Way of Life." Instead, they argued that the full and meaningful participation of black people under the terms of the U.S. Constitution would represent a transformation of the "American Way of Life," a democratization of it.[45]

As the state conference and the NCC sought to rally support for a campaign to break into the white primary, South Carolina's state legislature moved to head off the implications of the NAACP's ongoing legal efforts in Texas and the potential of a similar challenge within the state. In early 1943, shortly after the U.S. Supreme Court agreed to hear the Texas white primary case, *Smith v. Allwright*, the legislature repealed all laws pertaining to statewide primaries and passed a law providing that all political parties shall have the right to determine their own members. But on April 3, 1944, the U.S. Supreme Court, ruling in favor of the NAACP's case, found that because primary elections played such a recognized role in the election process itself, they constituted a practical delegation of state authority and thus could not exclude voters based on race without violating the Fifteenth Amendment.[46] By April, South Carolina newspapers had already begun raising the specter of "another Reconstruction" and put the public on notice that black South Carolinians were organizing to vote and challenge their exclusion from the primary. "We in South Carolina are going to do whatever we can," remarked South Carolina senator Burnet Maybank, "to protect our white primaries." Preparing for a reelection bid to the U.S. Senate, "Cotton Ed" Smith lambasted the U.S. Supreme Court's decision as the "culmination of the trend of the past

11 years." "I foresaw years ago the dangerous tendency of the New Deal," decried the man who had denounced the Party of Roosevelt and bolted from the Democratic Convention in 1938. "States rights have been usurped. And now, boldly, the Supreme Court has challenged the right of white supremacy in the political and social arena of my state."[47]

Not to be outdone, South Carolina's recently elected governor and U.S. Senate hopeful, Olin Johnston, called for a special legislative session in order to ensure that no laws pertaining to the white primary remained on the state's statute books. In his opening remarks to what became known as the "Extraordinary Session," Johnston declared, "White supremacy will be maintained in our primaries. Let the chips fall where they may." In words that reflected the extent to which the black struggle for voting rights represented a challenge to a world ordered by white male supremacy and simultaneously gave shape to white fears of the menace black political empowerment posed to their public *and* private lives, Johnston conjured up memories of the Reconstruction era. "Where you now sit," he needlessly reminded his audience, "there sat a majority of negroes [*sic*]. . . . The records will bear me out that fraud, corruption, immorality and graft existed during that regime that has never been paralleled in the history of our State." "History has taught us that we must keep our white Democratic primaries pure and unadulterated so that we might protect the welfare and home of all the people of our state," he continued. We must meet the challenge to the white primary "like men," he bellowed, and if the actions of the legislature were not enough, he added, "we South Carolinians will use the necessary methods to retain this white supremacy in our primaries and to safeguard the homes and happiness of our people." By the end of the five-day session, legislators had carefully poured over the state's statute books and removed every vestige of law pertaining to primaries and passed more than one hundred laws designed to separate the Democratic primary from the control of state government.[48]

As the special session of the state legislature met, the former and duly chastised president of the Charleston NAACP, John McCray, watched on with horror from the gallery of the state house as state officials reaffirmed their commitment to white supremacy and produced a virtual reenactment of the 1895 special session that had rewritten the state constitution to disfranchise African Americans. Black South

Carolinians did not need to wait, however, to formulate a response to vitriolic calls to keep South Carolina's politics white. Indeed, the special session was as much a response to ongoing black political activity as it was an attempt to head off a future lawsuit. As editor of *The Charleston Lighthouse*, McCray had undertaken a study of potential black voting power in South Carolina and found that black South Carolinians constituted a majority in three of the state's six congressional districts and in twenty-two of the state's forty-six counties. Through the combined efforts of Osceola McKaine and Modjeska Simkins, McCray's paper had merged with *The People's Informer*, edited by Esau Parker in Sumter, and relocated to Columbia as *The Lighthouse and Informer* in late 1941. By the spring of 1944 *The Lighthouse and Informer* had become the state conference's unofficial propaganda engine and Mc-Cray its chief propagandist. The paper championed the teacher salary fight and spread the word about the NAACP's activities across the state through distribution agents such as Levi Byrd, who sold the paper along with other national black publications. In March, McCray printed an editorial to rally support for the organization of Fourth Term for Roosevelt Clubs, to which the *Columbia Record* responded with a headline stating, "Negroes Plan Own Party in State Primary." That same month, the staunchly anti–New Deal *News and Courier* encouraged black South Carolinians to organize their own "Roosevelt or other 'Democratic party.'" "The white Roosevelt Democrats of South Carolina," it editorialized, "are about to be shown that they have got to ally themselves with the negro Roosevelt 'Democrats' in the South and in the North or else get out of that party." On the opening day of the special session, in the pages of *The Lighthouse and Informer*, McCray announced the creation of the South Carolina Colored Democratic Party and its intention to contest the validity "of the lily white party at the national (Democratic) convention" that summer and run candidates in November elections.[49]

From its inception the South Carolina Colored Democratic Party, which by the end of April would be renamed the Progressive Democratic Party (PDP), reflected and gave shape to the tensions and paradoxes, possibilities and limitations, of a rapidly expanding black civil rights struggle in South Carolina. Between 1943 and 1946 the number of NAACP branches more than tripled in the state, expanding from fifteen to forty-nine, and membership topped the ten thousand mark in 1945. Although the PDP operated as an independent political party, it was created through NAACP networks and claimed forty-five thousand members by the end of World War II. "The fact is," McCray later explained, "those in [the] NAACP, the Citizens Committee and in the Progressive Democrats were one and the same people." "The Progressive Democrats and the state NAACP Conference worked very close with each other. . . . By arrangement, the NAACP did all the legal work; the Progressive Democrats handled all the political action projects."[50] Like the NAACP, the PDP was created to do battle with white supremacy and Jim Crow, to demand full inclusion in American public life on terms of equality, and, yet, in practice, the PDP came into existence, as did NAACP branches, as an all-black organization. Indeed, at the same time that the organizational plans for the Colored Democratic Party explicitly restricted membership to black people "for protection against exploitation and persecution as well as suspicion," the organization laid claim to "the political creeds of the greater Democratic Party of the United States" and sought to provide South Carolina "with a two-party system always conducive to healthy government, the hope of a majority of white citizens and the 'force' Negroes need to end many of the flagrant discrimination against them." Faced with the exclusionary practices of the all-white state Democratic Party and the racial realities of life in South Carolina, the PDP demanded a social and political transformation of the existing racial order through the creation of a black political party. As symbolized by the change in name from the Colored Democratic Party to the Progressive Democratic Party, its founding members were well aware of the tension between the theory of racial inclusion and the strategic practice of race-based political organizing. McCray would later go to some length to emphasize, really fabricate, the interracial origins of the PDP, attributing the name change to the urgings of an elderly white woman who allegedly desired to join the Colored Democratic Party. But in 1944, McCray had deduced that the ends of full inclusion and equality, first and foremost, required the collective empowerment of black people as a group.[51]

In important respects, the creation of the PDP was a response to historical circumstances particular to the early 1940s. On the one hand, McCray had reasoned that despite the passing of a statewide black majority in 1930, black South Carolinians still constituted a majority of potential voters in twenty-two of the state's forty-six counties and represented a formidable voting bloc, even as black migration from the state continued as the long-term trend, threatening those majorities, and the unanimity of the potential black voting population remained unproved. "There is no reasonable explanation why in Calhoun county, for example, Negroes can not and have not established a political organization of their own," McCray argued. "And since government is based upon majority rule," he concluded, "Negroes can not lose in Calhoun or any of the twenty one other countries" with a majority black population. On the other hand, the creation of the PDP was a response to the waning hold of the Republican Party on the political loyalties of black South Carolinians and the political conundrum created by growing black support for the national Democratic Party in the face of continued exclusion from participation in local Democratic Party politics. For years the Republican Party in South Carolina had been divided between two factions that vied for national party recognition, namely Tireless Joe Tolbert's "Black and Tans," which maintained the support of a number of prominent African Americans, and the lily-white faction, led by Joe Hambright of Spartanburg. But as northern African Americans continued to leave the Party of Lincoln to support the Party of Roosevelt, under new leadership the lily-white faction began actively courting black supporters, dividing the loyalties of black South Carolina Republicans. "The traditionally 'Negro' Republican party in South Carolina is no longer effective," McCray wrote in 1944, "and can bring the Negro no political good in its present state." For McCray and a growing number of black South Carolinians the reconstruction of the Republican Party no longer appeared as a remedy to political disempowerment. "After all," McCray explained, "the Negro in South Carolina is at heart 'Democratic.'"[52]

As McCray was well aware, 1944 was also a pivotal year for the national Democratic Party. The war years witnessed a dramatic expansion of a broad-based social movement inspired by the New Deal and spurred forward by the growth of the CIO and the NAACP. By 1944 southern membership in the CIO reached 400,000, and the AFL grew to include 1.8 million members. Nationally, membership in the NAACP mushroomed to more than 350,000 by 1945, seven times the number of members in 1940 and nearly an eighteen-fold increase since 1929. At the same time, black migration to the urban North created an ever-expanding enfranchised black political constituency able to articulate its needs and interests in a way still impossible in the Jim Crow South.[53] As Patricia Sullivan has argued, the national Democratic Party stood at a metaphorical crossroads in 1944. How would the party respond to the growing power of northern black voters and increasingly organized black southerners? Would the party affirm its commitment to the leftward thrust of the liberal-labor coalition embodied by the vice presidential candidacy of Henry Wallace? Would it choose James Byrnes as Roosevelt's running mate, signaling the ascendancy of an emboldened southern white conservative constituency within the party? Or would it choose the middle path and select Harry S. Truman as Roosevelt's likely successor?[54] Recognizing the shifting political climate and unwilling to allow such decisions to be made for him or for black South Carolinians any longer, McCray sought to inject the issue of black political representation into the debate by challenging the seating of the all-white South Carolina delegation to that summer's Democratic National Convention in Chicago. "If it is not seated," he proclaimed in no uncertain words, "there will be the 'devil to play.' Refusal to recognize the delegation will draw immediate and pronounced retaliation from northern Negroes in support of the Democratic Party and, who by reason of their hold [on] the 'balance of power' that Party can not afford and does not intend to ignore."[55]

While the PDP was certainly a response to the particular circumstances of 1944, it was just as importantly an idea and institutional form that drew on a deeply rooted history of independent black political activism in which McCray was well schooled. Born in 1910, McCray was reared in Lincolnville, South Carolina, an all-black incorporated village located within Charleston County along the border between Berkeley and Dorchester counties. Created during Reconstruction by the Reverend R.H. Cain, an A.M.E. minister and black Republican Party leader who served two terms in the U.S. Congress in the 1870s, Lincolnville maintained a tradition of black self-governance into the 1940s. The town of approximately 350 black residents ran its own local government and, according to one resident, as a result, benefited from better schools and their own constabulary. "We don't have any of this business," he explained, "of a sheriff's deputy entering a house without a warrant or anything like that."[56] Although McCray directed his political efforts, from the NAACP to the PDP, toward the ultimate goal of full participation in and transformation of already existing and white-dominated institutions, he maintained a commitment to the principal of black self-determination. "What I am attempting to do" through the creation of the PDP, McCray explained, "is what impelled Richard Allen to found the AME church." Much as Allen had created the Bethel African Methodist Episcopal Church in Philadelphia in the wake of the American Revolution, amid continued and all the more glaring exclusion from and discrimination within white-dominated churches, McCray, himself a member of the A.M.E. Church, sought to provide black South Carolinians with an independent organization that could represent and safeguard their interests. In the context of the 1940s he insisted that black South Carolinians must also develop their own capacity to represent themselves. "I am interested," he explained, "in our people voting for their rights, tying up on certain specific elections with all other groups. Yet, when this is done, the [PDP] should not—and must not—sell its birthright; nor should any of the others."[57]

In substantial measure the PDP embodied McCray's quest for black self-determination and empowerment. On May 24, 1944, the PDP held its first statewide convention in the old Masonic Temple in Columbia to select a slate of eighteen delegates and two alternates to challenge the seating of the all-white South Carolina Democratic Party regulars at that summer's Democratic National Convention in Chicago.[58] The presence at the gathering of 179 delegates, representing thirty-nine of the state's forty-six counties, and a handful of observers who, according to McCray, hailed from the states of Georgia, North Carolina, Alabama, Mississippi, and Arkansas, was a testament to the organizational skill of party leaders and demonstrated the wide-ranging appeal of the party. Inside the Masonic Lodge, delegates were tied together by a call to support the war in Europe and the simultaneous demand to win freedom at home through self-assertive political action. Winning the right to vote, that is, the right of political representation, was at the forefront of an agenda that key leaders linked inextricably to questions of black self-respect and self-determination. "The 800 [N]egroes in South Carolina can no longer be lynched, segregated and Jim Crowed if South Carolina is to take her place with other states," an emboldened Reverend Hinton exclaimed before an energized audience. "We are living under greater dictatorship than Hitler has ever given and we don't like it. . . . Black boys are dying on the battlefields, and these South Carolina demagogues meet in extra sessions to further disfranchise what we are fighting for." "I want the world to know," he bellowed, "that among this group this afternoon there are red-blooded men and women who will fight for our constitutional rights no matter the price." In his keynote address, Osceola McKaine echoed Hinton's call for black self-assertion, and he invoked the history of black participation in state and federal politics during Reconstruction to call for a renewed quest for black self-respect. "There is only one way to fully regain our self-respect," he exclaimed, "and that is by participating again in our government. No longer may the Governor or the white people and master of the Negroes, and others, feel safe in saying, 'We give the Negroes what they need and should have.'"[59]

For McCray and, no doubt, many PDP members, the quest for self-determination and full inclusion represented no contradiction, but within the party the two goals coexisted in uneasy tension. Indeed, in his convention address, McKaine exposed the ideological and tactical fissure that had long proven a source of conflict within the black movement and would prove a ready source of conflict within the PDP in the years ahead. At the same time that he called for black people to "retrieve our lost self-respect" through black self-assertion, he suggested that the PDP ought to become a vehicle for the creation of an alliance between African Americans and the white working class. "Many underprivileged white men with red necks, pale faces and rough hands," he counseled, "have been exploited nearly as cruelly by the cynical, visible and invisible rulers of this State, as have the disfranchised and illiterate Negroes." "Many Negroes," he explained, "influenced by the propaganda of the ruling classes, dislike and distrust the poor whites instead of trying to make them friends and allies. The oneness of their cause with ours, if only they could be enlightened to realize it," he added "should make them our natural supporters." McKaine had lived an international life and two decades of crossing national and racial boundaries had shaped his political consciousness in profound ways. By 1944 he was increasingly active among the organizations and individuals animating the left wing of the New Deal liberal-labor coalition, also known as the Popular Front. And in 1945 he would become the first African American field representative for the Southern Conference for Human Welfare (SCHW), an organization founded in 1938 by southern white liberals inspired by the New Deal treatise *Report on the Economic Conditions of the South*, and dedicated to bringing economic and racial justice to the South. From his post with the SCHW, McKaine would immerse himself in a South-wide campaign to abolish the poll tax and organize workers on behalf of the Congress of Industrial Organizations-Political Action Committee (CIO-PAC). For McKaine, the PDP's role in this larger struggle was obvious, and he sought to encourage participants to view their struggle as a *natural* part of an interracial class struggle. But even as he did so, he implicitly acknowledged that the lived realities of black and white South Carolinians made class solidarity across lines of race more a dream for the future than a possibility for the present. Perhaps sensing the disbelief of his African American audience or perhaps recognizing the dissonance between his own vision of the future and the stark realities of white supremacy and racial oppression that brought his audience together that May day, McKaine felt the urge to explain himself further. "All of this in a keynote address may sound extraneous and out of place," he noted, "but I beg you to try to remember all that I have said about Negro–poor white relations. The future may prove to you that it was perhaps the most significant part of this speech."[60]

In May 1944, however, tensions and debates around the need for black self-organization and empowerment *and* the desire for broader alliances and interracial cooperation were temporarily smoothed over by the appeal of and shear exuberance for the Chicago convention challenge and winning the right to vote. That spring and summer, unseating the all-white state Democratic Party delegation at the Democratic National Convention and convincing national Democratic Party officials that the PDP represented the lawfully constituted and loyal Democratic representatives from the state of South Carolina absorbed the full attention of PDP members. In the weeks leading up to the July convention in Chicago, Democratic Party officials sought to persuade PDP leaders to abandon their convention challenge. Nevertheless, eighteen undeterred PDP delegates made their way to the Windy City to make their case before a convention subcommittee in mid-July. On Monday the seventeenth, nine delegates, including McCray and McKaine, appeared before a credentials subcommittee headed by Oscar R. Ewing, the vice chairman of the Democratic National Committee. In the hearing, PDP delegates faced down South Carolina senator Burnet Maybank, who presented the case for the all-white South Carolina delegation. After all sides were heard, the Democratic Party's Executive Committee, already occupied by the controversy surrounding the vice presidential nomination, voted to seat the all-white delegation.

The PDP, it ruled, had failed to follow proper procedures in establishing a party and in the selection of delegates. While some members of the PDP delegation wanted to push for a hearing before the full credentials committee or stage a more dramatic convention floor protest, ultimately the PDP delegation decided it was more important to demonstrate loyalty to the Democratic Party, and members returned to South Carolina with only vague promises of future federal government assistance in their voting rights efforts.[61]

Despite the failure to unseat the all-white South Carolina delegation, the PDP's 1944 challenge represented a remarkable demonstration of the desire and capacity of black southerners to organize collectively and demand full representation in the political decision-making processes that governed their lives. The NAACP's victory in *Smith v. Allwright* had marked a major turning point in the African American struggle for full citizenship rights and empowerment, but the PDP's convention challenge signaled that the battle for an end to the white primary and the struggle to secure the franchise would necessarily flow through South Carolina. During the war years the black struggle for civil rights in South Carolina expanded at rapid speed and began to garner national attention. A movement once rooted in numerous localized struggles and marked by the participation of a relatively narrow class of urban black professionals increasingly incorporated a range of new constituencies and interests. By virtue of its rapid growth, much as it had during a brief moment during the World War I years, the movement began to challenge the class and regional biases that had limited the efforts of an earlier generation of activists. At the same time, newfound national attention suggested that black South Carolinians would no longer need to wage their battles on their own. To be sure, during the World War II years, a new and ever-growing cadre of black activists pushed the ideology and practice of racial uplift to its limits and adopted a far more aggressive political posture that directly challenged white supremacy and the institutional structures of Jim Crow. The future of the bourgeoning black civil rights insurgency in South Carolina and the United States was, however, anything but certain during the waning days of the Second World War. Expanding constituencies also meant the potential for new conflicts. From their inception, the NAACP and the PDP incorporated a range of interests and ideological predispositions. Both organizations *contained* differences and conflicts among and between individuals, organizations, classes, genders, and regions. And both organizations drew strength from and were limited by the past they inherited. For decades, a select group of relatively privileged black South Carolinians worked within the racist and paternalistic terms of Jim Crow segregation and racial uplift to achieve a modicum of economic and social justice for black South Carolinians as a group, that is, *as a race*, even as many imagined a more equal and self-determining place within it. By the 1940s, after decades of struggle, black South Carolinians were increasingly capable and desirous of representing their own interests in the absence of the ritualized practice of white supremacy encoded in the politics of racial uplift. In an important sense, the formation of the State Conference of NAACP Branches and the PDP marked the fulfillment of an earlier generation's longings for greater black self-determination. At the same time, the creation of the two organizations posed new questions about the relationship between black empowerment and social justice, between the battle for racial equality and economic justice, and between the politics of race and the politics of class.

Born in 1891 and reared on a tobacco farm in Anson County, North Carolina, Levi G. Byrd began a lifetime of NAACP activism in Cheraw, South Carolina, in the early 1930s. A man of little formal education and a plumber by trade, Byrd was largely responsible for spearheading the formation of the South Carolina State Conference of NAACP Branches in 1939. Here Byrd is depicted in a studio image from the 1940s (above) and at work on his home in Cheraw during the 1950s (right). Courtesy of Alfred D. Byrd, Hampton, Virginia.

The caustic and fierce advocate of black self-representation in South Carolina and founder of the Progressive Democratic Party (PDP), John H. McCray. During the 1940s, McCray was the leading propagandist in the black fight for voting rights and equality. Courtesy of South Caroliniana Library, University of South Carolina, Columbia, S.C.

Modjeska Montieth Simkins became a leading figure in the State Conference of NAACP Branches in 1942 and for more than a decade served as the organization's secretary, a position she utilized to lambaste those who refused to stand strong for black equality and to cajole others to join the fight. Courtesy of South Caroliniana Library, University of South Carolina, Columbia, S.C.

The Reverend Joseph Armstrong De-Laine began organizing an underground branch of the NAACP in the repressive rural conditions of Clarendon County in the early 1940s and proved a leading figure in South Carolina's contribution to the U.S. Supreme Court's landmark *Brown v. Board of Education* (1954) decision, *Briggs v. Elliott* (1951). Here De-Laine is depicted in the St. James A.M.E. Church in Lake City, Florence County. The church was torched in October 1955 as massive resistance to black demands for equality escalated. Courtesy of South Caroliniana Library, University of South Carolina, Columbia, S.C.

Modjeska Simkins (left) and John McCray (far right) are depicted in 1957 with NAACP executive secretary Roy Wilkins (center), and the Reverend James M. Hinton (center-right). In addition to his work with the black-owned Pilgrim Health and Life Insurance Company and ministerial duties for Columbia's Second Calvary Baptist Church, Hinton served as the president of South Carolina's State Conference of NAACP Branches for more than a decade. Together, Simkins, Hinton, and McCray proved a formidable organizing team across the Palmetto State during the 1940s and early 1950s. Courtesy of South Caroliniana Library, University of South Carolina, Columbia, S.C.

(Above) World renowned singer, actor, and activist, Paul Robeson, arriving in Columbia for the Southern Negro Youth Congress's seventh youth legislature in October 1946. He is greeted by Allen University president S.B. Higgins and SNYC executive secretary Esther Cooper Jackson. Photo by E.C. Jones. Courtesy of James and Esther Jackson, Brooklyn, N.Y. *(Below)* More than nine hundred men, women, and children gathered in Columbia's Township Auditorium during the weekend of October 18, 1946, for the SNYC's seventh youth legislature. The gathering brought together leading advocates of social, political, and economic justice from across the U.S. South and the larger world. Photo by E.C. Jones. Courtesy of James and Esther Jackson, Brooklyn, N.Y.

Although a skeptic of Popular Front activism, John McCray addressed the SNYC's youth legislature, calling for an expanded fight against the Democratic White Primary. "We [have] shifted our responsibility and our charge to where we think it rightfully belongs," he explained. "Because nobody in the South has made any effort to put the National Democratic Party itself on the spot and hold it up before the world as a real rascal. We raised that question in 1944. That is why we went to Chicago. That is why we are going in 1948." Photo by E.C. Jones. Courtesy of South Caroliniana Library, University of South Carolina, Columbia, S.C.

Esther Cooper Jackson hands W.E.B. Du Bois a "Book of Reverence" for his lifelong work in the cause of black freedom and global justice. At the SNYC's seventh youth legislature Du Bois delivered an address entitled, "Behold the Land," in which he called for an alliance of southern workers, white and black, and declared that the southern struggle was "the firing line, not simply for the emancipation of the American Negro but for the emancipation of the African Negro and the Negroes of the West Indies; for the emancipation of the colored races; and for the emancipation of the white slaves of modern capitalist monopoly." Photo by E.C. Jones. Courtesy of James and Esther Jackson, Brooklyn, N.Y.

Theodore Baker of Haiti (left) attended the SNYC's 1946 gathering along with Osceola E. McKaine (right). As the first African American field representative of the Southern Conference for Human Welfare (SCHW), McKaine was the leading Popular Front figure in South Carolina who helped lead the NAACP's fight for equal pay for black teachers and an end to the White Primary. Shortly after the youth legislature, McKaine left his native South Carolina permanently, returning to Belgium to preside over "Mac's Place," a cabaret he established after serving in the U.S. Army in France during World War I. Photo by E.C. Jones. Courtesy of James and Esther Jackson, Brooklyn, N.Y.

John McCray, Pete Ingram, J.C. Artemus, and James Hinton, all leading figures of the NAACP and PDP, depicted in April 1948 as organizing efforts to put an end to the all-white Democratic Primary escalated across South Carolina. Courtesy of South Caroliniana Library, University of South Carolina, Columbia, S.C.

(Above) Black South Carolinians register to vote in Columbia as two legal decisions, *Elmore v. Rice* (1947) and *Brown v. Baskin* (1948), provided openings for ongoing efforts to secure the right to vote and access to the Democratic Primary. By the close of registration in July 1948, some thirty-five thousand African Americans had placed their names on the rolls of the Democratic Party, helping to swell the number of registered black voters across the state. Courtesy of South Caroliniana Library, University of South Carolina, Columbia, S.C. *(Below)* For the first time since Reconstruction, black South Carolinians made their way to the voting polls en masse in August 1948. Here black Columbians stand in line to vote in the formerly all-white Democratic Primary. Only four years earlier, then Governor Olin Johnston had declared, "White supremacy will be maintained in our primaries. Let the chips fall where they may." Courtesy of South Caroliniana Library, University of South Carolina, Columbia, S.C.

(Above) Rev. J.W. Seals, pastor of St. Mark's A.M.E. Church; J.S. Boyd; Rev. E.E. Richburg, pastor of Liberty Hill A.M.E. Church; and the Reverend J.A. DeLaine, leaders of the Clarendon County NAACP. In underground gatherings and mass meetings, these NAACP members rallied residents of Clarendon County to risk their livelihoods and lives to challenge Jim Crow and file *Briggs v. Elliott* in federal court, becoming the Deep South's sole representatives in the U.S. Supreme Court's landmark ruling, *Brown v. Board of Education.* Photo by E.C. Jones. Courtesy of South Caroliniana Library, University of South Carolina, Columbia, S.C. *(Below)* As Clarendon County NAACP officials secured signatures of county residents in support of a lawsuit demanding the equalization of white and black schools, white resistance to black demands turned increasingly violent. In October 1950, Reverend DeLaine's Summerton home burned to the ground as the local fire department watched. The Reverend DeLaine, his wife, Mattie, J.A. Jr., daughter, Ophelia, and son, B.B., survey the home's ruins. Photo by E.C. Jones. Courtesy of South Caroliniana Library, University of South Carolina, Columbia, S.C.

(Above) Mass meetings, such as the one depicted here at the Liberty Hill A.M.E. Church in 1951, sustained black Clarendon County residents as their fight for equality expanded and *Briggs v. Elliott* took their battle into the federal court system. Photo by E.C. Jones. Courtesy of South Caroliniana Library, University of South Carolina, Columbia, S.C. *(Below)* The Reverend E.E. Richburg stands with stalwart supporters of the Clarendon County civil rights insurgency inside St. James A.M.E. Church in Lake City (1952). Courtesy of South Caroliniana Library, University of South Carolina, Columbia, S.C.

NAACP special counsel Thurgood Marshall electrified black South Carolinians by boldly challenging Jim Crow in the courtroom. Here he arrives in Charleston in 1951 to argue *Briggs v. Elliott* before native Charlestonian Judge J. Waties Waring, and the U.S. District Court for the Eastern District of South Carolina. Photo by Cecil J. Williams. Courtesy of Cecil J. Williams, Orangeburg, S.C.

South Carolina NAACP Executive Committee chairman S.J. McDonald hands Harry Briggs a merit award. The two men are flanked by key NAACP figures. From left to right they are: Rev. E.E. Richburg, Modjeska Simkins, Rev. J.W. Seals, McDonald, Rev. J.A. DeLaine, Briggs, John McCray, J.S. Boyd, Rev. James Hinton, and Eugene A.R. Montgomery, the State Conference's first full-time and paid executive secretary (1951). Photo by E.C. Jones. Courtesy of South Caroliniana Library, University of South Carolina, Columbia, S.C.

(Above) During the winter of 1955–1956, black students at South Carolina State and Claflin College took the lead in efforts to combat repressive measures taken by Orangeburg's White Citizens' Council and state government officials to stem the rising tide of black demands for school integration and racial justice. Freedom Marches such as the one seen here in 1956, along with well-organized consumer boycotts, became potent tools in the ongoing civil rights movement. Photo by Cecil J. Williams. Courtesy of Cecil J. Williams, Orangeburg, S.C. *(Below)* As student-led sit-ins spread across the South in the spring of 1960, students in South Carolina took to the streets and staged sit-ins from Rock Hill, to Columbia, to Charleston. Here, students at South Carolina State and Claflin College march and draw attention to the struggles of generations past. Photo by Cecil J. Williams. Courtesy of Cecil J. Williams, Orangeburg, S.C.

(Above) In Orangeburg students readily linked an end to segregation to broader aspirations of freedom and justice (March 1960). Photo by Cecil J. Williams. Courtesy of Cecil J. Williams, Orangeburg, S.C. *(Below)* On March 15, 1960, Orangeburg law enforcement officials unleashed tear gas and fire hoses on student-led demonstrators. Nearly four hundred demonstrators were arrested and confined in a makeshift stockade outside the county jail known as the Pink Palace. Photographer Cecil Williams captured the event on film and also was arrested. A similar photograph by Williams appeared on the front page of *The New York Times* the following day. Photo by Cecil J. Williams. Courtesy of Cecil J. Williams, Orangeburg, S.C.

5 Popular Fronts:
From New Deal Coalition
to Black Rights Revolution

The notion of equality points the way to the essence of the democratic idea—the development of the realization of equality is the clue to the problem of democracy. The acid test of democracy in America is the inclusion of 15 million Negroes and other minority groups in the realization of the concept of equality.

> —From resolutions adopted by the South Carolina
> State Conference of NAACP Branches, 1948

Democracy and Equality are Inseparable.

> —Theme, annual meeting of the South Carolina
> State Conference of NAACP Branches, 1951

As World War II came to a close, African Americans in the North and South were increasingly able to articulate their needs and represent their interests on a regional and national scale in a way earlier generations could only imagine. Migration to the urban North, grassroots organizing and political mobilization, the growth of the NAACP, and the creation of seemingly countless voting rights organizations in the South, all signaled the powerful emergence of a previously submerged element in American life. At the same time, the wartime growth of the AFL and the CIO, a wave of nationwide strikes in 1945 and 1946, and the launching of the CIO's ambitious drive to organize the South, known as "Operation Dixie," provided an indication of the labor movement's expanded national influence and revealed the limits of labor's newfound power.[1] To be sure, the black struggle for civil rights and the labor movement did not emerge hermetically sealed off from one another. Many of the most promising moments in the history of each occurred when the two converged, forged alliances, and waged battles together. When afforded the opportunity, black workers regularly joined labor unions, especially CIO-affiliated ones, and battled to turn them into agents in their struggle for self-determination and equality. In an important sense, these moments of convergence represented the grand possibilities of the age so often celebrated by scholars; however, these moments also embodied the contingencies that filled the era with tension and conflict. The crisis of the Great Depression, the economic relief and reform efforts of the New Deal, and the war to defeat Fascism provided the critical context for a remarkable period of coalition-building among liberals and Communists, white and black workers, union and civil rights leaders, northern and southern Democrats. But the New Deal's economic reform agenda and the war to defeat Fascism simultaneously masked divisions along race, gender, regional, and organizational lines, smoothed over ideological differences, and postponed very real conflicts about the scope and meaning of past and future reform.[2] In postwar South Carolina, as in the postwar United States, changing circumstances required new strategies and tactics for reform, and while the left-wing of the New Deal coalition was to splinter from within and be ensnared and crushed by the emerging cold war, African Americans would push ahead on an agenda of democratic reform that represented a revision and extension of earlier reform efforts, not a turn away from them.

"We Shall Overcome"?: Black Tobacco Workers Strike American Tobacco Co.

Wednesday, October 3, 1945, began as did most days at the American Tobacco Company's cigar plant in Charleston. Approximately 1,400 white and black workers arrived at the corner of Columbus and Drake streets, filed into the dark red brick building along the banks of the Cooper River, and made their way to their respective and rigidly segregated departments to begin work. "Workers at the American Tobacco Company were very segregated," recalled Lillie Doster, "all the facilities were segregated—they were working on segregated floors." Like Doster, the vast majority of the plant's nine hundred black employees were women, and for weeks they had complained about the appalling working conditions in the factory. Workers at the plant had won the right to be represented by the United Cannery, Agricultural, Packing and Allied Workers of America (UCAPAWA-CIO) and secured their first union contract by December 1943. But despite a newly negotiated contract in September 1945, the majority of black workers, who occupied the lowest-paid, dirtiest, most labor-intensive, and hazardous job classifications in the plant, made only between fifty and sixty cents an hour. With time and a half for overtime, five hundred workers made a maximum of twenty-six dollars a week while another four hundred made just over thirty-one dollars. During the hot summer months the swampy conditions along the Cooper River made work inside the building extremely trying, while the winter months were marked by damp and drafty conditions. One asthmatic woman remarked that "even on the coldest days" she was not allowed to take a sweater into her department. "[C]onditions were very bad," remembered another. More importantly, black workers voiced their collective dismay at the arbitrary and unfair ways that they were treated by the white men and women who oversaw their work and had the power to discipline and fire them without cause. Verbal altercations with foremen and absences from work, even for sickness, no matter how many years of work at the plant, could and did result in the loss of a job.[3]

Despite the seemingly ordinary start to the day, that Wednesday black tobacco workers staged a sit-down strike from eleven in the morning until the closing of the plant that evening for the second time in recent months. According to one foreman, more than one hundred black women sat in his department "just idling their time away." Elsewhere groups of twelve to fifteen stopped work, gathered together, and sang hymns and spirituals. The immediate purpose of the strike was to protest the firing of a black man who was charged by a white forewoman with having had "familiarities" with black women under her supervision and the firing of a black woman who, her denials notwithstanding, had allegedly welcomed the man's sexual overtures. Emblematic of the type of control and arbitrary power wielded over their lives by white supervisors and management, alike, the firing of the two workers galvanized the plant's black workforce. The following day, when nine hundred black workers returned to the corner of Columbus and Drake streets, management declined to meet with union leaders and all nine hundred refused to enter the plant, ultimately returning home. Although later that day plant management agreed to begin talks with union leaders about the concerns of its black workforce and black workers returned to work on Friday, the two-day strike presaged considerable labor strife on the horizon.[4]

UCAPAWA's presence in Charleston, South Carolina's gateway to the Atlantic world, meant that the state would not avoid a rendezvous with the New Deal coalition's left flank, also known as the Popular Front. Organized in the summer of 1937 by a young Columbia University economics instructor and Communist Party member, Donald Henderson, UCAPAWA initially drew members from the Communist-led Trade Union Unity League (TUUL), the Cannery and Agricultural Workers Industrial Union, as well as a number of independent and AFL-affiliated agricultural unions. The left-led union immediately plunged into the arduous task of organizing some of the nation's most exploited workers in the fields of California and Florida. In the late 1930s it joined forces with the Southern Tenant Farmers Union (STFU) to organize Alabama cotton workers, only to encounter brutal repression and succumb to factional battles between Socialist Party and Communist Party members. Without the legal protection afforded industrial workers under the Wagner Act, organizing agricultural workers was an exceedingly difficult task, and by 1940 UCAPAWA had increasingly turned its attention to organizing workers in the food processing industry, including workers involved in the production of tobacco products. With the success of its organizing efforts among R.J. Reynolds Tobacco Company's black and white tobacco workers in Winston-Salem, North Carolina, and the creation of small beachheads in places like Charleston, UCAPAWA had positioned itself at the cutting edge of Popular Front activism by the end of 1943.[5]

Along with the CIO-affiliated National Maritime Union (NMU), UCAPAWA, which would soon be renamed the Food, Tobacco, Agricultural & Allied Workers Union (FTA), made Charleston a center of Popular Front activism by the summer of 1945 and a case study in the possibilities and limitations of the Left's long-sought-after black-white labor alliance. Reuel Stanfield, a white Midwesterner and Communist Party member, headed the NMU local and would become the president of the FTA Local #15. In 1934 Stanfield had been at the center of the maritime strikes that rocked the ports of California and landed him a five-year sentence in San Quentin for allegedly carrying dynamite in the trunk of his car while picketing on the docks of San Pedro. After serving his time in jail, he finally made his way to Charleston, where he spearheaded the organizing efforts of the CIO and Communist Party. Organizing tobacco workers was hard enough work, but the cigar plant's majority black and female workforce was also legally disfranchised, largely denied access to basic reading and writing skills, and, as a result, lacked the ability to represent their needs and interests through formal political channels. The lives of black and white workers on the job and in the broader community were, moreover, ordered in substantial measure by the legal strictures and social practices of Jim Crow segregation. Indeed, into the early fall months of 1945 Local #15's membership meetings were attended primarily by black workers and a few white union leaders.[6]

By the summer of 1945, however, Local #15 had made substantial progress organizing black workers and had begun attracting the interest of a number of young and idealistic, white, middle-class progressives. Karl Korstad, a native Minnesotan, was working as a staff sergeant in the U.S. Army Medical Corps in the public relations department of Charleston's Stark General Hospital that summer. As a graduate student in English at Syracuse University, during the 1930s Korstad delved into the writings of Karl Marx, Sigmund Freud, Kenneth Burke, and Malcolm Crowley, among others, and became, as he would later describe himself, a "Minnesota populist" and a member of the 1930s' "New Left Renaissance." While working in Stark Hospital's public relations office he encountered a cohort of like-minded progressives, including a New York University student named Sidney Fishman. Together they "talked constantly" about their hopes for the postwar era. "We had supported Henry A. Wallace and the progressive wing of the Democratic Party," Korstad recalled, "even after the city bosses and the labor leaders blocked Wallace's renomination for vice president in favor of the safer Harry S. Truman." For Korstad and Fishman, the labor movement, and the CIO in particular, represented the best hope for democracy in the South and a bulwark against what they understood as the growing power of the corporate sector and southern elites in the making of a postwar world. "If unions could continue to increase their numbers, if they could forge a stronger unity between blacks and whites, between men and women, among all religious and nationality groups," Korstad conjectured, "they could be crucial in moving America down the road that we envisioned: the fulfillment of the social programs of the New Deal, an end to colonialism, and a beginning of free independent nations worldwide. Moreover, if the workers of the South could build this kind of unity in their unions and in their community struggles, they would be able to free themselves from the poverty and deprivation forced upon them by Southern elites." Wanting "to be a part of that effort," Korstad and Fishman put their words into action, searched out Charleston's CIO locals, and began working as volunteers for Local #15, attending membership meetings, preparing leaflets and press releases, and helping to teach workers how to read and write.[7]

Then on October 22, less than three weeks following the sit-down strike, and one week after members of FTA Local #186 struck American Tobacco Company in Philadelphia, Pennsylvania, between 1,100 and 1,200 white and black employees went on strike against the American Tobacco Company in Charleston. Striking workers sought an across-the-board twenty-five cent wage increase, six days' sick leave with pay, improved working conditions, a no-discrimination clause, and a closed shop. When Local #56 in Trenton, New Jersey, followed suit and walked off the job on October 25, the implications of the strike became more clear as the collective North-South effort directly challenged the regional wage differentials that bolstered and helped rationalize Jim Crow segregation. In the weeks and months leading up to the strike, Local #15 had held separate meetings for white and black workers. White and black workers gathered on alternating evenings, white workers first, followed by black workers. But on Friday evening, October 26, four days into the strike, white and black workers held their first joint meeting. Although segregation continued to mediate life within and outside of the factory walls, as Lillie Doster explained, "We saw the need that we had to work together in a union to get benefits for all, because the more you have in an industrial union, the more benefit you can get."[8]

On the picket lines along the corner of Drake and Columbus streets it was clear that black women were in the lead of a strike that would drag on through the end of March 1946. Women like Lillie Martin, a mother and grandmother, assumed picket captain duties. Picket lines began in the early mornings and every evening the lines broke up with the singing of "We Shall Overcome," a song of protest adapted by the women from an old Negro spiritual, "I Will Overcome Someday." During most days, Lucille Simmons canvassed black neighborhoods in Charleston to rally support for the strikers, only to return to the picket lines in the evening to lead the singing of the song that strikers later taught to Zilphia Horton at the Highlander Folk School for labor organizers in Monteagle, Tennessee. At Highlander the song would be taught to the folk singers and activists Pete Seeger and Guy Carawan, who, in turn, taught it to a new generation of activists who made it an anthem of the 1960s civil rights movement. Within the union itself, black men and women sat on the executive board and represented the union in negotiations with American Tobacco Company. Lillie Martin, for one, was elected to the Executive Committee, while Celestine Bunch, a nineteen-year-old who had dropped out of school three years earlier to help support her disabled mother, was elected to the position of union vice president.[9]

For the band of activists inspired by the New Deal and who viewed the success of the CIO's organizing drive in the South as critical to the postwar reconstruction of America, the FTA's efforts in Charleston represented the possibilities of manifesting the long-hoped-for black-white labor alliance. "Deep in the grass roots," Osceola McKaine announced, "democracy is beginning to work effectively in the South." "For the first time in nearly 80 years," he exclaimed, "the laboring classes of both races" were getting together in South Carolina "to discuss their problems—as equals." "History was made," he noted, when one of the highest officials in the union "was a Negro." During the winter months, Korstad and Fishman organized "The New South" lecture series through the local CIO Political Action Committee. Meeting regularly in black churches on a nonsegregated basis, the lecture series brought many of the leading lights of the New Deal coalition's left-flank to Charleston to speak before, as Korstad recalled, regular crowds of four to five hundred African Americans and better than one hundred white Charlestonians "with workers, church people, and professionals—even a banker—in attendance." In February, with strike funds running low, Korstad traveled to Washington, D.C., and with the aid of Clark Foreman and Virginia Durr, both of the Southern Conference for Human Welfare (SCHW), established the Emergency Committee to Aid Families of American Tobacco Company Strikers. With the irascible Durr's assistance, Korstad was also able to win the support of Florida's senator Claude Pepper; the former director of the National Youth Administration, Aubrey Williams; Frank Porter Graham of the University of North Carolina; and the then-head of the National Council of Negro Women (NCNW), Mary McLeod Bethune, among others. That same month, Foreman helped organize a chapter of the SCHW in Charleston. John H. Potts, who had only recently been hired to handle the duties of principal at Avery Institute after a distinguished career as an educator in Columbia's black public school system, was elected president and Korstad's wife, Frances, a descendent of old Charleston families, was elected secretary. For Korstad, the strike and cooperation of white and black professionals signaled that a world of possibilities was in the making. "In Charleston," he fondly recalled, "it had become evident that the workers would fight to keep their unions. White and black FTA members appeared able to overcome their prejudices of their social environment and work together as equals. Furthermore," he added, "the lecture series seemed to point to the fact that there were middle-class whites who were willing to explore the possibilities of a new South in joint meetings with the black community."[10]

While McKaine and Korstad celebrated the strike for the hope it seemed to inspire for interracial cooperation, the strike's implications were far more ambiguous on the ground. White workers were never a monolithic group, and most of the nearly two hundred white workers who joined the American Tobacco Company's majority black workforce on the picket lines were white women who shared with black women, albeit in segregated departments, the labor-intensive work of stripping tobacco leaves and rolling cigars. During the nearly six-month-long strike, striking workers endured constant police harassment. Police smashed picket lines, and Reuel Stanfield was arrested. In what proved a double-edged sword for the FTA, *The News and Courier* kept the public informed of union activities and regularly published the names of union leaders, negotiating committees, and meeting places. FTA members received support from the NMU, but support from local all-white AFL unions never emerged. Moreover, cold winter months and economic hardship wore down the striking workers. "It was a very cold winter," recalled Lillie Doster, "and most of the ladies were bread winners for their families," making it exceedingly difficult to sustain the strike, let alone interracial alliances. Indeed, over the course of the winter, strikers slowly trickled back to work. By late March, before a strike settlement was reached, some one thousand strikers had returned to their jobs.[11] On March 30 members of Local #15 ratified an agreement to accept an eight-cent per hour wage increase, a fifteen percent raise, but a fraction of what they demanded. Even before the workers agreed to settlement terms, the recently organized, all-white AFL Tobacco Workers International Union

(TWIU), Local #257, representing the cigar plant's male machinists, lodged a complaint with the American Tobacco Company and the National Labor Relations Board (NLRB), challenging the FTA's right to represent the plant's workforce and to negotiate a contract with the company. Although a threatened machinist strike to protest the FTA's right to represent the plant's workers was averted, the TWIU's challenge to the legitimacy of the FTA provided a sign of future troubles.[12] Divisions among white workers along lines of gender, skill, and organizational affiliation, to say nothing of the ways in which Jim Crow segregation and black disfranchisement continued to support white supremacy and divisions between white and black workers, left an economically depressed workforce in a highly precarious position in postwar South Carolina.[13]

From Columbia John McCray watched events transpire in Charleston with a skeptical eye and a substantial degree of concern. For Korstad and McKaine, no matter how romantic their rendering of it, Popular Front activism in Charleston suggested the possibilities of interracial cooperation and represented the best hope for democracy in the South. McCray, on the other hand, viewed the Communist Party, the CIO-PAC, and the SCHW as a threat to the institutional integrity of the PDP and a challenge to the self-organization and self-representation of black South Carolinians. Never one to dismiss tactical, even interracial, alliances out of hand, by the spring of 1946 McCray had become convinced that McKaine's involvement with the SCHW and the CIO PAC and his connections to the Communist Party threatened to split the PDP internally, dilute what he deemed the PDP's most pressing objective, the organization of black South Carolinians, and subject the party and the struggle in South Carolina to control from outside of the state. While McKaine readily embraced the SCHW's offer to become its first African American field representative, McCray had earlier rejected the same offer. He not only worried that the SCHW responsibilities would curtail his work with *The Lighthouse and Informer* and the PDP. He also believed that the offer had been motivated by a desire on the part of the SCHW and the CIO-PAC to co-opt the party's agenda and capture its members. "I consider it significant that the PAC and CIO have chosen this state as a testing ground for a contemplated southern campaign," he wrote in September 1945. "I happen to know that the PDP's accomplishment was one inspiration to them and several attempts previously to get hold of its membership and hold its support having failed, they now resort to buying in persons they consider influential in the movement."[14]

Informed by a lifetime of international travels and associations, McKaine's vision of the PDP as a vehicle for the creation of a white-black labor alliance clashed with McCray's vision of the party as a means to the empowerment of black people, a vision that was shaped far more by his sense of self as a South Carolinian and his philosophical commitment to the principal of local self-determination. "I intend to live and die in South Carolina—if I don't get escorted to the border and expelled bodily," McCray explained. "Sure [the SCHW position] would offer contacts and fame but I am not interested in them. I'm not interested in publicity and big sounding titles and positions. They would scare me to death." Always a double-edged philosophy, McCray's insistence on local self-determination left him branded as an Uncle Tom and race traitor when he publicly opposed the NAACP's antilynching campaign in 1937. And yet, in the years following, McCray proved himself a forceful advocate of racial justice and helped turn South Carolina into a major front in America's own postwar struggle with democracy. For McCray the central issue was not, however, whether he was perceived as a race traitor or a race radical. Rather, he was concerned, first and foremost, with finding a means to empower black South Carolinians, and he believed that objective required black South Carolinians to take the lead in their own struggle for equality. "The PDP is under local (state) control," he insisted. "The PAC is not. I would oppose with all my vigor subjugation of our people to control from outside. The PAC's big weakness here," he added, "is that it shall be controlled by New York and other places." Unwilling to replace the paternalistic power dynamics of Jim Crow segregation with what he perceived as new forms of potential subjugation, McCray chafed at McKaine's willingness to devote increasing energy to organizational activities outside of South Carolina. McCray doubted that McKaine could work for the PDP and the CIO-PAC without sacrificing the work of the former for the latter. "The fact is cause for great concern," he wrote, "as it has not been proved yet that any man can serve two masters at the same time."[15]

Despite their philosophical and tactical disagreements, McCray and McKaine maintained a steadfast friendship until McKaine's death in 1955, but that friendship came with a cost in 1945 and 1946. Virtually from the moment PDP delegates left the Chicago Democratic

National Convention to return to South Carolina in the summer of 1944, divisions within the PDP began to percolate to the surface. Rumors swirled that McCray had sold out the PDP to Democratic Party officials for cash bribes and later had misused party funds for personal travel expenses.[16] Although McCray viewed the charges levied against him as part and parcel of organization politics as usual, they came at precisely the same moment that the PDP's efforts had begun attracting the attention of a number of organizations interested in making inroads in South Carolina and at a time when the PDP faced difficult choices about its own future. In the year following the convention challenge, the Communist Party sent a number of party members to South Carolina to meet with McCray, offer their assistance to the movement, and, as McCray recalled, encourage the PDP to align itself with "a worldwide struggle." Faced with internecine organizational battles and the daunting task of turning the PDP into a full-fledged political party, he saw the Communist Party's overtures as an effort to infiltrate and break up an indigenous people's movement. "Here in Columbia, for several months," he wrote in May 1945, "Communists, directed by New York, have attempted to seize the party." "I have stood firm against alliances with bodies foreign to the state," he continued, "bodies which over a period of years haven't been able to do any good for themselves. Other sources have stood in opposition, have conspired against us, have seized on our Chicago action—an action ordered by a majority vote—to apply the first code and creed of the Communist Party against out young body: DIVIDE AND CONQUER or cast into confusion." McKaine's connections to the Communist Party and his efforts, as McCray saw it, "to switch the [PDP] over to PAC and the Communists," proved a ready source of conflict within the party, and McCray's unwillingness to take action against McKaine further called his personal leadership into question. "I have caught veritable hell from loyal party members," McCray explained, "because I have known of the contrary and even treacherous behavior of McKaine, serving at my pleasure, and have done nothing about him." But McCray's unwillingness to expel McKaine from the PDP, as some members desired, did not stem from close personal ties alone. It also derived from an acknowledgement of the complexity and tenuousness of the *intra*-racial coalition that the PDP represented and within which McKaine maintained a substantial following. To force him from the organization, McCray deduced, "would provide ammunition necessary for general division and bedlam" within the party and signal that he had conceded victory to his opponents.[17]

The Southern Negro Youth Congress and the 1946 Columbia Youth Legislature

In the spring of 1946 the black struggle for civil rights in South Carolina confronted a host of opportunities *and* challenges. Across the South, black southerners were organized as never before in the twentieth century, and South Carolina represented an important strategic and symbolic site in the bourgeoning southern movement. Not only were black South Carolinians increasingly organized, a number of dedicated activists also pointed to the work of the FTA and the SCHW as an indication of the era's interracial possibilities, a seeming crack in the foundation of Jim Crow. At the same time, South Carolina's white political leadership led the charge to turn back New Deal era reform efforts, resist further challenges to Jim Crow segregation, and prevent the extension of full civil rights to African Americans. Within the state, violence remained an ever-present threat to black assertiveness and challenges to existing social and political hierarchies. In South Carolina's most publicized act of postwar racial violence, Isaac Woodard, a black soldier returning from military service in February, was arrested for an alleged altercation with a bus driver on his way to meet his wife in Winnsboro. While in police custody he was severely beaten and blinded in both eyes as a result. In Columbia, police regularly subjected black soldiers to harassment and physical brutality. In Bennettsville, the Ku Klux Klan burned a cross and made it known that participation in the NAACP would trigger further Klan activity. In August 1946 a mob lynched James Walker Jr. in Elko, and six months later a mob took the life of a twenty-five-year-old epileptic named Willie Earl in Pickens County. As it had in the past, the upsurge in racial violence combined with the downward spiral of South Carolina's cotton economy to make migration an attractive resistance strategy, and black migration from the state accelerated accordingly.[18] It was in this context that movement activists faced the task of rethinking older organizational practices and theoretical presuppositions in order to adapt to rapidly changing social, political, and economic circumstances.

In the spring of 1946, as the PDP seemed to falter and his personal leadership was called into question, McCray gave his support to a temporary organization called the Anti–Jim Crow Committee that called for a boycott of busses, streetcars, and other public places in Columbia on the first Sunday of every month to begin in March. Modeled, in part, on the rent strikes and consumer boycotts deployed in Harlem to protest discrimination in the 1930s, the planned strike to protest Jim Crow segregation drew explicitly on the philosophical and tactical tenets of nonviolence and passive resistance. "The Jim Crow protest is planned and wished to be devoid of hatred and bitterness," McCray wrote. "It is not aimed at any particular firm or persons. Rather, to awake—and only awake—citizens of both races to how injustices are perpetrated against Negro citizens under the disguise of necessary separation of the races." It was designed, he explained, "to protest in passive resistance any and all measures designed and calculated for the purpose of inflicting inequality upon the Negro." This included not only mistreatment on city busses and public places where black people, he noted, are "shunted into little corners as though they carried leprosy or other dangerous and contagious diseases [and] often times they are set upon while in these corners and physically abused," but also in the rapidly growing public employment sector of the economy. "Because of Jim Crowism," he continued, "there are no Negroes on the local police force or in any place of city employment beyond janitorial and garbage collecting capacities." The focus of the protest was, however, to be on the city busses that were fast replacing streetcars as central sites in the day-to-day battles over the meaning and practice of Jim Crow.[19]

Although the white press minimized the extent of the boycott, the Anti–Jim Crow Committee largely succeeded in keeping black Columbians off city busses on the first Sunday of March. Aided, in part, by private automobile owners who picked up would-be bus riders at various bus stops around the city, McKaine noted, "nearly all of the city busses were devoid of Negro passengers the entire day." Perhaps more importantly, though, the boycott signaled that McCray was willing, despite and because of challenges to his leadership, to experiment with new strategies, tactics, and alliances in the face of changing circumstances. While he initially accepted the duties of the committee's chairmanship over his "personal protest," as chairman he worked with the local NAACP Youth Council, a number of black churches, as well as the Socialist Workers Party. Indeed, in the wake of the Anti–Jim

Crow Sunday movement, he lent his support to the efforts of the Southern Negro Youth Congress (SNYC), a Communist-led and, in many ways, quintessential Popular Front organization, to organize in South Carolina and hold their annual youth legislature in Columbia that October.[20]

Organized in Richmond, Virginia, in February 1937, the SNYC owed its immediate inspiration to the organization of the National Negro Congress (NNC) only a year earlier. The NNC was, in large part, the creation of the Young Turks, including Ralph Bunche and John P. Davis, in partnership with the era's preeminent black labor leader, A. Philip Randolph. Its founding meeting in Chicago, Illinois, embodied the mid-1930s efforts of the self-fashioned black Left to reorient the black struggle for equality by foregrounding issues of class and economics and by promoting the vaunted alliance between labor and African Americans. For a number of young, black, twenty-something, southern-born activists in attendance, the organization of the NNC was an important event that highlighted the pressing economic problems of the time and advanced the cause of forging an alliance between African Americans and an incipient labor movement. But, these young southerners did not abide the NNC uncritically. Rather they called attention to what they understood as the all-too-articulate, even disconnected tenor of the NNC's older, thirty-something, northern leadership. "You northern-born Negroes don't know anything about your *roots*," the Arkansas-born militant James Ashford castigated his compatriots. "You don't know that our people aren't going to get anywhere until there's a militant mass movement in the South." At the urging of Ashford, Edward Strong, the NNC's Youth Section chairman, advocated the creation of a southern-based, youth-oriented organization that, the two believed, might better address the particular problems facing the majority of black Americans who still lived in the Jim Crow South. The very idea of the SNYC was conceived as a means to address the particularities of black oppression in the United States and to develop, in theory and practice, a social movement that did not reject the *radical*, labor- or class-based, solutions proposed from the North or what were, in the eyes of some, the seemingly more *conservative*, nationalistic or race-based, solutions emanating from the South.[21]

In numerous ways, the young men and women who became leaders of the SNYC embodied this tension between the North and the

South. Strong's personal history, for example, traversed regional, in-stitutional, and ideological lines. He was the son of a Baptist minister and spent the first twelve years of his life in Texarcana, Texas, where, for a time, he picked cotton and lived under the strictures of Jim Crow. Like thousands of other southerners, Strong's family migrated to the industrial Midwest in the 1920s, where some members found jobs in the industrial plants of Flint, Michigan. Strong became a youth lead-er in the Mount Olive Baptist Church, organized an NAACP Youth Council, and, while attending college in Chicago, became a member of the Communist Party.[22]

Like Strong, most of the SNYC's early leaders were members of the Communist Party, and their own politics were shaped in profound ways by their participation in the radical student movement of the 1930s.[23] Revolutionary Marxism and the politics of class and econom-ics animated their own thinking and activism. But neither the SNYC nor its principle members were products of single institutions, politi-cal traditions, or static theories.[24] The lives of its individual members crossed numerous institutional, geographic, racial, and ideological boundaries. James E. Jackson Jr. was one of the SNYC's key organizers and theorists and, perhaps, the organization's most committed Com-munist Party member. Yet his life is, like Strong's, representative of a general pattern of experiences shared by the organization's leadership. Born in Richmond's segregated Jackson Ward in 1914, Jackson was raised in a family that was, by all accounts, part of the city's educated, professional, black middle class. His father was a pharmacist and an NAACP activist. The younger Jackson received his early political edu-cation from "bull sessions" in the back room of his father's pharmacy, which doubled as an important social and political arena in black Rich-mond. While attending Virginia Union, a black Baptist college, Jack-son joined the Communist Party. He was a founding member of an interracial student organization, the Cooperative Independent Club, which, among other activities, marched onto the floor of the Virginia State Legislature to demand the abolition of segregation in public educa-tion. His sister, Alice Jackson, became a litigant in a lawsuit, inspired by the NAACP's campaign against discrimination in education, which challenged the University of Virginia's exclusion of African Americans from its graduate school. After graduating from Virginia Union in 1934, Jackson earned a degree in pharmacy from Howard University and then returned to Richmond to work with his father.[25]

Far from hindering his political development, Jackson's particular class position and life experiences facilitated his radicalization. The segregated confines of Jackson Ward schooled Jackson in the racial realities that regulated life in the South. More than driven by "status anxiety" or a desire to "reform" the black masses, Jackson came to understand his own prospects in life as tied to the political and economic fate of the masses of black people with whom he lived, socialized, and did business. As a college student and as a member of the Communist Party, Jackson made connections beyond the confines of segregated Richmond. His intellectual engagement with Marx, discussions about international struggles for justice, and interaction with progressive-minded white college students all played important parts in the making of Jackson's social and political consciousness. As the product of many, and some might argue contradictory, experiences, Jackson came to see simple solutions to complex problems as an anathema to progress. He believed that class antagonism and economic exploitation were central problems of his time, but he also viewed class-based antagonism as a problem implicated in, but not regulative of all forms of inequality and oppression. For Jackson, Marxism provided a critically important *developmental* theory to guide human beings through the maze of twentieth-century capitalism. "I have sought," he wrote, "to determine what is valid and useful in these writings as distinguished from what is in error, out-moded or inapplicable. It has always been my view that Marxism as a social science has to be studied as a science and not viewed as holy scripture; it recognizes one law above all others: that is, motion and development—old propositions and estimates giving way to new propositions."[26] Consistent with his compound identity, Jackson took his task and that of the SNYC as applying theory to particular and ever-changing circumstances. As activists *and* theorists, Jackson and members of the SNYC sought to plunge themselves into the messy business of transforming the world to meet their expectations of its potential for democracy. To do so, they readily placed their theory in dialogue with the practical realities of struggle.

Less than a month after their founding meeting in Richmond, Jackson and the newly formed SNYC began their first project in an effort to organize black workers in the Richmond area tobacco industry. Following a sit-down strike orchestrated by the black women who labored in the stemming division of the Carrington and Michaux tobacco plant, the SNYC moved in to offer organizational assistance. With the aid of C. Columbus Alston, a young and experienced union organizer from Detroit, Michigan, Jackson helped the workers organize an independent union, the Tobacco Stemmers and Laborers Union (TSLU), which rapidly won a wage increase, shorter hours, and union recognition. The union victory created a ripple effect throughout the Richmond area tobacco industry. In July 1938, the TSLU affiliated with the recently created UCAPAWA. In one successful effort, white members of the Amalgamated Workers of America (ACWA-CIO) joined black workers in a strike at the Brown and Williamson Tobacco Company.

Despite important victories, black workers remained in the industry's lowest-paid and least skilled jobs. A strike of the I.N. Vaugn Company in September 1938 led to the arrest of Jackson and triggered mass firings of black workers. Even before the strike, the tobacco industry had begun mechanizing its least skilled tasks performed largely by African Americans. Long on seniority and experience in industrial manufacturing, white workers readily moved into the newly mechanized jobs, while black workers were phased out along with the job classifications they occupied.[27] Although SNYC activists could take credit for the advances made in black unionization, they also were witnesses to the limits of their efforts. The needs and interests of black and female workers, they could readily deduce, differed in significant ways from those of their white counterparts. Even the "economic" interests of black workers were shaped in fundamental ways by racial discrimination and lack of political power. Jim Crow unions, segregated job classifications, lack of educational opportunities, disfranchisement, and limits on participation in the public life of the South all infringed on the capacity of black workers to earn a living and participate in the organization of industry.

Members of the SNYC carried their early observations and experiences with them to Birmingham, Alabama, a major center of New South industrialism and Popular Front activism, where they established their headquarters in 1939. Although women were active in the organization from the beginning, following the move to Birmingham they came to play increasingly visible roles in the congress. Dorothy Challenor Burnham, who was active in the radical student movement in New York City, joined the organization in Birmingham along with her husband, Louis Burnham. Rose Mae Catchings, who had roots in the YWCA, Thelma Dale Perkins, niece of Tuskegee University President,

F.D. Patterson, and Sallye Davis, mother of future black radical Angela Davis, all became active members by the early 1940s.

In early 1941 Esther Cooper married James Jackson and, shortly thereafter, at the urging of her male compatriots, became the SNYC's executive secretary. Cooper graduated from Oberlin College in 1938. While studying for her master's degree in sociology at Fisk University, under the direction of Charles S. Johnson, she joined the Communist Party. Her mother, a former president of the Arlington, Virginia, NAACP, encouraged Cooper to follow her love and political interests to Birmingham. Under Cooper's leadership and with the infusion of women into the organization (a number of whom were also married to fellow members), the SNYC moved the issue of domestic and organizational roles onto the organization's political agenda. As Cooper recalls, "It was part of the political development in the Congress for black males that women were on equal par."[28] For Cooper and others in the SNYC, the central leadership roles played by women in black communities, from club work, to church-based activities, appeared self-evident. Although their understanding of this reality did not move questions of patriarchy to the front of the political agenda, it substantially shaped the manner in which the SNYC sought to organize black communities.

As early as 1942 the SNYC expressed interest in organizing in South Carolina and made contact with Osceola McKaine. "We are in the midst of the fight for equal salaries for our teachers," McKaine informed the SNYC at the time, "but shall be most happy to push the movement at the same time if you will send us one or two directives." At McKaine's suggestion, the SNYC placed Modjeska Simkins on its national adult advisory board. Three years later, as the movement in South Carolina garnered national attention and numerous organizations sought to make inroads in the state, students at Benedict College, with the assistance of Annie Belle Weston, a well-respected professor of religious education and the secretary of the PDP, formed the first SNYC club in the state. And in 1946, recognizing the strategic and symbolic importance of the movement in South Carolina, the SNYC decided to hold its annual youth legislature in Columbia that fall. But in contrast to the other left-led organizations attempting to make inroads to the South Carolina movement, by the spring of 1946 the SNYC managed to win the support of McKaine, Simkins, *and* McCray, all of whom agreed to serve on the organization's local steering committee charged with making preparations for the fall legislature. Despite McCray's longstanding opposition to "outside" interference and wariness of the Communist Party, he provided the SNYC and its youth legislature with editorial support in the months and weeks leading up to the October gathering.[29]

Members of the SNYC were skilled organizers and their ability to win McCray's support reflected, in large measure, their understanding of the racial realities that regulated life in South Carolina and the revolutionary potential of already existing black institutions and the ongoing black civil rights insurgency. The SNYC was less interested in making itself a permanent fixture of institutional life in South Carolina, than it was injecting existing institutions with new energy and prodding them in new directions. With an astute awareness of the central roles that black women played in the associational and institutional life of southern black communities, the SNYC relied on Simkins and Weston to make their initial forays into the state. Rather than encouraging the creation of independent SNYC organizations, Louis Burnham, the SNYC's organizational secretary, suggested that organizers focus on encouraging already existing groups and individuals, including social clubs, campus fraternities and sororities, young men's civic organizations, as well as progressive ministers, and the "more wide awake hostesses at the USO," to affiliate with the SNYC, perhaps create a SNYC club, and support the organization's activities. In a strategy that was well-designed to tap into local traditions of club work and associational activity, the SNYC acknowledged the central roles that these organizations played in the lives of black South Carolinians, refused to dismiss them as mere harbingers of bourgeois nationalism, and sought to find a means of directing their energies to the cause of black liberation.[30]

In the summer of 1946, Simkins helped organize a SNYC Leadership Training School in Irmo, a small town only ten minutes outside Columbia, which became a center of SNYC youth activity in 1946 and 1947. The SNYC intended the Leadership Training School and affiliated SNYC clubs to serve as vehicles for educating young people and fostering their intellectual and cultural development. In a style and language familiar to many black South Carolinians, the SNYC suggested that clubs address "local" concerns such as access to quality educational equipment, community centers, and recreational facilities. Clubs were to promote healthy living, proper diet, and exercise.

Through plays, musical concerts, poetry readings, and lessons in black history, the clubs were to serve as a means of inculcating "an understanding and appreciation of national and inter-national problems," to "correct and combat distortions of Negro History," to "popularize inter-racial youth meeting," spur "participation in the realistic struggle for Negro freedom," and inspire "hope of freedom and the will to win freedom." In short, in the idiom of racial uplift, members of the SNYC worked to rally young people to the cause of racial equality and world justice. Through the club strategy, SNYC activists preserved rather than usurped older traditions of racial uplift and worked to create an opportunity to reorient those traditions in new, more activist—more overtly political—directions.[31]

Even more important than their willingness to work within and through existing black institutions, the SNYC's success in recruiting across the spectrum of black leadership in South Carolina stemmed from the willingness of its members to organize around issues that already animated the concerns of a broad cross section of black South Carolinians. While members of the SNYC maintained a commitment to the restructuring of the relationship between labor and capital, that is, to the democratization of economic relationships, they did not organize as if all significant political issues flowed from conflict at the point of industrial production. Partly as a result, the SNYC chose to make the issue of the vote the centerpiece of its fall youth legislature. The issue of the vote, organizers could well surmise, appealed to a mass constituency and had the potential to dramatize a host of other issues that flowed from questions of representation and political power.

After months of organizing, the SNYC's efforts came together in the production of their fall youth legislature. On October 18, 1946, more than nine hundred men, women, and children gathered in Columbia's Township Auditorium for the SNYC-sponsored event. As the legislature opened on Friday afternoon, black delegates representing each of the former Confederate states marched into the auditorium where they viewed an oversized American flag that only partially obscured from view a larger-than-life-size mural of the "freedom road."[32] Adorning the walls of the auditorium were portraits of the twenty-two black men who served in the U.S. Congress during the Reconstruction era and banners demanding land for "Landless Farm Workers," the abolition of segregation in public transportation, the end of police brutality and the Ku Klux Klan, and finally, support for Henry Wallace and "Big 3 Unity." Black as well as a number of white participants came to the legislature at the behest of the SNYC to "reassess the position of Negro youth in the South . . . plan further strategy . . . [and] demonstrate in a dramatic way" the resolve of youth to advance the cause of political and economic justice.[33] Over the weekend, those in attendance participated in workshops led by local and national activists, labor leaders, and civil rights organizers. They heard speeches, attended dramatic performances, and received lessons in the history of black activism and protest.

Held only a few weeks prior to the midterm election of representatives to the Eightieth U.S. Congress, a Congress that would be dominated by a powerful bloc of conservative northern Republicans and southern Democrats, the legislature brought together a number of nationally and internationally prominent individuals and organizations active in Popular Front circles during the New Deal and World War II years. Among the workshop leaders, performers, and speech makers were W.E.B. Du Bois, Paul Robeson, Clark Foreman of the Southern Conference for Human Welfare (SCHW), Henry O. Mayfield of the United Mine Workers of America (UMWA), Hosea Hudson of the United Steel Workers of America (USWA), the young historian Herbert Aptheker, the left-wing author Howard Fast, and native South Carolinian bluesman, Josh White. International guests included representatives from Haiti and India.[34]

The legislature was a showcase for the SNYC's vision of global democracy and represented an effort to translate its vision to a wider audience. Workshops and panels concerned with "Youth and Labor," "Peace," "Veterans," "Education," "Voting," and "Civil Liberties," included labor leaders, civil rights activists, community leaders, educators, and African American youth. The daily sessions held at Benedict College and neighboring Allen University reflected the SNYC's effort to promote a cross-class, interracial, intergenerational, multi-organizational, and multi-issued approach to social, political, and economic justice. The panel sessions debated issues of local, national, and international significance and drew up resolutions that were designed for submission to the Eightieth U.S. Congress and presented to the larger legislature.[35]

The centerpiece of the legislature was, of course, the issue of the vote. In effect, the SNYC choreographed the legislature to demon-

strate the ways in which the struggle for the vote was part and parcel of a larger struggle for political *and* economic democracy in the
South and ultimately around the world. In her opening address to
the legislature, Esther Cooper (Jackson) highlighted the centrality
of the vote to the future of progressive movements. "We have come
here to Columbia, in the heart of South Carolina, in the heart of the
South," she proclaimed, "to rearm ourselves with a deeper realization of our condition and our needs; we have come to give strength
and organizational power to the burning and unsilenceable demand of
our generation for the *right to live and prosper*." "The Justice Department," she charged, "has stood like an ostrich with its head in the sand
while armed bands of lynchers . . . maim and murder our veterans, our
women, our youth . . . and enshroud our eyes with fear for our lives."
Pointing to the portraits of Reconstruction leaders displayed around
the hall, she called for legislature participants to rearm themselves with
"their primary weapon in their fight for complete freedom—the right
to vote." In a refrain that would be heard throughout the legislature,
she invoked Reconstruction as a time "when white men and black
men shared political power in true representative state governments,
and administered wisely and progressively in the interest of the whole
people." The right to vote, she was saying, was not an end in itself, but
rather a critical means to the creation of a more just and democratic
world.[36]

In what was scheduled as an introduction to a keynote speech by
Reverend Adam Clayton Powell Jr., who pulled out of the legislature
at the last moment, McCray used his legislature address to focus on
the vote and champion the PDP as an example for black people to follow in other states.[37] Still ambivalent about the relationship between
the black movement in South Carolina and struggles elsewhere, Mc-
Cray increasingly viewed the problems facing black people in South
Carolina as intractable in the absence of national remedies. "I do not
know tonight what Negroes in Georgia, Alabama, Mississippi, Texas
or Arkansas are going to do," he explained:

> I only know what we of South Carolina are trying to do and what
> we have thus far succeeded in doing. . . . We are not worrying . . .
> about the men from the State parties, we have shifted our responsi-
> bility and our charge to where we think it rightfully belongs, where
> if National Democratic Committee . . . is interested in the fight of

the South, the southern white people and the southern Negroes as they always profess themselves to be, we wouldn't have the curse of a Democratic white primary. But why have we had it? Because nobody in the South has made any effort to put the National Democratic Party itself on the spot and hold it up before the world as a real rascal. We raised that question in 1944. That is why we went to Chicago. That is why we are going in 1948.

"In 1948," he continued, "I don't believe that South Carolina should be the only state considering or attempting this solution. I think that every southern state in which there is disfranchisement . . . should send full delegations to wherever that convention is being held."[38]

The SNYC sought, then, to make explicit the connections between the local and national contexts of struggle. One of the critical connections they sought to forge was with the labor movement. Echoing the call for an alliance between African Americans and white workers, the Youth and Labor panel resolved, "That the Southern Negro Youth Congress assist and aid wherever and whenever possible the southern organizational drive of labor unions, to maintain the basic principle of complete unity of Negro and white workers as a guarantee for the successful conclusion of the organizational drive—a drive which will bring to the southern worker a strong weapon with which to secure adequate wages and working conditions."

Simultaneously, the SNYC worked to expand the scope of the labor movement's concerns to incorporate black workers, particularly women, who labored disproportionately in nonindustrial occupations, including agriculture and domestic service. In her remarks to the panel, SNYC member Florence Valentine explained, "Women in general have been discriminated against and exploited through limitation of their opportunities for employment, through long hours, low wages, and harmful working conditions. These hardships have fallen upon Negro women with double harshness."[39] The panel's recommendations reflected the SNYC's sensitivity to the importance of an alliance between labor and African Americans, as well as their understanding that race and gender shaped the very ways in which black men and women entered the labor market and experienced economic exploitation.[40]

During the legislature, no single speaker or panel presented an explicit theoretical treatise on the relationship of race and class, but efforts to highlight the ways in which racial discrimination and white supremacy placed distinct limits on progressive movements hinted at an emerging, if still ambiguous, theoretical insight. On the one hand, legislature participants treated race as a mask behind which "real" economic interests and relationships lurked. In this conception, evil capitalists and opportunistic politicians imposed race on white workers and African Americans (whose interests were assumed to be essentially the same) as a means of economic exploitation. As the panel on "Civil Liberties" put it:

> We know that . . . unreasonable separation has existed not because of any difference between Negro and White youth, not because their souls, hearts and minds bear any innate hatred one for the other . . . But because the rulers and owners of the bread and butter of the nation's wealth would deny the masses of Americans, both Negro and White a decent way of life in order to satisfy their greed, seeking to rule by dividing our people.[41]

At the same time, legislature participants hinted implicitly at the possibility that race, and specifically Jim Crow, was a cross-class social construction produced and reproduced in the day-to-day lives of white people and African Americans of all economic classes.[42] The same panel on "Civil Liberties" explained it this way:

> [White and black youth] have been separated by barriers of jim crow laws, white supremacy ideologies, unfit and inadequate schools, denial of the use of the ballot, terroristic violence, and threat of violence from the Ku Klux Klan and other facist and vandalistic lynch mobs [sic].
>
> The continued existence of inequalities, the continued practices of acts of violence and intimidation directed against the Negro people and minority groups are evils which seriously weaken the whole fabric of our democratic way of life. There can be no real freedom for any group so long as these evils continue to exist.[43]

While their theory of race remained ambiguous—race was presented as both an illusion imposed on unwitting victims *and* as a socially produced reality through which white and black people made sense of the world—the SNYC did not treat race as either superfluous or intractable. Indeed, the SNYC sought to remake the existing racial order by bringing black and white people together, when possible, and by working to eradicate the legal and institutional divisions that served to buttress racist ideologies and practices.

The SNYC was concerned with more than simply convincing black people that their interests resided with white workers and the labor movement. They were also interested in convincing labor and white workers that the black struggle against Jim Crow and white supremacy more generally was in *their* interests. SCHW president Clark Foreman, a white Georgian, New Dealer, and coauthor of the classic New Deal treatise *Report on the Economic Conditions of the South*, informed the legislature audience, "The organization of prejudice is the prelude to fascism. . . . Segregation, prejudice and discrimination are part and parcel of the economic issue in the South."[44]

In keeping with their professed principles, the SNYC worked hard to bring white youth into the fold. During the legislature, Junius Scales, a white North Carolinian, Communist Party member, and labor organizer, became the SNYC's first white national officer. Never one to romanticize the possibility of forging interracial alliances, in his address before the legislature, W.E.B. Du Bois stressed the need for alliances across the color line and he worked to place the struggle in the South in a global context. "White youth in the south is peculiarly frustrated," Du Bois explained. "There is not a single great ideal to which they can express or aspire to, that does not bring them into flat contradiction with the Negro problem." He called for black youth to reach out to their potential allies in the white South. "This is the firing line," he counseled:

> not simply for the emancipation of the American Negro but for the emancipation of the African Negro and the Negroes of the West Indies; for the emancipation of the colored races; and for the emancipation of the white slaves of modern capitalist monopoly. . . . Slowly but surely the working people of the South, white and black, must come to remember that their emancipation depends upon their mutual cooperation; upon their acquaintanceship with each other; upon their friendship; upon their social intermingling.[45]

Du Bois and members of the SNYC did not view the forging of a broadly based interracial alliance as a simple task. Instead, as reflected in their words and actions, they viewed the making of such an alliance as part of a process, a process that was, in the mid-1940s, only beginning.[46]

Similarly, the SNYC worked to connect the black struggle for civil rights in South Carolina to a broader international arena of struggle. In the mid-1940s racial and economic inequality in South Carolina animated the concerns of the men and women that SNYC activists sought to organize.[47] For members of the SNYC global peace was, however, a necessary component in the long-term struggle for justice and democracy. "Among the highest aims and aspirations of American youth is the desire to live in a peaceful world," the "Peace" panel declared. "We endorse the principle that the root causes of war arise out of political, social, and economic oppression."[48] The Communist Party had, after all, provided SNYC activists with personal connections to an international arena of struggle. Internationalism had been part and parcel of their political development. SNYC members regularly traveled abroad, engaged in dialogue with activists from other nations, and participated in efforts to promote progressive global cooperation. In the year prior to the legislature, for example, Esther Cooper (Jackson) took part in the Women's Youth Brigade's effort to rebuild war-torn Stalingrad and attended the 1945 meeting of the Fifth Pan African Congress held in Manchester, England, where she met Kwame Nkrumah, a young graduate student and future revolutionary from Ghana.[49] But, recognizing how day-to-day realities shaped the concerns of black South Carolinians, SNYC members did not assume that their radical global consciousness was necessarily the same as those they sought to organize, and they worked to find ways to reconcile those differences.

The legislature, in effect, served as a vehicle for the SNYC to translate its global experiences and vision to a wider audience. During the course of the weekend-long gathering, speakers filled their speeches with references to South Carolina native and U.S. secretary of state, James F. Byrnes. Byrnes provided legislature participants with a tangible symbol of the contradiction between the United States's democratic rhetoric abroad and racial practices at home. "Mr. Byrnes, that favorite son of this commonwealth, and Secretary of State of the United States, is today occupying an indefensible position," Du Bois exclaimed. "He must begin to help establish in his own South Carolina something of that democracy which he has been recently so loudly preaching to Russia."[50] In speech and song, Paul Robeson worked to place the black movement in South Carolina in dialogue with freedom movements around the world. Between his soulful renditions of "Go Down Moses," "Old Man River," and "Scandalize My Name," he shared his life of international travel and reported on the status of workers in other parts of the world. "One must understand the unity of struggle," he explained. "We are laboring people. We come from toiling masses and have always seen as allies the toiling masses of the world. . . . I want to say that there are children in many parts of the world who know about you here, who know a lot about you. You wouldn't think that way across the water, they who have struggled think of your struggle."[51]

In an important sense, the legislature represented a rather stunning example of the SNYC's vision and organizational efforts. On the surface it suggested that the possibilities for future collaboration were in place. However, in the headlines and columns of local newspapers, signs of impending conflict were evident even before the close of the gathering. "Russia Is Praised At Negro Meeting" read one headline. "Governor Charges Negro Meeting Was Communist" read another. "It is regrettable," South Carolina's governor, Ransome J. Williams, stated, "that Communistic elements came boldly and brazenly into South Carolina in an effort to undermine Secretary of State Byrnes' position in the councils of the United States."[52] In a reply covered by the local press, the SNYC asserted that Governor Williams's "attempt to discredit the highly successful conference . . . will fail."[53] And yet, the force of anticommunist rhetoric and politics was only beginning to emerge as a major factor in American life in 1946. Indeed, over the next two years, the SNYC struggled to survive as it came under increasing attack for its ties to the Communist Party. By 1949 the organization ceased to exist and its members scrambled to survive a growing wave of anticommunist persecution.[54]

The organizational demise of the SNYC was not, however, simply a result of the onset of the cold war. Anti–Communist Party sentiment predated the end of the Roosevelt era. In 1940 the House Committee on Un-American Activities listed the SNYC as a Communist front organization and, thereafter, the Federal Bureau of Investigation kept the SNYC under its watchful surveillance.[55] Many left-liberals who had worked closely with Communist Party members in the 1930s began the 1940s doubting the honesty and commitment of their Communist Party allies who had broken with the antifascist movement to support Joseph Stalin's Nazi-Soviet Pact in 1939.[56] African American activists such as McCray proved willing to work with the SNYC because he perceived that its members were sincerely interested in advancing the interests of black South Carolinians. Even so, McCray never relinquished his wariness and distrust of the Communist Party. "Disliking any violent theory and even more 'underhanders' and 'undercoverers,'" he wrote in 1947, "we have never seen anything of worth in the Communist Party for the Southern Negroes."[57]

Since the inception of the SNYC, its members had found room within the hierarchical and authoritarian structure of the Communist Party International (CP) and CP-USA for tactical and theoretical experimentation. By the mid-1940s, however, whatever space for creativity and innovation SNYC members had found within the Communist Party rapidly closed as the party became increasingly sectarian and inflexible. Under the control of longtime party activist William Foster, the party ordered its members to organize openly on its behalf, in effect, calling off the collaborative efforts embodied by the Popular Front.[58] Such changes within the CP were registered on the closing day of the Columbia youth legislature when James Jackson announced his resignation from the staff of the SNYC to become the state chairman of the Communist Party in Louisiana. In Louisiana, he organized openly as a member of the party, was attacked by a police escorted mob, arrested, and finally forced to leave the state. In 1951, Jackson and a number of other CP leaders were indicted under provisions of the Alien Registration law of 1940, also known as the Smith Act, which prohibited the teaching or advocacy of the overthrow of the government by force or violence. Rather than face the charges in the hostile political climate of the early 1950s, on the direction of party officials, Jackson joined other Communist Party members in the CP's underground network. While he was underground, his wife and two children experienced economic hardship and were subjected to constant and intrusive FBI surveillance.[59] For the Jacksons and the SNYC, the anticommunist hysteria of the emerging cold war proved devastating. The demise of the organization and the horrors experienced by its members did not, however, signal the demise of the African American struggle for self-determination and equality and grand visions of democratic revolution.

By 1946 members of the SNYC recognized in their organizational practices, if not in a fully developed theory, that the economic reform agenda of the New Deal and the class-based politics that animated the concerns of the Popular Front, no longer could or did represent the cutting edge of reform in postwar America. In the 1930s and 1940s, white workers who already held jobs in the industrial sector of the American economy had disproportionately determined and benefited from the reforms of the New Deal and had become, in many instances, a bulwark against further reform efforts by the end of World War II.[60] At the same time, through migration to northern industrial centers and collective organization in the South, African Americans represented an increasingly active and powerful voice in American life that was pushing beyond the narrowly crafted economic reform agenda of the New Deal. For African Americans, economic justice required a frontal assault on the ideology and practice of white supremacy and its most glaring manifestation, Jim Crow. Political disfranchisement in the South, as well as segregated schools, neighborhoods, job markets, and union halls, on both sides of the Mason-Dixon line, militated against the creation of a postwar coalition akin to that forged during the economic crisis of the 1930s and the antifascist campaigns of the war years. Indeed, the continued disfranchisement of southern African Americans helped make possible the rise of a powerful conservative coalition in the U.S. Congress in 1946 that was intent on turning back the tide of New Deal era reforms. Although black South Carolinians remained divided in myriad ways, guaranteeing no ideological or political conformity in the absence of disfranchisement and Jim Crow, what the SNYC found was that the issue of winning the right to vote and the pursuit of full civil rights could, and did, provide a means of creating a powerful cross-class, *intra*-racial coalition dedicated to stretching the parameters of American democracy and offering hope for further reform efforts. Put another way, even before the formal onset of the cold war, the necessary terrain of social and political struggle had shifted. In postwar America, the nation's rendezvous with its history of racial exclusion, violence, and discrimination could no longer be postponed. And while the SNYC would not survive the transition to the postwar era and the Popular Front would splinter from within and be crushed by cold war hysteria, the African American fight to expand the scope and meaning of American democracy was only beginning to take the shape of a mass movement in the mid-1940s.

NAACP Revivalism and the Expanding
Civil Rights Insurgency

Like the SNYC, the Popular Front, if understood in terms of individuals and specific institutions such as the CIO, the SCHW, and the Communist Party, did not survive the transition to the postwar era in South Carolina. Its first serious blow was dealt in the aftermath of the SNYC's youth legislature when its erstwhile proponent, Osceola McKaine, boarded an ocean liner bound for France in early December never to return to the United States. In ailing health, McKaine ultimately made his way back to Belgium where he presided over his old cabaret, "Mac's Place," until his death in November 1955. By the fall 1946 legislature, he had already announced, in effect, his resignation from the struggle in the United States. His work with the PDP had come to an end and he had severed his ties with the SCHW over financial and strategic concerns. In Charleston the Popular Front's postwar travails were more deep-seated and reflected preexisting divisions among the city's working classes that the onset of the cold war helped to magnify. Nationally the FTA came under attack for its ties to the Communist Party. In April 1947 the Eightieth U.S. Congress passed the Taft-Hartley Act over President Truman's veto. In addition to prohibiting the closed shop and providing states carte blanche to pass right to work laws, Taft-Hartely required union leaders to sign noncommunist affidavits in order for their unions to receive NLRB protection, handing the FTA's opposition a useful weapon to wield in battles for worker loyalty. In early 1950, the embattled CIO expelled the FTA from its ranks for its Communist ties. Shortly thereafter, the rapidly declining FTA merged with the Distributive, Processing and Office Workers of America (DPOW), essentially an organization composed of other Communist-led unions that also had been purged from the CIO. At the local level, loyal members of Local #15 spent the late 1940s and early 1950s fending off attempts by the TWIU-AFL, as well as the United Steel Workers of America (USWA-CIO), to defeat their union. Although the TWIU's and USWA's red-baiting infused campaigns failed to win control of the Charleston cigar plant, the FTA's largest and strongest local in Winston-Salem had been crushed by 1951, the CIO had won the right to represent workers at the American Tobacco Company's plant in Philadelphia, and, as a result, Local #15 was left to wage future battles largely on its own. Add to this the largely failed efforts of the CIO's Operation Dixie to make substantive inroads to the state in the late 1940s and the Popular Front disappeared as an institutional force in South Carolina.[61]

By no means, however, did the decline of the Popular Front in the late 1940s signal a retrenchment of the black civil rights insurgency. To the contrary, the postwar era looked far more like a beginning than an ending for most black South Carolinians. The Popular Front never held a monopoly on activism dedicated to expanding the meaning and practice of American democracy, whether in South Carolina or elsewhere. And in South Carolina the black fight for equality, which the State Conference of NAACP Branches declared to be the "acid test of democracy in America," had only just begun to open up substantial fronts in an ongoing battle for meaningful political representation and an end to Jim Crow. Indeed, in the summer of 1946, a light-skinned cab driver and secretary of the Richland County PDP, George Elmore, walked into a small grocery store in Columbia's ninth ward and asked the middle-aged white woman tending the store if he could sign the registration book kept there. In doing so, he inaugurated another campaign for black voting rights, helped put an end to the white primary, and contributed to the expansion of the black struggle for civil rights.

During the summer of 1946, the Negro Citizens Committee organized teams of prospective black voters to spread out across Columbia in an attempt to sign their names to registration books in advance of the Democratic primary scheduled for that August. In the aftermath of the state legislature's 1944 Extraordinary Session, which repealed all laws pertaining to primary elections in an attempt to evade the implications of *Smith v. Allwright*, registering to vote as a Democrat had become especially difficult. As part of an effort to separate the Democratic Party from the formal apparatus of the state, local party officials presided over voter registration books in their private homes and businesses. In Columbia the books were kept in a number of locations, including a drugstore, private home, and liquor store. To build their case against the state Democratic Party, teams of black would-be voters stood watch outside respective registration sites until they observed that a white person placed his or her name on the books inside. Then team members moved in to enroll. In the summer of 1946 such efforts were rewarded with little success, until Elmore managed to slide in under the racial radar of one unsuspecting bookkeeper. Apparently fooled by Elmore's racially ambiguous appearance, the grocery store clerk/registrar welcomed Elmore's request to place his name on the Democratic Party rolls and even helped guide him through the registration process. When she noticed his street address, however, she exclaimed in utter exasperation, "Why you're a damned nigger, too!" Asked by party officials to carry the day-to-day burden of upholding the color line in the face of the NCC's ongoing registration campaign, on this day, the task proved too much and she allowed Elmore to register. Immediately following the exchange inside, Elmore triumphantly emerged from the store to inform the waiting team that the woman allowed him to place his name on the books and told him "to tell the rest of you damned niggers you can come in and register too." Those in wait, including Reverend Hinton and Columbia NAACP stalwart Robert W. Mance, proceeded to sign their names to the voter registration rolls, laying the groundwork for a planned assault on the white primary in August.[62]

When black voters, including Elmore, reported to vote in the August primary, Democratic Party officials summarily turned them away. Harold Boulware, the head of the state conference legal committee, filed a class-action lawsuit, *Elmore v. Rice*, in federal court to open up the Democratic primary to black voters soon thereafter. With the aid of NAACP attorneys Thurgood Marshall and Robert Carter, Boulware prepared the case for a hearing before Judge Waring in U.S. District Court in June 1947. Only months earlier, Waring had presided over the federal trial of Lynwood Shull, the police chief accused of blinding Isaac Woodard, and been horrified by the jury's not guilty verdict. The same month that Waring prepared to hear the most recent challenge to the white primary in South Carolina, he also prepared to hear the case of *Wrighten v. Board of Trustees of University of South Carolina*, a suit brought by Avery alumnus John H. Wrighten Jr. and the NAACP in an attempt to win admission to the all-white university's law school. On June 12, 1947, Waring issued decisions in both cases that would have profound effects on the future of the black civil rights struggle in South Carolina.

In the *Wrighten* case, Waring sided with the state. In short, defense lawyers argued that the state's belated attempts to establish a black law school at South Carolina State College satisfied the legal requirements of separate but equal and the existing legal precedent established in *Missouri ex rel. Gaines v. Canada* (1938), a suit brought by the NAACP in an effort to achieve integration by forcing states to pay for truly separate and equal educational facilities. The *Wrighten* decision led to the creation of a black law school in Orangeburg that would train some of the lawyers, including Wrighten and Matthew Perry, who later became shock troops in the civil rights movement of the 1950s and 1960s. At the same time, the seeming absurdity of the state's insistence on maintaining separate law schools and the apparent impossibility of actually creating truly equal institutions, provided Waring an insider's look at the limits of the separate but equal doctrine. But Waring maintained that the responsibility to make policy in matters of public education ought to rest with the state legislature, not with the court in the spring of 1947. In the matter of voting rights, however, Waring found that the Democratic Party, acting as the effective agent of the state, had abdicated its responsibility to ensure the rights of African Americans to participate freely in the state's election process and ruled in favor of the plaintiffs.

In *Elmore v. Rice*, the defense maintained that following the 1944 Extraordinary Session the South Carolina Democratic Party operated as a private club, akin to a sewing circle, a church, or a country club, and, therefore, could not be bound by the constitutional mandates of the Fourteenth or Fifteenth Amendments. While Waring (for the time being) thought that public education remained a private affair to be adjudicated through the legislative process, he ruled that the defense argument represented "pure sophistry." "[P]rivate clubs and business organizations," he argued, "do not vote and elect a President of the United States, and the Senators and members of the House of Representatives of our national congress." "When the General Assembly, answering the call of Governor Johnston, met in extraordinary session," he added, "it was wholly and solely for the purpose of preventing the Negro from gaining a right to vote in the primaries as granted under the doctrine of Smith v. Allwright." In words that further alienated him from many of his fellow white South Carolinians, Waring ordered the Democratic primary open to all South Carolinians. "It is time," he wrote, "for South Carolina to rejoin the Union. It is time to fall in step with the other states and to adopt the American way of conducting elections." Only weeks earlier, President Truman had addressed the NAACP's annual conference in Washington, D.C., and declared that the United States's "case for democracy" in the world "should be as strong as we can make it" and thus the nation could "no longer afford the luxury of a leisurely attack upon prejudice and discrimination." "[W]e cannot, any longer," he proclaimed, "await the growth of a will to action in the slowest state or the most backward community." Waring concluded his opinion by quoting from Truman's address, giving notice to white South Carolinians that the eyes of the nation and the world were upon them.[63]

Over the course of the next year, the South Carolina NAACP and its political arm, the NCC, battled a temporary stay of Waring's order to open the primary to black South Carolinians, defeated an appeal to the Fourth Circuit Court of Appeals presided over by the NAACP's old nemesis, Judge John J. Parker, and sustained another legal victory when the U.S. Supreme Court refused to hear the state's final appeal in April 1948. But in South Carolina, the battle to give meaning to *Elmore* had only just begun. In May 1948 the state Democratic Party met and, as they had in the past, devised another set of rules to maintain white supremacy and thwart the efforts of black South Carolinians to participate fully in the state's political decision-making process. Adroitly finessing the legal specificities of Waring's ruling in *Elmore*, which state Democratic Party officials argued barred the exclusion of African Americans from participation in the Democratic primary not from the Democratic Party itself, convention participants adopted new party rules and registration procedures. They limited membership in the party to whites only and created a two-tiered system of registration for primary elections. Under the new rules, members of the Democratic Party qualified to vote in primary elections by virtue of party membership alone. Non-party members, meaning African Americans, qualified to vote in primary elections only after obtaining registration certificates for the general election, preserving, in effect, the capacity of white registrars to serve as gatekeepers to the election process. Additionally, the party mandated that all voters take an oath pledging support for "states' rights," fidelity to "the social, religious and educational separation of the races," opposition to the proposed Federal Employment Protection Committee (FEPC), and that they were members of no other political party.[64]

Although the state Democratic Party worked hard to ensure white supremacy in the election process, black South Carolinians worked tirelessly to secure their right to participate fully in that process. In the wake of the Democratic Party's May convention, the PDP held its own state convention and selected twenty-eight delegates to, once again, take its case to the Democratic National Convention that July. In early July, as the PDP prepared to head to Philadelphia for its second unsuccessful bid to unseat the state's all-white delegation, the NAACP filed suit on behalf of David Brown, a service station attendant and PDP officer in Beaufort County, to win admission to the Democratic Party. Prior to the Democratic Party's May convention, Brown managed to place his name on the party rolls, but, soon afterward, party officials purged his name from the list. Waring scheduled a hearing for the case, *Brown v. Baskin*, on July 16, just three days after South Carolina governor Strom Thurmond led the defeat of the PDP challenge in Philadelphia and just one day before he strode to the platform at the founding convention of the States' Rights Democrats (also known as the Dixiecrats) in Birmingham, Alabama, and bellowed, "There's not enough troops in the Army to force the southern people to break down segregation and admit the Negro race into our theaters, into our swimming pools, into schools and into our homes." From the bench, Waring issued an injunction mandating that the state Democratic Party open its membership rolls and allow all parties, without regard to "race, color, creed, or condition," to participate in the impending August 10 primary. In remarks expressing his growing contempt for the willful failure of Democratic Party officials to abide by the letter and spirit of the *Elmore* decision, Waring castigated the defense. "It is important that once and for all," he wrote, "the members of this Party be made to understand—and that is the purpose of this opinion—that they will be required to obey and carry out the orders of this court, not only in the technical respects but in the spirit and true meaning of the same." Promising to jail those who further evaded his orders, Waring also ordered enrollment books to remain open for extended hours until July 31 and he struck down the Democratic Party's required oath.[65]

Before the registration books closed at the end of July, some thirty-five thousand African Americans placed their names on the rolls of the Democratic Party, swelling the ranks of registered black voters in the state. For the first time since the late-nineteenth century, substantial numbers of black South Carolinians made their way to the polls in August to vote in the only election that determined the outcome of state and national races, the Democratic primary. Of course, thirty-five thousand registered black voters represented only a fraction of the eligible black vote in South Carolina in 1948, even though the increase represented a 700 percent increase of the number registered in 1946.[66] But the significance of the rise in registered black voters cannot be quantified by mere statistical data alone. As Kari Frederickson has ably demonstrated, the NAACP- and PDP-orchestrated challenge to the exclusion of African Americans from the Democratic Party in South Carolina opened up a schism among white South Carolina Democrats that hastened the defection of the party's most conservative members and accelerated the process of ending one-party rule in the Palmetto State. Although it would take Thurmond an additional sixteen years to make his well-publicized switch to the Republican Party, his actions and those of his fellow Dixiecrats worked to drive a wedge within the state Democratic Party itself, helping to undermine the notion of a solid white South.

Disillusioned by the vitriol and intransigence of the state party's more reactionary leadership, a small group of white South Carolinians, many of them ministers and women affiliated with the South Carolina Council on Human Relations, presided over by Alice Spearman, formed the Citizens Democratic Party (CDP) in the spring of 1948. As Frederickson notes, CDP officials "took pains to point out that they did not endorse Truman's civil rights program." But its members did oppose the state party's efforts to circumvent *Elmore*, argued that qualified black voters ought to be able to participate in the Democratic primary, and sought to ensure the state party's support for national Democratic Party candidates. In July the CDP took its case to the Democratic National Convention in Philadelphia where their efforts to reign in the state party proved unsuccessful.[67]

Back in South Carolina, on a county-by-county basis, the solid wall of white opposition to black participation in the state's election process showed signs of cracking. By the time Waring heard testimony in *Brown v. Baskin*, Democratic Party officials in Greenville, Laurens, Pickens, and Richland counties had begun compliance with the letter if not the spirit of *Elmore*, in defiance of the state party. Whether county officials feared jail time, worried about poor publicity, earnestly believed that it was time for black South Carolinians to take part in the election process, or felt assured that the machinations of the registration process itself could effectively limit the number of *qualified* African American voters remains an open question. What is more certain, however, is that black South Carolinians had dramatically shifted the terms of the debate about black voting rights by the summer of 1948 and, in doing so, opened new institutional and discursive space for a frontal assault on Jim Crow and an expansion of the black struggle for civil rights.[68]

As much as the end of the white primary represented a substantial victory in the black fight for voting rights, NAACP leaders recognized the victory as just one step, albeit an important one, in their ongoing battle for self-determination and equality. Indeed, they were already working to reshape the agenda of the black civil rights insurgency and expand its base of participation by the spring of 1947 in anticipation of their triumph over the white primary. In 1947 and 1948, reflecting and giving shape to a shift in national office policy, NAACP leaders in South Carolina worked to push a direct attack on the legal doctrine and social practice of "separate but equal" to the front of its agenda. The national office had, in principle, long opposed segregation in all forms as an evil per se, but, in practice, had pursued a legal agenda that accommodated segregation as a means to its ultimate abolition. For their part, black South Carolinians played important roles in the NAACP's equalization campaign. However, as Wrighten's case made its way through the court system and the state prepared a segregated, makeshift law school in Orangeburg, state conference officials placed the weight of the South Carolina NAACP behind a campaign to end state imposed segregation *and* discrimination, which, as they had come to understand them, were inextricably bound together. "We are concerned about the denial of civil rights," state conference secretary, Modjeska Simkins, explained, "and the indignities experienced by us because of segregation." In his address to the annual gathering of the state conference in the fall of 1947, Reverend Hinton "made it definitively clear that no future cases will be filed and fought on the moth-eaten and futile 'separate but equal' subterfuge." Instead, he asserted, "the State Conference, in line with the national office directive would seek persistently to end segregation and discrimination in American life." Arguing that the Jim Crow "system" based on the doctrine of "SEPARATE but NEVER EQUAL" had "failed on its merits," Hinton boldly challenged NAACP members to embrace the battle to end segregation. "Now that the decision is made," he exclaimed, "I want to request anyone who is not fully willing to take a consistent stand against segregation and its evil to come up NOW and let us return to you your lousy dollar that you paid as a membership fee—or forever hereafter hold your peace."[69]

For state conference officers, the move to explicitly reject segregation was less a radical departure from past ideas and practices, than it was a bold adaptation to changing circumstances. From Gunnar Myrdal's *American Dilemma*, to the Truman administration–sponsored civil rights treatise, *To Secure These Rights*, to the shifting currents of the federal courts, as a social practice and legal doctrine, segregation appeared on the defensive in the late 1940s. South Carolina's NAACP leadership moved to occupy the terrain opened up by this marked institutional and ideological shift. As NAACP officials explained it, a frontal assault on segregation represented a means to equality that, they argued, was "the essence of the democratic idea." Equality, in their conception, entailed the realization of the full inclusion of black people in the political and economic life of the nation on a nondiscriminatory basis. More than demanding inclusion for inclusion's sake, however, NAACP leaders sought to secure, in practice, the rights of all black people to be more self-determining and recognized participants in the making of a more democratic America. "We are no longer satisfied with formal statements of support, pious platitudes or analyses of our plight and position as America's largest and most maligned minority," they resolved in the fall of 1948. "We demand deeds that will make the Bill of Rights a reality in American life." To that end, they sought an end to "the twin evils" of the poll tax and lynching. They sought "the fullest participation in the elective process of all citizens" and the passage of federal and state fair employment practice legislation. As they represented it, "the realization of the concept of equality" was not something out there waiting to be ushered in in a single revolutionary instant. It was, rather, a process, the development of which pointed human beings on the path toward a more democratic way of living. "The notion of equality points the way to the essence of the democratic idea," they stated, "[and] the development of the realization of equality is the clue to the problem of democracy."[70]

South Carolina NAACP officials knew well that a frontal assault on segregation represented a bold move, one that would be met by staunch white resistance and would require "supersalesmanship," as Hinton explained it, "to convert" many black leaders to the "antisegregation concept" itself. But, a frontal assault on segregation, as they conceived it, did not also mean an abandonment of the practice of black self-organization. To the contrary, the work of ending the legal and social practice of segregation required, in their estimation, a vociferous campaign of black self-organization. Put another way, NAACP activists recognized that the collective organization of black South Carolinians represented a necessary precondition for access to the individual rights embodied in the American Constitution and the Bill of Rights; group organization and individual rights were, to them, inextricably intertwined. Indeed, in the spring of 1947 the South Carolina State Conference of Branches endorsed plans to hire their first full-time and paid executive secretary, whose task was to be the expansion of the NAACP's organizational presence and the promotion of its program across the state.[71]

In July 1948 the state conference hired a twenty-five-year-old, Orangeburg native, Eugene Alonzo Randolph Montgomery, to lead the association's expansion efforts. Born in 1923 to a relatively well-off family, the young Montgomery was reared in a home on Treadwell Street in an Orangeburg neighborhood comprised largely of black professionals and located just a short walk across the nearby railroad tracks to the campuses of Claflin College and South Carolina State. Montgomery's father owned a grocery and meat market that served as a gathering place for many of the town's black residents until the Depression put him out of business and he died a short time later. Supported by his mother, who worked as a midwife after his father's passing, extended family members, and Claflin's first African American president, Alonzo B. Randolph, from whom he derived his middle names, Montgomery attended the Methodist school from the first grade through college and earned his bachelor's degree in sociology there in 1942. Although he was offered the principal post at a three-teacher school, he packed his bags and headed north for the promise, as he perceived it, of better wages and opportunity in the Pittsburgh, Pennsylvania, steel industry. What he encountered, however, was a tightly controlled union hierarchy. It was "very segregated," he recalled. So, he left Pittsburgh and found work as a welder in a Chester, Pennsylvania, shipyard. After a period of work there, he returned to South Carolina, volunteered for the Marine Corps, and served in the military until 1946. At the age of twenty-three he enrolled in a master's degree program at Atlanta University's school of social work, before, once again, returning to Orangeburg. With a Master's of Social Work in hand, Montgomery began looking for work in the college town in the midst of a declining black belt economy, until the Reverend I. DeQuincy Newman, the pastor at Orangeburg's Trinity Methodist Church, a PDP activist, and president of the local NAACP branch, suggested that he travel to Columbia to talk with Hinton about the available executive secretary position. Montgomery's social background and life experiences made him an ideal candidate for the task. At once a man of impeccable educational credentials and social pedigree *and* the embodiment of the values of hard work and respectability that held appeal across class lines among black South Carolinians, Montgomery began organizing on behalf of the state conference in the summer of 1948 and oversaw the tremendous expansion of the organization over the following three years.[72]

Montgomery, as it turned out, was a masterful organizer. For a starting salary of seventy-five dollars a week, Montgomery launched the NAACP's first full-fledged, coordinated, and statewide grassroots organizing effort in its thirty-odd-year history in South Carolina. In 1948 the state conference organized branches into regional divisions corresponding to existing U.S. congressional districts, and the NAACP's organizing campaign doubled as a voter registration drive. "Much of what we have won in the courts," Montgomery explained, "can be lost if we fail to work out a definitive program to get every qualified person to vote." Over the next two years, Montgomery traveled extensively throughout the state, as many as 1,800 miles in a single month and regularly more than 1,000. In 1946 NAACP records indicate that forty-nine branches operated in South Carolina, and by the end of 1948 black South Carolinians could claim the existence of sixty-nine branches. By 1951 state organizers boasted that more than one hundred branches existed statewide, even though national office records indicate the existence of only eighty-four. But national office statistics, while still impressive and representing a nearly six-fold increase since 1943, provide only a partial measure of the NAACP's expanded presence and appeal in the Palmetto State during the opening years of the cold war.[73]

Joining forces with Reverend Hinton, Montgomery took the NAACP, quite literally, into the backwoods, cotton fields, and rural county churches of South Carolina. The NAACP had long been associated with the black church in South Carolina. Not only were churches one of the few quasi-public meeting places available to black people and ministers played important leadership roles in the organization, but the very struggle for civil rights, the black fight for self-determination and equality, was imbued with religious meaning. "To deny any part of our citizenship of that freedom of unlimited participation in all things, equally shared and enjoyed by the majority," the state conference resolved, "is to destroy Democracy and Christianity." From the reorganization of a branch in Anderson, where NAACP activists had fled for their lives twenty years earlier, to the creation of new branches in more tucked away towns such as Ruffin, located just south of the Edisto River, and Yamassee, situated along the Combahee River, Hartsville in Darlington County, and Lake City in Florence County, to the formation of one large Clarendon County branch through the merger of two smaller branches in Summerton and Manning, Montgomery and Hinton carried out what must be understood as an NAACP revival. "Everybody knew Hinton" by 1948, Montgomery recalled. "You've got to remember, back then, when you were battling whitey and winning, you had one hell of a reputation." So when the two men made preparations to visit a small town or rural hamlet, interested local leaders "put the word out." When Hinton "was going to show up at that church," Montgomery explained, "out there in the back woods . . . the church was going to be full." "I have never in my life heard anybody speak like he could speak," he added. "When he got through speaking I had to do the work" of signing up members and organizing a branch. "But he made it easy. When he got through speaking, they were ready to go, to do whatever was necessary."[74]

Expanding and energizing the NAACP was hard and dangerous work. Although official NAACP statistics placed South Carolina's NAACP membership at a peak of 14,237 at the end of 1948, the number of black South Carolinians who participated in local branches and supported the NAACP, but never formally joined the organization, was far larger. "Nobody ever knew how many members [there were] in each branch," Montgomery noted. "We were the only ones who knew."[75] In places such as Moncks Corner, in Berkeley County, the local Progressive Club paralleled the town's NAACP branch. "Its program is the same as the NAACP's," Montgomery reported, "but because so many people are afraid to join NAACP they find it more expedient to operate as another organization." In places such as Clarendon County, sharecroppers were drawn to the NAACP, attended mass meetings in area churches, and sought to participate in its activities, "knowing full well the man [was] going to kick them off [their] place." To keep them involved and insulated from the reprisals of white landowners, organizers arranged tacit agreements to encourage the participation and support of sharecroppers while keeping their names off official membership rolls and petitions. As Montgomery explained, activists such as Hinton, as well as McCray and Simkins, both of whom made the NAACP revival rounds with Montgomery, all had a certain degree of independence from white South Carolinians that enabled their open and vigorous activism. "They couldn't touch them," he noted, "which was a key element in it." Nevertheless, Hinton was abducted from his home in Augusta, Georgia, by at least three white men in April 1949. Thrown to the floor of a car and held there by his neck, he was spirited to the countryside, dragged from the vehicle, hit in the face with a flashlight, and blindfolded. "You want to place Negroes in the College of Charleston," Hinton recalled one man saying. "Don't you know that cannot be done in South Carolina." Fortunately for Hinton, his attackers came to the conclusion, inexplicably so, that "[t]his is not the nigger" and left him face down in the countryside to find his way back to the home he kept in Augusta.[76]

Hinton's abduction was, in important respects, a foreshadowing of things to come. Indeed, as the black struggle for equality in South Carolina grew and the NAACP's legal victories mounted, resistance to the black insurgency grew as well. But just as piecing together a black movement dedicated to the expansion of American democracy required hard work, so too did the making of a collective movement resisting black advancement, and full-scale massive resistance to the expanding black movement had yet to crystallize in the early cold war years. Indeed, as the cold war worked to arrest the Popular Front alliances that animated left-wing activism during the New Deal era, a new kind of Popular Front, a black Popular Front, fast occupied the cutting edge of reform in postwar America. In South Carolina the black fight for self-determination and equality had only just begun to animate a mass-based constituency on a statewide basis and only just begun to launch a frontal assault on Jim Crow as the cold war emerged as a major force in American life. Amid the collapse of the Old Left, black South Carolinians continued to search for a means to secure their rights and expand the meaning and practice of democracy in America. Far from repudiating the struggles of the previous decade, black South Carolinians kept the democratic hopes of the earlier era alive in the shape of an expanding and increasingly national movement for black civil rights.

6 Cold War Civil Rights: *Brown v. Board of Education* and the Emerging Power of the Periphery

*People got tired of what was going on . . . and knowing how they came,
they wanted things better for their children.*
—Hauleen Green Smith, Clarendon County

*It is our belief that timing, and not time, is a dimension of social change,
and that it is the quality of the experience which matters in our common
associations, and not the length of time we are exposed to one another. As
a mode of human association, segregation prevents the realization of even
the most elementary demands of equality, making democracy impossible.
Consequently, we believe that the elimination of segregation from all aspects of life is the first step toward the realization of true democracy.*
—Statement of the eighteenth annual meeting of the
South Carolina State Conference of Branches, October 24, 1959

To think and write about the black struggle for civil rights in the
1950s, the period canonized as the era of the NAACP's legal victory in *Brown v. Board of Education*, the Montgomery Bus Boycott,
the rise of Martin Luther King Jr., and the school integration crisis
in Little Rock, Arkansas, without reference to the cold war would be
more than mere folly. It would be bad history. The United States's
conflict with the Soviet Union and its preoccupation with defeating
the forces of Communism abroad and at home shaped the black
struggle for self-determination and equality, just as it shaped American and world history. Scholars have left little doubt that the cold
war contributed significantly to a growing rhetorical, if not programmatic, commitment on the part of liberal policymakers and judges
to securing full civil rights for African Americans. At the same time,
historians have produced a growing body of scholarship that details

187

the damage cold war politics and anticommunist persecution inflicted upon black struggles for justice on a global scale. From the persecution of individuals like W.E.B. Du Bois and Paul Robeson, to the curtailment of civil liberties, to the muting of voices concerned with battling colonialism and forging solidarity with "Third-World" peoples, to declining concern with "structural reform" of the American economy, the costs of cold war commitments have been made clear. Or have they?[1]

In the cost accounting of cold war era politics, the NAACP has not escaped stinging criticism for the choices it made and the oftentimes ingratiating support it lent U.S. foreign policy in exchange for a gradualist approach to securing civil rights for African Americans. Her criticism pointedly directed toward Walter White and the NAACP, Penny von Eschen sums up the critique of the association's cold war commitments best. "By acquiescing in a narrowed civil rights agenda," she writes, "many civil rights leaders forfeited the means to address . . . structural changes" in America's racialized political economy. Much as when the national leadership of the NAACP met the challenge of the Young Turks in the mid-1930s in an effort to preserve the organization's overarching commitment to an attack on racial injustice through a creative refashioning of American law and political structures, the association faced yet another challenge to its historic mission by the opening months of 1946. Increasingly, shifting political currents pushed the organization to choose between winning civil rights for African Americans and committing to the kind of anticolonialism and sweeping economic reform agenda championed by Du Bois, Robeson, and organizations such as the SNYC. In July 1946, a full year before George Kennan's "Mr. X" article appeared in *Foreign Affairs*, casting the Soviet Union as an inherently expansionist menace to be "contained" "with unalterable counter-force at every point where they show signs of encroaching upon the interests of a peaceful and stable world," Arthur M. Schlesinger Jr. put the NAACP, and the nation, on notice that the Communist Party was busy "sinking tentacles" into the bourgeoning civil rights organization. By that time, Walter White and the Board of Directors were, once again, embroiled in conflict with Du Bois that spanned the personal, financial, and ideological. That conflict reached a crescendo in 1947 and 1948 as the association sought to insulate itself from charges of Communist subversion and Du Bois strengthened his personal ties to members of the CP-USA, including Doxey Wilkerson, Herbert Aptheker, and James and Esther Jackson.[2]

First commissioning Du Bois to prepare *An Appeal to the World: A Statement on the Denial of Human Rights to Minorities in the Case of Citizens of Negro Descent in the United States of America and an Appeal to the United Nations for Redress,* White worked, in conjunction with the United Nations (UN) secretariat under pressure from the United States, to delay its presentation to the UN and to hold up its release to the broader public. Then, spurned by the board's decision to send White to represent the association at a fall 1948 gathering of the UN General Assembly in Paris to discuss the "rights of subject peoples," Du Bois refused to brief the secretary on issues likely to be raised at the international meeting. Instead, Du Bois composed a memorandum that, David Levering Lewis writes, "skewered the secretary for having accepted the administration's invitation to serve as special consultant to the U.S. delegation to the UN" and charged him with placing the NAACP "in the lap of the United States government." In September the Board of Directors resolved to terminate Du Bois's contract, and by the end of the month Du Bois departed permanently from the ranks of the organization he had played such a prominent role in creating. By the spring of 1950, the NAACP had publicly repudiated Paul Robeson and passed a resolution at its annual convention prohibiting Communists from membership in the organization and strengthening the capacity of the board and national officers to deal with potential Communist subversion of its branches. White took pains to defend the organization's brand of anticommunism, arguing that its policies "had been effected by democratic methods . . . without hysteria or the unfair tactics used by individuals such as Senator Joseph McCarthy." But, when White wrote that "Communists can be rooted out by truly democratic methods," he gave shape and substance to the tortured logic of cold war politics.[3]

Propelled by adherents of the political Left, Right, and Center, the emerging cold war cultural climate tended to cast political choices in stark either/or terms. Capitalism or Socialism, democracy or totalitarianism, civil rights or structural economic reform, the politics of the cold war demanded that men and women choose sides. "Which side are you on?" became, in effect, a rallying cry that helped define the choices of both the Left and the Right. In an important sense, the NAACP contributed to this narrowed climate of political choices in the 1950s. If deeply committed activists and intellectuals like the Jacksons, Robeson, and Du Bois were willing to tolerate the increasingly apparent authoritarianism of the Communist Party in the service of social justice, an equally committed Walter White believed that the CP had little more to offer African Americans than the surest road to hell, and he and the NAACP compromised its historic commitment to civil liberties to insulate the association from its influence. For White, his own dictatorial proclivities notwithstanding, the CP was thoroughly tainted by its totalitarian tendencies. Assuming the voice of all black Americans, White explained, "[T]he Negro wants no part of any system in which arbitrary power is vested in one man or a small clique of men. This revulsion against dictatorship applies to all forms of totalitarian rule, whether they be Communist, Dixiecrat, or any other."[4]

Political calculation, principled opposition to totalitarianism, as well as historical animus dating back to the days of Scottsboro, all played roles in shaping the politics of the NAACP during the opening years of the cold war. But while the NAACP gave shape and substance to the cold war, it also worked to lay a critical pathway beyond the ossified political choices of the 1950s. As Charles Houston had counseled the Young Turks in the early 1930s, there were many NAACPs: the NAACP of the national office, which worked the high level struggles to secure constitutional rights for African Americans, to wring political concessions from the executive branch and from Congress, and to, more generally, create the conditions necessary for black people to become equal participants in the making of their own and the nation's collective future; and there was the NAACP of the branches, which represented the front lines of myriad day-to-day battles waged against black oppression and in the cause of black freedom. The many faces of the NAACP, Houston argued, were inextricably linked to one another; vibrant branches were crucial to the success of the association's legal agenda and the association's legal agenda was crucial to the larger African American quest for self-determination and equality.

Since the late 1930s, energized and supported by an expanding branch constituency, the NAACP and its legal arm, the Legal Defense and Education Fund, Inc. (Inc. Fund)—created in 1939 and headed by Thurgood Marshall—had begun striking with deadly force at the legal-constitutional support system of Jim Crow and white supremacy in America. At the same time, the association's legal work had helped galvanize a growing social movement among African Americans across

the South. By the end of the 1940s, the NAACP's hard-fought battles to knock the legs out from under Jim Crow seemed imminent,
though hardly guaranteed, and a mass-based social movement had
begun stretching beyond the organization's historic base of support
among urban, middle-class African Americans. Indeed, any assessment
of the choices made by the NAACP during the early years of the cold
war not only must take into account the organization's relationship to
national politics and policy. It also must take into full consideration
the relationship of the organization to its mass base in its many local
branches, branches that were in the process of creating the necessary conditions for a remaking of national politics and policy. From
the vantage point of the movement in South Carolina, Walter White
and the national officers of the NAACP made the difficult political
choices that allowed an expanding grassroots social insurgency to proceed apace and for the legal battle against Jim Crow to push ahead. In
their full context, there was little ironic or narrow in the association's
calculations or choices. Both were consistent with the organization's
history and the constantly shifting terrain of struggle confronted by
black people in America.

From Clarendon County to *Brown v. Board of Education*

At precisely the moment the cold war emerged as a major factor in
American life, an NAACP revival had commenced in the state of
South Carolina. Membership numbers swelled in the late 1940s and
black South Carolinians continued to charter new NAACP branches
across the state. Between 1946 and 1955, the number of branches
in the state nearly doubled from forty-nine to eighty-four. Never before had the organization established such a thorough presence in
the state and never to the same extent had the organization drawn its
membership and allegiance from the state's most rural, isolated, and
powerless regions. For the first time since the era of Reconstruction,
the African American civil rights insurgency was being waged and,
in critical respects, led by those on the margins of history and the
periphery of power. What had been an episodic and highly tentative
pattern emerging during World War I and the early 1920s became a
full-blown pattern by the early 1950s that would develop more fully in
the years ahead. In South Carolina, and the larger nation, events in rural
Clarendon County proved the embodiment of this trend, representing

both the promise of an empowered periphery and the failure to provide those on the margins with the justice they demanded.

It is hard to imagine a place in post–World War II America more
poor or brutally oppressive than Clarendon County, South Carolina.
And, yet, by 1947 the black residents of the county would emerge as
key leaders of the NAACP's campaign to destroy Jim Crow segregation, becoming the only representatives from the Deep South included in the landmark U.S. Supreme Court decision, *Brown v. Board of
Education* (1954). African Americans comprised better than 70 percent of the county's population in 1950, the highest percentage in
South Carolina. White people owned 85 percent of the land in the
county, where two-thirds of black households earned less than $1,000
a year and a mere 280 made as much as $2,000. Born in Summerton
in 1922, Minnie Ida Wright recalled the difficulties growing up in
Clarendon. "It was rough then," she explained, "because they bring
us up the rough way, hardway." Wright's father was a sharecropper
who plowed "from sunrise to sundown," and her mother worked as a
domestic servant for a white family. Disfranchised and living life under
the regime of white supremacy in the midst of the South Carolina
black belt, the Wrights battled in myriad ways to earn a living, build
and sustain networks of family and friends, and secure a better life for
themselves. The Wrights held education in high regard, but working in a chronically depressed cotton economy, they struggled to find
ways to send each of their eight children to the Scott's Branch School
in the town of Summerton. They sold corn to purchase clothes and
books for school and the children split time in the classroom and the
cotton fields, returning home at the end of each school day to labor in
the fields to support the family.[5]

Formal and state-funded schooling, however, was hard to come by
for the vast majority of Clarendon County's black residents. During
the 1949–1950 school year the state spent $179 for each white child
to attend twelve schools, while it spent only $43 for every black child
to attend some sixty-one single- and two-teacher schools scattered
across the county. Most of the schools were little more than makeshift structures, usually constructed in the shadow of a black church.
"That's how most of the schools got their name, because it started in
the church first," Joseph Richburg Sr. remembered. "Then the parents got together and built a little shack." Schools operated to the
rhythms of cotton production. While the county paid for a portion of

the school year, black parents pooled resources to extend it, a practice they called "running pay school." The eldest of ten children, Richburg was born in 1920 and reared on land owned by his grandfather, who rented plots of it to his children. The Richburg family was one of a handful of black families in Clarendon, including the Pearsons, Levys, Clarks, Fraziers, Davises, and Johnsons, who owned substantial tracts of land. Although land ownership elevated the Richburgs' economic and social status relative to families such as the Wrights, the hardships of agricultural life and the desire for education cut across lines of class. Richburg attended the two-room Spring Hill School, adjacent to the Spring Hill A.M.E. Church, through the fourth grade. Then he attended the Scott's Branch School, located behind St. Marks A.M.E. in Summerton, through the eighth grade. But the demands of cotton production and the patriarchal prerogatives of his father drew him back to the fields. "I finished the eighth grade," he noted, "and Daddy tell me I'll have to come home and feed the rest of the children. . . . I had to plow."[6] Voting, too, remained out of the question for the county's black residents as African Americans remained thoroughly disfranchised in Clarendon County at the end of a decade that witnessed the legal end of the white primary.[7]

Although black residents of Clarendon lived a life of extreme political and economic marginalization, such marginalization did not translate into a lack of political consciousness or a failure to fight to improve their lives. Whether residents pooled resources to survive a downturn in the cotton economy, raised funds to run "pay school," or attended one of the county's many black churches, they developed an ethic of struggle and sense of justice that provided fertile ground for more formal political action. Exceptional because his family owned nearly 250 acres of land, J.A. (Joseph Armstrong) DeLaine nevertheless exemplified the changing course of the civil rights struggle in South Carolina during the 1940s, linking marginalized rural voices, a sense of religious revivalism, and the NAACP's expanding battle to destroy the legal infrastructure of Jim Crow. Like most of the county's black residents, DeLaine grew up working the land and was schooled in the value of education. Born in July 1898 to Henry Charles and Tisbia Gamble DeLaine, he was reared on the family farm outside of the town of Manning, Clarendon's county seat. Henry DeLaine had been born into slavery, although one family version tells the story of his birth to an "indentured servant" named Maria, worked his way into the ministry, became pastor of Liberty Hill A.M.E. Church, and eventually owned a small grocery store and funeral parlor. A model of thrift and uplift, DeLaine pushed his children hard in all endeavors. In 1912, after refusing to accept punishment for fighting two white boys who had been harassing his sister, J.A. left his father's home for a period of four years and labored in "sweatshop" conditions in Atlanta and Baltimore. Upon his return to South Carolina, he enrolled in high school at Columbia's Allen University. There he graduated from high school, earned a B.A., and commenced work toward the eventual completion of a divinity degree in 1931. That year he married Mattie Belton and the two began teaching careers in Orangeburg. But like his father, J.A. soon turned to a career in the ministry. Between 1934 and 1939 he served as the pastor of the Spring Hill A.M.E. Church near Summerton. At the same time, he taught and held the principal's post at the three-teacher Bob Johnson School in the nearby village of Davis Station. In 1940 he was assigned to the A.M.E. Church's Pine Grove Circuit with responsibilities for ministering to the Pine Grove and Society Hill A.M.E. Churches in the lower end of Clarendon County. He also moved his family into a newly constructed home in Summerton, where he continued to work as a teacher at the Liberty Hill School, and where his spouse began work as an elementary school teacher at the Scott's Branch School. As Richard Kluger has noted, along with Joseph Richburg's uncle, the Reverend E.E. Richburg of Liberty Hill A.M.E., DeLaine fast became "one of the two best-known and most respected black ministers in the county."[8]

For DeLaine, the duties of minister and teacher readily translated to the work of social activism. With an understanding of ministerial leadership that could both unleash the latent potential of a congregation for self-representation and stifle it through its top-down and patriarchal style, DeLaine believed that it was his Christian duty to lead his congregation within and outside of the church. "It is the duty of those whose province is to Rule the Church of God to be foremost in every good work," he wrote. "In things that become the Christian the minister must become the example . . . in acts of love to the sick and aged and young and tender; in kindness to all; in public spirit and regards to the general welfare; in honor, truth and prudence and self-command." As he would explain it, "I want to be a good shepherd of the sheep which God has given me. It is my desire to promote tenderness and gain the confidence of the members so they will be free to tell me their needs and as best I can I will assist in guiding them." Much as the leadership of the state NAACP imbued their civil rights work with religious meaning, DeLaine looked to the association as a means to affect his vision of a just and Christian world.[9]

It was during the summer of 1942 that DeLaine became interested in the NAACP through Osceola McKaine's campaign for the equalization of teachers' salaries. That summer he joined McKaine's hometown branch in Sumter. By the beginning of the following year, the work of the Negro Citizens Committee to secure the right to vote, under the leadership of the A.M.E. minister E.A. Adams and Reverend Hinton, inspired DeLaine to create an NAACP branch in Clarendon, which became known in Clarendon as the Citizens Committee. "We use the name Citizens Committee," he explained, "but it is really the NAACP." In a letter to the national office he provided insight to the difficulties he confronted. "I want you to mail all mail to me in plain envelopes," he wrote. "You see I am a preacher in this county and a public school teacher too. My living largely depend[s] upon the ones that fear and hate the N.A.A.C.P. My activities have already been under question." Indeed, it would take DeLaine five additional years to secure a formal NAACP charter. The repressive rural context in which DeLaine organized, as it did elsewhere in the state, militated against turning the NAACP into a mass organization in Clarendon County. So, too, did DeLaine's health. By early 1944 DeLaine had begun suffering from pleurisy, a painful inflammation of the membrane surrounding the lungs, and his organizational work ground to a near standstill. "My work with the Church, School, and [the] effort to work the folks up to want full citizenship," he noted, "was more than I could take under the war strain and privation."[10]

Such difficulties did not mean that the NAACP ceased to exist or to serve as a harbinger of future mass action in Clarendon. During the mid-1940s, the NAACP continued to operate as a loosely jointed, underground organization, supported and maintained by a small band of dedicated individuals working through the association and its various organizational fronts. For the Richburgs, joining the NAACP was a family affair. Joseph joined on his own in the 1930s and recalls that his father, two uncles, L.B. Rivers and the Reverend Richburg, "all of us" were members of the organization. A. Maceo Anderson, the principal of the Scott's Branch School, helped lead efforts on the voting rights front through the Citizens Committee, while future NAACP branch vice president, Sarah Daniels, a home demonstration agent and president of the Clarendon County Teachers' Association, organized two women's auxiliaries of the PDP and led local voter registration efforts. "I am hoping to help every teacher of Clarendon County," she wrote in late 1946, "see the work of this organization and at least register."[11]

Although marginalized politically and economically, African Americans in Clarendon County were closely connected to the institutions and social forces giving shape to the expanding black civil rights insurgency of the 1940s. As early as 1943, the issue of adequate bus transportation to and from school became the subject of conversation between DeLaine and members of Clarendon's black community, including Levi Pearson, laying groundwork for the county's future connection to the NAACP's legal campaign for educational equality. Due to a lack of state-funded bus transportation, Pearson, a sizeable landowner, and his elder sons regularly drove area children in the back of an old pickup truck to the Mount Zion school, a four-classroom, cement block structure, located eight miles from their home, a routine made particularly galling because the county paid for bus transportation for area white children. By 1946, Pearson and his brother, Hammett, in consultation with DeLaine, had organized local parents to deal with the problem. They purchased an old school bus from the county, fixed it up "the best they could," pooled money to purchase gas and hire a driver, and began transporting children to the Scott's Branch School, where three of Pearson's children attended by that time.[12]

For Ferdinand Pearson, one of Levi's eldest sons, the issue of equal education opportunities confronted him the moment he returned home from overseas service in the U.S. Army during World War II. The war, as it had elsewhere, gave shape to the emerging movement in Clarendon County. At age twenty-three, Ferdinand Pearson's experience in the military sharpened his sense that life had to change in the county. "It made me feel like something was wrong with our society," he explained. "Came back here and found that America was still segregated . . . was just the same as it was before I went away." "I am over there putting my life on the line to help save a country," he continued, "that is goin' to segregate me back home. . . . I didn't want my sons and daughters to see those kind of conditions." Upon his return to South Carolina he became part of a cohort of black World

War II veterans, including his brother Jessie, dedicated to improving life in Clarendon County. With the aid of DeLaine, the veterans drew up a petition to secure state funding for agricultural training classes as part of the GI Bill and began adult education classes at the Scott's Branch School under DeLaine's tutelage. As Pearson recalled it, De-Laine used the GI Bill classes to provide veterans with information about the NAACP and to recruit new members.[13]

In the spring of 1947 the day-to-day and largely behind-the-scenes activism in Clarendon County converged with the NAACP's search for a suitable case to challenge inequities in public education for school children that would culminate in *Brown*. While attending the Benedict-Allen Summer School, where he was enrolled in George Singleton's "Race and Culture" course, DeLaine listened to an address delivered by Reverend Hinton to a gathering of summer school enrollees. Hinton decried the state of black schools in South Carolina, argued that black South Carolinians would never advance without quality education, and, as DeLaine remembered it, challenged his audience to take the lead in the fight against discrimination in the state's public schools. Virginians had already launched such a campaign, he declared. But "No teacher or preacher in South Carolina has the courage," he exclaimed, "to get a plaintiff to test the School Bus Transportation practices of discrimination against Negro children."[14] Prodded by Professor Singleton, DeLaine returned to Clarendon and that Sunday held a meeting with his son, Joseph A. DeLaine Jr., along with Levi and Hammett Pearson, to discuss a legal challenge to the problem of bus transportation. Eight days later, DeLaine and Levi Pearson traveled to Columbia to meet with state conference attorney Harold Boulware, Reverend Hinton, and A.J. Butler of the Sumter NAACP. Together they resolved to put the resources and energies of the state NAACP behind a campaign to end discrimination in public school bus transportation in Clarendon County. Afterward, DeLaine and Pearson returned home to file a petition in Pearson's name with the County Superintendent of Education, the County School Board, and the State Board of Education, requesting that the county provide school bus transportation for his children and the other black children residing in School District No. 26. In a note he later jotted at the bottom of a letter to Boulware, DeLaine declared, "This is the legal beginning of the movement set in motion by me for the benefit of Negro children." If he took too much personal credit for launching "the movement," his note proved correct on two counts: the movement in South Carolina would be fought in and through Clarendon County from 1947 forward and the NAACP's court action did represent the "legal beginning" of a much larger movement already underway.[15]

By 1947, both the South Carolina NAACP and the national office were rapidly moving to declare formal opposition to the support of legal cases aimed at equalization rather than outright opposition to the doctrine of "separate but equal," but for the time being they remained willing to challenge Jim Crow by demanding equalization of funding and facilities. Pearson's petition, however, proved an insufficient vehicle for either strategy. State officials simply ignored Pearson's petition for months. In Clarendon County, where the work of the NAACP remained clandestine, support for the bus transportation suit waned among African Americans. "Many questions are being asked me about when the Bus Transportation case will start," DeLaine wrote Reverend Hinton. "I had a pretty good sentiment worked up for financial help but everything is growing cold and wandering now." Still feeling the effects of illness and mindful that broad public knowledge of his NAACP activities would likely end his teaching career, DeLaine remained largely in the background. In a sign of utter resignation, DeLaine sent the balance of the branch's treasury, $83.20, to the state NAACP in early February 1948. "It looks like our officers," he wrote, "are not going to do anything further. In fact I think it will be well to get all of the money out of the hands of the officers." DeLaine felt certain that the bus transportation case could revive local activism. He also believed that those with the means, those who did not depend on white people for their livelihood, had to take the lead in the fight. "When the Bus Transportation case breaks to the public," he explained, "it will give courage to many who are waiting on leadership." Nevertheless, he added, "Nothing short of a new organization is needed here." "Who will take the leadership is a problem to me. There are a number of the folks about in the county who want to do something but don't have the ability to take the leadership."[16]

Pearson, as a large landowner, had agreed, of course, to lead the way and Harold Boulware and Thurgood Marshall filed suit on his behalf in the U.S. District Court in Florence that March. In the meantime, Reverend Hinton took matters into his own hands. He appointed Pearson "temporary president" of the Clarendon NAACP branch and asked him to notify Sarah Daniels that she was to serve as vice president, DeLaine as secretary, and the Reverend J.W. Seals of St. Mark's A.M.E. as treasurer. But even before the case, *Pearson v. County Board of Education*, reached the courtroom for its scheduled opening session on June 9, it was dismissed. Clarendon County officials had "discovered" that Pearson paid property taxes in School District No. 5, not in District No. 26. Pearson's property straddled the two districts, but the new evidence left him without legal standing to sue in the district where the NAACP charged his children were denied state-funded bus transportation. Although the case went nowhere, its immediate effect was to expose the undercover activities of the faltering NAACP branch in Clarendon and open local activists to reprisal. "Somebody had to suffer for the eyes of the people being opened," DeLaine later wrote, "so the School Board discharged Mr. A.M. Anderson the principal of Scott's Branch School during the last 18 years." Sarah Daniels, similarly, lost her post as a home demonstration agent. That spring, Pearson's credit was revoked at white-owned stores and banks. In the fall, white cotton gin owners refused to gin his cotton and white farmers declined to lend him equipment to harvest his crops. As a result, Pearson was forced to watch his wheat, oats, and beans rot in the field. Even some of the black "folks were afraid to be seen talking with him on the street or in public places," his son recalled.[17]

As a result of white reaction to rising black demands in Clarendon, further work on the civil rights front appeared unlikely by the beginning of the 1948–1949 school year. In addition to targeting specific activists, Summerton officials took new steps to enforce school district boundaries, demanding that parents submit applications to attend schools in their respective districts. They also hired I.S. Benson, a man without a college degree, to assume the duties of principal at the Scott's Branch School, replacing the former and beloved school head, Maceo Anderson. In late September, DeLaine wrote Hinton and Boulware informing them that something must be done quickly to jump-start the legal campaign. "We are getting knocks on every side," he explained. "I am trying to hold every thing together as best I can." With activism on the school issue in Clarendon at a seeming standstill, Thurgood Marshall and his legal staff prepared to cease their work in the Palmetto State and move on to other cases. As Eugene Montgomery remembered it, "Clarendon County almost never happened." "They were dragging their feet in New York," he recalled, until Hinton instructed him to get in touch with the national office and set them straight. The state NAACP wanted to know what the national office was going to do. "[I]f you're not going to go for it," they declared, "let us know. We'll drop the whole thing." Soon enough, however, Marshall and his staff held a meeting in Columbia with state NAACP officials and representatives from Clarendon County, including DeLaine. At the meeting, Marshall clearly established the terms and conditions of his legal staff's continued involvement in the rural county. He informed the Clarendon contingent that the NAACP would no longer support a fight to win equal bus transportation alone and announced that if the case in Clarendon were to proceed it would need to proceed as an effort to win "Equal Educational Opportunities and Facilities for Negro Children." As DeLaine remembered it, Marshall "threatened to pull up from Clarendon County" unless he could secure a sufficient number of plaintiffs willing to lend their names to the lawsuit. The terms clearly set, DeLaine and his compatriots took up the gauntlet. They returned to Clarendon and organized a series of community meetings in black churches to rally support for the equalization suit and to encourage parents to sign their names to a petition requesting that state officials equalize school facilities.[18]

In Clarendon, black churches were at the center of the NAACP's activities. Rousing mass meetings brought members of the community together across lines of economic status and privilege. Sharecroppers, day laborers, and domestic workers filled the churches, along with the small handful of landowners, teachers, and ministers. But despite a series of mass meetings, signatures for the NAACP lawsuit proved difficult to secure during the months of March and April. By the early weeks of June, however, students in the senior class at the Scott's Branch School took the lead in the fight for educational equality and helped jump-start the ailing movement in Clarendon.

The 1948–1949 school year was the first time that the Scott's Branch School offered a twelfth grade year to its students. For members of the school's first senior class, like Robert Georgia Jr. and Abraham Smith, the additional year of school came as a welcome surprise. Georgia and Smith were accustomed to hard work and sacrifice just to attend school on a regular basis. Milking cows, collecting wood, and working in the cotton fields before and after school was a normal part of their daily routine. But their senior year experience stretched the limits of their expectations for hard work and fairness. Although students regularly contributed out-of-pocket funds for school supplies and books, the school board's replacement principal for the beloved Maceo Anderson, I.S. Benson, raised fees and, students complained, failed to supply them with the promised equipment. Students and parents held rallies to raise funds for the school and they too seemed to vanish. Benson rarely showed himself in the classroom. As the end of the school year approached, he levied a $2.50 charge for state certificates for each student and threatened to withhold the transcripts of seniors who complained about the prohibitive fee. Benson, DeLaine explained, had "misjudged the feelings, intelligence and courage of students and parents." With DeLaine's assistance, students organized and drew up a petition detailing their charges against Benson and submitted them to the superintendents and trustees of School District No. 22 and Clarendon County. When officials ignored the petition, DeLaine noted, "a flame of anger" ignited the passions of students, teachers, and parents and led to a dramatic mass meeting on June 8.[19]

The mass meeting was held in the St. Mark's A.M.E. Church and proved to be, DeLaine wrote, "the Psychological Meeting which conditioned the minds of the mass of parents in District 22. This was the time when the effort shifted from Mr. Levi Pearson to Harry Briggs, et al." It was the meeting, in other words, that transformed the struggle in Clarendon County from an individual to a collective one. Ostensibly the purpose of the meeting was to air student grievances and secure the formal support of parents to, once again, petition the appropriate school officials for redress. But DeLaine, Reverend Seals, and Levi and Hammett Pearson saw the meeting as an opportunity to rally community support for the equalization suit. In important respects, student grievances vividly encapsulated a series of issues that concerned parents deeply and that the NAACP lawsuit sought to address. African Americans actually had created the Scott's Branch School as an extension of the St. Mark's A.M.E. Church. Despite and because of the state's refusal to adequately fund the school, the black community's investment in it had been substantial over the years. Parents, it became clear at the meeting, viewed Scott's Branch as an integral part of the community and vehicle for its future advancement. Thus, the school board's firing of Anderson and Benson's subsequent tenure as principal not only highlighted the blatant and persistent inequities between white and black schools in the county in terms of funding and facilities. They also laid bare the larger issues of representation and power in school affairs. For years, the Scott's Branch School had served as a focal point of civic life among the county's black residents. The departure of Anderson and the school board's replacement signaled that parents had been locked out of the school's decision-making process and, in effect, what little control they had over their children's futures. In the mass meeting, parents demanded an acknowledged role in the school's decision-making process and they made it clear that they viewed the school as a valued community possession. They wanted the right to hold civic meetings on school grounds and they wanted to have a role in the selection of the principal charged with ensuring that the educational needs of their children were met.[20]

As DeLaine had hoped, the mass meeting rapidly moved from an airing of collective grievances to a discussion of how to address them. First, those in attendance created a Committee on Action. Then in a ritualized performance between minister and congregation, De-Laine was nominated to chair the committee despite his initial refusal to assume such a prominent leadership role. "It would damage his reputation," he argued, "and the Parents would expect too much of the committee" and his actions could mean "the end of his teaching career and maybe his life." But with a packed church urging him on, shouting "You must take the lead!" DeLaine "reluctantly" agreed to chair the committee. Indeed, through his artful performance DeLaine soon won support for the NAACP's legal campaign by suggesting that the congregation's concern for the education of their children might require a battle all the way to the U.S. Supreme Court.[21]

In the short term, the efforts of the Committee on Action to address the concerns of African Americans in Clarendon County sparked another round of white reprisals aimed at preserving white supremacy that would serve as an ominous backdrop to the NAACP's legal campaign as it wound its way through the federal court system on the road to *Brown*. On June 9, DeLaine presented the parents' grievances to Clarendon school officials, and two days later he was relieved of his teaching and administrative duties at the Silver School. In July parents petitioned the superintendent and trustees of District 22 in an effort to stem the tide of school firings in the wake of their June actions. Although school officials refused to terminate Benson's employment, parents managed to force Benson's resignation by the following October. In the meantime, efforts to secure sufficient signatures for the NAACP's school equalization petition proceeded apace. In a last-ditch effort to put a stop to mounting black activism, the superintendent of schools, H.B. Betchman, offered DeLaine the principal's post at the Scott's Branch School. As DeLaine remembered it, Betchman did not hide his intentions. "You must stop this fight," he told DeLaine. "These colored people are doing what you tell them to do and you must give them a better leadership than this." After DeLaine refused the offer, his wife, Mattie, "was drafted" by the county to serve as the school's principal, a post which, over the course of the following school year, passed through the hands of four more temporary appointees as school officials desperately sought a way to put a stop to the rebellion emanating from the school.[22]

In December, DeLaine was informed that the Ku Klux Klan was "going to take him to ride if he didn't shut his mouth." By then DeLaine was posting armed guards outside his home and warning "innocent persons" not to approach his home at night for fear that he might inadvertently shoot them. Next, DeLaine became the target of a $20,000 slander suit stemming from the ouster of I.S. Benson and, ultimately, was ordered to pay $2,700 in damages to the former Scott's Branch principal. That spring, the A.M.E. synod transferred DeLaine to the St. James A.M.E. Church in Lake City, Florence County, at the same moment that the movement in Clarendon verged on total collapse. In October his Summerton home went up in flames as the local fire department stood by and watched it burn to the ground.[23]

DeLaine was not the only person targeted for reprisal. On November 11, 1949, after six earlier petitions citing specific issues related to Benson's tenure at the Scott's Branch School brought no relief, black parents submitted a petition to school officials asking for "equal opportunities for Negro children." The petition fulfilled DeLaine's promise to Marshall and launched, once again, the legal campaign to secure equal educational opportunities for black children. As DeLaine explained, upon the filing of the equalization petition a "malicious lie was broadcast that Negroes wanted to send their children to white schools." Shortly thereafter, a third round of mass reprisals ensued. Harry Briggs, the son of sharecroppers and a World War II veteran, signed the petition and was fired from his job as a gas station attendant at a local filling station. His wife, Eliza Briggs, lost her job as a maid at the Summerton Motel. So too did Annie Gibson. Massie Solomon lost her job as a maid and her family was thrown off their land. William "Bo" Stukes was fired from a local automobile repair shop, and James Brown was let go after ten years of working for the local Esso. William "Mich" Ragin and the Reverend Seals were teaching GI classes at the Scott's Branch School and their employment was terminated. At the end of the school term, those teachers who signed their names to the petition were not offered contract renewals. When Harry Briggs sought to make ends meet by working twenty acres of rented farmland, he was denied access to credit and could not find a gin owner willing to gin his cotton. Virtually across the board, those who dared to sign the petition faced crushing economic sanctions. Many lost access to credit and to farm and business supplies. Some were fired from their jobs, while others had bank loans called in or were thrown off their land. Harry Briggs attempted to remain in Summerton, but was forced to migrate to Florida in search of work to support his family by 1953. Indeed, to openly challenge white supremacy in Clarendon County quickly became associated with leaving town. "A lot of our colored people had to leave Summerton," Minnie Ida Wright recalled, "and go off from here to get jobs to make a living. Couldn't stay here." "A lot of people had to move off the white man's place," Milison Green remembered, "a good many." "As soon as they started asking for something, then, that [NAACP] was a bad name for the whites," Joseph Richburg explained. "If you was an NAACP man, if you was on that man's place sharecropping, or if you were renting, you had to move. . . . It wasn't funny."[24]

In an important sense, however, the winter of repression only marked the beginning of a struggle that would cut to the quick of the social and symbolic power of white supremacy in the United States. By May 1950 the equalization movement in Clarendon had come to a screeching halt and the NAACP branch virtually ceased to exist. "We really dont have a real branch," DeLaine wrote to the national office in May, and now "[m]ost of the Negroes are afraid to be connected in any way whatsoever." But as local efforts ground to a standstill and recourse to local institutions was exhausted, NAACP lawyers carried the battle, once again, into the federal court system. On behalf of twenty adult petitioners, including Harry Briggs, and forty-six children who managed to withstand (at least for the time being) the unrelenting intimidation and economic sanctions of the winter months, NAACP attorneys filed *Briggs v. Elliott* in U.S. District Court for the Eastern District of South Carolina and scheduled a preliminary hearing before Judge J. Waties Waring in November. In a matter of months, what had begun as a local challenge to the inequitable practice of Jim Crow would be transformed into a direct assault on the legal foundation of racial segregation, taking on broad regional, national, and international significance. Despite the brutal repression they faced, black residents of Clarendon County welcomed the direct attack on Jim Crow. After listening to Legal Defense Fund (LDF) attorney Robert Carter inform a mass meeting that "we had to fight segregation head-on," a "gray-headed sage" sitting in the jam-packed church exclaimed to roars of laughter and applause, "We wondered how long it would take you lawyers to reach that conclusion."[25]

By the time *Briggs v. Elliott* made its way into Waring's courtroom, the native Charlestonian judge was perhaps white South Carolinians' most despised public figure. In 1945 he had divorced his native Charlestonian wife of more than thirty years and married a northerner, Elizabeth Avery, who would soon emerge as an outspoken advocate of racial equality and integration. Simultaneously, with black South Carolinians prodding him at every turn, Waring had begun a judicial transformation, ruling first for the equalization of black and white teachers' salaries and then abolishing South Carolina's white primary system. With each decision, Waring became increasingly isolated from most of his fellow white South Carolinians and increasingly radical in his opposition to segregation and white supremacy. Time and again, the state's white political officials proved incapable of even the most modest racial reforms, convincing Waring that full citizenship rights for African Americans could not be achieved within the framework of the "false doctrine and patter called 'separate but equal.'" As early as the spring of 1949, Waring openly expressed a desire to see black South Carolinians launch a direct challenge to segregation. Thus, when Thurgood Marshall and the NAACP brought the *Briggs* case before Waring, perhaps in an effort to avoid a hearing before the staunchly conservative three-judge court required for such a challenge, and failed to sufficiently raise the issue of segregation's constitutionality, Waring directed Marshall to amend the complaint to confront the issue head on and refile it before a fully empanelled district court. For Waring, whose personal and judicial transformation mirrored and gave shape to the emerging post–World War II liberal consensus on race, legal segregation was an anathema to the American way of life that now required purging. The end of Jim Crow segregation had not only become critical to the advancement of racial equality in South Carolina, it had also become, in his view, an imperative of the cold war itself. "To me the situation is clear and important," he would write in what became his dissenting opinion in *Briggs*, "particularly at this time when our national leaders are called upon to show to the world that our democracy means what it says and that this is a true democracy and there is no under-cover suppression of the rights of any citizens because of the pigmentation of their skins."[26]

Although *Briggs v. Elliott* failed to secure a victory against Jim Crow at the district court level, the case became one of five cases included in the U.S. Supreme Court's May 1954 ruling striking down the doctrine of "separate but equal" in public education. "We conclude," Chief Justice Earl Warren wrote, "that in the field of public education the doctrine of 'separate but equal' has no place. Separate educational facilities are inherently unequal." In Warren's conception, education had fast become "perhaps the most important function of the state and local governments." It represented the cornerstone of "democratic society . . . the very foundation of good citizenship." Public schools, he argued, were key instruments "in awakening the child to cultural values, in preparing him for later professional training, and helping him to adjust normally to his environment." To separate black children from white children in them "solely because of their race," he explained in the decision's most controversial passage, "generates a feeling of inferiority as to their status in the community that may affect their hearts and minds in a way unlikely to ever be undone." In striking down the legal doctrine of "separate but equal," the Supreme Court dealt a resounding blow to the legal underpinnings of Jim Crow segregation and called for a democratization of the nation's key institution of learning, socialization, and economic opportunity. The decision marked a major turning point in American jurisprudence and, in theory at least, placed the law on the side of the black struggle for civil rights.[27]

For African Americans engaged in a grassroots civil rights insurgency, however, legal victories meant far less than lived realities. The South Carolina State Conference of NAACP Branches had been on record in favor of "INTEGRATION, instead of SEGREGATION" since it issued its "Exhortation for Voluntary Action" in 1941, and the state NAACP's leadership fully supported the national organization's efforts to directly confront Jim Crow beginning in 1947. But the goal for the state NAACP's leadership and the men and women of Clarendon County never had been just about achieving the legal end of

Jim Crow or, for that matter, ensuring that black students learn in the presence of white children. Full democratic participation, equality, and the capacity to shape individual and collective futures were the objectives that animated the activism of black South Carolinians and brought them into the orbit of the NAACP's legal campaign. Equality had been the watchword of the state conference and of the movement in Clarendon County. Time and again, black South Carolinians linked equality to the realization of democracy and made it plain that the elimination of segregation represented a first step toward the achievement of both. Moreover, the right and ability to interact freely with white people was generally construed as a means to these larger ends. The state conference put it this way five years after *Brown*:

> It is our belief that timing, and not time, is a dimension of social change, and that it is the quality of the experience which matters in our common associations, and not the length of time we are exposed to one another. As a mode of human association, segregation prevents the realization of even the most elementary demands of equality, making democracy impossible. Consequently, we believe that the elimination of segregation from all aspects of life is the first step toward the realization of true democracy.[28]

Toward a New Beginning?

For black South Carolinians, and African Americans across the South, the lived reality of the years immediately following the Supreme Court's landmark ruling proved more catastrophic than transformative. The legal end of Jim Crow did not usher in a new era of equality, democracy, or even enlightened racial reform. Rather, the effective impact of *Brown* and the Supreme Court's May 1955 "Ruling of Relief," which famously instructed lower courts to implement its decision with "all deliberate speed," was to inaugurate a vicious and sustained campaign to resist school integration, crush the NAACP, and curtail the black civil rights insurgency in South Carolina. White businessmen and other leading public officials began forming White Citizens' Councils across the Palmetto State in the summer of 1955 to stem the tide of the black insurgency through the collective deployment of economic and political pressure. Some fifty-five Citizens'

Councils were in operation by July 1956. At the same time, the South
Carolina legislature took steps to vigorously oppose the full implications of *Brown* and vanquish proponents of integration. At the behest
of the Gressette Committee, an advisory committee so named for its
chairman, State Senator L. Marion Gressette, the legislature repealed
the state's compulsory school attendance law. It provided local school
officials with authority to sell or lease school property and it prohibited automatic renewal of teacher contracts. Harkening back to the
Nullification Crisis of 1832, the legislature passed an "interposition
resolution" in 1956 declaring that the state of South Carolina maintained the right to "interpose" its authority "between its people and
the federal government."

The legislature then took aim at the NAACP, borrowing from the
tactics used to persecute alleged Communist Party members and sym-
pathizers earlier in the decade. It charged the organization with advocating an agenda "contrary to the principles upon which the economic
and social life of our state rests." Lawmakers unanimously adopted a
resolution requesting that the U.S. attorney general list the NAACP
"as a subversive organization so that it may be kept under the proper
surveillance and that all citizens of the United States may have ample
warning of the danger to our way of life which lurks in such an organization." Next, they barred NAACP members from employment in
local, county, and state government. As a condition of employment,
teachers were required to divulge their personal and family ties to the
association and declare their personal views on school integration.[29]

For black residents of Clarendon County the post-*Brown* racist counterinsurgency struck with particularly horrifying force. The
NAACP's campaign for equality in public education and an end to Jim
Crow reached a crescendo just as increasing numbers of small-scale
farmers, sharecroppers, and laborers found it virtually impossible to
make a living in South Carolina and across the region. In the twenty
years following the *Brown* decision, the number of black farmers in the
county plummeted, while the total black population, as a proportion
of the total population, slid by 10 percent. As the need for black labor
fell, little was left to hold back the onset of a merciless terror campaign. On October 5, 1955, DeLaine's Lake City church was torched.
Three days later he received a death threat warning him to leave town
voluntarily or by force of dynamite. Then, on the night of October
10, DeLaine and his wife were awakened by gunshots fired into their

home. After whisking his wife out the back door with the help of a neighbor, Webb Eaddy, DeLaine grabbed his rifle and stood guard outside under the cover of darkness. Once again, a passing car fired shots toward his home. This time, DeLaine returned fire. "Then," he recalled, "I made up my mind to run for my life." DeLaine jumped in his car and headed for safe harbor in the city of Florence, managing to elude would-be-assailants along the way. The next day he was reunited with his wife, and friends spirited the couple across the state border to Charlotte, North Carolina. Ultimately, DeLaine would make his way to New York where he learned that Florence officials had charged him with assault and battery with a deadly weapon. Now a fugitive from South Carolina justice, DeLaine remained in New York for the remainder of his life, never to return to the state he had fought so hard to change.[30]

While DeLaine was forced to make his final exit, the White Citizens' Council in Clarendon stepped up efforts to resist school integration and crush the local black insurgency. The force of white economic sanctions, the threat of massive violence, and the decline of necessary agricultural labor proved devastating to African Americans and wreaked havoc on the county's long-term social and economic well-being. "It dried Summerton up," Joseph Richburg explained, "it dried them up. . . . See, it wasn't much money out in the field, but it was so many of them, you know. A lot of people leave and went up North just like I did." Like so many others, Richburg and his family left Clarendon in search of a better life elsewhere. For the Briggs family, life in Clarendon turned increasingly bleak. Harry and Eliza Briggs had hoped that their efforts would improve their children's educational and life opportunities. "My children didn't get it," though, the education that is, Eliza Briggs later explained. Even worse, she thought, was that her husband's efforts and the crushing economic sanctions imposed on him in Clarendon, meant that their children "didn't have a chance to raise up with their daddy" because, of course, "he had to leave." Indeed, by the time Clarendon County finally submitted to a token desegregation plan in 1965, following yet another lawsuit brought by black parents, the Briggs children were grown. They had packed their bags and headed north to New York City. Harry and Eliza Briggs would eventually join them. Harry found work as a parking attendant and, as she had in Clarendon, Eliza took a job as a chambermaid. Back in Clarendon, white resistance to school integration persisted.

Under a 1970 court order designed to achieve a more equitable racial balance in the county school system, white parents entirely withdrew their support from the public schools. With a single exception, white children enrolled in Clarendon Hall, a Baptist parochial school, and other private academies, or left the county altogether.[31]

In the short term, the efforts of white South Carolinians to cripple the NAACP and the black fight for self-determination and equality were highly effective. Between 1955 and 1957 the number of NAACP branches in South Carolina fell from eighty-four to thirty-one, the lowest total since the organization began its rapid expansion in 1943. Accordingly, membership in the organization plunged from more than 8,266 to 2,202, threatening to return the organization to the brutal days and ineffectual ways of the 1920s and early 1930s.[32] At the same time, key members of the aging generation of civil rights activists who had been so instrumental in coordinating, expanding, and helping to promote the fighting spirit of the state organization in the 1940s had begun a slow retreat from the movement's front lines. In 1949 John McCray had covered the rape trial and subsequent execution of a twenty-four-year-old black man, Willie Tolbert, only to be charged with "maliciously and deliberately" maligning the character of the man's alleged victim, a white teenage girl, under the provisions of an antiquated criminal-libel statute. In 1952, after allegedly violating the terms of the probation he had agreed to serve to avoid jail time, McCray was sentenced to and served out a sixty-day term on the Newberry County chain gang. By the end of 1954 McCray's *Lighthouse and Informer*, the longtime propaganda arm of the state conference, had been put out of business, the casualty of mounting debt and growing personal animosity between McCray and Modjeska Simkins.[33]

For years, Simkins and her family-owned Victory Savings Bank had supported McCray's personal and business finances. Following McCray's term on the chain gang, Simkins helped keep the operations of the *Lighthouse and Informer* from collapsing. But when Simkins demanded that McCray begin paying off his unmet financial obligations in the spring of 1954, McCray lashed out. In a paranoid outburst reminiscent of his mid-1940s clash with Osceola McKaine, McCray publicly charged Simkins with dominating the activities of the state conference and attempting to "take over" the PDP. Simkins, in turn, resolved to put the ailing *Lighthouse and Informer* and its combative editor out of their (and her own) misery. Before year's end, she had the contents of the newspaper's home at 1022½ Washington Street, including the paper's then existing back issues, sold off to satisfy a portion of its debts. By then Simkins had herself become the target of a red-baiting campaign prosecuted by South Carolina political officials in cooperation with the *Charleston News and Courier*. Simkins would later deny that her ties to and vocal support of radical black activists, including Harlem city councilmen, Benjamin Davis, Paul Robeson, and W.E.B. Du Bois, contributed to her increasingly strained relationship with the NAACP. However, for the first time in seventeen years, Simkins was not nominated to serve as secretary of the state conference in 1957. As she understood it, the state conference had simply lost its edge in the repressive atmosphere of the mid-1950s. Only a year earlier James Hinton's Columbia home had been hit with a barrage of gunfire and, despite the swirl of events following in the wake of *Brown*, the association failed to call an executive board meeting or hold that year's annual state conference gathering. "It seems like some kind of pressure was put on [Hinton] from some element in the power structure," Simkins explained, "that caused him to . . . not push the program he had." By the fall of 1958 Hinton had formally resigned his post as state conference president, marking, along with Simkins's ouster and McCray's demise, a symbolic closing to a crucial chapter in the ongoing struggle for self-determination and equality in South Carolina.[34]

The NAACP's travails in South Carolina were by no means isolated. In the NAACP's southeast region alone, an area encompassing Florida, Georgia, Mississippi, Alabama, Tennessee, North Carolina, and South Carolina, massive resistance helped cut the organization's membership nearly in half between 1955 and 1957, dropping from 52,375 to 26,955. In Alabama the organization was banned, while in Louisiana and Texas state-imposed injunctions decimated NAACP activity and slashed membership rolls. Nationally, under pressure from southern members of Congress, the Internal Revenue Service launched an investigation into the relationship between Marshall's tax-exempt LDF and the tax-paying NAACP, forcing their complete separation. At precisely the moment when the NAACP ought to have been working to turn its monumental legal victory over Jim Crow into a sustained effort to mobilize a broader mass insurgency, the organization was thrown on the defensive. Rather than expanding its membership, publicizing its decades-long work on behalf of African Americans, and turning its revolutionary legal victory into meaningful reforms, the NAACP was forced to fight a rearguard battle against the forces of massive resistance.[35]

In important respects, *Brown* represented a culmination. It was the product of the NAACP's decades-long social and legal campaign to destroy Jim Crow segregation. What had begun in the crucible of the Progressive Era as a top-down campaign waged by a class of urban and professional reformers, both white and black, had become a battle that included a broad cross section of African Americans and stretched into some of the nation's poorest and least developed regions by the opening years of the 1950s. In South Carolina the NAACP had posed a challenge to the paternalistic dynamics of the ideology and practice of racial uplift. It had become a means of tying black South Carolinians together in new ways, connecting them to a broader national and international arena of struggle, and, in doing so, helped to loosen traditional hierarchies and power dynamics at the local level. By the 1940s the national association, in dynamic tension with local branches and their various organizational fronts, had begun chiseling away at the legal underpinnings of Jim Crow segregation and political disfranchisement, encouraging the growth and increasingly aggressive posture of the black struggle for self-determination and equality. Indeed, as the cold war worked to arrest the New Deal era Popular Front, a broad-based African American social insurgency rattled the very social and institutional foundations of white supremacy and overturned the legal basis of its most glaring manifestation, Jim Crow.

As significant as the NAACP's legal and symbolic victory in *Brown* was, however, the emerging presence and power of those on the margins of history and the periphery of power in the association's efforts was even more significant. *Brown* was made possible by a civil rights insurgency that had only just begun to give voice to the needs and concerns of the nation's most marginalized and powerless people as the cold war emerged as a significant force in American and international life. And for those engaged in this expanding social insurgency, the legal assault on Jim Crow and calls for an end to the practice of racial segregation were not understood as ends in themselves. African Americans in Clarendon County and the larger civil rights movement were guided by a desire for equality and the ability to shape their own futures. Both objectives, the South Carolina State Conference had long maintained, were essential for the "realization of true democracy." Massive resistance to *Brown*, no matter how effective in the short term, did not permanently arrest this larger movement that had given rise to the NAACP's landmark Supreme Court victory; black people had faced such opposition and terror many times before. To the contrary, in the aftermath of *Brown* and amid the rising tide of massive resistance, the movement began searching for new directions forward. In the process of struggle, the movement's mass base would expand once again, endowing the civil rights insurgency of the late 1950s and early 1960s with its greatest source of promise and greatest potential for power. It was a mass base that was both cause and effect of the NAACP's landmark legal victory and a mass base that would demand not only an end to the practice of Jim Crow, but a remaking of the nation's social, political, and economic structure.

Conclusion

Movement, Memory, and American Democracy

In South Carolina, the future of the movement was registered at the precise moment that the movement of the past seemed on the precipice of total collapse. As African Americans did across the South in the wake of *Brown*, black parents in Orangeburg, South Carolina, organized a petition drive through their local NAACP branch to demand an immediate end to segregation in the town's public schools. Orangeburg was home to South Carolina State and Claflin College and was fast emerging as a center of civil rights activism in the state and region. In the summer of 1955, fifty-seven adults signed the petition, including sharecroppers, domestic servants, business owners, and skilled craftsman. In short order, the local white-owned newspaper, *The Times and Democrat*, published the full text of the petition along with the names of those who signed it. What followed was a pattern repeated across the South in response to similar petition drives. Orangeburg's white business leaders gathered, organized a White Citizens' Council, and turned their economic power against the petitioners and members of the NAACP. Black employees were fired, sharecroppers evicted, credit and charge accounts revoked, and white-owned supply companies refused to deliver goods to black retailers. In nearby Clarendon County, black residents responded to similar tactics by organizing an informal boycott of businesses owned by Citizens' Council members, but met little success. In Orangeburg, by contrast, the counter-boycott lasted nearly a year. And while the overwhelming might of white economic and political power ultimately crushed it, the black consumer boycott reflected and gave shape to a post-*Brown* movement in the making.[1]

215

"Don't Buy Where You Can't Work" campaigns and other forms of consumer boycotts had been deployed throughout the urban North beginning in Chicago in 1929 and then spread to Detroit, Cleveland, and Harlem in the 1930s, as well as to Washington, D.C., Baltimore, and Richmond in the Upper South. While selective buying campaigns, including the 1946 Anti–Jim Crow Sunday protest in Columbia, were utilized episodically in the Deep South before the 1950s, the movement in Orangeburg marked the advent of the full-blown consumer boycott in the region and signaled the increasing exchange of ideas and tactics across North-South lines, as well as new ties made possible, in part, by a fast developing knowledge- and consumer-based national economy. In Orangeburg, African Americans targeted the particular businesses owned by Citizens' Council members, but they also called for broader boycotts of national brand-name products sold by the leaders of massive resistance. Orangeburg's mayor, Robert H. Jennings, was a leading member of the Citizens' Council and owner of the local Coca-Cola bottling company, the Palmetto Bakery, one of the largest bread suppliers in the state, and Orangeburg Fuel and Ice. Boycotters refused to patronize his businesses and added brand names such as Coca-Cola, Sunbeam Bread, Standard Oil, the Ford Motor Company, the Lance Company, maker of "Nabs," the Curtis Company, makers of "Baby Ruth" candy bars, and Lays, the popular potato chip and popcorn company, to its list of corporations not to patronize and products not to purchase. As their boycott took hold in Orangeburg, it garnered extensive coverage in the national black press and support from the state and national NAACP. Just as significantly, the tactic proved inspiring to an ultimately more successful effort underway in Montgomery, Alabama. At the request of the Reverend Ralph Abernathy, boycott leaders would travel to Alabama during the Montgomery Bus Boycott to share their experiences and answer questions at a mass meeting in Martin Luther King Jr.'s Dexter Avenue Baptist Church.[2]

By the winter of 1955–1956, the NAACP-sponsored consumer boycott began to give shape to a broader movement in Orangeburg and the nation when students at South Carolina State joined the campaign. Students refused to eat the bread and drink the milk supplied to the school's cafeteria by the Palmetto Bakery and Coble Dairy and demanded that the university discontinue serving the bread and milk in the cafeteria. When school officials refused, students boycotted the cafeteria altogether. And when state officials launched a probe into "subversive activities" on campus aimed at ferreting out NAACP members and supporters, South Carolina State faculty members overwhelmingly endorsed resolutions defending their academic freedom and right to support the NAACP. In response to the increasingly aggressive state investigation into subversive activities, 1,500 students boycotted classes and demanded the removal of state law enforcement officials. "This is not a mental institution nor penal institution," exclaimed student leader Fred Moore, "but an institution of higher learning, attended by free people in a free land." Student expulsions followed, but the student and faculty actions pointed toward the increasing significance of the university in the battles ahead, as well as the emergence of a new cohort of activists enrolled in the region's black colleges. In less than four years, Orangeburg became the site of a full-fledged student movement, led in part by Charles "Chuck" McDew, the future chairmen of the Student Nonviolent Coordinating Committee (SNCC). In the wake of the February 1, 1960, student sit-in in Greensboro, North Carolina, McDew and other students from South Carolina State helped lead the first wave of sit-ins in Orangeburg's Kress Department Store. In response to mass demonstrations in Orangeburg's downtown business district, local law enforcement officials unleashed water hoses and tear gas on the students and arrested four hundred demonstrators on March 15. The following day, *The New York Times* ran a front-page story with a picture of the wet and battered students confined in a makeshift outdoor stockade, helping to fan the flames of the sit-in movement across the region and nation.[3]

From consumer boycott to sit-in, black South Carolinians began the process of reinventing the movement through a creative refashioning of old institutions and ideas to meet the challenges of shifting circumstances. In 1957, James T. McCain, a cousin of Osceola McKaine and founding member and president of the Sumter NAACP, launched the Congress of Racial Equality's (CORE) first sustained organizing drive in the South. Founded in 1942 by a radical band of interracial pacifist intellectuals in Chicago, who drew inspiration from the Indian revolutionary Mahatma Gandhi, CORE had pioneered the use of nonviolent direct action tactics in a 1947 challenge to segregation in interstate bus transportation, known as the "Journey of Reconciliation." In an effort to reenergize the organization and begin a nonviolent campaign of direct action aimed at ending the practice of

Jim Crow, CORE hired McCain, whose work with the NAACP had already cost him a principal's post in violence-torn Clarendon County. Using his extensive NAACP contacts and ties to the Palmetto State Teachers' Association, McCain launched CORE's southern campaign in South Carolina. Between 1957 and 1959, McCain helped create nine CORE chapters in the state and began turning South Carolina into a laboratory for the use of nonviolent direct action. From Beaufort, to Charleston, to Florence, to Greenville, to Camden, Jasper, Marion, Sumter, and even Clarendon County, McCain canvassed in an effort to resuscitate a troubled movement. In June 1958, CORE held its national convention at Frogmore on St. Helena Island and by July a CORE chapter in Columbia began planning for nonviolent demonstrations on city busses and in eating facilities and shopping areas. In October, the Columbia CORE carried out its first "action program" by testing the eating facilities at the Columbia airport. On February 12, 1960, with McCain's assistance, students at Rock Hill, South Carolina's Friendship Junior College, launched the first round of sit-ins in the state, less than two weeks after events in Greensboro sparked the sit-in movement. It was in Rock Hill, less than a year later, that students at Friendship Junior College, along with CORE field secretary, Tom Gaither, refused to post bail after being arrested for sitting-in at a segregated lunch counter, helping to launch a "jail-in" movement that was joined by Diane Nash, Charles Jones, Ruby Doris Smith, and Charles Sherrod, all influential members of the recently created SNCC. Indeed, the protests in Rock Hill provided a spark to a student movement during a lull in activism and became, write August Meier and Elliott Rudwick, "the model for the jail-in strategy of the Freedom Rides of 1961, and several subsequent major campaigns which CORE conducted in the South."[4]

McCain's efforts in South Carolina did not, however, merely introduce CORE's brand of nonviolent direct action to the state. His efforts also introduced the militantly interracial CORE to black South Carolinians' ongoing struggle for self-determination and equality. Time and again, as McCain attempted to rally black Carolinians to a campaign of nonviolent direct action and to convince them to identify fully with the interracial congress, he found himself immersed in ongoing struggles to secure the right to vote—that is, to secure the right of self-representation. For black South Carolinians, interracial alliances and integration were rarely viewed as objectives independent of empowerment, and the right to represent themselves in the civic arena had long taken precedence over both. Much to the dismay of CORE's national leadership, McCain insisted that the struggle for the right to vote constituted a form of nonviolent direct action in the repressive conditions of South Carolina. He also encountered substantial difficulty creating CORE chapters that operated independently from existing NAACP branches and leadership. The leadership of CORE chapters in Spartanburg and Greenville, for example, it became quite clear, were "simply the leadership of the local NAACP wearing new hats." Despite their frustration, McCain's work in South Carolina proved an education for CORE's leadership. Reluctantly, they came to acknowledge the significance of the vote to the southern black struggle, as well as the direct action facets of the voter registration process. Even before CORE turned its attention to voter registration efforts in Mississippi in the summer of 1964, the organization was responsible for registering some sixteen thousand black voters and helped to infuse the black struggle for civil rights in South Carolina with the weapon of nonviolent direct action. And following passage of the 1965 Voting Rights Act, McCain and CORE managed to register thirty-seven thousand black South Carolinians in twenty-four counties. In Clarendon County, with CORE's assistance black voter registration increased from three hundred to five thousand between June 1965 and February 1966, and two African Americans ran unsuccessfully for town council. Statewide, black South Carolinians proved the balance of power in the election of Democratic candidates to Congress and the governor's office in the fall of 1966. By 1974 thirteen African Americans served in the state's House of Representatives.[5]

At the same time that McCain reenergized the black struggle for civil rights in South Carolina and the nation, Septima Poinsette Clark emerged once again as a leading light in the civil rights insurgency, connecting the past to the future and helping to crystallize the radical democratic significance of the civil rights movement. In 1945, a truck farmer on Johns Island named Esau Jenkins bought a bus to transport the island's children to the public schools of Charleston, a path Clark once traveled by boat. At the time, Jenkins was a member of the executive board of the Charleston NAACP and an activist in the Progressive Democratic Party. On his daily ventures to Charleston, Jenkins not only transported school children, but also began transporting black women employed as domestic servants and by the American

Tobacco Company's cigar plant, as well as men employed as long-shoreman on the city's wharves. By 1948 he had turned the bus into a roving voter education and registration vehicle and formed what he called the Progressive Club, a quasi-political organization that he also envisioned as a consumer cooperative. Tying together the issues of literacy, political empowerment, and economic cooperation, Jenkins's work represented an effort to put the NAACP's and PDP's challenge to the white primary into practice and to secure a better life for the residents of Johns Island.

As Jenkins pursued his initiatives, Septima Clark returned to teaching in Charleston with the assistance of Wil Lou Gray, one of the state's leading white educational reformers active in interracial work. In Charleston, Clark worked with the YWCA and the NAACP and was introduced to the Highlander Folk School, the New Deal era labor organizing center run by Miles and Zilphia Horton in Monteagle, Tennessee, by the YWCA's executive secretary in Charleston, a white woman named Anna Kelley. In late June 1954, Clark attended a workshop at Highlander, where the Hortons had begun turning the labor-organizing center into a center for civil rights activism. Later that summer Clark returned to Monteagle for another workshop with her colleague from the Charleston NAACP, Esau Jenkins. Increasingly intrigued by the rich history of low country activism, which included the 1945–1946 American Tobacco Company strike and Jenkins's on-going work on the Progressive Club, the Hortons investigated the possibility of turning Johns Island into a demonstration community for the establishment of a citizenship school. With funding from the Emil Schwartzhaupt Foundation, the Hortons began developing the citizenship school idea on the island, tapping into decades of activism and continuing the movement's trend toward empowering the voices of the nation's most marginalized and least empowered people. When her teaching contract was not renewed in 1956 because of her NAACP membership, Clark was hired by Highlander to run its workshops on the island she had grown to know well. Along with her cousin Bernice Robinson, Clark commenced full-time work at the Johns Island Citizenship School in 1957.[6]

Through the Highlander Folk School and Martin Luther King Jr.'s Southern Christian Leadership Conference (SCLC), which hired Clark to run its citizenship education and voting rights efforts in 1961, Clark and Robinson helped speed the process of developing an organizing tradition and philosophy that drew from and wove together decades of black women's club and social welfare work, labor organizing, and civil rights activism with profound implications for the movement and the larger world. At the center of their vision was the belief in the necessity of democratizing all human relationships and creating the social, political, and economic conditions that would allow all human beings to possess the necessary tools required to shape their world in accordance with their individual and collective sense of its possibilities. It was a vision that challenged the sectarian tendencies of radical struggles in the past and called for the development of "group-centered" leadership that represented a challenge to male-centered and top-down leadership styles. "We affirm our faith in democracy as a goal that will bring about dignity and freedom to all; in a democracy as an *expanding* concept encompassing human relationships from the smallest community organization to international structure; and *permeating all economic, social and political activities*," Clark wrote in a pamphlet for Highlander in 1960. "Democracy," she continued, "to us means that membership in the human family entitles all to freedom of thought and religion, to equal rights to livelihood, education, and health; to equal opportunity to participate in the cultural life of a community and to equal access to public services." Advocating unionization, farmers' cooperatives, and an end to "legally entrenched discrimination and segregation," Clark called for a "diversity of approach" to struggle. "With a democratic goal," she explained, "we are in a position to fight anything that gets in the way, whether it be totalitarian communism, or fascism or monopoly dominated capitalism." No single approach, no single institution, or static ideology, she was saying, could bring about the kind of democratic society she imagined. Building on her years engaged in struggle, she viewed democracy as a goal and a process—in short, a way of living.[7]

Clark's own thinking and activism had changed significantly since her first teaching job on the island she once thought "a strange land that might have been, for all I knew about it, on the other side of the Atlantic." In the process of struggle—in the movement for black civil rights—Clark came to embrace and sought to create a radical democratic vision of the United States and the larger world. Her vision was radical precisely because it sought to give voice to those without a voice and to empower those residing on the margins of history and the periphery of power. It was a radical vision because it sought the creation of the social, political, and economic conditions necessary to allow all human beings to be meaningful participants in the decision-making processes that govern human life and shape the course of the world's future. This was not a vision hatched in universities or drawn from the words of grand orators. Rather, it was a vision forged in struggle, nurtured in the ongoing quest for black self-determination and equality, and made possible by the shifting currents of the civil rights movement in South Carolina.

In the traditional telling and popular understanding of "The Civil Rights Movement," the radical democratic meaning of a movement dedicated to unchaining the capacity of ordinary people for self-representation is all too muted. In this traditional narrative, The Civil Rights Movement begins with the NAACP's 1954 Supreme Court victory in *Brown v. Board of Education* and ends in the wake of congressional passage of the Civil Rights Act of 1964 and Voting Rights Act of 1965. In between these legal and legislative triumphs, Martin Luther King Jr. is launched onto the national stage; black college students sit in at lunch counters around the South; CORE and SNCC launch the Freedom Rides and major voting rights campaigns; the racist southern sheriff Eugene "Bull" Connor attacks young black demonstrators with police dogs and fire hoses in Birmingham, Alabama; King delivers his "I Have a Dream Speech" at the March on Washington; and the American public and U.S. Congress are moved to put an end to the odious practice of Jim Crow segregation. Ultimately, American ideals are triumphant and the nation's democratic institutions are validated. Only growing black frustration in the urban North and increasingly radical calls for Black Power and economic justice put an end to a movement that elevated the consciousness of a nation and redeemed its soul.

For the past twenty years, scholars have worked to transform the traditional telling and popular understanding of The Civil Rights Movement. Rather than focusing on the primary leaders, major organizations, key events, and national institutions, they have sought to recover the "hidden" history of the movement, a movement of ordinary African Americans struggling for an expansive vision of freedom, not merely for an end to Jim Crow and the possession of formal civil rights. In doing so, scholars have uncovered a rich history of black protest and activism in communities throughout the United States that refuses to fit neatly within the traditional narrative of The Civil Rights

Movement. They have also stretched the chronology of the movement backward in time, discovering as Jacquelyn Dowd Hall writes,
"the story of a 'long civil rights movement' that took root in the
liberal and radical milieu of the late 1930s" and that "was intimately
tied to the 'rise and fall of the New Deal Order.'" It was in the years
of the Great Depression and World War II, the argument goes, that a
broadly based social movement of African Americans and their white
allies challenged not only racial discrimination in the southern United
States, but also economic exploitation and colonial subjugation on a
global scale. Joining together the forces of civil rights organizations,
including the National Negro Congress and the NAACP, with the
CIO and the Communist Party, this Popular Front coalition provided
a critique of capitalism, racism, and colonialism that galvanized black
activism for nearly a decade. Only the rising winds of the cold war and
emerging anticommunist hysteria led to the break up of this coalition
and contributed to a moderation of the black struggle for freedom,
which had become by the end of the 1940s, scholars contend, a more
narrow struggle for civil rights shaped principally by the NAACP's
legal, constitutionally based agenda, and animated by southern-based
protest organizations inspired by the black church. Such a shift, writes
Bob Korstad, "cast a long shadow over the second half of the twentieth century, [ensuring] that when the civil rights struggle of the 1960s
emerged it would have a different social character and different political agenda, which in the end proved inadequate to the immense social
problems that lay before it."[8]

In its emphasis on the constantly shifting, improvisational character of black activism and the centrality of black demands for self-
determination and equality to struggles for civil rights across the
divides of time and space, *Democracy Rising* represents a challenge to
the traditional narrative of The Civil Rights Movement and to the new
story of the "long civil rights movement." Although seldom considered in the same light as places such as Mississippi and Alabama, which
garnered national media attention during the ferment of the turbulent
1960s, or understood in relationship to the urban North and West,
South Carolina was crucial to the development of the black struggle
for civil rights in the South and the larger nation. In a very real sense,
the civil rights movement moved through the Palmetto State, and in
the Palmetto State the movement moved through the NAACP. By
the first years of the 1960s, the NAACP had been at the forefront of

the African American struggle for civil rights and America's ongoing struggle with democracy for more than forty years. During the mid-1940s, the era so romanticized by current-day scholarship, Jim Crow segregation and the near total denial of the right of self-representation to African Americans proved formidable obstacles to movements dedicated to an expansive conception of justice and democracy. But with black South Carolinians in the lead, the NAACP defeated the white primary, dismantled the legal underpinnings of Jim Crow, and by the first years of the 1950s created an opening for the nation's most marginalized and least powerful citizens to speak and act for themselves in a way and on a scale barely imaginable only decades before. With its victory in *Brown v. Board of Education*, the NAACP issued a dramatic challenge to white supremacy and to conceptions of America as a nation for white men only. In doing so, the association literally changed the terms of the debate and altered the very context in which the African American struggle for civil rights maneuvered.

Despite and because of the NAACP's victories, the organization and its legal-legislative agenda have been understood by critics, past and present, as the antithesis of radicalism. Born in Denmark, South Carolina, in 1944, the future black militant Cleveland Sellers came of age at precisely the moment at which the NAACP's greatest victories were enshrouded in the crush of massive resistance. Compared to the brashness of the student sit-ins and the forceful demands of Black Power, the NAACP appeared, he would write, "too slow, too courteous, too deferential and too ineffectual" for his generation. "Our parents had the NAACP," he explained, and while the association's practices of "pursuing 'test cases' through the courts, [and] using laws and the Constitution to fight racial discrimination" may have "suited their temperaments," his generation "needed something more." For Sellers, much like the Young Turks of the 1930s, the NAACP, and the rights struggle associated with it, was too legalistic and bureaucratic, too gradual and narrow in approach, and too defined by the existing institutional arrangements of American society to adequately address the nation's racial and economic inequalities. Today, many scholars offer a similar critique, counter-posing the supposed moderation of the NAACP and movement of the early 1960s, with the "forgotten" labor-based movement of the New Deal era and the radical demands of late 1960s Black Power. Although each critique represents a challenge to the traditional Civil Rights Movement narrative, they too misconstrue the full meaning and significance of the NAACP and the movement it shaped so profoundly.[9]

Democracy Rising provides a new way to think about and understand both the NAACP and the African American struggle for civil rights through its refusal to choose between a triumphant Civil Rights Movement narrative, one which excoriates the movement's radicalism, celebrates its restraint, and reinforces a conservative call for a "color blind" America, and a tragic narrative, which excoriates the movement's limits and romanticizes either a New Deal or Black Power era movement dedicated to the structural overhaul of American institutions. Black South Carolinians working in and through the NAACP seldom engaged in struggles for the sake of winning legal victories or for securing the possession of abstract constitutional rights. And seldom did black South Carolinians see the possibility or desirability of separating civil rights from the larger objective of exercising greater control over their own lives and fundamentally altering the distribution of opportunity and economic justice in America. To the contrary, the struggles of black South Carolinians have long been about a larger quest for self-determination and equality, about the right and ability to shape individual and collective lives in a manner consistent with the grandest visions of democracy. At its best, the African American civil rights insurgency confronted the world as black people encountered it, encouraged its participants to imagine new realities, and refused to be bound by existing institutional arrangements. For the men and women engaged in struggle, the challenge was to creatively utilize the means, methods, ideas, and institutions available to them to reshape their world. In struggles that spanned more than five decades, the NAACP proved the black civil rights insurgency's primary vehicle, giving shape to individual lives, local communities, South Carolina, the United States, and the larger world.

The NAACP's victory in *Brown v. Board of Education* and its subsequent efforts to secure passage of the Civil Rights Act of 1964 and Voting Rights Act of 1965 marked the legal and legislative end of racial discrimination in the United States. But these legal and legislative triumphs did not mark the end of racial or economic inequality, nor did they signal the end of the African American civil rights insurgency. Rather, they marked the onset of a new phase of struggle in which the ongoing quest for self-determination and equality could begin to assume new life. And that is what it did.[10]

In South Carolina, the African American civil rights insurgency has continued to move between victory and violence, progress and defeat. As racial violence escalated across the nation in the late 1960s and the Vietnam War raged abroad and in the streets of America, black South Carolinians remained at the forefront of the movement. Between 1965 and 1968, efforts to integrate Orangeburg's All-Star Bowling Lane gave shape to ongoing civil rights activism in the state and region. In the fall of 1967, after becoming a leading figure in SNCC and the larger Black Power movement, Cleveland Sellers returned to South Carolina to begin organizing black college students at South Carolina State and Claflin College. "By working with students," he explained, "I believed I could develop a movement focusing attention of the problems of poor blacks in South Carolina . . . [and] that my efforts might also encourage some of SNCC's members to return to the South and begin organizing again." Then on the night of February 8, 1968, as black students gathered at the edge of campus to protest the continued segregation of the bowling alley and the refusal of city officials to allow an organized demonstration of the "hated symbol of discrimination," state police fired shotguns and .38 caliber pistols into the crowd of demonstrators. Although students contributed to the conflict by throwing incendiary devices and other projectiles at the police, the hail of indiscriminate gunfire struck and killed three students, Samuel Hammond Jr., Delano Middleton, and Henry Smith, and wounded another twenty-seven. For his part in the demonstration, Sellers was charged with a series of offenses, including arson, inciting to riot, and assault and battery with the intent to kill. Two years later he would be convicted on a misdemeanor rioting charge. The "Orangeburg Massacre," as it became known, ensured that South Carolina would not avoid the racial violence that swept the nation in the late 1960s. It also stood as a visible reminder of the depth of the struggle still to be waged for racial justice in the Palmetto State.[11]

Just a year later, following the murder of Martin Luther King Jr. on a hotel balcony in Memphis and another summer of racial violence, hope for change emerged in Charleston when black hospital workers at the University of South Carolina's Medical College Hospital (MCH) demanded recognition of their union, 1199B of the New York–based Hospital Workers Union 1199. Like the sanitation workers' strike a year earlier in Memphis that garnered the support of King and the SCLC, black workers' demands for union recognition were closely linked to demands for dignity and respect. Sparked by the firing of twelve union activists, between March 20 and June 27 the black and largely female workforce at MCH waged a strike campaign for union recognition that highlighted the racial and economic inequities of the fast-growing healthcare industry, an industry at the heart of an emerging knowledge- and technology-driven national economy. The strike brought together labor, civil rights, and Black Power activists and turned national attention, once again, to the movement in South Carolina. A twenty-six-year-old nurse named Mary Moultrie, the daughter of a Charleston Navy Yard worker, led the strike. She was assisted by a number of longtime South Carolina activists, including Lillie Mae Doster, a leading figure in the FTA, who had been active in the 1945–1946 tobacco workers' strike; Isaiah Bennett, the president of the FTA's successor organization, the Retail, Wholesale, Department Store Union (RWDSU); and William Saunders, a thirty-seven-year-old army veteran and militant proponent of Black Power, whose activism was shaped by his experiences working with Esau Jenkins's voter registration efforts on Johns Island. Each provided crucial links between the strike and South Carolina's ongoing civil rights insurgency.[12]

The strike was punctuated on May 11, when the SCLC helped spearhead a "Mother's Day March," in which the United Automobile Workers' Walter Reuther and the SCLC's Ralph Abernathy and Coretta Scott King linked arms with the strikers who carried signs demanding "Human Dignity," "Justice," and "Human Rights." In the wake of King's assassination and the sanitation workers' campaign in Memphis, the SCLC chose Charleston as a site for a major civil disobedience campaign and worked closely with national and local leaders of 1199. Throughout the spring months, SCLC organizers, including Andrew Young and Hosea Williams, organized in support of the striking workers and carried out mass marches and confrontations with local authorities, resulting in mass arrests and a confrontation with National Guard troops. Throughout the campaign, the SCLC's constant declaration that "We Are Somebody" tapped into deeply held sentiment among strikers and a movement animated by a drive for self-determination and equality. "We are tired of asking and begging," Mary Moultrie explained in words that echoed across decades of struggle. "Now we are demanding."[13]

Ultimately, the strike achieved only modest concrete gains. The hospital rehired the fired workers, white nurses agreed to the return of the strikers to MCH, workers received a wage increase, and the union managed to secure a new grievance procedure along with vague promises of a voluntary union dues check-off system. But the failure of the workers to secure recognition of their union highlighted the continued denial of black South Carolinians' right of self-representation. Despite decades of struggle through the NAACP, the PDP, labor unions, and the myriad organizations chronicled in *Democracy Rising*, the right of self-representation remained the most pressing concern confronting black South Carolinians in the first years of the 1970s. Without it, many of their basic needs and visions of a more just and democratic future would remain disproportionately in the hands of others. As it had been for decades, that fight for self-representation was (and continues to be) inextricably tied to the right to vote and to full recognition of the humanity of black people.

From the Voting Rights Act of 1965 to the present day, the civil rights insurgency in South Carolina has battled for the right to vote and for full representation in the decision-making processes shaping local communities and the larger world. By 1974 thirteen African Americans had begun service in the state's House of Representatives, the first blacks to serve in South Carolina's General Assembly since 1902. It would not be until 1984, however, that longtime NAACP stalwart and veteran of the civil rights insurgency, I. DeQuincey Newman, would become the first African American to serve in the South Carolina State Senate since Reconstruction. Following the Voting Rights Act of 1965, South Carolina abandoned a system in which single senators served each of the state's forty-six counties, in favor of a system based largely on multi-member districts. In the 1940s, John McCray had envisioned the possibility of electing twenty senators from majority black counties and saw the PDP as a means to that objective. But the effect of the multi-member districts was to minimize the possibility of electing blacks to the most powerful branch of government in the state and to dilute the potential power of black majorities to determine election outcomes. It would not be until 1984 that the South Carolina legislature became the last state legislative body in the South to adopt a single-member district system, thus reviving the possibility of electing blacks to the powerful Senate.[14]

Partly as the result of the general assembly's adoption of single-member districts and ongoing efforts waged by the state NAACP to challenge at-large election systems in localities across the state since 1986, South Carolina boasted the sixth-highest percentage of black elected officials in the nation and the fourth-highest percentage in the former Confederacy by 2001. In the first years of the twenty-first century, black South Carolinians comprised 27 percent of the state's voting age population and held 534 elected offices, numbers that translated to 13.5 percent of all elected offices in the state. Of these offices, women held 32 percent, a figure that ranked South Carolina behind only Illinois as the state with the highest percentage of black women holding elected office in the nation. Although black South Carolinians continue to be grossly underrepresented in judicial, law enforcement, and federal offices, they have made major inroads in municipal government across the state, securing posts from school board representative to mayor, and blacks constitute 19.4 percent of the state House of Representatives and 15.2 percent of the Senate. In 1992, lifetime NAACP member James E. Clyburn earned a seat in the U.S. House of Representatives from South Carolina's Sixth Congressional District, becoming the first African American to serve in the state's congressional delegation since 1897. As the elected representative of South Carolina's Sixth District, Clyburn continues, in 2005, to serve fifteen counties in a region that includes Clarendon County and the heart of the state's black belt, as well as Columbia, Florence, Charleston and the low country.[15]

For black South Carolinians, however, the right to vote and elect representatives of their own choosing were never ends in themselves. Each was tied inextricably to emancipation from the evils of "social, economic, and political slavery," as the State Conference of NAACP Branches explained it in the 1940s. And yet, the basic right of self-representation, in the voting booth, in state and national legislative bodies, in places of employment, in union halls, and in everyday civic life, continues to elude black South Carolinians in the first years of the twenty-first century, frustrating visions of full emancipation and deliverance from the evils of "social, political, and economic slavery." Between 1991 and 1996, a series of church burnings in South Carolina and across the South proved highly visible reminders of racial hatred's stubborn and violent refusal to confine itself to the past. In 1999 the state conference called for a boycott of South Carolina's tourism industry in an effort to convince the state's political and business leaders to remove the Confederate battle flag from the dome atop the state's capitol building in Columbia, where it had flown since 1962. "The flag," explained state conference executive director Dwight James, "represents to many African Americans like myself the institution of slavery, an idea about the confederacy, that it stood for the continuation of slavery, [and] the segregation of African Americans in this country." Between January and July 2000, in conjunction with the national NAACP, the state conference carried out an economic boycott and staged a series of mass marches and demonstrations that captured national headlines, shaped the 2000 campaign for U.S. president, cost the state at least twenty million dollars in lost tourism revenue, and ultimately secured the removal of the flag from the capitol dome. For many black South Carolinians, however, the removal of the flag from the capitol dome proved a hollow victory as officials relocated the flag to a prominently located Confederate memorial on statehouse grounds. "As long as the Confederate Battle flag flies in a place of honor and maintains a cloak of currency," Representative Clyburn wrote, "lingering effects of our state's segregationist past will continue to infiltrate our daily lives and color our official conduct."[16]

In important ways, the struggle over the placement of the Confederate battle flag on the grounds of South Carolina's statehouse proved emblematic of the civil rights insurgency's quest for self-determination and equality by virtue of the NAACP's forceful demand for the respect of black South Carolinians, their history, desires, and basic humanity. That quest for respect remains inseparable from the larger struggle for social, political, and economic justice. At the dawn of the twenty-first century African Americans comprised 70 percent of South Carolina's prison population, black males remained disproportionately relegated to the lowest-paid and least prestigious jobs from the healthcare industry to the low-wage service sector more generally, while 25 percent of black families earned less than $15,450 a year compared to 7 percent of whites, and school districts with higher percentages of African Americans had access to $313 less to spend per student than districts with lower percentages. Put another way, the problems confronting the state of South Carolina, the nation, and the larger world remain daunting more than eighty years since the first NAACP branches took root in the Palmetto State, more than fifty years since the NAACP's landmark victory in *Brown v. Board of Education*, and more than forty years since the passage of the Civil Rights Act of 1964.[17]

Confronted with the plight of the present, today scholars are engaged in a debate over the meaning of the past. Sometimes they wonder where it all went wrong, contemplate roads not taken, and seek
to recover lost opportunities. Increasingly, scholars have found hope
in the present through the illumination of moments in the past when
labor unions and interracial alliances occupied the cutting edge of reform and a structural overhaul of American political and economic
institutions seemed possible, if not imminent. In this historical narrative, the onset of the cold war marked a critical turning point, closing
windows and slamming doors on the possibilities of the 1940s and
narrowing the democratic possibilities of the future. Although scholars continue to celebrate the civil rights movement of the 1950s and
early 1960s for its victories over Jim Crow and racial injustice in the
South, the movement's successes are tempered by *new* knowledge
of the more radical possibilities that resided in an earlier time and
that reemerged briefly during the Black Power era. As a result, the
deeper meaning and significance of the African American struggle
for civil rights has been flattened—demands for civil rights have
been separated from their intended purposes, the connection between
rights possession and rights application severed, the ties between legal-
legislative victories, black empowerment, and democratic transformation snapped.

The separation between civil rights demands and radical democratic transformation is not, however, merely the consequence of the
cold war or choices made by others in the past. This separation is
every bit as much (if not more so) the product of our own historical
narratives, those written from the Left, Right, and Center, and how
we have chosen to represent the past and its relationship to our own
time. Black South Carolinians engaged in civil rights struggles rarely
made sharp distinctions between civil rights gains and economic justice, between legal-legislative victories and democratic transformation.
Just as significantly, black South Carolinians rarely conceived of their
struggles for self-determination and equality in tragic *or* triumphant
terms—their struggles had no clear ending. For participants in the
ongoing civil rights insurgency, twists and turns, tensions and conflicts, hope and despair, victory and violence were part and parcel of
the daily battles they waged. Circumstances constantly shifted beneath
their feet and swift adjustments to new realities were essential for individual and collective survival. By positing hope for a better future in

the failed promises of the past, scholars seeking to chart a better future have missed the hope residing in the civil rights movement itself. It is a hope borne of the realization that ordinary human beings have changed the world by refusing to be bound by the constraints of the past and a hope made possible by the recognition that opportunities for change reside in the world as we find it, not just as we wish it to be. *Democracy Rising* is written in that spirit and offers that spirit as a way to narrate the history of the civil rights movement in America.

Notes

Introduction: The Politics of Civil Rights Struggle

1. The historiography on the civil rights movement continues to grow. For overviews, see my introduction in Lau, ed., *From the Grassroots to the Supreme Court*; Theoharis and Woodard, eds., *Freedom North*, especially the foreword by Evelyn Brooks Higginbotham and introduction by Theoharis; Lawson, "Freedom Then, Freedom Now"; Payne, *I've Got the Light of Freedom*, Bibliographic Essay, 413–441. Also, see two important collections of essays, Eagles, ed., *The Civil Rights Movement in America*; Robinson and Sullivan, eds., *New Directions in Civil Rights Studies*.

2. My thoughts on the civil rights movement as a process as opposed to an event borrows from the insights of Moses and Cobb, *Radical Equations*, especially the authors' introduction, 3–22; Martin, *No Coward Soldiers*, especially 1–43; Martin and Sullivan, eds., *Civil Rights in the United States*, editors' preface in Volume I, ix–xii; Du Bois, *Feminism & Suffrage*, 15–20. Also, see Fairclough, *Race and Democracy*; Sullivan, *Days of Hope*. On the centrality of slavery, race, and racial discrimination in the United States, see Morgan, *American Slavery, American Freedom*; Roediger, *Wages of Whiteness*; Huggins, "The Deforming Mirror of Truth." My thoughts here are also informed by the work of critical race theorists, including Bell, *Faces at the Bottom of the Well* and Williams, *The Alchemy of Race and Rights*.

3. For an overview of the growing civil rights scholarship concerned with the urban North, see Theoharis and Woodard, eds., *Freedom North*. Key monographs that emphasize the centrality of self-determination to African American civil rights struggles, North and South, include, Bates, *Pullman Porters and the Rise of Protest Politics in Black America*; Biondi, *To Stand and Fight*; Self, *American Babylon*; Tyson, *Radio Free Dixie*; Woodard, *A Nation within a Nation*. In *Civil Rights and the Idea of Freedom*, King writes that a quest for "genuine self-determination encompassing both individual and collective dimensions" was central to the African American struggle for civil rights (202). For a sweeping and insightful examination of the ways in which black civil rights struggles have challenged and called for a transformation of American democracy, see Singh, *Black Is a Country*. And for the important role of self-determination in traditions of African American thought and struggles, see Franklin, *Black Self-Determination*; Hahn, *A Nation under Our Feet*; Harding, *There Is a River*.

4. On slavery and planter ideology in South Carolina, see Burton, *In My Father's House Are Many Mansions*; Faust, *James Henry Hammond and the Old South* and *Mothers of Invention*; Fox-Genovese, *Within the Plantation Household*; Genovese, *Roll, Jordon, Roll*; Joyner, *Down by the Riverside*; Morgan, *Slave Counterpoint*; Sinha,

The Counter-Revolution of Slavery, quote on 5; Wood, *Black Majority*. On Reconstruction in South Carolina, see Holt, *Black over White*; Saville, *The Work of Reconstruction*, quote on 191; Schwalm, *A Hard Fight for We*; Williamson, *After Slavery*. My thoughts on the meaning of freedom for African Americans also draw on Berlin et al., *Slaves No More*.

5. Foner, *Nothing But Freedom* and *The Story of American Freedom*, 95–114, and *Reconstruction*, especially 251–61.

6. On black women's participation in Reconstruction in South Carolina, see Saville, *The Work of Reconstruction*; Schwalm, *A Hard Fight for We*. On class and social cleavages among African Americans and within the Republican Party, see Holt, *Black over White*. On achievements of the Republican Party in South Carolina, see Foner, *Reconstruction*, 316–22, 364, 366, 370–71, 373; Holt, *Black over White*, 1, 157.

7. On the Hamburg Massacre and the retreat from Reconstruction in South Carolina, see Kantrowitz, *Ben Tillman & the Reconstruction of White Supremacy*, 64–71, quote on 69; Foner, *Reconstruction*, 570–75; Holt, *Black over White*, 173–224; Williamson, *After Slavery*, 266–73.

8. On the disfranchisement movement in South Carolina, see Kousser, *The Shaping of Southern Politics*, 84–91, 145–52; Tindall, *South Carolina Negroes*, 68–91. Also, see I.A. Newby, *Black Carolinians*, 36–50.

9. On segregation in South Carolina, see Edgar, *South Carolina: A History*, 448–49; Tindall, *South Carolina Negroes*, 291–302. On the Phoenix "Riot," see Pranther, "The Origins of the Phoenix Racial Massacre of 1898"; Tindall, *South Carolina Negroes*, 256–58.

10. My thoughts on the reactionary/revolutionary tradition in South Carolina are informed by Sinha, *The Counter-Revolution of Slavery*, especially 1–7, 255–58. On the ongoing efforts to historicize white supremacy in the South, see Dailey et al., *Jumpin' Jim Crow*, especially the editors' introduction.

11. Important local and state studies include, Chafe, *Civilities and Civil Rights*; Colburn, *Racial Change and Community Crisis*; Dittmer, *Local People*; Fairclough, *Race and Democracy*; Honey, *Southern Labor and Black Civil Rights*; Lewis, *In Their Own Interests*; Morris, *The Origins of the Civil Rights Movement*; Norrell, *Reaping the Whirlwind*; Payne, *I've Got the Light of Freedom*. The literature on the black migration is extensive, and I take up the issue at length in Chapter Two. For an overview, see Trotter, ed., *The Great Migration in Historical Perspective*. Key works in African American women's history include, Brown, "Womanist Consciousness" and "Negotiating and Transforming the Public Sphere"; Chateauvert, *Marching Together*; Higginbotham, *Righteous Discontent*; Hine, *Hinesight*; Hunter, *To 'Joy My Freedom*; Robnett, *How Long? How Long?*; White, *Too Heavy a Load*. For two of the better theoretical explanations for the inseparability of social and political history, see Dailey, *Before Jim Crow* and Edwards, *Gendered Strife and Confusion*, especially 1–23.

12. On the creation of the NAACP, see Kellogg, *NAACP*; Lewis, *W.E.B. Du Bois: Biography of a Race*, 386–407; McPherson, *The Abolitionist Legacy: From Reconstruction to the NAACP*, 368–93; Ross, *J.E. Spingarn and the Rise of the NAACP*; Meier and Bracey, "The NAACP as a Reform Movement." On the corporate reorganization of American life and culture at the turn of the twentieth century, see Sklar, ed., *The United States as a Developing Country*, 1–36, 209–18 and *The Corporate Reconstruction of American Capitalism*; Livingston, *Pragmatism and the Political Economy of Cultural Revolution* and *Pragmatism, Feminism, and Democracy*, especially 1–14.

13. Bartley, *The New South*, 463. Key works that I am characterizing as tragic renderings of the history of post–World War II reform include, Korstad, *Civil Rights Unionism;* Korstad and Lichtenstein, "Opportunities Found and Lost"; Anderson, *Eyes Off the Prize*; Brinkley, *The End of Reform*; Fraser and Gerstle, eds., *The Rise and Fall of the New Deal Order*; Honey, *Southern Labor and Black Civil Rights*; Sullivan, *Days of Hope*; Von Eschen, *Race against Empire*. Hall's 2004 Organization of American Historians presidential address, "The Long Civil Rights Movement and the Political Uses of the Past," adopts this narrative, in effect announcing it as the new and dominant scholarly periodization of the civil rights movement.

Iriye's *Global Community* offers an important corrective to international and domestic studies that invest too much explanatory power in the cold war to determine the course of post–World War II U.S. and world history. Placing too much emphasis on the cold war, Iriye writes, can be "misleading," because, "It compels us to see all events and episodes at that time in the framework of the geopolitical drama and blinds us to the possibility that many developments in the world might have taken place regardless of the Cold War" (62).

14. My thoughts on historical narrative are informed by Brown, "Polyrhythms and Improvization"; Livingston, *Pragmatism and the Political Economy of Cultural Revolution*, xv–xxi and *Pragmatism, Feminism, and Democracy*, especially 85–114.

15. Chandra Mohanty has written a cogent theoretical explanation for the relationship of the center and periphery in Mohanty et al., *Third World Women and the Politics of Feminism*, 1–50 and 51–80. Key, *Southern Politics in State and Nation*, especially his chapter on South Carolina, 130–55.

1. Segregation and Self-Determination

Epigraph. Du Bois, *Dusk of Dawn*, 309–10.

1. Roy Nash, "The Lynching of Anthony Crawford," Part 7, Series A, Reel 16, NAACP Papers; W.T. Andrews to W.E.B. Du Bois, October 26, 1916, Part 7, Series A, Reel 16, NAACP Papers; Roy Nash to Elbert M. Stephens, March 22, 1917, NAACP Papers. For other accounts of the Crawford lynching, see *The Crisis* 13 (December 1917), 67; Ballard, *One More Day's Journey*, 156–59; Litwack, *Trouble in Mind*, 309–12.

2. On Blease and South Carolina politics during the "Progressive Era," see Carlton, *Mill and Town in South Carolina*, 215–72; Simon, *A Fabric of Defeat*, 11–35. Also, see Edgar, *South Carolina: A History*, 472–76; Key, *Southern Politics in State and Nation*, 142–45; Kousser, *The Shaping of Southern Politics*, 231–37.

3. On segregation in South Carolina's textile industry, see Newby, *Black Carolinians*, 134–35; Carlton, *Mill and Town in South Carolina*, 244–45. On the role of the textile industry in New South development, see Tindall, *The Emergence of the New South*, 70–110; Flamming, *Creating the Modern South*; Hall et al., *Like a Family*. On the textile industry in South Carolina, see Carlton, ibid.; Simon, *A Fabric of Defeat*, especially 11–58.

4. For lynching numbers in South Carolina I rely on White, *Rope and Faggot*, 258. Also, see Finnegan, "'At the Hands of Parties Unknown'"; Newby, *Black Carolinians*, 60.

5. Woodward, *Origins of the New South*. Also, see Woodward, *The Strange Career of Jim Crow*, "flexibility and tolerance" quote is from 34. Key works in the Wood-

wardian mold include: Goodwyn, *The Populist Moment*; Gilmore, *Gender and Jim Crow*; Dailey, *Before Jim Crow*.

6. Gilmore, *Gender and Jim Crow*, xxi, 178, 148, 210, xxi, 202.

7. General histories of Columbia and Charleston include, Moore, *Columbia and Richland County*; Fraser, *Charleston! Charleston!* On black life in Columbia, the best works include, Woods, "Black Woman Activist in Twentieth-Century South Carolina," esp. 14–85; Lofton, "A Social and Economic History of Columbia, South Carolina." On black life and politics in Charleston in the nineteenth century, see Powers, *Black Charlestonians*.

8. Quoted in Ovington, *The Walls Came Tumbling Down*, 105. On the organization and early years of the NAACP, see Kellogg, *NAACP*; Lewis, *W.E.B. Du Bois: Biography of a Race*, 297–534; Meier and Bracey, "The NAACP as a Reform Movement"; Meier and Rudwick, "The Rise of the Black Secretariat in the NAACP"; Ovington, "The National Association for the Advancement of Colored People"; Ovington, *The Walls Came Tumbling Down*, 100–243; Ross, *J.E. Spingarn and the Rise of the NAACP*.

9. Membership numbers are from, Report and Recommendations on Membership and Staff, 1957, III-A-37, NAACP Papers (Manuscript Division, Library of Congress, Washington, D.C.); *The Crisis* 17 (April 1919), 284–85; *The Crisis* 19 (March 1920), 241; Ovington, "The National Association for the Advancement of Colored People," 115. Butler W. Nance to W.E.B. Du Bois, June 5, 1915, I-G-196, NAACP Papers.

10. I deal in depth with the mass migration of African Americans from the South to the North in Chapter Two. Membership figure is from *The Crisis* 19 (March 1920), 241. On the shifting membership dynamics of the NAACP, see Meier and Rudwick, "The Rise of the Black Secretariat," especially 105; Meier and Bracey, "The NAACP as a Reform Movement." John R. Shillady Memorandum concerning the Need for Annual Income, 1918, Part I, Reel 23, NAACP Papers.

11. Du Bois, *Dusk of Dawn*, 243.

12. On the Amenia Conference, see Du Bois, *Dusk of Dawn*, 243–45; Lewis, *W.E.B. Du Bois: Biography of a Race*, 517–27; Kellogg, *NAACP*, 87–88; Ross, *J.E. Spingarn*, 46–48. On James Weldon Johnson, see Johnson, *Along This Way*; Kellogg, *NAACP*, 133–35; Levy, *James Weldon Johnson* and Levy, "James Weldon Johnson and the Development of the NAACP." On Du Bois and Johnson at the Amenia Conference, see Lewis, *W.E.B. Du Bois: Biography of a Race*, 524. On Johnson's significance as a legitimizing force for the NAACP, see Meier and Rudwick, "The Rise of the Black Secretariat," 105. Meier and Rudwick write, "[H]is ties with the Washingtonians legitimized the NAACP among many blacks previously suspicious of the organization. His political connections helped the NAACP's efforts to influence Republican party policy and national legislation."

13. Du Bois, *Dusk of Dawn*, 245. Johnson, *Along This Way*, 314–15. *The Crisis* 14 (May 1917), 18, 19; Johnson quoted on 19; Branch and membership statistics are on 19. Also, see Minutes of the Meeting of the Board of Directors, February 13, April 9, 1917, Part I, Reel 1, NAACP Papers; Kellogg, *NAACP*, 134–35. For more on Johnson's efforts to organize the "Dixie District" or "Southern Empire," see Johnson, *Along This Way*, 310–17; Levy, *James Weldon Johnson*, 186–215.

14. Address delivered by James Weldon Johnson, Thirteenth Annual Conference of the NAACP, June 19, 1922, Part I, Reel 8, NAACP Papers. On Johnson's vision

for the NAACP, also see Levy, *James Weldon Johnson*, 186–215; Meier and Rudwick, "The Rise of the Black Secretariat," especially 106, n. 64. The NAACP's legal, legislative, and publicity efforts in the nineteen-teens are chronicled in Kellogg, *NAACP*, 57–65, 103–46.

15. James Weldon Johnson to Mary White Ovington, August 20, 1919, Part I, Reel 17, NAACP Papers; Meier and Rudwick, "The Rise of the Black Secretariat," 106.

16. Newby, *Black Carolinians*, 86–90. Kuznets and Thomas, *Population Redistribution and Economic Growth*, 88–89. On Kuznets's methodology and problems with using census figures to arrive at black migration numbers, see Spear, *Black Chicago*, 138–39.

17. The literature concerned with the gendered sources of nineteenth-century subjectivity and citizenship is extensive. Works that have most influenced my thinking on the subject include, Cott, *The Grounding of Modern Feminism*; Du Bois, *Feminism & Suffrage*; Kerber, *No Constitutional Right to be Ladies*; Livingston, *Pragmatism and the Political Economy of Cultural Revolution*. On the raced and gendered sources of nineteenth-century subjectivity and citizenship, see especially Brown, "Negotiating and Transforming the Public Sphere"; Gilmore, *Gender and Jim Crow*; Higginbotham, *Righteous Discontent*; White, *Ar'n't I a Woman*. The patriarchal and racial dynamics of power in nineteenth-century South Carolina has achieved it clearest articulation in Kantrowitz, *Ben Tillman & The Reconstruction of White Supremacy*; McCurry, *Masters of Small Worlds*.

18. Butler W. Nance to W.E.B. Du Bois, June 15, 1915, Columbia Branch File, I-G-196, NAACP Papers; Butler W. Nance Address, Tenth Anniversary Conference of the NAACP, Report of Branches, June 28, 1919, Part I, Reel 8, NAACP Papers. An Address to the People of South Carolina, under the auspices of the Capital Civic League, 1915, Columbia Branch File, I-G-196, NAACP Papers.

19. Biographical Profile from the Nathaniel Jerome Frederick House, N.J. Frederick, Black History Vertical Files, South Caroliniana Library, University of South Carolina, Columbia; Nathaniel Jerome Frederick, "Negroes and the Law," ibid.; Meier and Rudwick, "Attorneys Black and White," 136. For brief histories of South Carolina's black schools, colleges, and universities, see Gordon, *Sketches of Negro Life*, 92–109.

20. On nineteenth-century conceptions of manhood and womanhood, see Bederman, *Manliness & Civilization*; Dailey, *Before Jim Crow*; Edwards, *Gendered Strife and Confusion*; Schwalm, *A Hard Fight for We*.

21. On the ways in which the particular legacies of slavery and the persistence of racism and racialized economic inequality have shaped the experiences of black people in relationship to the ideology and practice of Victorian values and separate spheres, see Brown, "'What Has Happened Here'"; Brown, "Negotiating and Transforming the Public Sphere"; Higginbotham, "African-American Women's History and the Metalanguage of Race." On the politics of respectability as accommodation and resistance, see Higginbotham, *Righteous Discontent*.

22. An Address to the People of South Carolina. Cott, *The Grounding of Modern Feminism*, 6.

23. There is no existing copy of the Columbia, South Carolina, NAACP branch charter. The Charleston branch held its organizational meeting on February 27, 1917. Application for Charter, Charleston, South Carolina, February 27, 1917, Charleston

Branch File, I-G-196, NAACP Papers. The Charleston and Columbia branches were organized on Johnson's southern trip (January 15–March 15, 1917). *The Crisis* 14 (May 1917), 18–19. The national office received the applications for charters from the Charleston and Columbia branches by April 1917. Minutes of the Meeting of the Board of Directors, April 9, 1917, Part I, Reel 1, NAACP Papers. For one account of the founding of the Columbia NAACP branch, see Woods, "Black Woman Activist," 154–58.

24. Nance Address, Tenth Anniversary Conference of the NAACP, Report of Branches, June 28, 1919, Part I, Reel 8, NAACP Papers.

25. On Hull, the history of the Monteith family, and the involvement of women in the early NAACP, see Woods, "Black Woman Activist," 14–85, especially 37–66.

26. D.B. Brooks to Lealtad, September 20, 1920, Columbia Branch File, I-G-196, NAACP Papers; William Pickens, "The Women Voter Hits the Color Line," *The Nation* 111 (October 6, 1920), 372–73; Terborg-Penn, *African American Women in the Struggle for the Vote*, 153.

27. D.B. Brooks to Lealtad, September 20, 1920, NAACP Papers; Pickens, "The Woman Voter Hits the Color Line," *The Nation,* 372.

28. Butler W. Nance to Walter White, September 11, 1920, Columbia Branch File, I-G-196, NAACP Papers.

29. Terborg-Penn, *African American Women in the Struggle for the Vote*, 154.

30. On the rise of the New Negro and its impact on the concerns and interests of black women, see White, *Too Heavy a Load*, esp., 110–41. Also, see Bair, "True Women, Real Men."

31. Du Bois, *The Crisis* 13 (April 1917), 269. On Du Bois's visit to Charleston, see Lewis, *W.E.B. Du Bois: Biography of a Race*, 526–28.

32. Application for Charter, Charleston, South Carolina, NAACP Papers.

33. On free black people in Charleston during the antebellum era, see Berlin, *Slaves without Masters*; Johnson and Roark, *Black Masters*; Powers, *Black Charlestonians*, especially 36–72. The 1860 population figure is from Powers, 37. On the influence of the "aristocrats of color" in postbellum South Carolina and Charleston, see Powers, *Black Charlestonians*, 73–225; Holt, *Black over White*, especially 43–71. Holt, in short, argues that the socioeconomic differences (including considerations of class, color, occupation, and educational background) among South Carolina's black leaders were crucial factors in the fall of Reconstruction era Republican government in the state, 4, 208–24. On Charleston's "aristocrats of color" and their lasting reputation for "snobbery and colorphobia," see Gatewood, *Aristocrats of Color*, 80, 81–82, 156–57, 281–82; Gordon, *Sketches of Negro Life*, 69. On emerging patterns of racially segregated neighborhoods, see Fraser, *Charleston! Charleston!*, 307; Powers, *Black Charlestonians*, 250–53. On the rise of Jim Crow in Charleston, see Fraser, *Charleston! Charleston!*, 308; Fields, *Lemon Swamp and Other Places*, 51–65, especially 57–58. On the erosion of the intra-racial color line in Charleston, see Drago, *Initiative, Paternalism, and Race Relations*. Drago writes, "Paradoxically, racial radicalism not only helped create a black professional class by pressing segregation but also undermined the economic basis of the color line. The old elite, basically artisans, held jobs that afforded them some economic opportunity. As long as their livelihood and economic advantages rested on their serving the white elite, they were encouraged to maintain a caste-and-color line. However, the segregation wrought by racial radicalism led to Charleston blacks' losing skilled jobs to whites. . . . The loss of jobs to whites eroded the economic base of the old elite and the pragmatic validity for their

practicing the color line" (184). On the transformation of the economic basis of the black upper class in another Deep South city, see Meier and Lewis, "History of the Negro Upper Class in Atlanta."

34. Application for Charter, Charleston, South Carolina, NAACP Papers.

35. Drago, *Initiative, Paternalism, and Race Relations*, 172, 175; Gordon, *Sketches of Negro Life*, 140. Also, see Ball, *The Sweet Hell Inside*, 60–63, 80–89.

36. Application for Charter, Charleston, South Carolina, NAACP Papers; Drago, *Initiative, Paternalism, and Race Relations*, 99, 101, 172. Drago's *Initiative, Paternalism, and Race Relations* is the definitive history of Avery Normal Institute. My discussion here draws from his work, as well as Edmund L. Drago and Eugene C. Hunt, "A History of Avery Normal Institute from 1865–1954," Avery Research Center, College of Charleston, Charleston, South Carolina.

37. Fields, *Lemon Swamp*, 13. Drago, *Initiative, Paternalism, and Race Relations*, 4–5. On Cox's effort to combat caste and class prejudice, see Drago, ibid., 139–40.

38. On the organization of the SCFCWC, see 40th Anniversary of the South Carolina Federation of Colored Women's Clubs, 1909–1949, Program Guide, Part I, Reel 22, NACW Records; 50th Anniversary, S.C. Federation of Colored Women's Clubs, Program Guide, South Caroliniana Library, University of South Carolina, Columbia; Gordon, *Sketches of Negro Life*, 178–87. On the organization of the NACW, see White, *Too Heavy a Load*, 21–55, quote on 24; Shaw, *What a Woman Ought to Be and Do*.

39. Gordon, *Sketches of Negro Life*, 184. On black women's club work and its relationship to interracial cooperation, see Gilmore, *Gender and Jim Crow*; Hall, *Revolt against Chivalry*, especially 59–106.

40. 40th Anniversary of the South Carolina Federation of Colored Women's Clubs, 1909–1949, Program Guide, NACW Records. On Terrell's visit and its influence, see Fields, *Lemon Swamp*, 189–90; White, *Too Heavy a Load*, 21–24; Jeannette Cox, "A History—by administration—of the Phyllis Wheatley Literary and Social Club," Phyllis Wheatley and Social Club Collection, Avery Research Center, College of Charleston, Charleston, South Carolina, hereafter cited as Cox, "A History of the Phyllis Wheatley."

41. Cox, "A History of the Phyllis Wheatley"; Application for Charter, Charleston, South Carolina, NAACP Papers; Drago, *Initiative, Paternalism, and Race Relations*, 149–50, 168.

42. Cox, "A History of the Phyllis Wheatley."

43. On the history of the Modern Priscilla, see 40th Anniversary of the South Carolina Federation of Colored Women's Clubs, 1909–1949, Program Guide, NACW Records; Fields, *Lemon Swamp*, 197–99, 202–3. Also, see Drago, *Initiative, Paternalism, and Race Relations*, 193; White, *Too Heavy a Load*, 23–24.

44. Holt, "Marking," 10. It is worth thinking about identity, as Holt suggests, in terms of a practice, in terms of something that is produced, malleable, incomplete, and, therefore, open to contest and change. For other important statements to this effect, see Dimock and Gilmore, eds., *Rethinking Class*, especially, 1–104; Edwards, *The Practice of Diaspora*; Hall, "Cultural Identity and Diaspora"; Hanchard, *Orpheus and Power*, 3–30.

45. U.S. Bureau of the Census, *Fourteenth Census of the United States, Vol. II, Population, 1920*, 78.

46. Richard H. Mickey to Dear Sir, May 10, 1917, Charleston Branch File, I-G-196, NAACP Papers.

47. Nelson to R.A. Skinner, June 26, 1917, Charleston Branch File, I-G-196, NAACP Papers; Daniel to Van Dyke, July 2, 1917, Charleston Branch File, I-G-196, NAACP Papers; Edwin A. Harleston to John R. Shillady, November 2, 1918, Charleston Branch File, I-G-196, NAACP Papers; *The Crisis* 17 (April 1919), 281.

48. Membership Report Blank, March 1, 1918, Charleston Branch File, I-G-196, NAACP Papers.

49. *The Crisis* 13 (April 1917), 270.

50. Quote is from Drago and Hunt, "A History of Avery Normal Institute."

51. On Charleston's public schools, see Drago, *Initiative, Paternalism, and Race Relations,* 71–72, 124, 181; Gordon, *Sketches of Negro Life,* 269.

52. Fields, *Lemon Swamp,* 41–43.

53. Edwin A. Harleston, Address, Tenth Anniversary Conference of the NAACP, Report of Branches, June 28, 1919, Part I, Reel 8, NAACP Papers.

54. Richard Mickey to NAACP, December 21, 1917, Charleston Branch File, I-G-196, NAACP Papers; Edwin Harleston to John R. Shillady, November 2, 1918, NAACP Papers; Harleston Address, Tenth Anniversary Conference of the NAACP, NAACP Papers.

55. Edwin Harleston to John R. Shillady, November 2, 1918, NAACP Papers.

56. City Board of School Commissioners Minute Book, January 9, 1919, Office of Archives and Records, Charleston County School District, Charleston, South Carolina; Harleston Address, Tenth Anniversary Conference of the NAACP, NAACP Papers.

57. Thomas E. Miller, et al. to His Excellency, R.A. Cooper, et al., January 18, 1919, Columbia Branch File, I-G-196, NAACP Papers. Miller's biography is derived from Holt, *Black over White,* 54; Tindall, *South Carolina Negroes,* 56.

58. Butler Nance to Mary White Ovington, February 5, 1919, Part I, Reel 8, NAACP Papers; Harleston Address, Tenth Anniversary Conference of the NAACP, Report of Branches, June 28, 1919, Part I, Reel 8, NAACP Papers; "Colored Teachers in Charleston Schools," *The Crisis* 22 (June 1921), 60.

59. Fields, *Lemon Swamp,* 203; Harleston Address, Tenth Anniversary Conference of the NAACP, June 28, 1919, Part I, Reel 8, NAACP Papers.

60. Clark, *Echo in My Soul,* 33. For a biographical portrait of Clark, see McFadden, "Septima P. Clark." Also, see Clark, *Septima Clark and the Civil Rights Movement.*

61. On the life and history of Johns Island, see Carawan and Carawan, eds., *Ain't you got the right to the tree of life?*; Clark, *Echo in My Soul,* 142. For Clark's and Fields's own retelling of their teaching experiences on Johns Island, see Clark, *Echo in My Soul,* especially 32–58; Fields, *Lemon Swamp,* 110–40.

62. Clark, *Echo in My Soul,* 59–61.

63. Ibid., 60–61.

64. "Colored Teachers in Charleston Schools," *The Crisis* 22 (June 1921), 60. *The Crisis* puts the number of petition signatures at twenty-five thousand. Clark remembers collecting more than ten thousand signatures herself. See *Echo in My Soul,* 61.

65. Harleston Address, Tenth Anniversary Conference of the NAACP, June 28, 1919, Part I, Reel 8, NAACP Papers.

66. The meeting was reported in *The State*, February 5, 1919, 2. Glenda Gilmore has suggested that the African American crossover from the Republican Party to the Democratic Party generally attributed to the New Deal, and specifically dated to the national elections of 1936, is better understood in light of changes begun in the 1920s, including Lily White Republicanism, women's suffrage, the emergence of the NAACP, and black migration to the North. Gilmore, "False Friends and Avowed Enemies: Southern African Americans and Party Allegiances in the 1920s," in Dailey et al., eds., *Jumpin' Jim Crow*, 219–38. Chappelle's vision of black South Carolinians' wielding the "balance of power" and Edwin Harleston's desire to create a "black primary" intimate, however, that the roots of the shift lie even deeper than Gilmore suggests. They also require a rethinking of the ways in which African Americans viewed the dominant political parties and continually sought creative ways to achieve representation through them. I take up both issues at length in Chapter Four.

67. NAACP to E.L. Ball, Sept. 21, 1918, Aiken Branch File, I-G-196, NAACP Papers; Application for Charter, Anderson, South Carolina, March 11, 1919, Anderson Branch File, I-G-196, NAACP Papers; Application for Charter, Beaufort, South Carolina, June 11, 1919, Beaufort Branch File, I-G-196, NAACP Papers; Application for Charter, Darlington, South Carolina, April 7, 1918, Darlington Branch File, I-G-196, NAACP Papers; Application for Charter, Florence, South Carolina, March 26, 1919, Florence Branch File, I-G-196, NAACP Papers; Application for Charter, Orangeburg, South Carolina, June 25, 1919, Orangeburg Branch File, I-G-197, NAACP Papers.

2. Riot and Reaction

Epigraphs. Bishop John Hurst, Address, Tenth Anniversary Conference of the National Association for the Advancement of Colored People, June 22, 1919, Part I, Reel 8, NAACP Papers; Jacques-Garvey, *Philosophy and Opinions of Marcus Garvey*, 5.

1. Du Bois, "Returning Soldiers," *The Crisis* 18 (May 1919), 13–14. Also see Lewis, *W.E.B. Du Bois: Biography of a Race*, 578; Lewis, *W.E.B. Du Bois: The Fight for Equality*, 3–7.

2. On the June 1919 annual convention of the NAACP, see Kellogg, *NAACP*, 236; Ovington, *The Walls Came Tumbling Down*, 167–71; List of Delegates, Tenth Anniversary Conference of the NAACP, Report of Branches, 1919, Part I, Reel 8, NAACP Papers.

3. My account of the Charleston Race Riot draws upon the following: *Charleston News and Courier*, May 11, 1919, 1,3; Ibid., May 12, 1919, 8; Ibid., May 13, 1919, 12; Ibid., May 16, 1919, 10; Ibid., May 17, 1919, 10; *New York Times*, May 11, 1919, 3–4; Report on the Race Riot at Charleston on the night of May 10 and 11, 1919, Federal Surveillance of Afro-Americans, Reel 20; Francis Grimké, Address, Tenth Anniversary Conference of the NAACP, Report of Branches, June 28, 1919, Part I, Reel 8, NAACP Papers; Edwin A. Harleston, Address, Tenth Anniversary Conference of the NAACP, Report of Branches, June 28, 1919, NAACP Papers. Also, see Drago, *Initiative, Paternalism, and Race Relations*, 174; Fraser, *Charleston! Charleston!*, 363.

4. *Charleston News and Courier*, May 12, 1919, 8, reported seventeen injured black civilians based on numbers from Charleston's Roper Hospital. Based on reports sent to him by the Charleston NAACP, which included an investigation of hospital

records and a canvassing of black neighborhoods, Francis Grimké reported forty injured black civilians, Address, Tenth Anniversary of the NAACP, Report of Branches, June 28, 1919, NAACP Papers. On the NAACP's post-riot investigation, see Harleston, Address, Tenth Anniversary of the NAACP, Report of Branches, June 28, 1919, NAACP Papers.

5. *Charleston News and Courier*, May 16, 1919, 10.

6. Harleston, Address, Tenth Anniversary of the NAACP, Report of Branches, June 28, 1919, NAACP Papers. Also, see Grimké, Address, Tenth Anniversary of the NAACP, Report of Branches, June 28, 1919, NAACP Papers.

7. *Charleston News and Courier*, May 25, 1919, H-8.

8. Fraser, *Charleston! Charleston!*, 363.

9. On the Red Summer of 1919, see Lewis, *When Harlem Was in Vogue*, 16–24; Schrecker, *Many Are the Crimes*; Tuttle, *Race Riot*. Also, see Murray, *Red Scare*; Preston, *Aliens and Dissenters*.

10. Harleston, Address, Tenth Anniversary of the NAACP, Report of Branches, June 28, 1919, NAACP Papers.

11. Application for Charter, Anderson, South Carolina, March 11, 1919, Anderson Branch File, I-G-196, NAACP Papers. Gassaway's report on the activities of the Anderson branch quoted in, "Modern Exiles," 71.

12. "Modern Exiles," 71–72; James Weldon Johnson to Mary White Ovington, August 20, 1919, Part I, Reel 17, NAACP Papers; Butler W. Nance to James Weldon Johnson, October 26, 1919, Columbia Branch File, I-G-196, NAACP Papers; List of Delegates, 1919 Annual Convention, Part I, Reel 8, NAACP Papers.

13. On the decision to hold the 1920 annual convention in Atlanta, see Kellogg, *NAACP*, 245–46; Ovington, *The Walls Came Tumbling Down*, 177–78.

14. "Modern Exiles," 70.

15. Report of Field Secretary, July 8, 1920, Part I, Reel 4, NAACP Papers.

16. On the NAACP in Texas during World War I, see Reich, "Soldiers of Democracy," especially, 1491–1505, membership numbers on 1501 and 1503; Gillette, "The NAACP in Texas."

17. On Shillady and his investigation in Texas, see Kellogg, *NAACP*, 239–41; Ovington, *The Walls Came Tumbling Down*, 171–75; Reich, "Soldiers of Democracy," 1500–1501.

18. Reich, "Soldiers of Democracy," 1501, 1502.

19. Report of the Secretary, May 1920, Part I, Reel 4, NAACP Papers; *The Crisis* 21 (March 1921), 204; McMillen, *Dark Journey*, 314–15.

20. Dittmer, *Black Georgia in the Progressive Era*, 206–7.

21. Fairclough, *Race and Democracy*, 20.

22. On the decline of NAACP branch growth in the 1920s, see McAdam, *Political Process and the Development of Black Insurgency*, 104. According to McAdam's figures, between 1916 and 1920 southern branches made up 30 percent of all new branches formed. Although the number of new branches declined in both the North and South during the 1920s, between 1921 and 1925 only 5 percent of new NAACP branches were formed in the South.

23. *Congressional Record*, 66th Congress, 1st Session, 4302–5.

24. On James Byrnes and his early life and political career, see Robertson, *Sly and Able*, 1–120, quote on 41. On Ben Tillman and his politics of white supremacy, see Kantrowitz, *Ben Tillman & the Reconstruction of White Supremacy*.

25. *Congressional Record*, 66th Congress, 1st Session, 4305.

26. Walter White to Dr. C.C. Johnson, June 7, 1918, Aiken Branch File, I-G-196, NAACP Papers; Shillady to E.L. Ball, September, 1918, Aiken Branch File, I-G-196, NAACP Papers; Note attached to Bagnall to Branch President and Secretary, February 8, 1923, Aiken Branch File, I-G-196, NAACP Papers; Application for Charter, Aiken, South Carolina, December 6, 1938, Aiken Branch File, I-G-196, NAACP Papers.

27. White, *Rope and Faggot*, Table VII, 258; Newby, *Black Carolinians*, 192. Also, on lynching in South Carolina, see Finnegan, "'At the Hands of Parties Unknown.'"

28. The best work on the reemergence of the Klan in the 1920s is MacLean, *Behind the Mask of Chivalry*. Also, see Chalmers, *Hooded Americanism*; Jackson, *Ku Klux Klan in the City*. On the arrival of the Klan in South Carolina, see "The Ku Klux Are Riding Again!" 229–31; Report of the Secretary, December 1920, Part 1, Reel 4, NAACP Papers; Hux, "The Ku Klux Klan and Collective Violence in Horry County"; Edgar, *South Carolina: A History*, 484.

29. *Charleston News and Courier*, May 23, 1923, 1.

30. Bagnall, "Lights and Shadows," 125.

31. Quoted in Hux, "The Ku Klux Klan and Collective Violence in Horry County," 217.

32. There are many accounts of the events leading up to the arrest of the Lowman family as well as the subsequent events leading to the lynching of Demon, Clarence, and Bertha Lowman. I draw on the following accounts: Newby, *Black Carolinians*, 242–45; White, "The Shambles of South Carolina," 72–75; White, *Rope and Faggot*, 29–33; Statement Made by N.J. Frederick, Columbia, SC, n.d., Part 7, Series A, Reel 16, NAACP Papers; *New York Times*, October 9, 1926, 1; *New York Times*, October 17, 1926, Section 9, 7.

33. Statement Made by N.J. Frederick, Columbia, S.C., n.d., Part 7, Series A, Reel 16, NAACP Papers.

34. Ibid.

35. Affidavit signed by Lucy Mooney, November 2, 1926, Part 7, Series A, Reel 16, NAACP Papers; Affidavit signed by Charles Lee, November 2, 1926, Part 7, Series A, Reel 16, NAACP Papers. The jailor, Rupert Taylor, vigorously denied willing involvement. See *New York Times*, October 9, 1926, 1; *New York Times*, October 10, 1926, 28.

36. *New York Times*, October 10, 1926, 28; Ibid., November 10, 1926, 2; Ibid., January 29, 1927, 30; Newby, *Black Carolinians*, 245; White, "The Shambles of South Carolina," 72; "South Carolina Public Condemns Aiken Affair," Reel 53, Commission on Interracial Cooperation Papers.

37. The literature on the migration as a strategy for survival and as a social movement of revolutionary import is immense. For examples that have particularly influenced my thinking, see Clark-Lewis, *Living In, Living Out*; Griffin, *"Who set you flowin'?"*; Grossman, *Land of Hope*; Hine, "Rape and the Inner Lives of Black Women"; Hine, "The Black Migration to the Urban Midwest"; Hunter, *To 'Joy My Freedom*; Lewis, *In Their Own Interests*; Painter, *Exodusters*; Trotter, *Coal, Class, and Color*; Wright, *Old South, New South*; Trotter, ed., *The Great Migration in Historical Perspective*.

38. U.S. Bureau of the Census, *Fourteenth Census of the United States*, vol. 2,

Population, 1920; U.S. Bureau of the Census, *Fifteenth Census of the United States*, vol. 3, *Population, 1930*.

39. On the collapse of the cotton economy in the South, see Tindall, *The Emergence of the New South*, 111–42; Vance, *Human Factors in Cotton Culture*; Wright, *Old South, New South*, 198–274; Johnson et al., *The Collapse of Cotton Tenancy*. On the collapse of the cotton economy in South Carolina, also see Kiser, *Sea Island to City*; Newby, *Black Carolinians*, 199–201; Woofter, *Black Yeomanry*.

40. On the boll weevil's arrival in South Carolina, see Kiser, *Sea Island to City*, 108; Tindall, *The Emergence of the New South*, 121; Vance, *Human Factors in Cotton Culture*, 95; Woofter, *Black Yeomanry*, 132.

41. *Thirty-First Annual Report of the South Carolina Experiment Station of Clemson Agricultural College for the Year Ended June 30, 1922*, 39–43; "South Carolina Agricultural Experimental Station Circular 82," 3, 21. On declining farm wage rates, see Wright, *Old South, New South*, 202.

42. Quoted in Bethel, *Promisedland*, 114.

43. *The State*, June 19, 1923, 13; *Charleston News and Courier*, June 20, 1923, 8; *New York Times*, June 20, 1923, 14; *New York Times*, April 24, 1923, 20; *New York Times*, April 29, 1923, Section 8, 1.

44. *New York Times*, April 17, 1923, 37. Also, see U.S. Bureau of the Census, *Fifteenth Census of the United States*, vol. 3, 775.

45. Kuznets et al., *Population Redistribution and Economic Growth*, 89–90.

46. Quoted in Kiser, *Sea Island to City*, 111.

47. See note 37 above on migration, especially, Grossman, *Land of Hope*; Hine, "Rape and the Inner Lives of Black Women."

48. Woofter, *Black Yeomanry*, 94–95.

49. On the emergence of a community of black South Carolinians in Philadelphia, see Ballard, *One More Day's Journey*. On the emergence of a black South Carolina community in Harlem, see Kiser, *Sea Island to City*.

50. Ballard, *One More Day's Journey*, 8–9. By 1930, for the first time, more non-white native South Carolinians lived in the states of Pennsylvania and New York than in any southern state with the exception of North Carolina. Kuznets et al., *Population Redistribution and Economic Growth*, 337.

51. The importance of letter writing and visiting in the migration process has been demonstrated in most recent histories of black migration. For evidence of letter writing and visiting among and between black South Carolinians, see Bethel, *Promisedland*, 174–94; Clark-Lewis, *Living In, Living Out*, 51–67; Ballard, *One More Day's Journey*, 172–82.

52. Ballard, *One More Day's Journey*, 174–75.

53. Quoted in Clark-Lewis, *Living In, Living Out*, 75.

54. Kiser, *Sea Island to City*, 198.

55. Ibid., 132.

56. Ibid., 133.

57. Ibid., 132. On similar experiences shared by white ethnic immigrant girls and women in New York City, see Peiss, *Cheap Amusements*. On the ways in which black women carved out space for pleasure and self-expression in the urban South and how migration provided new outlets for that expression, see Hunter, *To 'Joy My Freedom*, especially 145–86, 219–40.

58. Grossman, *Land of Hope*, 37.

59. On the revolutionary import of black migration and its relationship to the development of the modern civil rights movement, see Denning *The Cultural Front*, especially 7, 36–37, 466–77; Kelley, *Yo' Mama's Disfunctional!*, 125–58; Lewis, "The Origins and Causes of the Civil Rights Movement"; Wright, *Old South, New South*, 239–74.

60. James, *Holding Aloft the Banner of Ethiopia*, 135. Branch statistics are from Hill et al., *The Marcus Garvey and Universal Negro Improvement Association Papers, Vol. III*, 1001–2. Also, see James, *Holding Aloft the Banner of Ethiopia*, 365; Martin, *Race First*, 15. On the UNIA in Georgia, see Rolinson, "The Universal Improvement Association in Georgia"; in Mississippi, see McMillen, *Dark Journey*, 312–13; in Norfolk, Virginia, see Lewis, *In Their Own Interests*, 72–77; in southern West Virginia, see Trotter, *Coal, Class, and Color*, 243–45. Steven Hahn notes this prevalence of UNIA divisions in the rural South in making his case for the persistence of nineteenth-century visions of black solidarity and identity in the early twentieth century. *A Nation under Our Feet*, 465–76.

61. *Negro World*, February 4, 1922, 10; Hill et al., *The Marcus Garvey and Universal Negro Improvement Association Papers*, 995, 1000.

62. *Negro World*, March 12, 1921; Hill et al., *The Marcus Garvey and Universal Negro Improvement Association Papers*, 404. In Charleston, UNIA membership drew from the ranks of the city's domestic laborers, common laborers, ministers, and skilled craftsmen. Carpenters comprised a disproportionate share of its membership and the local black carpenter's union hall served as one of its principal meeting places, along with black churches. My sketch of Charleston's UNIA membership composition is derived from a list of names gleaned from the *Negro World* between 1921 and 1924 that was then cross-referenced with *Walsh's Charleston City Directory* for 1923 and 1924.

63. E.B. Burroughs to Robert Bagnall, May 11, 1929, Charleston Branch File, I-G-196, NAACP Papers. On periodic surges in membership, see Membership Reports in Charleston Branch File, I-G-196, NAACP Papers.

64. R.W. Jackson to Robert Bagnall, August 14, 1923, Columbia Branch File, I-G-196, NAACP Papers; "Columbia Branch–S.C." report, 1927, Columbia Branch File, I-G-196, NAACP Papers; Robert Bagnall to A.A. Nelson, August 1, 1927, Columbia Branch File, I-G-196, NAACP Papers; N.J. Frederick to Robert Bagnall, October 6, 1928, Columbia Branch File, I-G-196, NAACP Papers; Sam Wallace to Robert Bagnall, March 10, 1928, Columbia Branch File, I-G-196, NAACP Papers. In May 1924 a group of women in New York City organized the Women's Auxiliary to the NAACP. Organized in part to support the fundraising efforts of the national office, its membership included the wives of such NAACP leaders as Robert Bagnall, W.E.B. Du Bois, James Weldon Johnson, William Pickens, and Walter White. Other notables included Essie Goode Robeson, the wife of Paul Robeson; A'Lelia Walker, daughter of Madam C.J. Walker; Lucile Randolph, the wife of A. Philip Randolph; and the young writer Jessie Fauset. See Memorandum from Miss Randolph to Mrs. McClendon, June 15, 1925, Women's Auxiliary to the NAACP, I-C-196, NAACP Papers; Women's Auxiliary N.A.A.C.P. membership list, March 1925, I-C-196, NAACP Papers.

65. Branches that obtained charters and became inactive include: Aiken, Anderson, Darlington, Florence, Greenville, Lone Star (Calhoun County), Orangeburg, Rock Hill, and Walterboro. Attempts to establish branches occurred in Bamberg, Camden, Georgetown, Hardeeville, Spartanburg, Union, Varnville, as well as at Benedict College, and Voorhees Normal and Industrial Institute in Denmark. South Caro-

lina Branch Files, I-G-196 and I-G-197, NAACP Papers. In contrast to the UNIA, which established no membership quotas as a condition for creating a branch, the NAACP required fifty members to establish an officially chartered branch. Membership fees were $1 per year and membership had to be renewed each year.

66. Application for Charter, Walterboro (Colleton County), South Carolina, October 6, 1921, Walterboro Branch File, I-G-197, NAACP Papers; J.H. Holmes to James Weldon Johnson, November 13, 1923, Walterboro Branch File, I-G-197, NAACP Papers. On soil and lumber industry, see *South Carolina: A Handbook*, 304–5.

67. Application for Charter, Beaufort, South Carolina, June 11, 1919, Beaufort Branch File, I-G-196, NAACP Papers; Charles E. Washington to James Weldon Johnson, July 26, 1927, Beaufort Branch File, I-G-196, NAACP Papers. For revival of branches in the 1940s, see Chapters Four and Five.

68. *South Carolina: A Handbook*, 296–97; Application for Charter, Calhoun County, South Carolina, November 19, 1925, Lone Star Branch File, I-G-197, NAACP Papers; A.D. Wright to Robert Bagnall, February 25, 1929, Lone Star Branch File, I-G-197, NAACP Papers; T.J. Lemon to Robert Bagnall, June 22, 1930, Lone Star Branch File, I-G-197, NAACP Papers. Despite its rich portrayal of rural black political life, Steven Hahn's *A Nation under Our Feet* falls prey to old and unproved views of the NAACP. "The perspective of the fledgling National Association for the Advancement of Colored People (NAACP)," Hahn writes, "had little appeal (and the NAACP had little interest in moving outside the urban South, where it recruited among a sympathetic black middle class), whereas Garvey's views comported with their own experiences" (472).

69. "South Carolina Agricultural Experiment Station Circular 82," 3; Wright, *Old South, New South*, 202–3.

70. Kuznets et al., *Population Redistribution and Economic Growth*, 89–90.

71. On Gillespie's early life, see Gillespie, *to Be, or not . . . to Bop*, 1–47; Shipton, *Groovin' High*, 3–20.

72. *South Carolina: A Handbook*, 301–2; Historical Society of Chesterfield County, *Images of America*; Edgar, *South Carolina: The WPA Guide to the Palmetto State*, 303–6, 339–40, 465–66. Gillespie was likely the great-grandson of James A. Powe's grandfather, who fathered children with Gillespie's enslaved great-great grandmother, Nora. Gillespie, *to Be or not . . . to Bop*, 441–43; Shipton, *Groovin' High*, 303. On the influence of the Sanctified Church, see Gillespie, ibid., 31.

73. Gillespie, *to Be, or not . . . to Bop*, 1–2.

74. Ibid., 13.

75. *Cheraw Chronicle*, Bicentennial Edition, July 1, 1976, 6E; Tindall, *The Emergence of the New South*, 354; Edgar, *South Carolina*, 485–89, 499.

76. Gillespie, *to Be, or not . . . to Bop*, 14.

77. Shipton, *Groovin' High*, 25; Gillespie, *to Be, or not . . . to Bop*, 54–55.

78. Shipton, *Groovin' High*, 27.

79. On Gillespie's early years in Philadelphia and his role in the creation of bebop, see Gillespie, *to Be, or not . . . to Bop*, 48–221; Shipton, *Groovin' High*, 21–157.

80. Murray, *Stomping the Blues*, 245.

3. Radicalism and Liberal Reform

Epigraphs. Robert F. Wagner, Address before the Annual Conference of the National Association for the Advancement of Colored People, January 4, 1931, Part I, Reel 14, NAACP Papers; Du Bois, "Segregation," (January 1934), 20.

1. On the NAACP's role in the Harlem Renaissance, see Lewis, *When Harlem Was in Vogue* and *W.E.B. Du Bois: The Fight for Equality*, 153–82. On the NAACP's legislative and legal battles in the 1920s, see Hine, *Black Victory*, especially 72–108; Goings, *"The NAACP Comes of Age,"* especially 15–18; Meier and Rudwick, "Attorneys Black and White"; Ross, *J.E. Spingarn*, 103–24; Zangrando, *The NAACP Crusade against Lynching*.

2. Historians who focus on the internal dynamics of national office politics and the organization's national legal/legislative agenda have tended to conclude that by 1930 the NAACP had firmly established itself, institutionally if not also programmatically. See Goings, *"The NAACP Comes of Age"*; Ross, *J.E. Spingarn*. Ross argues that during the 1920s the NAACP "passed from organizational to institutional status," developing "a distinct 'character,' a self." "Its distinctive character, its goals, its response to patterns to external stimuli were," she writes, "becoming set," 103, 104, 108. I suggest, here, that the organization and its program were far from stable or "fixed" in the early 1930s.

3. The NAACP recorded a membership of 21,402 in 1929. The number likely dipped lower in the early 1930s, only beginning to make a recovery at the national level in the middle of the decade. Membership numbers from, Report and Recommendations on Membership and Staff, 1957, III-A-37, NAACP Papers. On the circulation decline of *The Crisis* and the problems it posed for the organization, see Minutes of the Meeting of the Board of Directors, June 14, 1930, Part I, Reel 2, NAACP Papers; Du Bois, *Dusk of Dawn*, quote on 295; Lewis, *W.E.B. Du Bois: The Fight for Equality*, 154–55, 266–301; Ross, *J.E. Spingarn*, 139–43.

4. Janken, *White*, especially 29–87, 129–66; Meier and Rudwick, "The Rise of the Black Secretariat in the NAACP," 113.

5. "Critical Period Faces Negro, Walter White Tells Meeting," Press Release, Annual Mass Meeting, January 5 [1931], Part I, Reel 14, NAACP Papers.

6. Walter White to Lorenzo H. King, December 30, 1932, Part I, Reel 14, NAACP Papers.

7. On the NAACP's financial crisis in the early 1930s, see Ross, *J.E. Spingarn and the Rise of the NAACP*, 125–43. On the important role of Jews in the NAACP and particularly in the support of the organization during the early 1930s, see Weiss, "Long-distance Runners of the Civil Rights Movement," especially 136–37. Also, see Lewis, "Parallels and Divergences"; Meier and Rudwick, "Attorneys Black and White." On the Garland Fund, see Minutes of the Meeting of the Board of Directors, June 9, 1930, Part I, Reel 2, NAACP Papers; Tushnet, *The NAACP Legal Strategy against Segregated Education*, 1–20.

8. Walter White to Lorenzo H. King, December 30, 1932, Part I, Reel 14, NAACP Papers; Report of Committee on Budget for Fiscal Year Beginning January 1, 1933 and Ending December 31, 1933, Part I, Reel 5, NAACP Papers; Remarks of Mr. J.E. Spingarn, President, to the Annual Business Meeting of the N.A.A.C.P., January 9, 1933, Part I, Reel 5, NAACP Papers; Minutes of the Meeting of the Board of Directors, January 9, 1933, Part I, Reel 2, NAACP Papers; Ross, *J.E. Spingarn*, 132–36.

9. Meier and Rudwick, "The Rise of the Black Secretariat," 114–15.

10. On Roosevelt's Hundred Days, see Kennedy, *Freedom from Fear*, 131–59; Leuchtenburg, *Franklin D. Roosevelt and the New Deal*, 41–62.

11. On the NAACP, the Communist Party, and Scottsboro, see Carter, *Scottsboro*, quotes from 59–67. Also, see Goodman, *Stories of Scottsboro*.

12. Minutes of the Meeting of the Board of Directors, May 9, 1932, Part I, Reel 2, NAACP Papers; Minutes of the Meeting of the Board of Directors, March 14, 1933, Part I, Reel 2, NAACP Papers. Joel Spingarn, according to B. Joyce Ross, played an important role in convincing reluctant executives, possibly Walter White and board members, to approve of the Conference. *J.E. Spingarn*, 168–78.

13. The standard treatments of the second Amenia Conference are, Ross, *J.E. Spingarn*, 159–85; Wolters, *Negroes and the Great Depression*, 219–29. Also, see Holloway, *Confronting the Veil*, 4–16; Lewis, *W.E.B. Du Bois: The Fight for Equality*, 318–25; Young, *Black Writers of the Thirties*, 3–63.

14. Wolters, *Negroes and the Great Depression*, 222; Du Bois, "Youth and Age at Amenia."

15. Lewis, *W.E.B. Du Bois: The Fight for Equality*, 319–20.

16. Ibid., 307 and 630, n 307.

17. Spero and Harris, *The Black Worker*, 464, 463.

18. On the influence of developments in social science in the shaping of black racial ideology, especially with respect to the work of Franz Boas, see Bay, *The White Image in the Black Mind*, 187–217; Young, *Black Writers of the Thirties*, especially 35–63. Young makes an important distinction between the Young Turks' public pronunciations and writings, which called for a "moratorium on race," and their more privately held belief that race remained a pressing concern to the future of black people. That said, Young concludes that their rigid public stance on the primacy of class and economics helped foster a climate of misunderstanding and conflict with an older generation of "race men" and contributed to a debate about race and class that was couched in decidedly either/or terms. "Too often," he writes, "this [economic] orientation carried the young academics as far away from reality as an out-dated provinciality had carried some of their elders. Just as the older race men often advised an escape into race, these young radicals advocated escape—escape from the reality of race into a theoretical class" (239). For a fine summary of the Young Turks' embrace of class politics and their criticism of the NAACP, also see Myrdal, *An American Dilemma*, 788–90, 833–34.

19. Bunche, *A World View of Race*, 4, 21, 25, 67.

20. Ibid., 89, 91.

21. Ibid., 32, 92.

22. Du Bois, "Youth and Age at Amenia"; Lewis, *W.E.B. Du Bois: The Fight for Equality*, 323; Wolters, *Negroes and the Great Depression*, 221–27.

23. The standard treatments of the Report on the Future Plan and Program are: Ross, *J.E. Spingarn*, 217–45; Wolters, *Negroes and the Great Depression*, 302–52. Also, see Holloway, *Confronting the Veil*, 93–103.

24. The Future Plan and Program of the N.A.A.C.P., Part I, Reel 9, NAACP Papers; Bunche, "Critical Analysis of the Tactics and Programs of Minority Groups," 315.

25. The Future Plan and Program of the N.A.A.C.P., Part I, Reel 9, NAACP Papers. In Harris's "Preliminary Report of the Committee on the Future Plan and Program of the N.A.A.C.P.," he explicitly called for the creation of workers' and farmers' councils to carry out his program of economic education. The suggestion was cut from the final draft. The Preliminary Report can be found in "Committee Correspondence," Plan and Program Committee, July–Aug. 1934, I-A-29, NAACP Papers.

26. The Future Plan and Program of the N.A.A.C.P., Part I, Reel 9, NAACP Pa-

pers; Ross, *J.E. Spingarn*, 50–51, 236. In 1936 the NAACP amended its constitution to stipulate that members would select three members of the nominating committee, the board would select three, and the chairman of the board would become a permanent member of the committee.

27. Lewis, *W.E.B. Du Bois: The Fight for Equality*, 278–85; Ross, *J.E. Spingarn*, 198–216.

28. Lewis, *W.E.B. Du Bois: The Fight for Equality*, 263, 302–48.

29. Du Bois, *The Souls of Black Folk*, 39. On Du Bois and his conception of double-consciousness, see Bruce, "W.E.B. Du Bois and the Idea of Double Consciousness"; Lewis, *W.E.B. Du Bois: Biography of a Race*, 282–83. For a dissenting view of the meaning and significance of Du Bois's conception of double-consciousness and the political project flowing from it, see Reed, *W.E.B. Du Bois and American Political Thought*, 93–126. Reed is certainly correct to argue that Du Bois's notion of double-consciousness drew on a late-nineteenth century, neo-Lamarkian conception of "race, evolution, and social hierarchy" that Du Bois, himself, would later repudiate. But Reed fails to give adequate credence to the notion that *The Souls of Black Folk* simultaneously marked a departure from nineteenth-century thinking about race, that Du Bois began articulating a new understanding of racial identity as rooted in history, not biology and that he sought to fashion a political project designed to relativize race, to make racial identity only one of a number of social identities available to human beings.

30. On Du Bois's efforts to formulate "a new racial philosophy" and the writing and significance of *Black Reconstruction in America*, see Lewis, *W.E.B. Du Bois: The Fight for Equality*, 302–48, 349–87. Also, see Du Bois, *Black Reconstruction in America*; Foner, *Reconstruction*, xix–xxvii. The Young Turks' criticism of Du Bois's emerging philosophy for racial advancement is best summed up in Benjamin Stolberg's "Black Chauvinism," 570–71, which Sterling Brown, Ralph J. Bunche, Emmett Dorsey, and E. Franklin Frazier defended in a later edition of *The Nation*, 141 (July 3, 1935), 17. Harris quoted from his review of *Black Reconstruction* published in *The New Republic* LXXXIII (August 7, 1935), 367. On the Young Turks' stinging criticism of *Black Reconstruction* and Du Bois's use of Marx, see Lewis, ibid., 373–75; Du Bois, "Karl Marx and the Negro," 56.

31. Du Bois, "A Negro Nation within the Nation," 265–66.

32. The literature concerned with the development and nature of postindustrial society is immense. Works that have most influenced my thinking include: Bell, *The Coming of Post-Industrial Society*; Livingston, *Pragmatism, Feminsm, and Democracy*; Sklar, *The United States as a Developing Country*, 143–96; Wilson, *The Declining Significance of Race*.

33. Du Bois, "On Being Ashamed of Oneself," 200.

34. Ibid.

35. Du Bois, "Segregation" (January 1934), 20. Du Bois would develop this argument in greater depth in *Dusk of Dawn*, 173–220.

36. W.E.B. Du Bois quoted from his reply to Francis J. Grimké, "Segregation," *The Crisis* 41 (June 1934), 173–74. Quote on 174. For an insightful, though more pessimistic and critical, view of Du Bois's mid-1930s thinking about race-consciousness and civil rights struggle, see Guterl, *The Color of Race in America*, 148–53.

37. Lewis, *W.E.B. Du Bois: The Fight for Equality*, 338.

38. Du Bois, "Segregation," 20.

39. Du Bois, "Social Planning for the Negro," 125. Papers delivered at the "National Conference on the Economic Crisis and the Negro" were reprinted in the January 1936 edition of the *Journal of Negro Education.*

40. Minutes of the Meeting of the Board of Directors, April 9, 1934, Part I, Reel 2, NAACP Papers. Also, see *The Crisis* 41 (May 1934), 149.

41. On the particulars of Du Bois's resignation, see Lewis, *W.E.B. Du Bois: The Fight for Equality,* 340–48; Ross, *J.E. Spingarn,* 207–16; Wolters, *Negroes and the Great Depression,* 266–94.

42. On Harris's resignation from the NAACP Board of Directors, see Wolters, *Negroes and the Great Depression,* 327–28.

43. Charles H. Houston, Address Delivered before the Twenty-fourth Annual Conference of the National Association for the Advancement of Colored People, Chicago, Illinois, July 2, 1933, Part I, Reel 5, NAACP Papers. For an astute discussion of the NAACP's structure and the role of the national office and the branches, see Myrdal, *An American Dilemma,* 819–31, 1403, n. 41.

44. On Houston's efforts to transform the Howard University Law School into a laboratory for social activism and his formulation of the NAACP's legal strategy as a constitutive part of a broader social insurgency, see McNeil, *Groundwork,* 76–127, especially 116–17. Also, see Sullivan, *Days of Hope,* 84–91; Tushnet, *The NAACP Legal Strategy against Segregated Education,* 21–48.

45. Houston, Address, July 2, 1933, Part I, Reel 5, NAACP Papers.

46. Ibid.

47. On the George Green Lynching, see Joseph A. Tolbert to Roy Wilkins, January 4, 1934, Legal Files, I-D-58, NAACP Papers; Joseph A. Tolbert to Roy Wilkins, November 5, 1934, Subject Files, I-C-366, NAACP Papers; *Palmetto Leader,* November 9, 1935, Subject Files, I-C-366, NAACP Papers; Finnegan, "'At the Hands of Parties Unknown,'" 298–99. Norris Dendy was lynched on July 5, 1933, in Clinton, South Carolina, and Bennie Thompson was lynched on October 8, 1933, in Ninety-Six, South Carolina, Report of the Secretary, July 1933, Part I, Reel 5, NAACP Papers; Report of the Secretary, November 1933, Part I, Reel 5, NAACP Papers. On the chain gang lynching, see Joseph A. Tolbert to Walter White, November 27, 1933, Subject Files, I-C-366, NAACP Papers; Roy Wilkins to Arthur Spingarn, January 3, 1934, Subject Files, I-C-366, NAACP Papers; Joseph A. Tolbert to Roy Wilkins, January 4, 1934, Legal Files, I-D-58, NAACP Papers; Roy Wilkins to Arthur B. Spingarn, May 7, 1934, Legal Files, I-D-58, NAACP Papers; Joseph A. Tolbert to Roy Wilkins, May 19, 1934, Legal Files, I-D-58, NAACP Papers. Wilkins quoted from, Roy Wilkins to J.E. Spingarn, February 4, 1934, Part I, Reel 27, NAACP Papers.

48. For a history of Greenville County during the 1920s and 1930s, see Huff, *Greenville,* 292–373. On the South Carolina textile mill industry, see Simon, *A Fabric of Defeat.* Population figures and description are derived from, U.S. Bureau of the Census, *Sixteenth Census of the United States, Population, Vol. II, Part 6, South Carolina, 1940,* 383; Huff, *Greenville,* 333; George C. Stoney, Memorandum entitled "Greenville, S.C., Political Notes" submitted to Ralph J. Bunche, 1940, Box 38, File 7, Bunche Papers, The Schomburg Center for Research in Black Culture, New York, New York.

49. On the class and occupational makeup of black Greenville, see Huff, *Greenville,* 313–15, 355. Description of living conditions are derived from a study undertaken by the Greenville County Council for Community Development through

the Social Science Department at Furman University in conjunction with student researchers from Greenville's black Sterling High School, Negro Housing in Metropolitan Greenville, June 1938, Box 1, GCCCD Papers, James B. Duke Library, Furman University, Greenville, South Carolina; Recreational Facilities for Negroes in Greenville, Box 2, Negro Council, 1938–1941, GCCCD Papers; B.E. Geer to Leo M. Favrot, April 29, 1935, Box 433, Folder 4546, GEB Papers, Record Group 950, Rockefeller Archive Center, Sleepy Hollow, New York.

50. Interview with John Bolt Culbertson, by George C. Stoney, 1940, Box 38, File 7, Bunche Papers.

51. Interview with John Bolt Culbertson, by Wilhelmina Jackson, 1940, Box 36, File 3, Bunche Papers.

52. On Hattie Logan Duckett and the founding of the Phillis Wheatley Center, see "A Visit to Remember," Hattie Logan Duckett Biographical File, South Carolina Room, Greenville County Public Library, Greenville, South Carolina; Dedicatory Exercises, Hattie Duckett Elementary School, Sunday, April 24, 1966, Phillis Wheatley Center File, South Carolina Room, Greenville County Public Library, Greenville, South Carolina; 50th Anniversary, S.C. Federation of Colored Women's Clubs, Program Guide; Phillis Wheatley Ass'n Memoranda, December 31, 1925, Phillis Wheatley Center File; Phillis Wheatley Association: Purpose, Phillis Wheatley Center File; Huff, *Greenville*, 313–15. On Jane Edna Hunter and the founding of the Phillis Wheatley Association, see Hine, *Hinesight*, 109–28.

53. Phillis Wheatley Ass'n Memoranda; Phyllis Wheatley Association Annual Reports, 1937–1941, Phillis Wheatley Center File; 1939 At Phillis Wheatley: A Year of Progress and Achievement, Phillis Wheatley Center File; Phillis Wheatley Association Annual Report, May 1, 1937-June 1, 1938, Box 2, Interracial Cooperation, 1937–1939, GCCCD Papers.

54. Attendance List for a Meeting of the CIC in Greenville, South Carolina, March 23, 1931, Reel 53, Commission on Interracial Cooperation/Association of Southern Women for the Prevention of Lynching Papers, hereafter cited as CIC Papers; F. Clyde Helms to Friends and Members of the S.C. Interracial Council, CIC Papers. On the creation of the CIC, see Jacquelyn Dowd Hall, *Revolt against Chivalry*, 60–65, quote on 61; Tindall, *The Emergence of the New South*, 177–83. On the CIC in South Carolina, see Gordon, *Sketches of Negro Life*, 220–22; Fields, *Lemon Swamp and Other Places*, 192–95.

55. On the NRA and the strike activity of 1933–1934 in South Carolina, see Simon, *A Fabric of Defeat*, 90–122. On union and strike activity in Greenville, see Huff, *Greenville*, 350–55; Simon, *A Fabric of Defeat*, 114–15. The definitive work on the NRA remains Hawley, *The New Deal and the Problem of Monopoly*. On the NRA with respect to the southern textile industry, see Hodges, *New Deal Labor Policy*, 3–140.

56. On Geer and the Bruere Board, see Hodges, *New Deal Labor Policy*, 62–118; Huff, *Greenville*, 278–79; B.E. Geer to R.W. Bruere, October 21, 1933, Box 10, Geer, B.E., NRA Records, RG 69, Series 397, National Archives, Washington, D.C.; Telephone Communication, August 28, 1934, RG 69, Series 397, NRA Records. On Geer's tenure as president of Furman University, see Reid, *Furman University*, 62–99. On the New South "industrial spirit," see Tindall, *Emergence of the New South*, especially 70–80. On Frank Porter Graham and his tenure at the University of North Carolina, see Egerton, *Speak Now against the Day*, 130–34. For Geer's concerns about and vision for Furman, see B.E. Geer to Jackson Davis, October 10, 1935, Box

433, Folder 4547, GEB Papers. On Geer's early contacts with the GEB, see Conference, President B.E. Geer with Jackson Davis, May 28, 1934, Box 433, Folder 4546, GEB Papers; Interview, Leo M. Favrot with Dr. B.E. Geer, March 30, 1935, Box 433, Folder 4546, GEB Papers; B.E. Geer to Jackson Davis, October 10, 1935, Box 433, Folder 4547, GEB Papers. Quote about "happy community life" from Favrot interview of Geer. On the founding and activities of the GEB, see Fosdick, *Adventure in Giving*. On the creation and mission of the GCCCD, see Initial Grant Proposal, Box 1, GCCCD Papers; A Proposed Program for a County Adult Education Program and an Adult Community Leadership Project at Furman University, Greenville, South Carolina, May 15, 1935, Box 433, Folder 4546, GEB Papers; Leo M. Favrot to Edmund E. Day, June 8, 1935, Box 433, Folder 4547, GEB Papers; B.E. Geer to Leo M. Favrot, March 23, 1936, Box 433, Folder 4548, GEB Papers; Inter-office Correspondence, July 8, 1936, Box 433, Folder 4549, GEB Papers. On the Parker District School system and Lawrence Peter Hollis, see Huff, *Greenville*, 296–98. On adult education reform in South Carolina generally, see Leon Fink's chapter on South Carolina's leading adult education reformer, Wil Lou Gray, in Fink, *Progressive Intellectuals*, 242–74. On Ebaugh, see Laura Smith Ebaugh Biographical File, South Carolina Room, Greenville County Public Library, Greenville, South Carolina. On Blackwell, see Interview with Gordon Blackwell, by Brent Glass, Southern Oral History Collection.

57. Initial Grant Proposal, Box 1, GCCCD Papers; Annual Report (1st), 1936–1937, Box 1, GCCCD Papers; Annual Report (2nd), 1937–1938, Box 1, GCCCD Papers.

58. Initial Grant Proposal, Box 1, GEB Papers; Phillis Wheatley Ass'n Memoranda, December 31, 1925, Phillis Wheatley Center File; Leo M. Favrot to B.E. Geer, April 10, 1935, Box 433, Folder 4546, GEB Papers; B.E. Geer to Leo M. Favrot, April 12, 1935, GEB Papers; Annual Report (1st), 1936–1937, Box 1, GCCCD Papers; Annual Report (3rd), 1938–1939, GCCCD Papers. On black nursing and its significance to black communities, see Hine, *Black Women in White* and *Hinesight*, 163–82. For the importance of healthcare work in laying the groundwork for political activism, see Woods, "Modjeska Simkins and the South Carolina Conference of the NAACP."

59. Annual Report (1st), 1936–1937, Box 1, GCCCD Papers; A Description of the Buildings and Grounds of the Rural Schools for Negroes in Greenville County, December 1936, Box 435, Folder 4562, GEB Papers; Report on the Second Meeting of the County Council for White Leaders on Negro Education, December 2, 1937, Box 433, Folder 4550, GEB Papers .

60. Annual Report (2nd), 1937–1938, Box 1, GCCCD Papers; Annual Report (3rd), 1938–1939, Box 1, GCCCD Papers; Interview with Gordon Blackwell, by Brent Glass, Southern Oral History Collection; Negro Housing in Metropolitan Greenville, June 1938, Box 1, GCCCD Papers; Annual Report (1st), 1936–1937, Box 1, GCCCD Papers.

61. Annual Report (3rd), 1938–1939, Box 1, GCCCD Papers; Albert R. Mann Report, October 4, 1938, Box 434, Folder 4551, GEB Papers; Fred McCuistion and Selskar M. Gunn, "Report and Evaluation of the Work of the Greenville County Council for Community Development," October 29, 1940, Box 434, Folder 4551, GEB Papers; Negro Council Membership List, Box 2, Negro Council, 1938–1941, GCCCD Papers; "Recreational Facilities for Negroes in Greenville," Box 2, Negro

Council, 1938–1941, GCCCD Papers; "Crime in Greenville," Box 2, Negro Council, 1938–1941, GCCCD Papers; "The Counselor: Voice of the Negro Council for Community Development," Box 2, Negro Council, 1938–1941, GCCCD Papers.

62. Reid, *Furman University*, 83–96; Interview with Gordon Blackwell, by Brent Glass, Southern Oral History Collection; Interview with R.O. Johnson, by George C. Stoney, in George C. Stoney, "Greenville, S.C., Political Notes," Box 38, File 7, Bunche Papers; Interview with R.O. Johnson, by Wilhelmina Jackson, 1940, Box 36, File 3, Bunche Papers.

63. On the 1934 governor's race and Governor Johnston's relationship to white textile mill workers, see Simon, *A Fabric of Defeat*, 123–87. On the Wagner Act, see Bernstein, *The New Deal Collective Bargaining Policy*. On the creation of TWOC and its efforts to organize in South Carolina, see, respectively, Fraser, *Labor Will Rule*, 378–81; Simon, *A Fabric of Defeat*, 198–203.

64. Interview, President, S.C. League for Progressive Democracy (Labor's Non-Partisan League) Bradford, and Ralph Simmerson, T.W.U.A. organizer for Greenville, by George C. Stoney, 1940, Box 38, File 7, Bunche Papers, hereafter cited as Interview with Bradford and Simmerson, by George Stoney. Quotes are from Simmerson's conversation with Stoney in a discussion without Bradford present, hereafter cited as Interview with Simmerson, by George Stoney, Bunche Papers; Interview with King and Hayes, by George C. Stoney, 1940, Box 38, File 7, Bunche Papers, quote from King.

65. Most recent historians of the New Deal argue that its efforts to reform the American economy, notably but not exclusively through the National Recovery Act and its antecedent, the Wagner Act, authorized a specifically class-based form of politics. Only as New Deal liberals retreated from their earlier concern with the problems of monopoly and economic disorder by the 1940s, they maintain, did a broad conception of interest group– or rights-based politics emerge. For examples, see Brinkley, *The End of Reform*; Fraser and Gerstle, eds., *The Rise and Fall of the New Deal Order*, especially the editors' introduction; Fraser, *Labor Will Rule*; Gerstle, *Working-Class Americanism*; Korstad, *Civil Rights Unionism*; Lichtenstein, *The Most Dangerous Man in Detroit*. An earlier generation of historians demonstrated, however, that the New Dealers acknowledged the legitimacy of the large-scale corporation and empowered certain interest groups, including staple crop farmers, industrial workers, some ethnic groups, and a new intellectual-administrative class as a means of checking corporate power and reforming American society, but failed to do the same for all groups, including African Americans, sharecroppers, and domestic workers. Especially, see Leuchtenburg, *Franklin D. Roosevelt and the New Deal*, 63–94, 326–48. Also, see Bernstein, *The New Deal Collective Bargaining Policy*; Hawley, *The New Deal and the Problem of Monopoly*; Hofstadter, *The Age of Reform*, 302–28.

66. Robert W. Bagnall to Will Payne, March 1929, Greenville Branch File, I-G-197, NAACP Papers; Robert W. Bagnall to E.B. Halloway, January 21, 1931, Greenville Branch File, I-G-197, NAACP Papers; Lucille Black to Robert W. Bagnall, January 30, 1931, with attached list of branch officers, Part I, Reel 15, NAACP Papers; C.A. Williams Jr., to Robert W. Bagnall, June 21, 1934, Greenville Branch File, I-G-197, NAACP Papers; Robert W. Bagnall to C.A. Williams Jr., June 27, 1934, Greenville Branch File, I-G-197, NAACP Papers. On Bagnall's efforts to organize NAACP branches in 1931, see Robert W. Bagnall, "N.A.A.C.P. Branch Activities," *The Crisis* 39 (February 1932), 53; Robert W. Bagnall, "Lights and Shadows in the South," *The Crisis* 39 (April 1932).

67. Historical Sketch of the Greenville Branch NAACP in The NAACP's 15th Annual Southeast Regional Program Guide, Box 3, Programs, State Conferences, 1951–1967, Modjeska M. Simkins Papers, Modern Political Collections, University of South Carolina, Columbia; Application for Charter, Greenville, South Carolina, July 24, 1938, Greenville Branch File, I-G-197, NAACP Papers; *Hill's Greenville City Directory, 1938*; Membership Report, March 4, 1939, Greenville Branch File, I-G-197, NAACP Papers; J.A. Brier to NAACP National Office, August 5, 1938, Greenville Branch File, I-G-197, NAACP Papers. James A. Briar apparently used Briar and Brier interchangeably as the spelling of his last name. Often his letters to the National Office were signed J.A. Brier, but his name appears in NAACP publications as J.A. Briar. For purposes of clarity, I use the spelling "Briar" in the text. On battles for citizenship rights couched in claims to "Best Man" status in the nineteenth century, see Edwards, *Gendered Strife and Confusion*, especially 218–54; Gilmore, *Gender and Jim Crow*, especially 61–89. Also, see my discussion in Chapters One and Two concerning the ways in which struggles for citizenship rights and black liberation continue to be waged on and through the terrain of race and gender in the twentieth century.

68. *The Crisis* 47 (January 1940), 20; Baker, "The 'Hoover Scare' in South Carolina," 268, 282; Interview with J.A. Brier, by Wilhelmina Jackson, February 7, 1940, Box 36, File 3, Bunche Papers.

69. Briar and the men of the Greenville NAACP, it should be noted, did not simply represent the return of the repressed. As Elizabeth Faue and Robin Kelley have argued concerning working-class Finnish Americans, Communists, and black nationalists, radical movements organized along class and race lines often shared a highly masculinist understanding of struggle during the 1930s. "The language of class struggle and 'race' struggle," Kelley writes, "employed a highly masculinist imagery that relied on metaphors from war and emphasized violence as a form of male redemption. Thus on the terrain of gender, Communists and Black nationalists found common ground—a ground which rendered women invisible or constructed them in an auxiliary relationship." Kelley, "'Afric's Sons with Banner Red,'" 49; Faue, *Community of Suffering & Struggle*, especially 15–18, 71.

70. William Pickens to J.A. Brier, August 8, 1938, Greenville Branch File, I-G-197, NAACP Papers; William Pickens to J.A. Johnson, August 12, 1938, Greenville Branch File, I-G-197, NAACP Papers. On Daisy Lampkin, see McKenzie, "Daisy Elizabeth Adams Lampkin."

71. Membership Report, January 2, 1939, Greenville Branch File, I-G-197, NAACP Papers; Report of the Election of Officers, January 3, 1939, Greenville Branch File, I-G-197, NAACP Papers; Membership Report, November 6, 1939, Greenville Branch File, I-G-197, NAACP Papers; Interview with Henry Percival, Sr., by George C. Stoney, Box 38, File 7, Bunche Papers; Interview with John Bolt Culbertson, by Wilhelmina Jackson, 1940, Box 36, File 3, Bunche Papers.

72. Interview with Henry Percival, Sr., by Wilhelmina Jackson, February 6, 1940, Box 36, File 3, Bunche Papers; Interview with R.O. Johnson, by Wilhelmina Jackson, February 3, 1940, Box 36, File 3, Bunche Papers.

73. Interview with R.O. Johnson, by Wilhelmina Jackson, Bunche Papers; Interview with J.A. Brier, by Wilhelmina Jackson, Bunche Papers. Also, see Interview with R.O. Johnson, by George C. Stoney, Bunche Papers.

74. "Educating People to Help Themselves" Invitation Flier, Box 434, Folder 4552, GEB Papers.

75. Executive Committee Meeting Minutes, March 6, 1939, Box 2, Interracial Cooperation, 1937–1939, GCCCD Papers; B.E. Geer to Edmund de S. Brunner, March 11, 1939, Box 434, Folder 4557, GEB Papers.

76. Interview with R.O. Johnson, by Wilhelmina Jackson, Bunche Papers; Proceedings of the First Southeastern Regional Conference on Cooperation, "Educating People to Help Themselves," Address: "The Philosophy of Cooperative Action," by Arthur Raper, Box 434, Folder 4554, GEB Papers.

77. Interview with R.O. Johnson, by Wilhelmina Jackson, Bunche Papers; Interview with Henry Percival, Sr., by Wilhelmina Jackson, Bunche Papers; Interview with Henry Percival, Sr., by George C. Stoney, Bunche Papers; William Hill to NAACP National Office, June 12, 1939, South Carolina State Conference File, I-G-196, NAACP Papers; Interview with R.O. Johnson, by Wilhelmina Jackson, Bunche Papers; George C. Stoney, "Greenville, S.C., Political Notes," Bunche Papers; Interview with Henry Percival, Sr., by Wilhelmina Jackson, Bunche Papers; Interview with John Bolt Culbertson, by Wilhelmina Jackson, Bunche Papers.

78. *Greenville News*, July 6, 1939; Ibid., July 7, 1939. Briar blamed Anderson's boasting for exposing the NAACP's covert voter registration efforts, Interview with J.A. Brier, by Wilhelmina Jackson, Bunche Papers; *Greenville News*, July 7, 1939; *Greenville News*, July 8, 1939. Also, see Hoffman, "Genesis," 366–67.

79. Interview with R.O. Johnson, by Wilhelmina Jackson, Bunche Papers; Hoffman, "Genesis," 366; *Greenville News*, July 19, July 21, July 25, September 8, September 9, September 10, 1939; *The Crisis* 40 (January 1940), 20; Interview with Henry Percival, Sr., by George C. Stoney, Bunche Papers; Interview with J.A. Brier, Wilhelmina Jackson, Bunche Papers.

80. Executive Committee Meeting Minutes, July 19, 1939, Box 2, Interracial Cooperation, 1937–1939, GCCCD Papers; Interview with Henry Percival, Sr., by George C. Stoney, Bunche Papers.

81. Interview with John Bolt Culbertson, by Wilhelmina Jackson, Bunche Papers; Interview with Henry Percival, Sr., by Wilhelmina Jackson, Bunche Papers; *Greenville News*, July 8 and September 14, 1939; Interview with Ralph Simmerson, by George C. Stoney, Bunche Papers. Also, see Interview with King and Hayes, by George C. Stoney, Bunche Papers.

82. *Greenville News*, September 7, September 13, September 25, 1939; Associated Negro Press Report, no date, Reel 53, CIC Papers; *Greenville News*, November 22, 1939; Interview with Joseph Tolbert, by Wilhelmina Jackson, Box 36, File 3, Bunche Papers. On violence across the piedmont, see *Greenville News*, November 16 and 18, 1939.

83. *Greenville News*, November 16, 1939; Interview with J.A. Brier, by Wilhelmina Jackson, Bunche Papers; Interview with A.J. Whittenberg, by Peter F. Lau, PFL; *Greenville News*, December 1 and December 15, 1939; *The Crisis* 47 (January 1940), 20. On African American traditions of armed self-defense, see Tyson, *Radio Free Dixie*.

84. On the Youth Council response to the Greenville movement, see *The Crisis* 46 (October 1939), 312–13. On Greenville's influence in South Carolina, see Chapter Four. On the NAACP's voting rights initiative, see *The Crisis* 47 (May 1940), 149. Also, see Hine, *Black Victory*.

4. Civil Rights and Collective Action

Epigraphs. "Faith of Our Fathers," quoted from the program guide to the Second Annual Conference, South Carolina Branches, National Association for the Advancement of Colored People, June 15 and 16, 1941, South Carolina State Conference of Branches File, II-C-181, NAACP Papers. The conference opened on the fifteenth with the singing of "Faith of Our Fathers"; Progressive Democratic Party flier, "YOU'VE TRIED THE OTHERS, NOW TRY THE BEST!," likely penned by John H. McCray and distributed in 1944, Politics: General, Reel 7, McCray Papers, South Caroliniana Library, University of South Carolina, Columbia.

1. Byrd quoted in, *Cheraw Chronicle*, December 23, 1971, 1. Byrd's biography is drawn from the following sources: *Cheraw Chronicle*, September 28, 1972, in Black History File, Cheraw Town Hall, Cheraw, South Carolina; *Cheraw Chronicle*, September 12, 1985, 19A; *Cheraw Chronicle*, January 23, 1986; Funeral Services for Levi G. Byrd, September 12, 1985, from the personal files of Alfred D. Byrd, Hampton, Virginia; Interview with Alfred D. Byrd, by Peter F. Lau, PFL; Interview with Bernice S. Robinson, by Peter F. Lau, PFL.

2. Gillespie, *to Be, or not . . . to BOP*, 30.

3. Lucille Black to Levi G. Byrd, June 14, 1933, Cheraw Branch File, I-G-196, NAACP Papers; Interview with Alfred D. Byrd, by Peter F. Lau.

4. Levi G. Byrd to Walter White, June 16, 1933, Cheraw Branch File, I-G-196, NAACP Papers; Levi G. Byrd to National Office, June 27, 1933, Cheraw Branch File, I-G-196, NAACP Papers. Byrd's writings (typed and handwritten) reflect his lack of formal schooling and the immediacy with which he wrote the national office. I do my best to quote him verbatim.

5. *Cheraw Chronicle*, "The Chesterfield County Development Edition," May 31, 1934, 1. On Gillespie, see Chapter Two. In his work on South Africa's South-Western Transvaal, Charles Van Onselen has argued that relations of power premised on the ideology and social practice of paternalism, that is, on relations of power premised on the real and imagined relationships of the patriarchal household, between the father and his dependents, are particularly subject to outbursts of violence when the imagined family-like relationship is challenged. Van Onselen, "The Social and Economic Underpinnings of Paternalism and Violence on the Maize Farms of the South-Western Transvaal." He writes, "With the established racial order in the countryside being challenged by smart-talking city-folk from the outside, and time-honored social practices on the farms being questioned by previously loyal quasi-kin from the inside, white anger was fueled almost as much by a sense of treachery and betrayal as it was by feelings of insecurity and vulnerability. It was precisely *because* the roots of paternalism were so deeply embedded in the social soil of the triangle that the potential for inter-racial violence was so great" (148).

6. On religion and behavior as key markers of class in African American communities, see Higginbotham, *Righteous Discontent*, especially, 185–230; Clark-Lewis, *Living In, Living Out*. Also, see Chapter Three for a discussion of class as a social construction, which, I argue, is, like race, an identity that cannot exist independently from its performance or human articulation and, therefore, cannot be reduced, in the first or last instance, to its mere relationship to the means of production. Gillespie quoted in Gillespie, *to Be, or not . . . to Bop*, 30–31. On the Coulter Memorial Academy, see *Cheraw Chronicle*, "The Bicentennial Edition," July 1, 1976, 4D; Miles S. Richards, "A Chronicle of Coulter Memorial Academy," Coulter Academy, Black

History Vertical Files, South Caroliniana Library, University of South Carolina, Columbia, South Carolina. On the Robert Small Graded and Junior High School, see *Cheraw Chronicle*, May 31, 1934, 5.

7. *Cheraw Chronicle*, September 28, 1972; Levi G. Byrd to National Office, June 16, 1933, Cheraw Branch File, I-G-196, NAACP Papers; Interview with Alfred D. Byrd by Peter Lau; Interview with Bernice S. Robinson by Peter Lau.

8. Levi G. Byrd to National Office, November 1, 1933, Cheraw Branch File, I-G-196, NAACP Papers; Levi G. Byrd to National Office, June 16, 1933, Cheraw Branch File, I-G-196, NAACP Papers; Lucille Black to Rev. G.W. Long, November 2, 1933, Cheraw Branch File, I-G-196, NAACP Papers; Lucille Black to Prof. Henry Marshall, Cheraw Branch File, I-G-196, NAACP Papers; Lucille Black to Rev. F.W. Prince, Cheraw Branch File, I-G-196, NAACP Papers; Lucille Black to Rev. J.E. Mc-Coy, Cheraw Branch File, I-G-196, NAACP Papers.

9. Levi G. Byrd to National Office, July 19, 1933, Cheraw Branch File, I-G-196, NAACP Papers.

10. Interview with Alfred D. Byrd by Peter Lau; Interview with Bernice S. Robinson by Peter Lau. On the NAACP's 1937 antilynching campaign, see Zangrando, *The NAACP Crusade against Lynching*, 139–65; On the significance of button-wearing among CIO members, see Cohen, *Making a New Deal*, 339–40. Black women also boldly wore buttons during Reconstruction to proclaim their political allegiances. See Hunter, *To 'Joy My Freedom*, 32.

11. Interview with Alfred D. Byrd by Peter Lau; Interview with Bernice S. Robinson by Peter Lau.

12. Dickson quoted in Hoffman, "Genesis," 367; Application for Charter, Cheraw and Chesterfield County, South Carolina, May 19, 1939, Cheraw Branch File, I-G-196, NAACP Papers; 40th Anniversary, S.C. Federation of Colored Women's Clubs, 1909–1949, Program Guide, Part I, Reel 22, NACW Records; Levi G. Byrd to National Office, May 23, 1939, Cheraw Branch File, I-G-196, NAACP Papers; Hoffman, "Genesis," 367.

13. On the inactivity of the NAACP in Columbia and Charleston in the 1930s, see Bagnall, "Lights and Shadows," 124–25; William Pickens to E.B. Burroughs, April 24, 1934, Charleston Branch File, I-G-196, NAACP Papers; Memorandum from Mr. Morrow to Mr. White, Mr. Wilkins, Mr. Pickens, August 29, 1938, Part 12, Series G, Reel 19, NAACP Papers; William Pickens to Norman F. Fitzpatrick et al., September 14, 1938, Part 12, Series G, Reel 19, NAACP Papers; A.J. Clement Jr., to Walter White, January 2, 1936, Charleston Branch File, I-G-196, NAACP Papers. Also, see Hoffman, "Genesis" 346–69. On Frederick's challenge to the white primary, see N.J. Frederick to Walter White, April 23, 1932, Part 4, Series C, Reel 2, NAACP Papers; N.J. Frederick to Walter White, May 7, 1932, Part 4, Series C, Reel 2, NAACP Papers; N.J. Frederick to James Marshall, July 2, 1932, Part 4, Series C, Reel 2, NAACP Papers; Complaint filed in the State of South Carolina, County of Richland, Court of Common Pleas, Part 4, Series C, Reel 2, NAACP Papers; Minutes of the Meeting of the Board of Directors, July 11, 1932, Part 1, Reel 2, NAACP Papers. On McCray's reputation as a radical, see Wilhelmina Jackson, Charleston Memorandum, 1940, Box 36, Folder 1, Bunche Papers. On McCray's 1937 editorial, see John H. McCray, "States the Position of Southern Negroes," *Charleston News and Courier*, April 13, 1937, clipping in Charleston Branch File, I-G-196, NAACP Papers; Louise Purvis Bell to The Editor, *Charleston News and Courier*, April 16, 1937, clipping in Charles-

ton Branch File, I-G-196, NAACP Papers; Louise Purvis Bell to Walter White, April 16, 1937, Charleston Branch File, I-G-196, NAACP Papers; Walter White to John H. McCray, April 24, 1937, Charleston Branch File, I-G-196, NAACP Papers; A.J. Clement Jr., to The Editor, *Charleston News and Courier*, n.d., clipping in Charleston Branch File, I-G-196, NAACP Papers.

14. Levi G. Byrd to William Pickens, May 29, 1939, Cheraw Branch File, I-G-196, NAACP Papers; Levi G. Byrd to William Pickens, July 9, 1939, Cheraw Branch File, I-G-196, NAACP Papers.

15. Report of the Department of Branches, December 1929, Part I, Reel 5, NAACP Papers. On the organization of the Texas State Conference in 1937, see Gillette, "The NAACP in Texas."

16. Levi G. Byrd to William Pickens, July 9, 1939, Cheraw Branch File, I-G-196, NAACP Papers.

17. William Pickens to Levi G. Byrd, July 10, 1939, Cheraw Branch File, I-G-196, NAACP Papers; Levi G. Byrd to William Pickens, July 26, 1939, Cheraw Branch File, I-G-196, NAACP Papers; Levi G. Byrd to William Pickens, September 18, 1939, Cheraw Branch File, I-G-196, NAACP Papers; Levi G. Byrd to National Office, October 16, 1939, Cheraw Branch File, I-G-196, NAACP Papers; Hinton quoted in Wilhelmina Jackson, Columbia Memorandum, 1940, Box 36, Folder 2, Bunche Papers; James M. Hinton to William Pickens, June 13, 1940, Columbia Branch File, II-C-177, NAACP Papers. On the Columbia branch's reluctance to join because of financial concerns, also see William Pickens to R.W. Jackson, November 20, 1939, Part 12, Series G, Reel 18, NAACP Papers.

18. "A Salute to James Miles Hinton, Sr.," *Pilgrim Progress*, April 25, 1962, Reel 9, McCray Papers; Dedication and Commemoration, Reverend James M. Hinton, Sr., James M. Hinton, Black History Vertical Files, South Caroliniana Library, University of South Carolina, Columbia; Obituary, James M. Hinton, Black History Vertical Files, South Caroliniana Library; R. Wright Spears, "The Reverend Mr. James M. Hinton," September 3, 1969, James M. Hinton, Black History Vertical Files, South Caroliniana Library.

19. "Ain't ready yet boys" reference noted by Modjeska M. Simkins in *Cheraw Chronicle*, December 23, 1971, 12-A.

20. Levi G. Byrd to William Pickens, September 18, 1939, Cheraw Branch File, I-G-196, NAACP Papers; Levi G. Byrd to National Office, October 16, 1939, Cheraw Branch File, I-G-196, NAACP Papers. On Rev. Arthur Jerome Wright, see Edelman, *Lanterns*, 1–9, 175. On Rev. J.J. Starks, see Newby, *Black Carolinians*, 230.

21. Drawing on oral history interviews with Modjeska Simkins and historical sketches from the South Carolina State Conference of NAACP Branches annual convention program guides, Barbara Woods has concluded that the founding meeting of the state conference was held on October 10, 1939, and that both Reverend Hinton and Modjeska Simkins were present. See Woods, "Black Woman Activist," 166–67; Woods, "Modjeska Simkins," 106. Documentary evidence from the NAACP Papers not cited by Woods contradict this version of the story, as does Byrd's own rendering of the history in an oral history interview conducted in 1956. See Levi G. Byrd to William Pickens, November 10, 1939, S.C. State Conference File, I-G-196, NAACP Papers, also can be found in Part 12, Series G, Reel 18, NAACP Papers; Report of Election, The South Carolina Branch, November 10, 1939, Cheraw Branch File, I-G-196, NAACP Papers; Lucille Black, Memorandum to *The Crisis*, November 14,

1939, Part 12, Series G, Reel 18, NAACP Papers; J.A. Johnson to William Pickens, October 21, 1939, Part 12, Series G, Reel 18, NAACP Papers; William Pickens to J.A. Johnson, October 26, 1939, Part 12, Series G, Reel 18, NAACP Papers; A.W. Wright to William Pickens, November 12, 1939, Part 12, Series G, Reel 18, NAACP Papers; William Pickens to Levi G. Byrd, November 14, 1939, Part 12, Series G, Reel 18, NAACP Papers. Byrd's version is recounted in Hoffman's "Genesis," 368. Although members of the Columbia branch ultimately came to play a central role in the state conference, it was not until after 1941 that they did so. Their prominence in the organization from that point forward and their power within the organization to record its history is likely the cause of the hazy rendering of the organization's founding.

22. On Briar, see Chapter Three; Levi G. Byrd to Walter White, June 18, 1941, State Conference File, II-C-181, NAACP Papers; James M. Hinton to Gloster B. Current, July 27, 1948, Greenville Branch File, II-C-178, NAACP Papers; Leroy E. Carter to James M. Hinton, August 23, 1948, Greenville Branch File, II-C-178, NAACP Papers; Eugene A.R. Montgomery, November 16, 1948, Greenville Branch File, II-C-178, NAACP Papers; D.T. Prioleau to William Pickens, February 1, 1940, Georgetown Branch File, II-C-178, NAACP Papers. The Georgetown County branch was chartered on March 1, 1939, and would become one of the largest and most active branches in the state in the 1940s. See Georgetown Branch File, I-G-197 and II-C-178, NAACP Papers; A.W. Wright to William Pickens, May 2, 1940, State Conference File, II-C-181, NAACP Papers.

23. R.W. Jackson to William Pickens, February 8, 1940, Columbia Branch File, II-C-177, NAACP Papers; Wilhelmina Jackson, Columbia Memorandum, 1940, Box 36, Folder 2, Bunche Papers.

24. Woods, "Black Woman Activist," 167–69. Byrd quoted in note 36. Also, see Rev. James M. Hinton to Levi G. Byrd, May 31, 1962, from personal files of Alfred D. Byrd, Hampton, Virginia; Levi G. Byrd to Walter White, December 22, 1941, State Conference File, II-C-181, NAACP Papers; Official Program of the First Annual Conference of the South Carolina Conference of Branches N A A C P, May 17, 1940, State Conference File, II-C-181, NAACP Papers; Program guide from the Second Annual Conference, South Carolina Branches, National Association for the Advancement of Colored People, June 15 and 16, 1941, State Conference File, II-C-181, NAACP Papers; Program, Third Annual Conference of South Carolina Branches of the National Association for the Advancement of Colored People, June 14 and June 15, 1942, State Conference File, II-C-181, NAACP Papers. According to Byrd, after learning about Maggie Robinson's involvement with the state conference and the local NAACP, the trial judge denounced the NAACP in court and sentenced Robinson to a jail term rather than ordering her to pay a fine. Levi G. Byrd to Walter White, April 29, 1942, Cheraw Branch File, II-C-176, NAACP Papers; Levi G. Byrd to Thurgood Marshall, June 6, 1942, Cheraw Branch File, II-C-176, NAACP Papers; Memorandum to Mr. Marshall from Mr. White, June 10, 1942, Cheraw Branch File, II-C-176, NAACP Papers.

25. "Exhortation for Solid Voluntary Action by All the People of Cheraw, S.C. In the Matter of Support for the Only and Greatest Organizational Champion of Negro Rights in America—National Association for the Advancement of Colored People," State Conference File, II-C-181, NAACP Papers; Levi G. Byrd to William Pickens, March 10, 1941, State Conference File, II-C-181, NAACP Papers. In his

1959 article, "Genesis," Hoffman credited the Cheraw branch with authorship of the pamphlet and cited 1939 as the probable date of its publication. However, Byrd's March 10, 1941, letter to William Pickens and clues internal to the pamphlet date the pamphlet to the spring of 1941 and suggest that its authorship was a collaborative effort on the part of the state conference. A copy of "Exhortation for Solid Voluntary Action by the People of Charleston, S.C." also can be found in Charleston Branch File, I-C-176, NAACP Papers, indicating that the same pamphlet was printed in the name of branches other than Cheraw. Unless otherwise indicated, the following quotations are taken from "Exhortation for Solid Voluntary Action." On Du Bois, see Chapter Three, as well as *Dusk of Dawn* (1940); Cruse, *The Crisis of the Negro Intellectual*. Cruse writes, "America, which idealizes the rights of the individual above everything else, is in reality, a nation dominated by the social power of groups, classes, in-groups and cliques—both ethnic and religious. The individual in America has few rights that are not backed up by the political, economic and social power of one group or another" (7).

26. Logan, ed., *What the Negro Wants*. On the publication and significance of *What the Negro Wants*, see Janken, *Rayford W. Logan and the Dilemma of the African American Intellectual*, 145–66.

27. On New Deal spending and impact in South Carolina, see Hayes, "South Carolina and the New Deal," 523–49; Edgar, *South Carolina*, 501–11, and Robertson, *Sly and Able*, 201–43. On wartime mobilization, see Myers, "Black, White, and Olive Drab," 12–18; Moore, *Columbia and Richland County*, 392–93; Hamer, "A Southern City Enters the Twentieth Century," 44–68; Fraser, *Charleston! Charleston!*, 387–88; Edgar, *South Carolina*, 514–15.

28. On the mechanization of agricultural production in South Carolina, see Wright, *Old South, New South*, 234, Table 7.12. On the long-term decline in agricultural opportunities in South Carolina, see Fite, *Cotton Fields No More*, 163–204, especially see 238, Table A6. Toward the end of World War II, South Carolina experienced an increase in the number of nonwhite sharecroppers, likely due to war-induced circumstances that allowed for more profitable share arrangements, but that momentary spike upward began to decline by war's end. See Street, *The New Revolution in the Cotton Economy*, 213–14. On long-term trends in southern agriculture after 1940, also see Wright, *Old South, New South*, 239–74. Population numbers are from Kuznets, *Population Redistribution and Economic Growth*, 90; *A Report of the Seventeenth Decennial Census of the United States, Census of Population: 1950, Vol. II, Characteristics of the Population, Part 40, South Carolina*, 40–26.

29. Charles Jervey Ravenel to W.M. Hampton, October 24, 1942, Folder 19, Richard M. Jeffries Papers, South Caroliniana Library, University of South Carolina, Columbia, South Carolina; W.M. Frampton to Governor R.M. Jeffries, November 20, 1942, Folder 20, Richard M. Jeffries Papers; J.B. Walker to Governor R.N. Jefferes, October 23, 1942, Folder 18, Richard M. Jeffries Papers; Johnnie R. Smith to Gov. R.M. Jefferies, November 11, 1942, Folder 20, Richard M. Jeffries Papers; J.N. Hydrick to Chief S.J. Pratt, October 21, 1942, Folder 18, Richard M. Jeffries Papers. For more evidence of concerns of a labor shortage on a statewide scale, see Howard Cooper to Marion B. Holman, December 28, 1942, with accompanying statements from farmers in Greenwood, in Folder 21, Richard M. Jeffries Papers. Also, see telegrams in Folder 20, Richard M. Jeffries Papers.

30. W.S. Sanders to S.J. Pratt, September 4, 1942, Folder 50, Richard M. Jef-

fries Papers; Roland T. Clary to S.J. Pratt, September 5, 1942, Folder 52, Richard M. Jeffries Papers; Bryan McAbee to S.J. Pratt, October 17, 1942, Folder 52, Richard M. Jeffries Papers; S.J. Pratt to R.M. Jefferies, October 9, 1942, Folder 51, Richard M. Jeffries Papers. My reference to the materials in the Jeffries Papers came from, Richards, "Osceola E. McKaine and the Struggle for Black Civil Rights," 117–20. The University of North Carolina social scientist Howard Odum investigated and collected thousands of the stories and rumors that circulated among white southerners in the early war years. Along with FBI investigators, he concluded that black women were not forming "Eleanor Societies" and black people were not stockpiling guns and ammunition or ice picks for an impending Negro revolt, although he maintained that such rumors were symptomatic of changes underway in the southern social order. See Odum, *Race and Rumors of Race* (reprint, 1997), including the useful introduction by Bryant Simon, especially xi. The investigation undertaken by Governor Jeffries and the South Carolina Constabulary similarly suggests that rumors of arms stockpiling and impending insurrection were untrue, but they are less conclusive about conflicts around domestic labor. Thus it is quite possible that "Eleanor Societies" were products of the imaginings of white employers while the conflicts with domestic workers were anything but imaginary. It is also worth noting that a number of the rumors collected by Odum in South Carolina appear to directly draw on memories of the violence-plagued black voter registration effort and Klan terror in Greenville during the summer and fall of 1939. For examples, see 62–63. In addition to the reports already cited, see the Richard M. Jeffries Papers, Folders 50–52. On the relationship between labor strife in domestic service and industrial production, see Van Onselen, *Studies in the Social and Economic History of the Witwatersrand*, 1–73. Also, see Hunter, *To 'Joy My Freedom*. My thoughts here are also informed by Berlin et al., *Slaves No More*. Revolutionary moments brought on by events such as wars and economic crisis, the authors explain, "expose as few human events the foundations upon which societies rest. . . . Only in the upheaval of accustomed routine can the lower orders give voice to the assumptions that guide their world as it is and they wish it to be," x.

31. On wartime job discrimination in Charleston, see Weaver, *Negro Labor*, 23, 54–55; Hamer, "A Southern City Enters the Twentieth Century," 67–72. On the pressures on black neighborhoods and businesses in Charleston and Columbia during World War II, see Hamer, ibid., 44–45, 157–83; Fraser, *Charleston! Charleston!*, 388–91; Myers, "Black, White, and Olive Drab," 128–69. On police harassment and the activities of the Colored Citizens Committee, see Myers, ibid., Hinton quoted on 150.

32. Anderson, *A. Philip Randolph*, 241–61; Bates, *Pullman Porters and the Rise of Protest Politics in Black America*, 148–74; Dalfiume, "The 'Forgotten Years' of the Negro Revolution," 298–31; Reed, *Seedtime for the Modern Civil Rights Movement*.

33. "Exhortation for Solid Voluntary Action," State Conference File, II-C-181, NAACP Papers; Program, Third Annual Conference South Carolina Branches of the National Association for the Advancement of Colored People, June 14 and 15, 1942, State Conference File, II-C-181, NAACP Papers.

34. In *Pullman Car Porters and the Rise of Protest Politics in Black America*, Beth Tompkins Bates similarly identifies the early World War II years as a key point of departure that signaled the rise of black "protest politics." I differ with Bates about the extent to which the shift was brought about by forces external to the NAACP and my findings question the explanatory power of the "new-crowd"/"old-crowd"

dichotomy she adopts. I have found circumstances to be far more fluid on the ground than her work suggests. The language and conception of historical change invoked here draws explicitly from Sklar, *The Corporate Reconstruction of American Capitalism*, especially 431–41, and Livingston, *Pragmatism, Feminism, and Democracy*, especially the introduction.

35. Work on black transnationalism has suggested that travel and border crossing, real and imagined, by choice or force, has played a constitutive role in the making of a radical black politics. See Gilroy, *The Black Atlantic* and Edwards, *The Practice of Diaspora*. For Edwards, there is nothing essentially radical about movement across borders. Rather, he argues, it is the active process or practice of negotiating "the condition of diaspora" that allows for the *possibility* of radical politics (317). The U.S. domestic corollary includes the literature of black migration from the 1890s through the 1960s discussed at length in Chapter Two.

36. On the NAACP's legal campaign against discrimination in public education, see Tushnet, *The NAACP Legal Strategy against Segregated Education*; Houston, "Educational Inequalities Must Go!" 300. On Charles B. Bailey's attempt to integrate the School of Law of the University of South Carolina, see Bailey's correspondence with the National Office in American Fund for Public Service, University of South Carolina, 1938–1940, File I-C-202, NAACP Papers. On Osceola E. McKaine and his early efforts to promote the NAACP campaign for the equalization of teachers' salaries, see Richards, "Osceola E. McKaine," especially 103–50.

37. The fight for equalization of teachers' salaries in South Carolina is well documented. I rely on Tushnet, *The NAACP Legal Strategy against Segregated Education*, 92–93, and Yarbrough, *A Passion for Justice*, 42–46, for the legal battle and the response of South Carolina state officials. Marshall is quoted in Yarbrough, 43. Also, see McCray, "30 Glorious S.C. Years." Both teachers' salary cases were, however, more than legal decisions; they involved substantial community activism and support and while victories in the courtroom were significant, the efforts to give the judicial decisions meaning in practice involved additional struggle and the victories were more ambiguous. For works that explore the battle for salary equalization more fully, see Baker, "Ambiguous Legacies," 15–97; Brown, "Civil Rights Activism in Charleston," 28–43; Drago, *Initiative, Paternalism, and Race Relations*, 240–42. For an insightful analysis of Waring's personal and judicial thinking, see Schmidt, "J. Waties Waring."

38. Clark, *Echo in My Soul*, 75–89, 111, 148.

39. On the life and activism of Modjeska Simkins, see Woods, "Black Woman Activist"; Woods, "Modjeska Simkins," quote on 104. On the Civic Welfare League, see Hoffman, "Genesis," 365; Jackson, Columbia Memorandum, 1940, Box 36, Folder 2, Bunche Papers.

40. Report of the election of officers, Columbia, South Carolina Branch, November 1939, Part 12, Series G, Reel 19, NAACP Papers; Program guide from the Second Annual Conference, South Carolina Branches, National Association for the Advancement of Colored People, June 15 and 16, 1941, State Conference File II-C-181, NAACP Papers; Program, Third Annual Conference of South Carolina Branches of the National Association for the Advancement of Colored People, June 14 and June 15, 1942, State Conference File, II-C-181, NAACP Papers. Simkins is quoted in Woods, "Modjeska Simkins," 107; and in Interview with Modjeska Simkins, by Jacquelyn Hall, Southern Oral History Collection, copy also in Simkins Papers, Box 1, Modern Political Collection, University of South Carolina, Columbia.

41. Woods, "Modjeska Simkins," 107.

42. On Simkins's work on the teacher salary campaign, see Woods, "Black Woman Activist," 176–94, quote from 185. For collaboration with McKaine, also see Richards, "Osceola E. McKaine," 128. For an insightful analysis of the role religion played in Simkins's thinking and activism, see Chappell, *A Stone of Hope*, 63–66.

43. James M. Hinton to National Office, June 17, 1942, State Conference File, II-C-181, NAACP Papers; John H. McCray to Reverend I. DeQuincy Newman, December 20, 1967, Correspondence: John McCray, Box 2, Arthur J. Clement Jr., Papers, South Caroliniana Library, University of South Carolina, Columbia; McCray, "30 Glorious S.C. Years"; Thurgood Marshall Memorandum to Messrs. White, Wilkins, and Morrow, June 17, 1942, State Conference File, II-C-181, NAACP Papers.

44. Negro Citizens Committee of South Carolina pamphlet, "WHICH DO YOU WANT—DEMOCRACY OR 'THE AMERICAN WAY OF LIFE,'" ca. 1942–1943, State Conference File, II-C-181, NAACP Papers.

45. Ibid.

46. On the response of the South Carolina state legislature to the filing of *Smith v. Allwright*, see Farmer, "The End of the White Primary in South Carolina," 21. On *Smith v. Allwright*, see Hine, *Black Victory*, 212–32; Lawson, *Black Ballots*, 41–49.

47. *News and Courier*, March 27, 1944, 4; Ibid., March 29, 1944, 4; Ibid., April 4, 1944, 1; *The State*, April 5, 1944, 1; *News and Courier*, April 8, 1944, 1; Maybank quoted in *News and Courier*, April 5, 1944, 2; Smith quoted in *News and Courier*, April 7, 1944, 1. For statewide responses, see Farmer, "The End of the White Primary in South Carolina," 25–29.

48. On the "Extraordinary Session," see Farmer, "The End of the White Primary in South Carolina," 30–42; *News and Courier*, April 13, 1944, 1; *The State*, April 13, 1944, 1; *News and Courier*, April 15–21, 1944; *The State*, April 15–21, 1944. Johnston quoted in Farmer, 35, and in the *News and Courier*, April 15, 1944, 1.

49. The story of McCray's viewing the proceedings of the special session is recounted in Sullivan, *Days of Hope*, 169–70. On McCray's move to Columbia and the beginnings of the PDP, see McCray, "30 Glorious S.C. Years"; John H. McCray to Rev. I. DeQuincy Newman, December 20, 1967, Correspondence: John McCray, Box 2, Clement Papers; Richards, "Osceola E. McKaine," 105–9, 162–68; Frederickson, "The Dixiecrat Movement," 166–68. On McCray's move to Columbia, also see Woods, "Black Woman Activist," 173–74. Only scattered editions of the *Lighthouse and Informer* are still extant. McCray recounts the story of the March editorial in McCray, "30 Glorious S.C. Years"; John H. McCray to Rev. I. DeQuincy Newman, December 20, 1967, Clement Papers. Also, see *Columbia Record*, March 17, 1944, 11; *News and Courier*, March 27, 1944, 4; *News and Courier*, April 15, 1944, 1.

50. On NAACP membership numbers, see Membership Branch Statistics, II-C-380, NAACP Papers; Report and Recommendations on Membership and Staff, 1957, III-A-37, NAACP Papers. McCray's claim of forty-five thousand members cited from Sullivan, *Days of Hope*, 170. On the interrelationship of the NAACP and the PDP, see McCray, "30 Glorious S.C. Years"; John H. McCray to Rev. I. DeQuincy Newman, December 20, 1967, Correspondence: John McCray, Box 2, Clement Papers. Also, compare list of Progressive Democratic Party Personnel Sixth District, September 19, 1945, Politics: General, Reel 10, McCray Papers, to NAACP Branch Files for Flor-

ence and Georgetown, II-C-178, NAACP Papers. It was not uncommon for McCray to help organize NAACP branches and PDP clubs simultaneously, leading to some confusion as to whether or not the organizations were one and the same or separate entities. For example, see John H. McCray to R.A. Brown, March 21, 1945, Places: Williamsburg County, Reel 12, McCray Papers; John H. McCray to John Graham, July 5, 1945, Places: Williamsburg County, Reel 12, McCray Papers. Graham wrote to McCray, "My roster of members and officers: yes, everyone are P.D.P. members also (NAACP) that is every reason that there are [sic] no distinction." John Graham to McCray, July 12, 1945, Places: Williamsburg County, Reel 12, McCray Papers.

51. On the formation of the PDP as an all-black political party, see The South Carolina Colored Democratic Party: Organizational Plans formed by the *Lighthouse and Informer*, 1022½ Washington Street, Columbia (20), S.C., as a public service, 1944, Politics: General, Reel 7, McCray Papers, hereafter cited as SCCDP Organizational Plans. The document was certainly written by McCray. By May the PDP had adopted an open membership policy and in later years McCray would attribute the change in name to the Progressive Democratic Party to an elderly white women named Mrs. Howe as a way to highlight its "interracial" origins. However, in 1944, the PDP remained a black political party for a combination of practical and ideological purposes. On the PDP's open membership policy, see "YOU'VE TRIED THE OTHERS, NOW TRY THE BEST!" 1944, Politics: General, Reel 7, McCray Papers; "THE PLATFORM OF THE PROGRESSIVE DEMOCRATIC PARTY," May 24, 1944, II-B-213, NAACP Papers. On the PDP as a black political party, see John H. McCray, "The Progressive Democratic Party in South Carolina," reprinted from the *Southern Frontier*, August 1944, II-B-213, NAACP Papers. In "The Progressive Democratic Party in South Carolina," McCray writes, "The Progressive Democratic Party expects to remain a permanent organization, even though South Carolina's pattern falls before the U.S. Supreme Court. Future plans include a state-wide organization among Negroes so long as it shall be necessary to have *group action* in the matter of *group rights and privileges*." Italics added. On McCray's recounting of the name change, see McCray, "30 Glorious S.C. Years" and John H. McCray to Reverend I. DeQuincy Newman, December 20, 1967, Correspondence: John McCray, Box 2, Clement Papers.

52. McCray quoted from SCCDP Organizational Plans, Politics: General, Reel 7, McCray Papers. On the rationale for the creation of the SCCDP, see ibid.; McCray, "The Progressive Democratic Party in South Carolina," August 1944, II-B-213, NAACP Papers; John H. McCray to Thurgood Marshall, November 9, 1944, II-B-209, NAACP Papers. Also, see McCray, "30 Glorious S.C. Years" and John H. McCray to Reverend I. DeQuincy Newman, December 20, 1967, Correspondence: John McCray, Box 2, Clement Papers.

53. On the expansion of the CIO and AFL in the South during the World War II years, see Honey, *Southern Labor and Black Civil Rights*, 214; Sullivan, *Days of Hope*, 188. At the national level, see Fraser, *Labor Will Rule*, 441–575; Zeiger, *The CIO*, 141–90; Korstad and Lichtenstein, "Opportunities Found and Lost." For NAACP membership numbers, see Membership Branch Statistics, II-C-380, NAACP Papers; Report and Recommendations on Membership and Staff, 1957, III-A-37, NAACP Papers. On the emergence of African Americans as a major political force in the urban North, see Lemann, *The Promised Land*; Lewis, "The Origins and Causes of the Civil

Rights Movement"; Sitkoff, *A New Deal for Blacks*, 84–101; Weiss, *Farewell to the Party of Lincoln*. Also, see Theoharis and Woodard, *Freedom North*, for additional views on northern black politics in post–World War II America.

54. Sullivan, *Days of Hope*, 169–91.

55. SCCDP Organizational Plans, Politics: General, Reel 7, McCray Papers.

56. For a brief biographical sketch of John McCray, see John H. McCray to Arthur J. Clement Jr., August 4, 1952, Correspondence: John McCray, Box 2, Clement Papers. On the origins of Lincolnville during Reconstruction, see Williamson, *After Slavery*, 206–7. Quote from George C. Stoney Report for Bontecou and Bunche, 1940, Box 38, File 1, Bunche Papers.

57. John H. McCray to Rev. R.A. Brown, March 21, 1945, Places: Williamsburg County, Reel 12, McCray Papers; John H. McCray to G.S. Porcher, February 13, 1946, Places: Georgetown, Reel 11, McCray Papers.

58. The PDP and its 1944 challenge to the all-white South Carolina Democratic Party delegation at the 1944 Democratic National Convention has become the subject of much scholarly interest. Works include, Egerton, *Speak Now against the Day*, 227–28; Kari Frederickson, *The Dixiecrat Revolt*, 42–46; Frederickson, "The Dixiecrat Movement," 165–89, 349–53; Richards, "Osceola E. McKaine," 155–206; Sullivan, *Days of Hope*, 133–92. Also, see McCray, "30 Glorious S.C. Years"; John H. McCray to Reverend I. DeQuincy Newman, December 20, 1967, Correspondence: John McCray, Box 2, Clement Papers.

59. McCray, "30 Glorious S.C. Years"; John H. McCray to Reverend I. DeQuincy Newman, December 20, 1967, Correspondence: John McCray, Box 2, Clement Papers. The *News and Courier*, May 25, 1944, 1, claimed that 150 delegates representing 38 counties attended the gathering. Hinton quoted in the *News and Courier*, May 25, 1944, 1. Keynote Speech by Osceola E. McKaine, May 24, 1944, Progressive Democratic Party, Box 8, Clement Papers.

60. Keynote Speech by Osceola E. McKaine, May 24, 1944, Progressive Democratic Party, Box 8, Clement Papers. On McKaine's growing organizational responsibilities and work with the SCHW, see Richards, "Osceola E. McKaine," 180–87. On the creation of the SCHW, including McKaine's connection to it, see Sullivan, *Days of Hope*, 97–101, 195–220. Writing about the largest group of white industrial workers in South Carolina during the 1940s, Bryant Simon explains, "Unable to picture, even for a moment, a world where race did not matter, [white textile mill workers] could see African Americans only as enemies, as emasculating sexual predators and constant threats to their social position and economic status. Despite their economic liberalism, they could not imagine a biracial labor movement or a political challenge of the have-nots, black and white across the color line" (Simon, *A Fabric of Defeat*, 238).

61. The story of the PDP's 1944 convention challenge is recounted in Egerton, *Speak Now against the Day*, 227–8; Frederickson, *The Dixiecrat Revolt*, 42–46; Richards, "Osceola E. McKaine," 173–86; Sullivan, *Days of Hope*, 170–71. Also, see McCray, "30 Glorious S.C. Years"; John H. McCray to Reverend I. DeQuincy Newman, December 20, 1967, Correspondence: John McCray, Box 2, Clement Papers. The challenge garnered substantial attention from the national black press. For examples, see *Chicago Defender*, May 27, 1944, 1; Ibid., July 15, 1944, 1; Ibid., July 22, 1944, 1; *Norfolk Journal and Guide*, April 15, 1944, 6; Ibid., April 22, 1944, 6; Ibid., May 20, 1944, 4; Ibid., July 22, 1944, 1.

5. Popular Fronts

Epigraphs. Resolutions Adopted by the South Carolina Conference of the N.A.A.C.P., October 1948, South Carolina State Conference of Branches File, II-C-181, NAACP Papers; Program, Eleventh Annual Meeting of the South Carolina Conference, NAACP, October 13–14, 1951, Sumter, South Carolina, NAACP General, Box 2, Simkins Papers.

1. On the expansion of black voting rights organizations in the South, see Moon, *Balance of Power*; Heard, *A Two-Party South?*, especially 188–99; Sullivan, *Days of Hope*, especially 193–220. On the wartime growth of the labor movement and the strike-wave of 1945–1946, see Fraser, *Labor Will Rule*, especially 441–575; Lichtenstein, *Labor's War at Home*, especially, 202–32; Lipsitz, *Rainbow at Midnight*, 99–154; Zeiger, *The CIO*, 141–252; Korstad and Lichtenstein, "Opportunities Found and Lost." On Operation Dixie and its failures, see Griffith, *The Crisis of American Labor*; Minchin, *What Do We Need a Union For?*; Zeiger, *The CIO*, 227–41. For a study that complicates the traditional view of Operation Dixie as an unmitigated failure, see Jones, "Black Workers and the CIO's Turn toward Racial Radicalism." Also, see Jones, "Cutting through Jim Crow."

2. Much of the recent literature concerned with labor and politics during the New Deal era holds that the "universal" reform agenda of the New Deal, one interested primarily in the structural reform of the American economy, enabled the creation of a coalition of white workers and African Americans that pushed the United States in a more social democratic direction. In this rendering of the era, the CIO emerged as the primary engine of a class-based social movement that addressed issues of economic *and* racial injustice until, that is, liberal policymakers, labor leaders, and civil rights advocates shifted course in the postwar era and pushed a program of Keynesian-growth economics, rights-based reform, and anticommunism to the front of its agenda in the face of a general conservative ascendancy in American life. Examples include, Korstad and Lichtenstein, "Opportunities Found and Lost"; Brinkley, *The End of Reform*; Kazin, *The Populist Persuasion*; Korstad, *Civil Rights Unionism*; Lichtenstein, *The Most Dangerous Man in Detroit*; Bartley, *The New South*; Fraser, *Labor Will Rule*; Gerstle, *Working-Class Americanism*; Fraser and Gerstle, eds., *The Rise and Fall of the New Deal Order*, especially the editors' "Introduction" and Ira Katznelson's "Was the Great Society a Lost Opportunity?" By stressing the social democratic potential of this class-based coalition, this literature de-emphasizes the differences, disagreements, and tensions within the coalition itself and minimizes the erasures that accompanied the New Deal's ostensibly universal reforms. This tendency romanticizes the possibilities of the era and leads historians to view the growing emphasis on black civil rights in the postwar era, and the seemingly more fractious nature of the American Left, as part of a general retreat from or narrowing of the social democratic possibilities of the New Deal period. For works that emphasize differences and tensions within the CIO and the left-wing of the New Deal coalition, see Nelson, *Divided We Stand* and his exchange with Elizabeth Faue and Thomas J. Sugrue in Nelson, "Class, Race and Democracy in the CIO"; Norrell, "Caste in Steel"; Zeiger, *The CIO*. The limitations of the labor movement, and the CIO in particular, on questions of race, have long been a concern of Herbert Hill. For an overview of his thinking, see Hill, "The Problem of Race in American Labor History." On the limitations of the New Deal's ostensibly universal reforms, see Gordon, *Pitied But Not Entitled*; Kessler-Harris, "In the Nation's Image"; Sugrue, *The Origins of the Urban Crisis*. In *Days of Hope*, Sul-

livan maintains no romance with the CIO, but argues correctly, I believe, that the rise of the cold war helped arrest what were already tenuous and provisional interracial alliances forged by the hard work of some of the most visionary members of the New Deal coalition's left-flank, also known as the Popular Front. My argument represents an effort, in part, to reconcile the paradox contained in her conclusion, which identifies a decline of interracial possibilities, on the one hand, and makes an argument that views black civil rights activism as the critical democratizing force of the 1960s, on the other. It just might be that the decline of interracial possibilities in the 1940s contributed to the development of an independent black political voice capable of bringing the nation's most glaring manifestation of white supremacy, Jim Crow, to its knees, thus opening unprecedented opportunities for multiracial alliances in our own time, indeed, demanding them. As much as New Deal era reforms implicitly challenged entrenched patterns of white supremacy and segregation, it was not until the late 1940s, at precisely the same moment that the cold war emerged as a major factor in American life, that African Americans achieved a level of organization sufficient to place the issue of black voting rights and Jim Crow segregation on the national agenda. Indeed, in his important book, *Building a Democratic Political Order*, David Plotke argues that it was precisely the inability of the Democratic Party in the 1940s to sufficiently address and absorb the concerns of African Americans into its agenda that wreaked havoc on the party in the years to come. Without adequate recourse to the two-party system, African Americans were left to the courts and the streets to seek redress for their needs and interests, virtually assuring crisis and violent conflict in the future. See, especially, 262–97.

3. For working conditions in the American Tobacco Company's Charleston cigar plant, see Recollections of Lillie Doster, "South Carolina Voices of the Civil Rights Movement" Collection, Avery Research Center, The College of Charleston, Charleston, South Carolina; *Charleston News and Courier*, October 23, 1945, 1, 3. For the organization of the plant in 1943, see *The State*, December 3, 1943, 2; "We're Sticking Together," from *FTA Vanguard*, ca. 1950, Reel 18, Operation Dixie Papers.

4. *Charleston News and Courier*, October 4, 1945, 1; Ibid., October 5, 1945, 1.

5. On the history of UCAPAWA, see Korstad and Lichtenstein, "Opportunities Found and Lost"; Korstad, *Civil Rights Unionism*; Korstad, "Black and White Together"; Kelley, *Hammer and Hoe*, 173–75; Reid, "Food, Tobacco, Agricultural and Allied Workers Union of America (FTA)"; Ruiz, *Cannery Women, Cannery Lives*. By defining the Popular Front as the left-wing of the New Deal coalition, I am following the lead of Michael Denning who argues convincingly that the Popular Front was much more than a product of Communist Party strategy and design. Denning writes, "The Popular Front was the insurgent social movement forged from the labor militancy of the fledgling CIO, the anti-fascist solidarity with Spain, Ethiopia, China, and the refugees from Hitler, and the political struggles of the left wing of the New Deal. Born out of the social upheavals of 1934 and coinciding with the Communist Party's period of greatest influence in US society, the Popular Front became a radical historical bloc uniting industrial unionists, Communists, independent socialists, community activists, and émigré anti-fascists around laborist social democracy, anti-fascism, and anti-lynching" (*The Cultural Front*, 4).

6. Korstad, "Black and White Together," 73.

7. Ibid., 69–73.

8. *Charleston News and Courier*, October 23, 1945, 1; *Norfolk Journal and Guide*, February 2, 1946, 4; Harold J. Lane to FTA International Vice Presidents, Regional Directors, et al., November 2, 1945, Folder 6, Isaiah Bennett Collection, Avery Research Center, College of Charleston, Charleston, South Carolina; McKaine, "The Palmetto State," *Norfolk Journal and Guide*, November 10, 1945, 11; Recollections of Lillie Doster, "South Carolina Voices of the Civil Rights Movement" Collection. On the relationship between regional wage differentials and Jim Crow, see Jones, "Cutting through Jim Crow," 130–74; Wright, *Old South, New South*.

9. *Norfolk Journal and Guide*, February 2, 1946, 4; Recollections of Lillie Doster, "South Carolina Voices of the Civil Rights Movement" Collection; Korstad, "Black and White Together," 74; *Charleston News and Courier*, October 23, 1945, 1; Ibid., February 19, 1946, 1; Ibid., March 28, 1946, 10. Also, see picture of pickets in *Charleston News and Courier*, October 24, 1945, 3. On black women workers in the tobacco industry, see Janiewski, "Seeking 'a New Day and a New Way.'" On the history of "We Shall Overcome," see Korstad, "Black and White Together," 74–75; Carawan and Carawan, *Sing for Freedom*, 4, 15.

10. McKaine, "The Palmetto State," *Norfolk Journal and Guide*, November 11, 1945, 11; Korstad, "Black and White Together," 73–74; McKaine, *Norfolk Journal and Guide*, March 2, 1946, 9; Korstad, "Black and White Together," 75. On Potts, see Drago, *Initiative, Paternalism, and Race Relations*, 221–23. The SCHW was organized in Charleston's Morris Street Baptist Church on February 19, 1946. In addition to Potts, Foreman, and Korstad, Simkins and McKaine attended and the meeting was presided over by Reuel Stanfield. McKaine, *Norfolk Journal and Guide*, March 2, 1946, 9.

11. For examples of harassment, see *Charleston News and Courier*, October 24, 1945, 1; Ibid., November 3, 1945, 1; *Norfolk Journal and Guide*, February 2, 1946, 4. On *Charleston News and Courier* coverage, see October 23 and 24, 1945, 1; November 4, 1945, 10; February 19, 1946, 1; March 28, 1946, 10. On lack of AFL support, see *Norfolk Journal and Guide*, February 2, 1946, 4. Quote from Recollections of Lillie Doster, "South Carolina Voices of the Civil Rights Movement" Collection. On workers returning to work before the end of the strike, see Recollections of Lillie Doster, "South Carolina Voices of the Civil Rights Movement" Collection; *Charleston News and Courier*, March 28, 1946, 10.

12. On the TWIU's challenge to Local #15, see *Charleston News and Courier*, March 29, 1946, 1; Ibid., March 31, 1946, 1; Ibid., April 1, 1946, 6.

13. My argument reflects Bruce Nelson's insight that labor's travails in the cold war era were the result of factors internal and external to the labor movement itself. See Nelson, "Class, Race and Democracy in the CIO," and *Divided We Stand*.

14. John H. McCray to Arthur J. Clement Jr., September 7, 1945, Persons: Arthur Clement, Reel 9, McCray Papers.

15. Ibid.; John H. McCray to G.S. Porcher, February 13, 1946, Places: Georgetown, Reel 11, McCray Papers; John H. McCray to Arthur J. Clement Jr., Persons: Arthur Clement, Reel 9, McCray Papers.

16. John H. McCray to Arthur J. Clement Jr., May 14, 1945, Progressive Democratic Party, Box 8, Clement Papers. Also, see Levi G. Byrd to John H. McCray, March 7, 1946, Reel 10, McCray Papers.

17. John H. McCray to Reverend I. DeQuincy Newman, December 20, 1967, Correspondence: John McCray, Box 2, Clement Papers; John H. McCray to Arthur

J. Clement Jr., May 14, 1945, Progressive Democratic Party, Box 8, Clement Papers; John H. McCray to Arthur J. Clement Jr., May 14, 1945, Correspondence: John McCray, Box 2, Clement Papers; John H. McCray to Arthur J. Clement Jr., March 5, 1946, Correspondence: John McCray, Box 2, Clement Papers; Arthur J. Clement Jr., to John H. McCray, March 6, 1946, Persons: Osceola McKaine, Reel 9, McCray Papers. Challenges to McCray and the PDP also came from the Republican Party, notably from the Lincoln Emancipation Club, headed by the wealthy black undertaker I.S. Leevy, who, along with two other black Republicans, entered races for city offices in Columbia in the spring of 1946. See McKaine, "The Palmetto State," *Norfolk Journal and Guide*, May 18, 1946; Ibid., April 20, 1946. McKaine noted that, according to the Richland County registrar, most of those black people who registered did so as Republicans, although black Republicans remained divided, even then, by two factions within the Republican Party.

18. On South Carolina's white political leadership and their resistance to the New Deal and civil rights reform, see Patterson, *Congressional Conservatism*; Cohodas, *Strom Thurmond*; Frederickson, *The Dixiecrat Revolt*; Robertson, *Sly and Able*. On postwar racial violence in South Carolina, see "Along the Color Line," *The Crisis* 53 (September 1946): 276; John H. McCray to Governor Ransom J. Williams, June 12, 1946, Reel 7, McCray Papers; James M. Hinton to John H. McCray, February 18, 1946, Reel 14, McCray Papers; McKaine, "The Palmetto State," *Norfolk Journal and Guide*, March 30, 1946, 9. For a full accounting of the Woodard beating and the Earl lynching, see Frederickson, "The Dixiecrat Movement," 55–76. On the decline of the cotton economy and black migration in the 1940s, see Chapter Four, note 28.

19. A Call for Unity, Anti–Jim Crow Committee, Box 4, McCray Papers; John H. McCray to W.L. Liddell, March 11, 1946, Anti–Jim Crow Committee, Box 4, McCray Papers; John H. McCray to E.R. Lewis, March 5, 1946, Politics: General, Reel 7, McCray Papers. On earlier streetcar battles in South Carolina, see Chapter Two. On rising conflicts on busses in Columbia, see Myers, "Black, White, and Olive Drab," 341. On streetcars and busses as critical sites of struggle over Jim Crow, see Kelley, "'We Are Not What We Seem,'" 35–54; Meier and Rudwick, "The Origins of Nonviolent Direct Action in Afro-American Protest," 355–56.

20. *The State*, March 4, 1946, 2; *Charleston News and Courier*, March 4, 1946, 1; Ibid., March 5, 1946, 7; Ibid., April 8, 1946, 1; McKaine, "The Palmetto State," *Norfolk Journal and Guide*, March 23, 1946, 9; Ibid., March 30, 1946, 9; John H. McCray to E.R. Lewis, March 5, 1946, McCray Papers; NAACP to Modjeska Simkins, March 8, 1946, II-C-177, NAACP Papers; "A Practical Program to Kill Jim Crow," Anti–Jim Crow Committee, Box 4, McCray Papers.

21. On the origins and activities of the SNYC, see Kelley, *Hammer and Hoe*, 195–219; Richards, "The Southern Negro Youth Congress"; Augusta Strong, "Southern Youth's Proud Heritage." On the National Negro Congress, see Bates, *Pullman Porters and the Rise of Protest Politics in Black America*, 135–47 and "The New Crowd"; Griffler, *What Price Alliance?*; Kirby, *Black Americans in the Roosevelt Era*, 164–89; Wolters, *Negroes and the Great Depression*, 353–82. On the young southerners' disenchantment with the NNC, see Richards, "The Southern Negro Youth Congress," 20–21; Interview with James E. Jackson Jr., Esther Cooper Jackson, and Dorothy Burnham, by Peter F. Lau, PFL. James Ashford quoted in Lloyd Brown, "Southern Youth's Heritage," 252. In an important sense, the young activists took up the theoretical and programmatic conundrum articulated by W.E.B. Du Bois

at the turn of the twentieth century. "To-day the two groups of Negroes, the one in the North, the other in the South, represent divergent ethical tendencies, the first tending toward radicalism, the other toward hypocritical compromise," he wrote. "Between the two extreme types of ethical attitude which I have thus sought to make clear wavers the mass of millions of Negroes, North and South" (Du Bois, *The Souls of Black Folk*, 222–23, 225).

22. On Edward Strong, see Strong, "Southern Youth's Proud Heritage," 38–39.

23. On the student movement of the 1930s, see Cohen, *When the Old Left Was Young*.

24. On this point, see Kelley, "'Afric's Sons with Banner Red,'" 37. Kelley writes, "African-Americans who joined the Party in the 1920s and 1930s were as much the creation of American Communism as of Black nationalism; as much the product of African-American vernacular cultures and radical traditions as of Euro-American radical thought." My argument is that members of the SNYC were products of African American vernacular cultures, radical Euro-American radical thought, *and* American liberal thought and politics.

25. Interview with Jacksons and Burnham, by Peter F. Lau; Richards, "The Southern Negro Youth Congress," 17; Kelley, *Hammer and Hoe*, 200; Sullivan, *Days of Hope*, 82–83.

26. James E. Jackson Jr., "Statement before Sentencing," September 17, 1956, from the private files of James and Esther Jackson, copy in author's possession.

27. Interview with Jacksons and Burnham, by Peter F. Lau; Augusta V. Jackson, "A New Deal for Tobacco Workers"; Love, "In Defiance of Custom and Tradition"; Love, "The Cigarette Capital of the World," 181–214.

28. Interview with Jacksons and Burnham, by Peter F. Lau; also see Kelley, *Hammer and Hoe*, 206–7.

29. Osceola E. McKaine to SNYC, October 7, 1942, Correspondence, Box 3, SNYC Papers, Moorland-Spingarn Collection, Howard University, Washington, D.C.; McKaine, "The Palmetto State," *Norfolk Journal and Guide*, November 17, 1945, 11; Ibid., December 8, 1945, 11; Ibid., February 16, 1946, 9. On Weston, see Annie B. Weston, Black History Vertical Files, South Caroliniana Library, University of South Carolina, Columbia. Copies of the *Lighthouse and Informer* do not exist for the year 1946, but Louis Burnham, the SNYC's organizational secretary, wrote McCray thanking him for his editorial support leading up to and following the 1946 youth legislature. Louis Burnham to John H. McCray, October 29, 1946, Reel 14, McCray Papers.

30. Louis Burnham to Annie Belle Weston, April 20, 1946, Membership Drive, May 1946, Box 1, SNYC Papers.

31. Program Guide for the Southern Negro Youth Congress's Seventh Youth Legislature, Columbia, South Carolina, October 1946, 7th Conference, 1946, Box 6, SNYC Papers; Berkeley Wildcat, Newsletter of Berkeley Training School, 7th Conference, 1946, Box 6, SNYC Papers; "S.N.Y.C. High School Program" and "Southern Negro Youth Congress College Program," Speeches, Box 5, Simkins Papers. On the ways in which black Communists (including members of the SNYC) organized around the particular and often local concerns of African Americans and worked to mobilize them in a broader movement for social justice, see Kelley, *Hammer and Hoe*, especially 92–116.

32. The "freedom road" mural was likely an allusion to Howard Fast's novel

Freedom Road. The 1944 novel provided a heroic rendering of the black struggle for freedom during the Reconstruction era.

33. Strong, "Southern Youth's Proud Heritage," 47. Other published eyewitness accounts of the legislature include, Fast, "They're Marching Up Freedom Road"; Scales, *Cause at Heart*, 163. My visual depiction also draws from local press coverage of the legislature, especially the *Columbia Record*, October 17, 18, 1946, and *The (Columbia, S.C.) State*, October 18, 1946.

34. Program Guide for the Southern Negro Youth Congress's Seventh Youth Legislature, Columbia, South Carolina, October 1946, 7th Conference, 1946, Box 6, SNYC Papers. Also, see "Thank You Notes," October 29, 1946, SNYC Papers; *Columbia Record*, October 17, 1946; *The (Columbia, S.C.) State*, October 19, 1946.

35. The panel on labor, for example, included Henry Mayfield of the United Mine Workers of America, Mike Ross of the United Furniture Workers, Raymond Tillman of the United Transport Workers, Thomas Richardson of the United Public Workers, and Florence Valentine of the SNYC's Miami Council. The panel on education included Edward Weaver of Alabama State Teacher's College, Charles G. Gomillion of Tuskegee Institute, and Modjeska Simkins, while Hosea Hudson of the United Steel Workers of America, C.A. Scott of the *Atlanta Daily World*, Osceola McKaine, James Jackson, and Maenetta Steele of the Fairfield, Alabama SNYC were members of the panel on Voting. Program Guide for the Southern Negro Youth Congress's Seventh Youth Legislature, Columbia, South Carolina, October 1946, 7th Conference, 1946, Box 6, SNYC Papers. Also, see "Thank You Notes," October 29, 1946, 7th Conference, 1946, Box 6, SNYC Papers.

36. Press Release of Esther Cooper's Opening Address to the 7th Youth Legislature, Columbia, South Carolina, October 18, 1946, Box 6, SNYC Papers.

37. Although Powell was scheduled to deliver the legislature's keynote address he failed to make an appearance in Columbia. Sickness, fatigue, fear, and political calculation are all possible explanations for his failure to attend. I find it difficult to dismiss, however, the looming mid-term congressional elections as one possible cause for his absence. CIO president Philip Murray declined the SNYC's invitation to participate, citing previous commitments. Philip Murray to SNYC, July 9, 1946, 7th Conference, Speakers, Box 6, SNYC Papers.

38. John H. McCray's Address to Legislature, 7th Conference, 1946, Box 7, SNYC Papers. Also, see McCray's account of his own speech, John H. McCray to James A. Smith, April 10, 1972, Correspondence: John McCray, Box 2, Clement Papers.

39. Committee Hearing: Youth and Labor, October 19, 1946, 7th Conference, 1946, Box 6, SNYC Papers; Florence Valentine, "Remarks on JOBS AND JOB TRAINING FOR NEGRO WOMEN," Committee Hearing: Youth and Labor, October 18, 1946, 7th Conference, 1946, Box 6, SNYC Papers.

40. In important ways, the SNYC anticipated present-day concerns about the historical construction of class. For examples of present-day works that explore the historicity of class, see Dimock and Gilmore, eds., *Rethinking Class*, especially, 1–106; Kelley, *Race Rebels*; Roediger, *Wages of Whiteness*; Scott, "Experience."

41. Hearing on Civil Liberties, 7th Conference, 1946, Box 7, SNYC Papers. Also, see the SNYC's Executive Board Meeting: President's Report on the Perspective of Political Climate, 1947, Box 1, SNYC Papers. The report reads, "SNYC members clearly see and recognize racist theories as a façade behind which anti-democratic

forces operate against the entire mass of American people."

42. On race as a cross-class social construction produced in and through the day-to-day lives of white and black people, see among others Hall, "Cultural Identity and Diaspora"; Holt, "Marking"; Lewis, "Connecting Memory, Self, and the Power of Place in African American Urban History"; Williams, *The Alchemy of Race and Rights*.

43. Hearing on Civil Liberties, 7th Conference, 1946, Box 7, SNYC Papers.

44. Clark Foreman Address, October 18, 1946, 7th Conference, 1946, Box 6, SNYC Papers. On Foreman, see Sullivan, *Days of Hope*, 24–26, 64–65.

45. Address Delivered by W.E.B. Du Bois, "Behold the Land," Box 6, SNYC Papers. The speech was reprinted in *Freedomways: A Quarterly Review of the Negro Freedom Movement* 4 (Winter 1964), 8–15. On Du Bois's appearance at the youth legislature and his relationship to members of the SNYC, see Lewis, *W.E.B. Du Bois: The Fight for Equality*, 518–28, especially 524.

46. The SNYC's leadership was acutely aware of the differences among black people in the U.S. and international context, and among working-class people, generally. For them, constituting a radical black internationalism or even broader radical internationalism was necessarily a process. They saw nothing natural about identity or alliances, which they conceived as always in the process of becoming. For the best articulation of this kind of thinking and practice, see Edwards, *The Practice of Diaspora*.

47. For an argument that emphasizes the primacy of internationalist thought in black struggles during the 1940s, see Von Eschen, *Race against Empire*. Von Eschen argues that in the mid-1940s an "internationalist anticolonial discourse" animated African American politics and that, following the onset of the cold war, concern with the international context of black politics was "neglected in favor of an exclusive emphasis on domestic political and civil rights," 2–3, 186–87. My argument here is that Von Eschen overstates the extent to which an internationalist anticolonialism animated African American activism in the 1940s, and likely overstates, therefore, its disappearance after the onset of the cold war. In the 1940s, "local" concerns remained of utmost importance, animating, as it were, black struggles for justice in places like South Carolina. This is not to say that international concerns played no role, but that the depths of local racial and economic inequality necessarily weighed more heavily on the day-to-day lives of most black southerners. For a similar critique, see Savage, *Broadcasting Freedom*, 346, n. 125.

48. Committee Hearing: Peace, October 19, 1946, 7th Conference, 1946, Box 7, SNYC Papers.

49. Interview with Jacksons and Burnham, by Peter F. Lau.

50. Address Delivered by W.E.B. Du Bois, "Behold the Land," Box 6, SNYC Papers. Also, see Clark Foreman Address, October 18, 1946, 7th Conference, 1946, Box 6, SNYC Papers; Paul Robeson Address, October 19, 1946, 7th Conference, Box 6, SNYC Papers. Local papers in Columbia seized on the legislature's criticism of Byrnes. For examples, see *The (Columbia, S.C.) State*, October 19 and 21, 1946; *Columbia Record*, October 19, 21, and 22, 1946.

51. Paul Robeson Address, October 19, 1946, 7th Conference, 1946, Box 6, SNYC Papers. On Paul Robeson's life and activism, see Martin Duberman, *Paul Robeson*.

52. *Columbia Record*, October 19 and 20, 1946. Quote from October 20, 1946.

53. SNYC to Honorable Ransome J. Williams, October 21, 1946, Reel 14, Mc-Cray Papers; *Columbia Record*, October 22, 1946.

54. On anticommunism in the South in the late 1940s, see Fairclough, *Race and Democracy*, 135–63; Honey, *Southern Labor and Black Civil Rights*, 145–76; Sullivan, *Days of Hope*, 221–48. On the harassment and dissolution of the SNYC, see Richards, "The Southern Negro Youth Congress," 130–98; Kelley, *Hammer and Hoe*, 220–31.

55. Richards, "The Southern Negro Youth Congress," 137.

56. On the Nazi-Soviet Pact and its impact on the CP-USA, see Cohen, *When the Old Left Was Young*, xvi, 281–82; Klehr, *The Heyday of American Communism*, 386–416.

57. John H. McCray, "The Wicked Fleeth in Discord," *Lighthouse and Informer*, April 13, 1947. I thank Wim Roefs for the citation.

58. On the changes and conflicts within the CP-USA, see Isserman, *Which Side Were You On?*; Kelley, *Hammer and Hoe*, 220–26; Johanningsmeier, *Forging American Communism*, 293–332; Klehr, et al., *The Secret World of American Communism*, 3–19; Starobin, *American Communism in Crisis*, especially 71–120, 155–80.

59. Esther Cooper Jackson, "This Is My Husband," from the private files of James and Esther Jackson; Author's interview with Jacksons and Burnham.

60. On white working class resistance to racial reform in the postwar era, see Norrell, "Caste in Steel"; Nelson, *Divided We Stand*, 89–141, 185–250; Sugrue, *The Origins of the Urban Crisis*.

61. On McKaine's break with the PDP and the SCHW and his return to Europe, see Richards, "Osceola E. McKaine," 243–51, 257–66. On the demise of the FTA nationally and in Winston-Salem, see Korstad, *Civil Rights Unionism*, 368–415; Korstad, "Daybreak of Freedom," 276–410; Korstad, "Black and White Together," 86–94. On the CIO's expulsion of Communist-led unions, including the FTA, and efforts to "raid" their local affiliates, see Zeiger, *The CIO*, 277–93. On the postwar travails of Local #15, see Recollections of Lillie Doster, "South Carolina Voices of the Civil Rights Movement" Collection; Korstad, "Black and White Together," 88, 91–92; Reul Stanfield to Friends, February 10, 1947, Reel 22, Operation Dixie Papers; TWIU Newsletter, 1948, Reel 22, Operation Dixie Papers; FTA Flier, "FTA-CIO Contract Speaks for Itself," February 16, 1948, Reel 22, Operation Dixie Papers; Lloyd P. Vaughan to George Craig, December 11, 1950, Reel 18, Operation Dixie Papers; "NEWS FROM CIO" flier, 1951, Reel 18, Operation Dixie Papers; "LO-CAL #15, F.T.A. SIGNS ANOTHER CONTRACT," flier, 1951, Reel 18, Operation Dixie Papers. On the failures of Operation Dixie in South Carolina, see Griffith, *The Crisis of American Labor*, 22–45, especially 36; Minchin, *What Do We Need a Union For?*, 26–47.

62. Story recounted by McCray in John H. McCray to Reverend I. DeQuincy Newman, December 20, 1967, Correspondence: John McCray, Box 2, Clement Papers.

63. *Wrighten v. Board of Trustees of University of South Carolina*, 72 F. Supp. 948 (D.C.S.C, 1947); *Elmore v. Rice* 72 F. Supp. 516 (D.C.S.C. 1947). On Waring and his road to *Elmore*, see Schmidt, "J. Waties Waring"; Yarbrough, *A Passion for Justice*, 42–67, esp. 48–67. On *Elmore v. Rice*, also see Frederickson, *The Dixiecrat Revolt*, 109–10; Lawson, *Black Ballots*, 50–51. On the *Wrighten* and *Elmore* cases, also see Bender, "One Week That Changed the State."

64. Progressive Democratic Party et al. vs. The South Carolina Democratic Party et al., Before the Democratic National Convention, July 1948, II-B-213, NAACP Papers; Problem Presented by South Carolina: Brown v. Baskin, II-B-213, NAACP Papers; Frederickson, *The Dixiecrat Revolt*, 110–11; Yarbrough, *A Passion for Justice*, 69.

65. On the PDP's 1948 Democratic National Convention challenge, see Frederickson, *The Dixiecrat Revolt*, 111–12, 124–28, Thurmond quoted on 140. *Brown v. Baskin* 78 F. Supp. 933 (D.C.S.C. 1948). On *Brown v. Baskin*, also see Yarbrough, *A Passion for Justice*, 69–75.

66. Lawson, *Black Ballots*, 53–54. Also, see Problem Presented by South Carolina: Brown v. Baskin, II-B-213, NAACP Papers; Heard, *A Two-Party South?*,193 and 302–303 n. 1; Yarbrough, *A Passion for Justice*, 93. The number of registered voters in 1946 is found in Key, *Southern Politics in State and Nation*, 523.

67. See, generally, Frederickson, *The Dixiecrat Revolt*. The brief history of the CDP is recounted on 112–13. Also, see John H. McCray to Rev. I DeQuincy Newman, December 20, 1967, Correspondence: John McCray, Box 2, Clement Papers.

68. Problem Presented by South Carolina: Brown v. Baskin, II-B-213, NAACP Papers; Frederickson, *The Dixiecrat Revolt*, 113; Yarbrough, *A Passion for Justice*, 74–75.

69. Minutes—Seventh Annual Meeting of the S.C. Conference of the NAACP, October 19 and 20, 1947, South Carolina State Conference of Branches File, II-C-181, NAACP Papers; Press Release, S.C. Conference of the NAACP, October 24, 1947, South Carolina State Conference of Branches File, II-C-181, NAACP Papers. On the national office's move to prioritize a frontal assault on segregation, see Tushnet, *The NAACP Legal Strategy against Segregated Education*, 105–37, 138–66. Also, see Tushnet, *Making Civil Rights Law*, 150–67, especially 155–56.

70. Resolutions Adopted by the South Carolina Conference of the N.A.A.C.P., October 1948, South Carolina State Conference of Branches File, II-C-181, NAACP Papers.

71. Minutes—Seventh Annual Meeting of the S.C. Conference of the NAACP, October 19 and 20, 1947, South Carolina State Conference of Branches File, II-C-181, NAACP Papers; Press Release, S.C. Conference of the NAACP, October 24, 1947, South Carolina State Conference of Branches File, II-C-181, NAACP Papers. For more on the understanding of the need for an expansion of black self-organization, see membership campaign flier, composed by Modjeska Simkins, April 10, 1947, Columbia Branch File, II-C-177, NAACP Papers.

72. Interview with Eugene Alonzo Randolph Montgomery, by Charles H. Houston Jr., Behind the Veil Collection. Tape of interview also can be found at South Carolina State University Historical Collection, Orangeburg, South Carolina. Also, see Minutes, Eighth Annual Meeting of the South Carolina Conference, N.A.A.C.P., October 9–11, 1948, South Carolina State Conference of Branches File, II-C-181, NAACP Papers; James M. Hinton address, Annual Meeting of the South Carolina State Conference of NAACP, October 1959, Persons: James Hinton, Reel 9, McCray Papers.

73. James M. Hinton address, ibid. Montgomery quoted from his minutes from a meeting with NAACP officers in South Carolina's First Congressional District, January 15, 1949, South Carolina State Conference of Branches File, II-C-181, NAACP Papers. National office branch statistics are cited from, Membership Branch Statistics,

II-C-380, NAACP Papers; Report and Recommendations on Membership and Staff, 1957, III-A-37, NAACP Papers; Membership Status of South Carolina Branches, October 10, 1947, South Carolina State Conference of Branches File, II-C-181, NAACP Papers; 1949 Membership and 40th Anniversary Goals, South Carolina, South Carolina State Conference of Branches File, II-C-181, NAACP Papers. In his interview with Houston, Montgomery claims a peak of between 90 and 100 branches in South Carolina. John McCray claimed that "By the late '40s we had over 110 active branches." Interview with John McCray, by Worth Long, quote on 14; McCray, "30 Glorious S.C. Years."

74. For the crucial role of religious revivalism in the African American struggle for civil rights, see Chappell, *A Stone of Hope*, which includes a fine discussion of South Carolina activist Modjeska Simkins, 63–66. On Montgomery's organizing efforts during 1948 and 1949, see his monthly Memoranda to the Director of Branches, NAACP, Gloster B. Current, South Carolina State Conference of Branches File, II-C-181, NAACP Papers. And, see Interview with Eugene A.R. Montgomery, by Charles H. Houston Jr., Behind the Veil Collection. Quote on "Democracy and Christianity" from, Program, Eleventh Annual Meeting of the South Carolina Conference, NAACP, October 13–14, 1951, Sumter, South Carolina, NAACP General, Box 2, Simkins Papers. On the organization of specific branches noted, see James M. Hinton to Gloster Current, July 12, 1948, South Carolina State Conference of Branches File, II-C-181, NAACP Papers; Montgomery's monthly memoranda for July 1948, February 1949, and November 1948, respectively, South Carolina State Conference of Branches File, II-C-181, NAACP Papers. Also, see specific branch files in II-C-177 through II-C-181, NAACP Papers. Montgomery quoted from Interview with Eugene A.R. Montgomery, by Charles H. Houston Jr., Behind the Veil Collection.

75. Membership Branch Statistics, II-C-380, NAACP Papers; 1949 Membership and 40th Anniversary Goals, South Carolina, II-C-380, NAACP Papers. Quote from, Interview with Eugene A.R. Montgomery, by Charles H. Houston Jr., Behind the Veil Collection.

76. On the Monck's Corner Progressive Club, see Montgomery's monthly memorandum, November 1948, South Carolina State Conference of Branches File, II-C-181, NAACP Papers. On the NAACP in Clarendon County, see Interview with Eugene A.R. Montgomery, by Charles H. Houston Jr., Behind the Veil Collection, and Chapter Six. Montgomery quoted from Interview with Eugene A.R. Montgomery, by Charles H. Houston Jr., Behind the Veil Collection. On Hinton's abduction, see James M. Hinton to Thurgood Marshall, May 26, 1949, South Carolina State Conference of Branches File, II-C-182, NAACP Papers; FBI Report in James M. Hinton File #44–9900, Department of Justice, Federal Bureau of Investigation, Washington, D.C.

6. Cold War Civil Rights

Epigraphs. Interview with Hauleen Green Smith, by Kisha Turner, Behind the Veil Collection; South Carolina State Conference File, 1958–1959, III-C-143, NAACP Papers.

1. I have taken issue with much of this literature in Chapter Five. On the relationship between the cold war and liberal policymakers' growing concern with civil rights reform, see Dudziak, "Desegregation as a Cold War Imperative," and *Cold War*

Civil Rights. The costs of the cold war are summarized best in Schrecker, *Many Are the Crimes.* But also, see Horne, *Black & Red* and *Communist Front?*

2. Von Eschen, *Race against Empire,* 149. For similar views of the NAACP, see Anderson, *Eyes Off the Prize;* Janken *White,* especially 297–323, and "From Colonial Liberation to Cold War Liberalism." On the NAACP's response to the rising tide of domestic anticommunist fears and persecution, also see Horne's *Black & Red,* 49–111; Lewis, *W.E.B. Du Bois: The Fight for Equality,* 507–56; Record, *Race and Radicalism,* 132–68. Quotations are from, George F. Kennan, "Sources of Soviet Conduct," *Foreign Affairs,* XXV (July 1947), reprinted in Kennan, *American Diplomacy,* 104; Arthur M. Schlesinger Jr., "The U.S. Communist Party."

3. The account of Du Bois's conflict with White and the NAACP derives largely from Lewis, *W.E.B. Du Bois: The Fight for Equality,* especially 528–34, quote on 534. On White's explanation for his and the NAACP's brand of anticommunism, see White, *How Far the Promised Land?,* especially 212–27, quote on 223.

4. On the cold war's either/or logic, see Livingston, *Pragmatism, Feminism, and Democracy,* 85–114; White, *How Far the Promised Land?,* quote on 216. Also, on the NAACP's historical and principled ideological opposition to the Communist Party, see Record, *Race and Radicalism,* 132–221.

5. Kluger, *Simple Justice,* 5–8; Interview with Minnie Ida Wright, by Gregory Hunter, Behind the Veil Collection.

6. Interview with Joseph Richburg Sr., by Mary Hebert, Behind the Veil Collection. Also, see Interview with Moses Levy Sr., by Kisha Turner and Blair Murphy, Behind the Veil Collection. A special thanks and debt of gratitude are owed to Blair Murphy Kelley for her field work, conversations, and a paper she wrote on oral history and Clarendon County, "To Tell a Bigger Story," for a panel we did together at the Organization of American Historians' Annual Meeting in 2000.

7. Kluger, *Simple Justice,* 6–8. On the failed voter registration efforts, see J.A. DeLaine to Harold Boulware, March 6, 1948, Folder 2, DeLaine Collection, South Caroliniana Library, University of South Carolina, Columbia; J.A. DeLaine to Harold Boulware, April 9, 1948, DeLaine Collection.

8. DeLaine's personal history is detailed in, Kluger, *Simple Justice,* 3–14. For a more recent account informed by new documents and conversations with family members, see Lochbaum, "The World Made Flesh," especially 75–85. The account here also has benefited from Joseph A. DeLaine Jr.'s, "Recollections of His Father," and the author's conversations with Joseph DeLaine Jr.

9. DeLaine quoted in Lochbaum, "The World Made Flesh," 29–30.

10. J.A. DeLaine, "August 1962—Some Reminiscence of My Life: Vacation Reflections," Persons: J.A. DeLaine, Reel 9, McCray Papers, hereafter cited as "Reminiscence"; Richards, "Osceola E. McKaine," 117; DeLaine Jr., "Recollections of his Father," in author's possession. The DeLaine family dates the creation of the Clarendon County branch to 1941. Quotes are from: J.A. DeLaine to Flutie Boyd, April 7, 1948, Folder 2, DeLaine Collection; J.A. DeLaine to NAACP, January 17, 1943, Clarendon County Branch File, II-C-177, NAACP Papers; J.A. DeLaine, "Reminiscence," Persons: 5A.DeLaine, Reel 9, McCray Papers.

11. Interview with Joseph Richburg Sr., by Mary Hebert, Behind the Veil Collection; Officers of South Carolina Branches, January 20, 1944, State Conference Files, II-C-176, NAACP Papers; Report of Election of Officers, Clarendon County, September 2, 1948, Clarendon County Branch File, II-C-177, NAACP Papers; Bes-

sie House to John H. McCray, February 19, 1945, Places: Clarendon County, Reel 10, McCray Papers; Sarah E. Daniels to John H. McCray, December 1, 1946, Places: Clarendon County, Reel 10, McCray Papers.

12 Interview with Ferdinand Pearson, by Blair L. Murphy and Kisha Turner, Behind the Veil Collection.

13. Ibid.; Jessie Pearson et. al. to W.A. Schiffley, July 6, 1946, Folder 1, DeLaine Collection; Lochbaum, "The World Made Flesh," 84–85.

14. Kluger, *Simple Justice*, 13–14; quote from J.A. DeLaine and Others, "The Clarendon County School Segregation Case," in Joseph A. DeLaine, File Number: 9–28873, Federal Bureau of Investigation, Freedom of Information/Privacy Acts Section, Washington, D.C.

15. J.A. DeLaine to John H. McCray, December 14, 1961, McCray Papers; Kluger, *Simple Justice*, 13–14; Harold Boulware to J.A. DeLaine, July 29, 1947, Folder 1, DeLaine Collection (DeLaine's hand notes).

16. J.A. DeLaine to James Hinton, February 5, 1948, Folder 1, DeLaine Collection; Harold Boulware to J.A. DeLaine, February 16, 1948, Folder 2, DeLaine Collection (DeLaine's hand notes); J.A. DeLaine to Harold Boulware, April 9, 1948, Folder 2, DeLaine Collection.

17. James M. Hinton to Levi Pearson, March 12, 1948, Folder 2, DeLaine Collection; Harold Boulware to J.A. DeLaine, February 16, 1948, Folder 2, DeLaine Collection (hand notes); J.A. DeLaine to Harold Boulware, March 6, 1948, Folder 2, DeLaine Collection; J.A. DeLaine to Harold Boulware, April 9, 1948, Folder 2, DeLaine Collection; Kluger, *Simple Justice*, 17; Interview with Ferdinand Pearson, by Blair L. Murphy and Kisha Turner, Behind the Veil Collection.

18. J.A. DeLaine to James Hinton and Harold Boulware, September 30, 1948, Folder 3, DeLaine Collection; Interview with Eugene A.R. Montgomery, by Charles Houston Jr., Behind the Veil Collection; DeLaine and Others, "The Clarendon County School Segregation Case," in Joseph A. DeLaine, File Number: 9–28873, Federal Bureau of Investigation; Harold Boulware to J.A. DeLaine, March 8, 1949, Folder 3, DeLaine Collection (hand notes). Also, see Tushnet, *Making Civil Rights Law*, 154.

19. Interview with Robert James Georgia Jr. and Abraham Smith, by Mary Hebert and Blair L. Murphy, Behind the Veil Collection; Interview with Hauleen Green Smith, by Kisha Turner, Behind the Veil Collection; Petition submitted to Superintendents and Trustees of Clarendon County and District Number 22, 1949, Clarendon County Board of Education Complaints Against Principles, 1949–1950, South Carolina Department of Archives and History, Columbia, South Carolina, herafter cited as Complaint Files.

20. DeLaine and Others, "The Clarendon County School Segregation Case," in Joseph A. DeLaine, File Number: 9–28873, Federal Bureau of Investigation; Minutes of June 8, 1949 Meeting taken by the Reverend E.E. Richburg, Folder 3, DeLaine Collection, hereafter cited as Richburg Minutes. For more on the concerns of black parents in Clarendon County schools, see Complaint Files, South Carolina Department of Archives and History.

21. DeLaine and Others, "The Clarendon County School Segregation Case," in Joseph A. DeLaine, File Number: 9–28873, Federal Bureau of Investigation; Richburg Minutes, DeLaine Collection; Harold Boulware to J.A. DeLaine, March 8, 1949, Folder 3, DeLaine Collection (hand notes).

22. Robert Georgia, et al. to County Board of Education, July 9, 1949, Com-

plaint Files, South Carolina Department of Archives and History; R.M. Elliott et al., Summary of June 24, 1949 Meeting, Complaint Files, South Carolina Department of Archives and History; Parents of Scott's Branch School Petition to Superintendent and Trustees, July 25, 1949, Complaint Files, South Carolina Department of Archives and History; Parents of School District 22 to Trustees of School District 22, Trustees of County Board, & State Board of Education, September 18, 1950, Complaint Files, South Carolina Department of Archives and History; Parent Committee on Action to Superintendent and Trustees, April 13, 1950, Complaint Files, South Carolina Department of Archives and History. DeLaine quoted from "The Clarendon County School Segregation Case," in Joseph A. DeLaine, File Number: 9–28873, Federal Bureau of Investigation.

23. "Please Announce This In Your Church," ca. December 1949, Folder 3, DeLaine Collection (hand notes); DeLaine and Others, "The Clarendon County School Segregation Case," in Joseph A. DeLaine, File Number: 9–28873, Federal Bureau of Investigation; Kluger, *Simple Justice*, 25; Lochbaum, "The World Made Flesh," 121–22, 129–30.

24. DeLaine and Others, "The Clarendon County School Segregation Case," in Joseph A. DeLaine, File Number: 9–28873, Federal Bureau of Investigation; J.A. DeLaine, "An Open Letter: A Summary of Incidents in the Summerton School Affair," January 1950, Folder 4, DeLaine Collection, hereafter cited as "An Open Letter"; Interview with Eliza Gemble Briggs, by Mary Hebert, Behind the Veil Collection; Interview with Robert Georgia Jr., and Abraham Smith, by Mary Hebert and Blair L. Murphy, Behind the Veil Collection; Kluger, *Simple Justice*, 23–24; Interview with Minnie Ida Wright, by Gregory Hunter, Behind the Veil Collection; Interview with Melison Beatrice Green, by Mary Hebert, Behind the Veil Collection; Interview with Joseph Richburg Sr., by Mary Hebert, Behind the Veil Collection.

25. J.A. DeLaine to NAACP, May 3, 1950, Clarendon County Branch File, II-C-177, NAACP Papers. The story of the "gray-headed sage" is recounted in Carter, *A Matter of Law*, 97–98.

26. On Waring and his personal and judicial transformation, see Schmidt, "J. Waties Waring"; Yarbrough, *A Passion for Justice*, especially 127–71 and 172–212. On desegregation as a cold war imperative, see Dudziak, "Desegregation as a Cold War Imperative" and *Cold War Civil Rights*. Quotes are from Waring's dissenting opinion, in *Briggs v. Elliott* 98 F. Supp. 529, D.C.S.C. 1951.

27. Warren quoted from his majority opinion in *Brown v. Board of Education*, reprinted in Martin, *Brown v. Board of Education*, 168–84. On *Brown*'s significance as legal doctrine, see, for example, Garrow, "From *Brown* to *Casey*," quote on 74; Tushnet, "What Really Happened in *Brown v. Board of Education*." On its significance viewed across academic fields and decades, see Lau, *From the Grassroots to the Supreme Court*.

28. Statement of the 18th Annual Meeting of the South Carolina State Conference of Branches, October 24, 1959, South Carolina State Conference File, 1958–1959, III-C-143, NAACP Papers.

29. The most cogent argument on the devastating short-term effects of *Brown* in the South is Klarman, "How *Brown* Changed Race Relations" and *From Jim Crow to Civil Rights*. On the formation of White Citizens' Councils in South Carolina, see Quint, *Profile in Black and White*, 45–54. On the creation of White Citizens' Councils across the South, see Bartley, *The Rise of Massive Resistance*; McMillen, *The*

Citizens' Council. On the Gressette Committee and the state's legislative efforts to smash the NAACP, see Quint, *Profile in Black and White*, 103, 105–10.

30. Statistical data is from Wolters, *The Burden of Brown*, 130–31. On economic changes across the South, see Wright, *Old South, New South*, 239–74. Economic changes in South Carolina are detailed in Coclanis and Ford, "The South Carolina Economy Reconstructed and Reconsidered." On DeLaine's final exit, see Joseph A. DeLaine Jr.'s,"Details regarding Rev. De Laine's escape via Florence, SC," 1996, copy in author's possession; Lochbaum, "The World Made Flesh," 130–37; Kluger, *Simple Justice*, 3, 525; Quint, *Profile in Black and White*, 36; DeLaine and Others, "The Clarendon County School Segregation Case," in Joseph A. DeLaine, File Number: 9–28873, Federal Bureau of Investigation; J.A. DeLaine to J. Edgar Hoover, October 13, 1955, in Joseph A. DeLaine, FBI File. A copy of the death threat can be found in Folder 8, DeLaine Collection.

31. Interview with Joseph Richburg Sr., by Mary Hebert, Behind the Veil Collection; Interview with Eliza Briggs, by Mary Hebert, Behind the Veil Collection. On desegregation efforts in Clarendon County, see Wolters, *The Burden of Brown*, 150–51, 166.

32. Membership numbers are from, Report and Recommendations on Membership and Staff, 1957, III-A-37, NAACP Papers.

33. Membership numbers are from, Report and Recommendations on Membership and Staff, 1957, III-A-37, NAACP Papers. On McCray's legal travails, see "John McCray Jailed: Citizens Blaze with Anger," November 1951, along with other documents found in, Greenwood County Libel Case, Reel 13, McCray Papers. Also, see John Bolt Culbertson to Walter Reuther, September 10, 1953, Persons: John Bolt Culbertson, Reel 9, McCray Papers.

34. On the personal and financial conflict between Simkins and McCray, see Mrs. Andrew W. Simkins to John H. McCray, February 4, 1954, General Papers, 1951–1956, Box 1, Simkins Papers; Mrs. Andrew W. Simkins to John H. McCray, July 14, 1954, NAACP General, 1953–1954, Box 2, Simkins Papers; John H. McCray to Raymond E. Lark Jr., February 25, 1974, Correspondence: John McCray, Box 2, Clement Papers. On the efforts to red-bait Simkins and Simkins's view of the mid-1950s demise of the state conference, see Woods, "Black Woman Activist," 248–60. Evidence of the behind-the-scenes efforts to expose Simkins's "subversive" associations and activities can also be found in the NAACP, SC File, Box 20, William D. Workman Jr., Papers, Modern Political Collections, University of South Carolina, Columbia. Simkins quoted from Interview with Modjeska Simkins, by Jacqueline Hall, Southern Oral History Collection. Hinton's letter of resignation, September 12, 1958, can be found in South Carolina State Conference File, 1958–1959, III-C-143, NAACP Papers. On the difficulties faced generally by the state conference in the wake of *Brown*, see "Historical Sketch of South Carolina Conference of Branches of the National Association for the Advancement of Colored People," South Carolina Conference of NAACP Branches, Twenty-third Annual Convention Program, Programs, State Conference, 1951–1967, Box 3, Simkins Papers.

35. Report and Recommendations on Membership and Staff, 1957, III-A-37, NAACP Papers. On the repression of the NAACP in the South, see Carter, *A Matter of Law*, 147–63; Morris, *The Origins of the Civil Rights Movement*, 30–35; Tushnet, *Making Civil Rights Law*, 247–300. On NAACP repression in Louisiana and Mississippi following *Brown*, see, respectively, Fairclough, *Race and Democracy*, 187–233;

Dittmer, *Local People*, 41–89. On the LDF-NAACP split, see Tushnet, *Making Civil Rights Law*, 310–13; and Brown-Nagin, "The Impact of Lawyer-Client Disengagement."

Conclusion: Movement, Memory, and American Democracy

1. Accounts of the Orangeburg boycott include, Gore, *On a Hilltop High*, 199–205; Hine, "Civil Rights and Campus Wrongs"; Meier and Rudwick, "The Origins of Nonviolent Direct Action in Afro-American Protest," 364–65. Also, see Modjeska Simkins, "The Orangeburg-Elloree (SC) Story (Cont.) (Second Installment)," Box 3, NAACP General, n/d, Simkins Papers; James M. Hinton and Mrs. Andrew W. Simkins to State NAACP Membership, October 18, 1955, Box 2, NAACP General, October–December 1955, Simkins Papers.

2. On the history of "Don't Buy Where You Can't Work" campaigns, see Meier and Rudwick, "The Origins of Nonviolent Direct Action in Afro-American Protest," 314–32, especially Table II, 316. Detailed notes on the Orangeburg boycott and extensive documentary evidence, including reams of newspaper clippings, are collected in Box 15, Folder 11, Meier Papers, Manuscripts, Archives and Rare Books Division, Schomburg Center for Research in Black Culture, New York, New York. Before his death, Meier graciously guided me through his papers, a treasure trove for researchers. The list of products targeted by the boycotters can be found in the *Pittsburgh Courier*, September 24, 1955, 1, Box 15, Folder 11, Meier Papers. The boycott leaders' travels to Montgomery, Alabama, is recounted in Interview with Earl Matthew Middleton, by Charles H. Houston Jr., Behind the Veil Collection. The interview can also be found at the South Carolina State University Historical Collection, Orangeburg, South Carolina. On the emergence of a knowledge economy, see Bell, *The Coming of Post-Industrial Society*. On the emergence of a consumer nation in post–World War II America, see Cohen, *A Consumers' Republic*.

3. Hine, "Civil Rights and Campus Wrongs," 318, 323; *New York Times*, March 16, 1960, 1; Zinn, *SNCC*, 18; Meier and Rudwick, *CORE*, 119.

4. McCain's organizing efforts are all detailed in his reports filed with CORE's national office and his notebooks dating from December 1957 to December 1960, McCain Collection, South Caroliniana Library, University of South Carolina, Columbia. On CORE and McCain's organizing efforts on its behalf, see Meier and Rudwick, *CORE*, especially 77–90.

5. McCain's organizational efforts and the prominence of voter registration to them are chronicled in his notebooks in McCain Collection. Meier and Rudwick have fully detailed McCain's exchange with CORE's national leadership in *CORE*, 87–90, quote on 90. CORE's voter registration campaign in South Carolina also is recounted in Meier and Rudwick, *CORE*, 356–57. House of Representative numbers are in Edgar, *South Carolina*, 542.

6. On Esau Jenkins, Septima Clark, Highlander Folk School, and the origins of the Citizenship School on Johns Island, see Clark, *Echo in My Soul*, 89, 111–21, 135–44, 192; Esau Jenkins, Handwritten Composition, September 14 and September 24, 1966, Folder 1, Jenkins Collection, Avery Research Center, College of Charleston, Charleston, South Carolina; Esau Jenkins (Community Developer, Educator and Fighter for Human Rights) (1910–1972), Folder 6, Jenkins Collection; Nan Woodruff, "Esau Jenkins: A Retrospective View of the Man and His Times,"

Esau Jenkins Vertical File, Avery Research Center; Ling, "Local Leadership in the Early Civil Rights Movement," especially 405–15; Morris, *Origins of the Civil Rights Movement*, 139–62; Glen, *Highlander: No Ordinary School*; Tjerandsen, *Education for Citizenship*.

7. On the radical significance of the organizing tradition developed by Clark, see Grant, *Ella J. Baker*; Morris, *Origins of the Civil Rights Movement*; Payne, *I've Got the Light of Freedom*; Ransby, *Ella Baker and the Black Freedom Movement*; Robnett, *How Long? How Long?*

8. Hall, "The Long Civil Rights Movement," 4; Korstad, *Civil Rights Unionism*, 11.

9. Sellers, *The River of No Return*, 19.

10. On the NAACP's role in passage of the Civil Rights and Voting Rights Acts, see Jonas, *Freedom's Sword*, 169–230; Lawson, *Black Ballots* and *In Pursuit of Power*; Wilkins, *Standing Fast*, 290–326.

11. The definitive study of the Orangeburg Massacre remains, Nelson and Bass, *The Orangeburg Massacre*. Also, see Hine, "Civil Rights and Campus Wrongs"; Sellers, *The River of No Return*, 206–28, quotes on 206 and 209; Williams, *Freedom & Justice*, 221–229.

12. My account of the 1969 hospital workers strike is drawn from Fink and Greenberg, *Upheaval in the Quiet Zone*, 128–58; Williams, *Freedom & Justice*, 231–38. On the Memphis sanitation workers strike, see Green, "Battling the Plantation Mentality."

13. Moultrie quoted in Fink and Greenberg, *Upheaval in the Quiet Zone*, 136.

14. On changes in African American political representation in South Carolina, see Beazley, "Public Life," 101–14. On battles over single and multi-member legislative districts, see Burton et al., "South Carolina," 202–14.

15. Bositis, "Black Elected Officials"; Clyburn, "Biography."

16. On church burnings, see Center for Democratic Renewal, "Report of Six Month Preliminary Investigation" and Edgar, *South Carolina*, 568. On the Confederate flag, see Cabel, "South Carolina takes Confederate flag down from Capital dome"; Ifill, "Stars and Bars"; Clyburn, "Race is Still an Issue." James quoted in Ifill.

17. Sheheen, " . . . *And Miles to Go Before I Sleep*," 9; Swinton, "Economic Research Paper," 205, 210; Clyburn, "Setting History Straight on *Brown v. Board*."

Bibliography

Interviews

Abbreviations

Southern Oral History Collection. Wilson Library. University of North Carolina at Chapel Hill (SHC).

Behind the Veil: Documenting African-American Life in the Jim Crow South. Center for Documentary Studies at Duke University. Rare Book, Manuscript, and Special Collections Library, Duke University (BTV).

Peter F. Lau (PFL).

Adams, Benjamin Edward. Interview by Charles H. Houston Jr. Columbia, SC, July 20, 1994. BTV.

Adams, Fannie Phelps. Interview by Charles H. Houston Jr. Columbia, SC, July 28, 1994. BTV.

Allen, Johnny and Ida Belle. Interview by Blair L. Murphy. Sumter, SC, June 20, 1995. BTV.

Bethune, Thelmer. Interview by Kisha Turner. Silver, SC, July 6, 1995. BTV.

Blackwell, Gordon. Interview by Brent Glass. January 5, 1976. SHC.

Briggs, Eliza Gemble. Interview by Mary Hebert. Summerton, SC, June 16, 1995. BTV.

Briggs, Willie Mae. Interview by Kisha Turner. Summerton, SC, June 22, 1995. BTV.

Brooks, Charles Thomas, Sr. Interview by Charles H. Houston Jr. Columbia, SC, July 28, 1994. BTV.

Brunson, John Edward. Interview by Charles H. Houston Jr. Orangeburg, SC, July 26, 1994. BTV.

Butler, B.O. Interview by Kisha Turner and Blair L. Murphy. Summerton, SC, June 29, 1995. BTV.

Byrd, Alfred D. Interview by Peter F. Lau. Hampton, VA, March 1, 2000. PFL.

Caldwell, Rossie Juanita Lucille Brower. Interview by Charles H. Houston Jr. Orangeburg, SC, August 8, 1994. BTV.

DeLaine, Marguirite. Interview by Kisha Turner. Charleston, SC, July 8, 1995. BTV.

Dow, Willine Bosier. Interview by Blair L. Murphy. Pinewood, SC, June 21, 1995. BTV.

Felder, Julius. Interview by Charles H. Houston Jr. Cayce, SC, July 27, 1994. BTV.

Flemming, Abraham A.B. Interview by Kisha Turner. New Zion, SC, July 3, 1995. BTV.

Flood, John Marion. Interview by Mary Hebert. Summerton, SC, June 20, 1995. BTV.

Georgia, Robert, Jr., and Abraham Smith. Interview by Mary Hebert and Blair L. Murphy. Summerton, SC, June 14, 1995. BTV.

Gore, Blinzy Lee. Interview by Charles H. Houston Jr. Orangeburg, SC, August 5, 1994. BTV.

Gray, Reuben L. Interview by Blair L. Murphy and Kisha Turner. Sumter, SC, July 5, 1995. BTV.

Green, Melison Beatrice. Interview by Mary Hebert. Summerton, SC, July 4, 1995. BTV.

Gregory, Celestine Nelson. Interview by Kisha Turner. Summerton, SC, July 9, 1995. BTV.

Harper, John Roy, III. Interview by Charles H. Houston Jr. Columbia, SC, July 16 and August 12, 1994. BTV.

Hassell, Betty Ann. Interview by Charles H. Houston Jr. Richland City, SC, July 25, 1994. BTV.

Howard, Sallie Mae. Interview by Kisha Turner. New Zion, SC, June 28, 1995. BTV.

Hubbard, Robert James. Interview by Charles H. Houston Jr. Orangeburg, SC, July 21, 1994. BTV.

Jackson, James E., Jr., Esther Cooper Jackson, and Dorothy Burnham. Interview by Peter F. Lau. Brooklyn, NY, March 14, 1997. PFL.

Jamison, Annie Marion. Interview by Charles H. Houston Jr. Orangeburg, SC, July 13, 1994. BTV.

Jenkins, Barbara Jean. Interview by Charles H. Houston Jr. Orangeburg, SC, August 2, 1994. BTV.

Levy, Moses, Sr. Interview by Kisha Turner and Blair L. Murphy. Summerton, SC, June 29, 1995. BTV.

Lott, Sudie. Interview by Sally S. Graham. Saluda, SC, July 14, 1994. BTV.

McCollom, James Earl. Interview by Charles H. Houston Jr. Orangeburg, SC, August 5, 1994. BTV.

McCray, John H. Interview by Worth Long with Randall Williams, reprinted in *Southern Changes* 19 (Spring 1997): 13–15.

McCray, Josephine Dickey. Interview by Mary Hebert. Summerton, SC, June 27, 1995. BTV.

Middleton, Earl Matthew. Interview by Charles H. Houston Jr. Orangeburg, SC, July 19, 1994. BTV.

Mitchell, Rachel Lottie. Interview by Sally S. Graham. Manning, SC, July 15, 1994. BTV.

Montgomery, Eugene Alonzo Randolph. Interview by Charles H. Houston Jr. Orangeburg, SC, August 2, 1994, BTV.

Pearson, Ferdinand. Interview by Blair L. Murphy and Kisha Turner. Manning, SC, June 14, 1995. BTV.

Richardson, Ruth J. Interview by Blair L. Murphy. Pinewood, SC, June 19, 1995. BTV.

Richburg, Joseph, Sr. Interview by Mary Hebert. Summerton, SC, June 26, 1995. BTV.

Robinson, Bernice S. Interview by Peter F. Lau. Cheraw, SC, August 3, 1999. PFL.

Roland, Harold. Interview by Charles H. Houston Jr. Orangeburg, SC, August 4, 1994. BTV.

Simkins, Modjeska Monteith. Interview by Jacquelyn Hall. Columbia, SC, July 28–31, 1976. SHC.

Smith, Hauleen Green. Interview by Kisha Turner. Summerton, SC, June 14, 1995. BTV.

Sultan, James Emile, Sr. Interview by Charles H. Houston Jr. Orangeburg, SC, July 22, 1994. BTV.

Washington, Sallie. Interview by Blair L. Murphy. Summerton, SC, June 21, 1995. BTV.

Whittenberg, A.J. Interview by Peter F. Lau. Greenville, SC, August 2, 1999. PFL.

Williams, Cornelius C. Interview by Mary Hebert. Summerton, SC, June 22, 1995. BTV.

Williams, Ethel L. Interview by Charles H. Houston Jr. Orangeburg, SC, July 18, 1994. BTV.

Wright, Minnie Ida. Interview by Gregory Hunter. Summerton, SC, n.d. BTV.

Young, Samuel. Interview by Mary Hebert. Pinewood, SC, June 22, 1995. BTV.

Zimmerman, Geraldyne Pierce. Interview by Charles H. Houston Jr. Orangeburg, SC, July 14, 1994. BTV.

Manuscript Sources

Brooklyn, New York

Personal Files of Esther Cooper Jackson and James E. Jackson Jr.

Charleston, South Carolina

Avery Research Center, College of Charleston

J. Arthur Brown Papers
Isaiah Bennett Collection
Septima Poinsette Clark and Bernice Robinson Papers Collection
Esau Jenkins Collection
Bernice Robinson Collection
"South Carolina Voices of the Civil Rights Movement" Collection
Vertical Files
Phyllis Wheatley and Social Club Collection

Robert Scott Smalls Library, Special Collections, College of Charleston

Septima Poinsette Clark Papers

Office of Archives and Records, Charleston County School District

City Board of School Commissioners Minute Book
South Carolina Room, Charleston County Public Library
Walsh's Charleston City Directory

Cheraw, South Carolina

Chamber of Commerce
Matheson Memorial Library
Town Hall

Columbia, South Carolina

Personal Files of Carrie Allen McCray
South Carolina Department of Archives and History

South Caroliniana Library, University of South Carolina

Eugene A. Adams Collection
Arthur J. Clement Jr., Papers
Joseph A. DeLaine Collection
Richard M. Jeffries Papers
James T. McCain Collection
John H. McCray Papers
National Association for the Advancement of Colored People, Sumter Branch Minute
    Book, April 1942–September 1952
Black History Vertical Files
Annie B. Weston
Coulter Academy
James M. Hinton
N.J. Frederick

Modern Political Collection, University of South Carolina

Modjeska M. Simkins Papers
William D. Workman Jr., Papers

Hampton, Virginia

Personal Files of Alfred D. Byrd

Greenville, South Carolina

James B. Duke Library, Furman University

Papers of the Greenville County Council for Community Development
    (GCCCD)

South Carolina Room, Greenville County Public Library

Hattie Logan Duckett Biographical File
Laura Smith Ebaugh Biographical File
Phillis Wheatley Center File
Hill's Greenville City Directory

New York, New York

Schomburg Center for Research in Black Culture

Ralph J. Bunche Papers
Carnegie-Myrdal Collection
August Meier Papers
William Pickens Papers

Orangeburg, South Carolina

Miller F. Whittaker Library, South Carolina State University Historical Collection

Behind the Veil: Documenting African-American Life in the Jim Crow South

Sleepy Hollow, New York

Rockefeller Archive Center

General Education Board (GEB) Papers

Washington, D.C.

Library of Congress, Manuscript Division

Brotherhood of Sleeping-Car Porters Papers
National Association for the Advancement of Colored People (NAACP) Papers
National Urban League Papers

Moorland-Spingarn Research Center, Howard University

Papers of the Southern Negro Youth Congress (SNYC Papers)

National Archives

Cotton Textile National Industrial Relations Board
National Industrial Relations Board Records
National Recovery Administration (NRA) Records
Records of the National Youth Administration

Microfilm

Commission on Interracial Cooperation/Association of Southern Women for the
   Prevention of Lynching (CIC) Papers
Federal Surveillance of Afro-Americans (1917–1924): The First World War, the Red
   Scare, and the Garvey Movement
John H. McCray Papers
Operation Dixie: The C.I.O. Organizing Committee Papers, 1946–1953 (Operation
   Dixie Papers)
Papers of the National Association for the Advancement of Colored People (NAACP
   Papers)
Records of the National Association of Colored Women's Clubs (NACW Records)

Government Publications and Records

U.S. Bureau of the Census. *Fourteenth Census of the United States, 1920. Population*, vol. 2. Washington, D.C.: Government Printing Office, 1923.
————. *Fifteenth Census of the United States, 1930. Population*, vol. 3. Washington, D.C.: Government Printing Office, 1932.
————. *Sixteenth Census of the United States, 1940. Population: Part 6*, vol. 2. Washington, D.C.: Government Printing Office, 1943.
————. *A Report of the Seventeenth Decennial Census of the United States, Census of Population: 1950, Vol. II, Characteristics of the Population, Part 40, South Carolina*, vol. 2. Washington, D.C.: Government Printing Office, 1952.
Septima Poinsette Clark, File Number 44–14876, Department of Justice, Federal Bureau of Investigation, Washington, D.C.
U.S. Department of Commerce. *Statistical Abstracts of the United States*. 112th ed. Washington, D.C.: Government Printing Office, 1992.
Congressional Record, 66th Congress, 1st Session, 4302-5.
Joseph A. DeLaine, File Number 9–28873, Department of Justice, Federal Bureau of Investigation, Washington, D.C.
James M. Hinton, File Number 44–9900, Department of Justice, Federal Bureau of Investigation, Washington, D.C.
Modjeska Monteith Simkins, File Number 355398, Department of Justice, Federal Bureau of Investigation, Washington, D.C.

Legal Cases

Elmore v. Rice. 72 F. Supp. 516. D.C.S.C., 1947.
Briggs v. Elliott. 98 F. Supp. 529. D.C.S.C., 1951.
Brown v. Baskin. 78 F. Supp. 933. D.C.S.C., 1948.
Brown v. Board of Education. 347. U.S. 483, 1954.
Wrighten v. Board of Trustees of the University of South Carolina. 72 F. Supp. 948. D.C.S.C., 1947.

Newspapers and Periodicals

Baltimore Afro-American
Charleston News and Courier
Cheraw (S.C.) *Chronicle*
Chicago Defender
Columbia (S.C.) *Record*
Greenville (S.C.) *News*
Journal of Negro Education
Journal of Negro History
Lighthouse and Informer (Columbia, S.C.)
Negro World
New York Times
Norfolk (Va.) *Journal and Guide*
Palmetto Leader (Columbia, S.C.)
Pittsburgh Courier
The Crisis (Journal of the National Association for the Advancement of Colored People)

The Nation
The New Republic
The (Columbia, S.C.) *State*

Books, Articles, Dissertations, and Theses

"Along the Color Line." *The Crisis* 53 (September 1946): 276.

Anderson, Benedict. *Imagined Communities: Reflections on the Origin and Spread of Nationalism.* New York: Verso, 1991.

Anderson, Carol. *Eyes Off the Prize: The United Nations and the African American Struggle for Human Rights, 1944–1955.* New York: Cambridge University Press, 2003.

Anderson, James D. *The Education of Blacks in the South, 1860–1935.* Chapel Hill: University of North Carolina Press, 1988.

Anderson, Jervis. *A. Philip Randolph: A Biographical Portrait.* New York: Harcourt Brace Jovanovich, Inc., 1973.

Applebome, Peter. *Rising Dixie: How the South Is Shaping American Values, Politics, and Culture.* New York: Times Books, 1996.

Arensen, Eric. "Following the Color Line of Labor: Black Workers and the Labor Movement before 1930." *Radical History Review* 55 (Winter 1993): 53–87.

———. *Waterfront Workers of New Orleans: Race, Class, and Politics, 1863–1923.* New York: Oxford University Press, 1991.

Ashmore, Harry S. *An Epitaph for Dixie.* New York: Norton, 1958.

Auerbach, Jerorld S. *Labor and Liberty: The La Follette Committee and the New Deal.* Indianapolis: Bobbs-Merrill, 1966.

Ayers, Edward L. *The Promise of the New South: Life after Reconstruction.* New York: Oxford University Press, 1992.

———. *Vengeance and Justice: Crime and Punishment in the Nineteenth-Century American South.* New York: Oxford University Press, 1984.

Badger, Anthony J. *The New Deal: The Depression Years, 1933–1940.* New York: Noonday Press, 1989.

Bagnall, Robert W. "Lights and Shadows in the South." *The Crisis* 39 (April 1932).

———. "N.A.A.C.P. Branch Activities." *The Crisis* 39 (February 1932): 53.

Bair, Barbara. "True Women, Real Men: Gender, Ideology, and Social Roles in the Garvey Movement." In *Gendered Domains: Rethinking Public and Private in Women's History*, edited by Dorothy O. Helley and Susan Reverby. Ithaca: Cornell University Press, 1992, 154–66.

Baker, Bruce E. "The 'Hoover Scare' in South Carolina, 1887: An Attempt to Organize Black Farm Labor." *Labor History* 40 (August 1999): 261–82.

Baker, Scott R. "Ambiguous Legacies: The NAACP's Legal Campaign against Segregation in Charleston, South Carolina, 1935–1975." Ph.D. diss., Columbia University, 1993.

Balkin, Jack M., ed. *What "Brown v. Board of Education" Should Have Said: The Nation's Top Legal Experts Rewrite America's Landmark Civil Rights Decision.* New York: New York University Press, 2001.

Ball, Edward. *The Sweet Hell Inside: A Family History.* New York: William Morrow, 2001.

Ballard, Alan B. *One More Day's Journey: The Story of a Family and a People.* New York: McGraw-Hill Book Company, 1984.

Bartley, Numan V. *The New South, 1945–1980*. Baton Rouge: Louisiana State University Press, 1995.

———. *The Rise of Massive Resistance: Race and Politics in the South during the 1950's*. Baton Rouge: Louisiana University Press, 1999.

Bates, Beth Tompkins. "A New Crowd Challenges the Agenda of the Old Guard in the NAACP, 1933–1941." *American Historical Review* 102 (April 1997): 340–77.

———.*Pullman Porters and the Rise of Protest Politics in Black America, 1925–1945*. Chapel Hill: The University of North Carolina Press, 2001.

Bay, Mia. *The White Image in the Black Mind: African-American Ideas about White People, 1830–1925*. New York: Oxford University Press, 2000.

Beazley, Paul W. "Public Life: Participation in Public Life c. 1940–2003." In *". . . And Miles to Go before I Sleep,"* edited by Fred R. Sheheen. Columbia: University of South Carolina College of Liberal Arts's Institute for Public Service and Policy Research, 2004. <http://ipspr.sc.edu/brown/AndMilesToGo.pdf> Accessed April 8, 2005.

Bederman, Gail. *Manliness & Civilization: A Cultural History of Gender and Race in the United States, 1880–1917*. Chicago: The University of Chicago Press, 1995.

Bell, Daniel. *The Coming of Post-Industrial Society: A Venture in Social Forecasting*. New York: Basic Books, 1999.

Bell, Derrick. *Faces at the Bottom of the Well: The Permanence of Racism*. New York: Basic Books, 1992.

Bender, Jay. "One Week That Changed the State." *South Carolina Lawyer* (November/December, 1999): 34–37.

Berlin, Ira. *Many Thousands Gone: The First Two Centuries of Slavery in North America*. Cambridge: The Belknap Press of Harvard University Press, 1998.

———. "Time, Space, and the Evolution of Afro-American Society on British Mainland North America." *American Historical Review* 85 (February 1980): 44–78.

———. *Slaves without Masters: The Free Negro in the Antebellum South*. New York: The New Press, 1974.

Berlin, Ira, Barbara J. Fields, Steven Miller, Joseph P. Reidy, and Leslie Rowland, eds. *Slaves No More: Three Essays on Emancipation and Civil War*. New York: Cambridge University Press, 1992.

Bernstein, Barton J., ed. *Towards a New Past: Dissenting Essays in American History*. New York: Pantheon, 1968.

Bernstein, Irving. *The New Deal Collective Bargaining Policy*. Berkeley: University of California Press, 1950.

———. *The Turbulent Years: A History of the American Worker, 1933–1941*. Boston: Houghton Mifflin, 1970.

Bethel, Elizabeth Rauh. *Promisedland: A Century of Life in a Negro Community*. Columbia: University of South Carolina Press, 1997.

Biles, Roger. *The South and the New Deal*. Lexington: University Press of Kentucky, 1994.

Biondi, Martha. *To Stand and Fight: The Struggle for Civil Rights in Postwar New York City*. Cambridge: Harvard University Press, 2003.

Black, Earl, and Merle Black. *Politics and Society in the South*. Cambridge: Harvard University Press, 1987.

Blum, John Morton. *V Was for Victory: Politics and American Culture during World War II*. New York: Harcourt Brace Janovich, 1976.

Borstelmann, Thomas. *The Cold War and the Color Line: American Race Relations in the Global Arena*. Cambridge: Harvard University Press, 2001.

Bositis, David A. "Black Elected Officials: A Statistical Summary 2001." Joint Center For Political and Economic Studies, 2001.<http://www.jointcenter.org/DB/ detail/BEO.htm> Accessed March 14, 2005.

Boydston, Jeane. *Home and Work: Housework, Wages, and the Ideology of Labor in the Early Republic.* New York: Oxford University Press, 1990.

Boyle, Kevin. *Arc of Justice: A Saga of Race, Civil Rights, and Murder in the Jazz Age.* New York: Henry Holt and Co., 2004.

———. "'There Are No Sorrows That the Union Can't Heal': The Struggle for Racial Equality in the United Automobile Workers, 1940–1960." *Labor History* 36 (Winter 1995): 5–23.

———. *The UAW and the Heyday of American Liberalism, 1945–1968.* Ithaca: Cornell University Press, 1995.

Brinkley, Alan. *The End of Reform: New Deal Liberalism in Recession and War.* New York: Vintage Books, 1995.

———. *Voices of Protest: Huey Long, Father Coughlin, and the Great Depression.* New York: Knopf, 1982.

Brown, Elsa Barkley. "African-American Women's Quilting: A Framework for Conceptualizing and Teaching African-American Women's History." *Signs* 14 (Summer 1989): 921–29.

———. "Negotiating and Transforming the Public Sphere: African American Political Life in the Transition from Slavery to Freedom." In *The Black Public Sphere: A Public Culture Book*, edited by the Black Public Sphere Collective. Chicago: The University of Chicago Press, 1995, 111–50.

———. "Polyrhythms and Improvization: Lessons for Women's History." *History Workshop Journal* 31 (Spring 1991): 85–90.

———. "To Catch the Vision of Freedom: Reconstructing Southern Black Women's Political History, 1865–1880." In *African American Women and the Vote, 1837–1965*, edited by Ann D. Gordon, Bettye Collier-Thomas, John H. Bracey Jr., Arlene Voski Avakian, and Joyce Avrech Berkman. Amherst: University of Massachusetts Press, 1997, 66–99.

———. "'What Has Happened Here': The Politics of Difference in Women's History and Feminist Politics." *Feminist Studies* 18 (Summer 1992): 295–312.

———. "Womanist Consciousness: Maggie Lena Walker and the Independent Order of Saint Luke." *Signs* 14 (1989): 610–33.

Brown, Elsa Barkely, and Gregg D. Kinball. "Mapping the Terrain of Black Richmond." *Journal of Urban History* 21 (March 1995): 296–346.

Brown, Lloyd. "Southern Youth's Heritage." *Freedomways: A Quarterly Review of the Negro Freedom Movement* 4 (Spring 1964).

Brown, Millicent Ellison. "Civil Rights Activism in Charleston, South Carolina, 1940–1970." Ph.D. diss., Florida State University, 1997.

Brown-Nagin, Tomiko. "The Impact of Lawyer-Client Disengagement on the NAACP's Campaign to Implement *Brown v. Board of Education* in Atlanta." In *From the Grassroots to the Supreme Court: Brown v. Board of Education and American Democracy*, edited by Peter F. Lau. Durham: Duke University Press, 2004.

Bruce, Dickson, Jr. "W.E.B. Du Bois and the Idea of Double Consciousness." *American Literature* 64 (June 1992): 299–309.

Brundage, W. Fitzhugh. *Lynching in the New South: Georgia and Virginia, 1880–1930.* Urbana: University of Illinois Press, 1993.

Bunche, Ralph J. "A Brief and Tentative Analysis of Negro Leadership," 1940. Carn-
egie-Myrdal Collection, The Schomburg Center for Research in Black Culture.
New York, NY.
———. "Conceptions and Ideologies of the Negro Problem," 1940. Carnegie-
Myrdal Collection, The Schomburg Center for Research in Black Culture. New
York, NY.
———. "Critical Analysis of the Tactics and Programs of Minority Groups." *Journal
of Negro Education* 4 (July 1935): 308–20.
———. *The Political Status of the Negro in the Age of FDR.* Chicago: University of
Chicago Press, 1973.
———. "The Programs, Ideologies, Tactics and Achievements of the Negro Better-
ment and Interracial Organizations," 1940. Carnegie-Myrdal Collection. The
Schomburg Center for Research in Black Culture. New York, NY.
———. *A World View of Race.* Port Washington, NY: Kennikat Press, 1968.
Burkett, Randall K. *Black Redemption: Churchmen Speak for the Garvey Movement.*
Philadelphia: Temple University Press, 1978.
———. *Garveyism as a Religious Movement: The Institutionalization of a Black Civil
Religion.* Metuchen, NJ: Scarecrow Press, Inc., 1978.
Burkett, Randall K., and Richard Newman. *Black Apostles: Afro-American Clergy
Confront the Twentieth Century.* Boston: G.K. Hall & Co., 1978.
Burton, Orville Vernon. "'The Black Squint of the Law': Racism in South Carolina."
In *The Meaning of South Carolina History: Essays in Honor of George C. Rogers
Jr.*, edited by David R. Chesnutt and Clyde N. Wilson. Columbia: University of
South Carolina Press, 1991, 161–85.
———. *In My Father's House Are Many Mansions: Family and Community in Edgefield
County South Carolina.* Chapel Hill: University of North Carolina Press, 1985.
Burton, Orville Vernon, Terence R. Finnegan, Peyton McCrary, and James Loewen.
"South Carolina." In *Quiet Revolution in the South: The Impact of the Voting
Rights Act, 1965–1990*, edited by Chandler Davidson and Bernard Grofman.
Princeton: Princeton University Press, 1994, 126–51.
Burton, Orville Vernon, and Robert McMath, eds. *Toward a New South? Stud-
ies in Post Civil War Southern Communities.* Westport, CT: Greenwood Press,
1982.
Butler, Judith. *Bodies That Matter: On the Discursive Limits of "Sex."* New York: Rout-
ledge, 1993.
Butterfield, Fox. *All God's Dangers: The Bosket Family and the American Tradition of
Violence.* New York: Knopf, 1995.
Byrnes, James F. *All in One Lifetime.* New York: Harper, 1958.
Cabell, Brian and Associated Press. "South Carolina takes Confederate flag down
from Capital dome." *CNN.com*, July 1, 2000. <http://www.cnnstudentnews.
cnn.com/2000/US/07/01/scflag.01/> Accessed June 14, 2005.
Cann, Marvin. "Burnet Maybank and Charleston Politics in the New Deal Era." *Pro-
ceedings of the South Carolina Historical Association* (1970): 39–48.
———. "Burnet Rhett Maybank and the New Deal in South Carolina, 1931–1941."
Ph.D. diss., University of North Carolina, Chapel Hill, 1967.
———. "The End of a Political Myth: The South Carolina Gubernatorial Campaign
of 1938." *South Carolina Historical Magazine* 72 (July 1971): 139–49.
Cann, Mary Katherine Davis. "The Morning After: South Carolina in the Jazz Age."
Ph.D. diss., University of South Carolina, 1984.

Carawan, Guy and Candie Carawan, eds. *Ain't you got the right to the tree of life? The People of Johns Island, South Carolina—Their Faces, Their Words, and Their Songs.* Athens: The University of Georgia Press, 1989.

———. *Sing for Freedom: The Story of the Civil Rights Movement through Its Songs.* Bethlehem, PA: A Sing Out Publication, 1990.

Carlton, David L. *Mill and Town in South Carolina, 1880–1920.* Baton Rouge: Louisiana State University Press, 1982.

Carson, Claybourne. "Civil Rights Reform and the Black Freedom Struggle." In *The Civil Rights Movement in America*, edited by Charles W. Eagles. Jackson: University Press of Mississippi, 1986, 19–37.

Carter, Dan T. *The Politics of Rage: George Wallace, the Origins of the New Conservatism, and the Transformation of American Politics.* New York: Simon and Schuster, 1995.

———. *Scottsboro: A Tragedy of the American South.* Baton Rouge: Louisiana State University Press, 1969.

Carter, Robert L. *A Matter of Law: A Memoir of Struggle in the Cause of Equal Rights.* New York: The New Press, 2005.

Cayton, Horace R., and George S. Mitchell. *Black Workers and the New Unions.* College Park, MD: McGrath Publishing Company, 1969.

Cecelski, David S. *Along Freedom Road: Hyde County, North Carolina and the Fate of Black Schools in the South.* Chapel Hill: University of North Carolina Press, 1994.

Center for Democratic Renewal. "Report of Six Month Preliminary Investigation: Black Church Burnings in the South," June 10, 1996. In *African American Mosaic: A Documentary History from the Slave Trade to the Twenty-first Century, Volume Two: From 1865 to the Present*, edited by John H. Bracey Jr. and Manisha Sinha. New Jersey: Pearson Prentice Hall, 2004.

Chafe, William. *Civilities and Civil Rights: Greensboro, North Carolina and the Black Struggle for Freedom.* New York: Oxford University Press, 1980.

Chalmers, David M. *Hooded Americanism: The History of the Ku Klux Klan.* New York: Franklin Watts, 1981.

Chappell, David L. *A Stone of Hope: Prophetic Religion and the Death of Jim Crow.* Chapel Hill: The University of North Carolina Press, 2004.

Chateauvert, M. Melinda. *Marching Together: Women of the Brotherhood of Sleeping Car Porters.* Urbana: University of Illinois Press, 1997.

Clark, Septima Poinsette, with Cynthia Stokes Brown. *Septima Clark and the Civil Rights Movement: Ready from Within.* Navarro, CA: Wild Tree Press, 1986.

Clark, Septima Poinsette, with LeGette Blythe. *Echo in My Soul.* New York: Dutton and Company, 1962.

Clark-Lewis, Elizabeth. *Living In, Living Out: African American Domestics and the Great Migration.* New York: Kodansha International, 1994.

Clyburn, James E. "Biography." James E. Clyburn Home Page. <http://www.house.gov/clyburn/biography.htm> Accessed June 14, 2005.

———. "Race Is Still an Issue." James E. Clyburn Home Page, July 11, 2003. <http://www.house.gov/apps/list/speech/sc06_clyburn/030711raceanissue.html> Accessed June 14, 2005.

———. "Setting History Straight on *Brown v. Board*." James E. Clyburn Home Page, May 22, 2003. <http://www.house.gov/apps/list/speech/sc06_clyburn/030522brownvboard.html> Accessed June 14, 2005.

Cobb, James C., and Michael Namorato, eds. *The New Deal and the South*. Oxford: University of Mississippi Press, 1984.

Coclanis, Peter A., and Lacy K. Ford. "The South Carolina Economy Reconstructed and Reconsidered: Structure, Output, and Performance, 1670–1985." In *Developing Dixie: Modernization in a Traditional Society*, edited by Winfred B. Moore Jr., Joseph F. Tripp, and Lyon G. Tyler Jr. New York: Greenwood Press, 1988, 93–110.

Cohen, Robert. *When the Old Left Was Young: Student Radicals and America's First Mass Student Movement, 1929–1941*. New York: Oxford University Press, 1993.

Cohen, Lizabeth. *A Consumers' Republic: The Politics of Mass Consumption in Postwar America*. New York: Vintage Press, 2003.

———. *Making a New Deal: Industrial Workers in Chicago, 1919–1939*. New York: Cambridge University Press, 1990.

Cohodas, Nadine. *Strom Thurmond and the Politics of Southern Change*. New York: Simon and Schuster, 1993.

Colburn, David. *Racial Change and Community Crisis, St. Augustine, Florida, 1877–1980*. New York: Columbia University Press, 1985.

Cott, Nancy. *The Grounding of Modern Feminism*. New Haven: Yale University Press, 1987.

Crawford, Vicki L., Jacqueline Anne Rouse, and Barbara Woods, eds. *Women in the Civil Rights Movement: Trailblazers and Torchbearers, 1941–1965*. Bloomington: Indiana University Press, 1993.

Cruse, Harold. *The Crisis of the Negro Intellectual: A Historical Analysis of the Failure of Black Leadership*. New York: Quill, 1984.

Culver, John C., and John Hyde. *American Dreamer: A Life of Henry Wallace*. New York: W. W. Norton & Company, Inc., 2000.

Dailey, Jane. *Before Jim Crow: The Politics of Postemancipation Virginia*. Chapel Hill: The University of North Carolina Press, 2000.

Dailey, Jane, Glenda Gilmore, and Bryant Simon, eds. *Jumpin' Jim Crow: Southern Politics from the Civil War to Civil Rights*. Princeton: Princeton University Press, 2000.

Dalfiume, Richard. "The 'Forgotten Years' of the Negro Revolution." In *The Negro in Depression and War: Prelude to Revolution, 1930–1945*, edited by Bernard Sternsher. Chicago: Quadrangle Books, 1969, 298–316.

Daniel, Pete. *Lost Revolutions: The South in the 1950s*. Chapel Hill: The University of North Carolina Press, 2000.

Davis, Angela Y. *Blues Legacies and Black Feminism: Gertrude "Ma" Rainey, Bessie Smith, and Billie Holiday*. New York: Vintage Books, 1999.

———. "Angela Davis: Reflections on Race, Class, and Gender in the USA," Interview with Lisa Lowe. In *The Politics of Culture in the Shadow of Capital*, edited by Lisa Lowe and David Lloyd. Durham: Duke University Press, 1997, 303–23.

Davis, John P. "NRA Codifies Wage Slavery." *The Crisis* (October 1934).

DeLaine, Joseph A, Jr. "Details Regarding Rev. DeLaine's Escape via Florence, SC." 1996. Copy in possession of Peter F. Lau.

———. "Recollections of His Father, Reverend Joseph Armstrong DeLaine, Sr. and the Civil Rights Struggle of Clarendon County, SC." Copy in possession of Peter F. Lau.

Denning, Michael. *The Cultural Front: The Laboring of American Culture in the Twentieth Century*. London: Verso, 1998.

Devlin, George A. *South Carolina and Black Migration, 1865–1940*. New York: Garland Publishing, Inc., 1989.

Dimock, Wai Chee, and Michael T. Gilmore, eds. *Rethinking Class: Literary Studies and Social Formations*. New York: Columbia University Press, 1994.

Dittmer, John. *Black Georgia in the Progressive Era, 1900–1920*. Urbana: University of Illinois Press, 1977.

———. *Local People: The Struggle for Civil Rights in Mississippi*. Urbana: University of Illinois Press, 1994.

Drago, Edmund L. *Initiative, Paternalism, and Race Relations: Charleston's Avery Normal Institute*. Athens: University of Georgia Press, 1990.

Duberman, Martin. *Paul Robeson: A Biography*. New York: The New Press, 1989.

Du Bois, Ellen Carol. *Feminism & Suffrage: The Emergence of an Independent Women's Movement in America, 1848–1869*. Ithaca: Cornell University Press, 1999.

Du Bois, W.E.B. *Black Reconstruction in America, 1860–1880*. New York: Atheneum, 1992.

———. *Dusk of Dawn: An Essay toward an Autobiography of a Race Concept*. New Brunswick: Transaction Publishers, 1991.

———. "Karl Marx and the Negro." *The Crisis* (March 1933): 55–56.

———. "A Negro Nation within the Nation." *Current History* 42 (June 1935): 265–70.

———. "On Being Ashamed of Oneself: An Essay on Race Pride." *The Crisis* 40 (September 1933): 200.

———. "Returning Soldiers." *The Crisis* 18 (May 1919): 13–14.

———. "Segregation." *The Crisis* 41 (January 1934): 20.

———. "Segregation." *The Crisis* 41 (June 1934): 173–74.

———. "Social Planning for the Negro, Past and Present." *Journal of Negro Education* 5 (January 1936).

———. *The Souls of Black Folk*. New York: Penguin Books, 1982.

———. "Youth and Age at Amenia." *The Crisis* 40 (October 1933): 226–27.

Dudziak, Mary L. *Cold War Civil Rights: Race and the Image of American Democracy*. Princeton: Princeton University Press, 2000.

———. "Desegregation as a Cold War Imperative." *Stanford Law Review* 41 (November 1988): 61–120.

Eagles, Charles W., ed. *The Civil Rights Movement in America*. Jackson: University of Mississippi Press, 1986.

Edelman, Marian Wright. *Lanterns: A Memoir of Mentors*. Boston: Beacon Press, 1999.

Edgar, Walter. *South Carolina: A History*. Columbia: University of South Carolina Press, 1998.

———. ed. *South Carolina: The WPA Guide to the Palmetto State*. Columbia: University of South Carolina Press, 1988.

Edsall, Thomas Bryne, and Mary D. Edsall. *Chain Reaction: The Impact of Race, Rights, and Taxes on American Politics*. New York: W.W. Norton, 1992.

Edwards, Brent Hayes. *The Practice of Diaspora: Literature, Translation, and the Rise of Black Internationalism*. Cambridge: Harvard University Press, 2003.

Edwards, Laura F. *Gendered Strife and Confusion: The Political Culture of Reconstruction*. Urbana: University of Illinois Press, 1997.

Egerton, John. *Speak Now against the Day: The Generation before the Civil Rights Movement*. Chapel Hill: University of North Carolina Press, 1994.

Emmons, Caroline Scott. "The Flame of Resistance: The NAACP in Florida, 1910–1960." Ph.D. diss., Florida State University, 1998.

Eskew, Glenn T. *But for Birmingham: The Local and National Movements in the Civil Rights Struggle.* Chapel Hill: The University of North Carolina Press, 1997.

Fairclough, Adam. *Race and Democracy: The Civil Rights Struggle in Louisiana, 1915–1972.* Athens: University of Georgia Press, 1995.

Farmer, James O. "The End of the White Primary in South Carolina: A Southern State's Fight to Keep Its Politics White." M.A. thesis, University of South Carolina, 1969.

Fast, Howard. *Freedom Road.* New York: Duell, Sloan and Pearce, 1944.

———. "They're Marching Up Freedom Road." *New Masses* 61 (November 5, 1946): 20.

Faue, Elizabeth. *Community of Suffering & Struggle: Women, Men, and the Labor Movement in Minneapolis, 1915–1945.* Chapel Hill: The University of North Carolina Press, 1991.

Faust, Drew Gilpin. *James Henry Hammond and the Old South: A Design of Mastery.* Baton Rouge: The Louisiana State University Press, 1982.

———. *Mothers of Invention: Women of the Slaveholding South in the American Civil War.* Chapel Hill: The University of North Carolina Press, 1996.

Fields, Barbara J. "Ideology and Race in American History." In *Region, Race, and Reconstruction: Essays in Honor of C. Vann Woodward*, edited by J. Morgan Kouser and James McPherson. New York: Oxford University Press, 1982, 143–77.

———. "Slavery, Race and Ideology in the United States of America." *The New Left Review* 181 (1990): 95–118.

Fields, Mamie Garvin, with Karen Fields. *Lemon Swamp and Other Places: A Carolina Memoir.* New York: Free Press, 1983.

Fink, Gary M., ed. *Labor Unions.* Westport, CT: Greenwood Press, 1977.

Fink, Leon. "The New Labor History and the Powers of Historical Pessimism: Consensus, Hegemony, and the Case of the Knights of Labor." *Journal of American History* 75 (June 1988): 115–36.

———. *Progressive Intellectuals and the Dilemmas of Democratic Commitment.* Cambridge: Harvard University Press, 1997.

———. *Workingmen's Democracy: The Knights of Labor and American Politics.* Urbana: University of Illinois Press, 1983.

Fink, Leon, and Brian Greenberg. *Upheaval in the Quiet Zone: A History of Hospital Workers' Union, Local 1199.* Urbana: University of Illinois Press, 1989

Finnegan, Terrance R. "'At the Hands of Parties Unknown': Lynching in Mississippi and South Carolina, 1881–1940." Ph.D. diss., University of Illinois, 1993.

Fite, Gilbert C. *Cotton Fields No More: Southern Agriculture, 1865–1980.* Lexington: University Press of Kentucky, 1984.

Flamming, Douglas. *Creating the Modern South: Millhands & Managers in Dalton, Georgia, 1884–1984.* Chapel Hill: The University of North Carolina Press, 1992.

Foner, Eric. *Nothing But Freedom: Emancipation and Its Legacies.* Baton Rouge: Louisiana University Press, 1983.

———. *Reconstruction: America's Unfinished Revolution, 1863–1877.* New York: Harper and Row, 1988.

———. *The Story of American Freedom.* New York: W.W. Norton, 1998.

Foreman, Clark. "Decade of Hope." *Phylon* 12 (1951): 1937–50.

Fosdick, Raymond B. *Adventure in Giving: The Story of the General Education Board.* New York: Harper & Row Publishers, 1962.

Fox-Genovese, Elizabeth. *Within the Plantation Household: Black and White Women of the Old South.* Chapel Hill: The University of North Carolina Press, 1988.

Fox-Genovese, Elizabeth, and Eugene D. Genovese. "The Political Crisis of Social History: A Marxian Perspective." *Journal of Social History* 10 (Winter 1976): 205–20.

Franklin, John Hope, and August Meier, eds. *Black Leaders of the Twentieth Century.* Urbana: University of Illinois Press, 1982.

Franklin, V.P. *Black Self-Determination: A Cultural History of the Faith of the Fathers* Westport, CT: Lawrence Hill, 1984.

Fraser, Nancy. *Justice Interruptus: Critical Reflections on the "Postsocialist" Condition.* New York: Routledge, 1997.

———. "Rethinking the Public Sphere: A Continuation to the Critique of Actually Existing Democracy." *Social Text* 25/26 (1990): 56–80.

Fraser, Steve. *Labor Will Rule: Sidney Hillman and the Rise of American Labor.* New York: Free Press, 1991.

Fraser, Steve, and Gary Gerstle, eds. *The Rise and Fall of the New Deal Order, 1930–1980.* Princeton: Princeton University Press, 1989.

Fraser, Walter J., Jr. *Charleston! Charleston! The History of a South Carolina City.* Columbia: University of South Carolina Press, 1989.

Frazier, E. Franklin. *Black Bourgeoisie.* New York: Free Press, 1997.

Frederickson, Kari. "The Dixiecrat Movement and the Origins of Massive Resistance: Race, Politics, and Political Culture in the Deep South, 1932–1955." Ph.D. diss., Rutgers, The State University of New Jersey, 1996.

———. *The Dixiecrat Revolt and the End of the Solid South, 1932–1968.* Chapel Hill: The University of North Carolina Press, 2001.

———. "'The Slowest State' and the 'Most Backward Community': Federal Civil Rights Legislation, 1946–1948." *South Carolina Historical Magazine* 98 (April 1997): 177–202.

Gaines, Kevin K. *Uplifting the Race: Black Leadership, Politics, and Culture in the Twentieth Century.* Chapel Hill: The University of North Carolina Press, 1996.

Gardner, Lloyd. *Economic Aspects of New Deal Diplomacy.* Madison: The University of Wisconsin Press, 1964.

Garris, Susan Page. "The Decline of Lynching in South Carolina, 1915–1947." M.A. thesis, University of South Carolina, 1973.

Garrow, David J. "From *Brown* to *Casey*: The U.S. Supreme Court and the Burdens of History." In *Race, Law, and Culture: Reflections on Brown v. Board of Education*, edited by Austin Sarat. New York: Oxford University Press, 1997, 74–88.

Gatewood, William B. *Aristocrats of Color: The Black Elite, 1880–1920.* Bloomington: University of Indiana Press, 1990.

Gavins, Raymond. "The NAACP in North Carolina during the Age of Segregation." In *New Directions in Civil Rights Studies*, edited by Armstead L. Robinson and Patricia Sullivan. Charlottesville: University Press of Virginia, 1991, 105–25.

Genovese, Eugene D. *Roll, Jordon, Roll: The World the Slaves Made.* New York: Vintage, 1974.

Genovese, Eugene D., and Elizabeth Fox-Genovese, eds. *Fruits of Merchant Capital: Slavery and Bourgeois Property in the Rise and Expansion of Capitalism.* New York: Oxford University Press, 1983.

Gerstle, Gary. "The Protean Character of American Liberalism." *American Historical Review* 99 (October 1994): 1043–73.

———. *Working-Class Americanism: The Politics of Labor in a Textile City, 1914–1960.* New York: Cambridge University Press, 1989.

Gillespie, Dizzy, with Al Fraser. *to Be, or not . . . to Bop: Memoirs.* New York: Doubleday and Company, Inc., 1979.

Gillette, Michael Lowery. "The NAACP in Texas, 1937–1957." Ph.D. diss., The University of Texas, 1984.

Gillon, Steven. *Politics and Vision: The ADA and American Liberalism, 1947–1985.* New York: Oxford University Press, 1988.

Gilmore, Glenda Elizabeth. "False Friends and Avowed Enemies: Southern African Americans and Party Allegiances in the 1920s." In *Jumpin' Jim Crow: Southern Politics from the Civil War to Civil Rights,* edited by Jane Dailey et al. Princeton: Princeton University Press, 2000, 219–38.

———. *Gender and Jim Crow: Women and the Politics of White Supremacy in North Carolina, 1896–1920.* Chapel Hill: University of North Carolina Press, 1996.

Gilroy, Paul. *The Black Atlantic: Modernity and Double Consciousness.* Cambridge: Harvard University Press, 1993.

———. *'There Ain't No Black in the Union Jack': The Cultural Politics of Race and Nation.* Chicago: The University Press of Chicago, 1987.

Glen, John M. *Highlander: No Ordinary School, 1932–1962.* Lexington: University Press of Kentucky, 1988.

Goings, Kenneth W. *"The NAACP Comes of Age": The Defeat of Judge John J. Parker.* Bloomington: Indiana University Press, 1990.

Goodman, James. *Stories of Scottsboro.* New York: Pantheon Books, 1994.

Goodwyn, Lawrence. *The Populist Moment: A Short History of Agrarian Revolt in America.* New York: Oxford University Press, 1978.

Gordon, Asa H. *Sketches of Negro Life and History in South Carolina.* Industrial College: GA, 1929; reprint, Columbia: University of South Carolina Press, 1971.

Gordon, Colin. *New Deals: Business, Labor, and Politics in America, 1920–1935.* New York: Cambridge University Press, 1994.

Gordon, Linda. *Pitied But Not Entitled: Single Mothers and the History of Social Welfare.* Cambridge: Harvard University Press, 1994.

Gore, Blinzy L. *On a Hilltop High: The Origins and History of Claflin College to 1984.* Spartanburg, SC: The Reprint Company, 1994.

Grant, Joanne. *Ella J. Baker: Freedom Bound.* New York: John Wiley and Sons, Inc., 1998.

Green, Laurie B. "Battling the Plantation Mentality: Consciousness, Culture, and the Politics of Race, Class and Gender in Memphis, 1940–1968." Ph.D. diss., University of Chicago, 1999.

Greene, Christina. *Our Separate Ways: Women and the Black Freedom Movement in Durham, North Carolina.* Chapel Hill: The University of North Carolina Press, 2005.

Griffin, Farah Jasmine. *"Who set you flowin'?": The African-American Migration Narrative.* New York: Oxford University Press, 1995.

Griffin, Larry J., and Robert Korstad. "Class as Race and Gender: Making and Breaking Labor Unions in the Jim Crow South." *Social Science History* 19 (Winter 1995): 425–54.

Griffith, Barbara S. *The Crisis of American Labor: Operation Dixie and the Defeat of the CIO.* Philadelphia: Temple University Press, 1988.

Griffler, Keith P. *What Price Alliance? Black Radicals Confront White Labor, 1918–1938.* New York: Garland Publishing, Inc., 1995.

Grossman, James R. *Land of Hope: Chicago, Black Southerners, and the Great Migration.* Chicago: The University of Chicago Press, 1989.

Guterl, Matthew Pratt. *The Color of Race in America, 1900–1940.* Cambridge: Harvard University Press, 2001.

Gutman, Herbert G. *Work, Culture, and Society in Industrializing America: Essays in American Working-Class and Social History.* New York: Vintage Books, 1977.

Hahn, Steven. *A Nation under Our Feet: Black Political Struggles in the Rural South from Slavery to the Great Migration.* Cambridge: Belknap Press of Harvard University Press, 2003.

Hale, Grace Elizabeth. *Making Whiteness: The Culture of Segregation in the South, 1890–1940.* New York: Pantheon Books, 1998.

Hall, Jacquelyn Dowd. "Disorderly Women: Gender and Labor Militancy in the Appalachian South." *Journal of American History* 73 (September 1986): 354–82.

———. "The Long Civil Rights Movement and the Political Uses of the Past." *Journal of American History* 91 (March 2005): 1233–63.

———. "O. Delight Smith's Progressive Era: Labor, Feminism, and Reform in the Urban South—Atlanta, Georgia, 1907–1915." In *Visible Women: New Essays on American Activism*, edited by Nancy Hewitt and Suzanne Lebsock. Urbana: University of Illinois Press, 1993, 166–98.

———. *Revolt against Chivalry: Jessie Daniel Ames and the Women's Campaign against Lynching.* New York: Columbia University Press, 1979.

Hall, Jacquelyn Dowd, James Leloudis, Robert Korstad, Mary Murphy, Lu Ann Jones, and Christopher B. Daly. *Like a Family: The Making of a Southern Cotton Mill World.* Chapel Hill: The University of North Carolina Press, 1987.

Hall, Stuart. "Cultural Identity and Diaspora." In *Identity, Community, Culture, Difference*, edited by Jonathan Rutherford. London: Lawrence and Wishart, 1990, 222–37.

———. "Gramsci's Relevance for the Study of Race and Ethnicity." *Journal of Communication Inquiry* 10 (1986): 5–27.

———. "Subjects in History: Making Diasporic Identities." In *The House That Race Built*, edited by Wahneema Lubiano. New York: Vintage Books, 1998, 289–300.

———. "What Is This 'Black' in Black Popular Culture." In *Black Popular Culture*, edited by Gina Dent. Seattle: Bay Press, 1992, 21–33.

Hamby, Alonzo. *Beyond the New Deal: Harry S. Truman and American Liberalism.* New York: Columbia University Press, 1973.

Hamer, Fritz Peter. "A Southern City Enters the Twentieth Century: Charleston, Its Navy Yard, and World War II, 1940–1948." Ph.D. diss., University of South Carolina, 1998.

Hanchard, Michael George. *Orpheus and Power: The Movimiento Negro of Rio de Janeiro and São Paulo, Brazil, 1945–1988.* Princeton: Princeton University Press, 1994.

Harding, Vincent. *There Is a River: The Black Struggle for Freedom in America.* New York: Vintage, 1983.

Harris, Abram. "The Future Plan and Program of the NAACP." Part I, Reel 9, NAACP Papers, 1934.

———. "Preliminary Report of the Committee on the Future Plan and Program of the N.A.A.C.P." Committee Correspondence, Plan and Program Committee, July–Aug. 1934, I-A-29, NAACP Papers.

Harris, William H. *Keeping the Faith: A. Philip Randolf, Milton P. Webster, and the Brother-hood of Sleeping Car Porters, 1925–1937.* Urbana: University of Illinois Press, 1977.

Hawley, Ellis W. *The New Deal and the Problem of Monopoly: A Study in Economic Ambivalence.* New York: Fordham University Press, 1995.

Hayes, Jack Irby, Jr. "South Carolina and the New Deal, 1932–1938." Ph.D. diss., University of South Carolina, 1972.

Heard, Alexander. *A Two-Party South?* Chapel Hill: The University of North Carolina Press, 1952.

Hemmingway, Theodore. "Beneath the Yoke of Bondage: A History of Black Folks in South Carolina, 1900–1940." Ph.D. diss., University of South Carolina, 1976.

Hewitt, Nancy. "Reflections from a Departing Editor: Recasting Images of Marginality." *Gender and History* 4 (Summer 1992): 3–9.

Higginbotham, Evelyn Brooks. "African-American Women's History and the Meta-language of Race." *Signs* 17 (Winter 1992): 251–74.

———. "Clubwomen and Electoral Politics in the 1920s." In *African American Women and the Vote 1835–1965,* edited by Ann D. Gordon with Bettye Collier-Thomas. Amherst: University of Massachusetts Press, 1997, 134–55.

———. "Rethinking Vernacular Culture: Black Religion and Race Records in the 1920s and 1930s." In *The House That Race Built,* edited by Wahneema Lubiano. New York: Vintage Books, 1998, 157–77.

———. *Righteous Discontent: The Women's Movement in the Black Baptist Church, 1880–1920.* Cambridge: Harvard University Press, 1993.

Hill, Herbert. *Black Labor and the American Legal System: Race, Work, and the Law.* Madison: University of Wisconsin Press, 1985.

———. "Lichtenstein's Fictions: Meany, Reuther and the 1964 Civil Rights Act." *New Politics* 7 (Summer 1998): 82–107.

———. "Lichtenstein's Fictions Revisited: Race and the New Labor History." *New Politics* 7 (Winter 1999): 148–63.

———. "The Problem of Race in American Labor History." *Reviews in American History* 24 (1996): 189–208.

Hill, Robert, Barbara Bair, and Edith Johnson, eds. *The Marcus Garvey and Universal Negro Improvement Association Papers, Vol III.* Berkeley: University of California Press, 1990.

Hine, Darlene Clark. "The Black Migration to the Urban Midwest: The Gender Dimension, 1915–1945." In *Hinesight: Black Women and the Reconstruction of American History.* Bloomington: Indiana University Press, 1994, 87–139.

———. *Black Victory: The Rise and Fall of the White Primary in Texas.* Millwood, New York: KTO Press, 1979.

———. *Black Women in White: Racial Conflict and Cooperation in the Nursing Profession, 1890–1950.* Bloomington: Indiana University Press, 1989.

———. *Hinesight: Black Women and the Reconstruction of American History.* Bloomington: Indiana University Press, 1994.

———. "Rape and the Inner Lives of Black Women: Preliminary Thoughts on the Culture of Dissemblance." *Signs* 14 (Summer 1989): 118–22.

Hine, Darlene Clark, Elsa Barkley Brown, and Rosalyn Terborg-Penn, eds. *Black Women in America: An Historical Encyclopedia,* 2 Vols. Bloomington: Indiana University Press, 1994.

Hine, William C. "Civil Rights and Campus Wrongs: South Carolina State College Students Protest, 1955–1968." *South Carolina Historical Magazine* 97 (October 1996): 310–31.

Historical Society of Chesterfield County. *Images of America: Chesterfield County.* Dover, NH: Arcadia Publishing, 1997.

Hoare, Quintin, and Geoffrey Nowell Smith, eds. *Selections from the Prison Notebooks of Antonio Gramsci.* New York: International Publishers, 1971.

Hodes, Martha. *White Women, Black Men: Illicit Sex in the 19th-Century South.* New Haven: Yale University Press, 1997.

Hodges, James A. *The New Deal Labor Policy and the Southern Cotton Textile Industry, 1933–1941.* Knoxville: University of Tennessee Press, 1986.

Hoffman, Edwin D. "The Genesis of the Modern Movement for Equal Rights in South Carolina." *The Journal of Negro History* 44 (October 1959): 346–69.

Hofstadter, Richard. *The Age of Reform: From Bryan to F.D.R.* New York: Vintage, 1955.

Holloway, Jonathan Scott. *Confronting the Veil: Abram Harris Jr., E. Franklin Frazier, and Ralph Bunche, 1919–1941.* Chapel Hill: The University of North Carolina Press, 2002.

Holt, Thomas C. *Black over White: Negro Political Leadership in South Carolina during Reconstruction.* Urbana: University of Illinois Press, 1977.

———. "Marking: Race, Race-making, and the Writing of History." *The American Historical Review* 100 (February 1995): 1–20.

———. *The Problem of Freedom: Race, Labor, and Politics in Jamaica and Britain.* Baltimore: Johns Hopkins University Press, 1992.

Honey, Michael. *Southern Labor and Black Civil Rights: Organizing Memphis Workers.* Urbana: University of Illinois Press, 1993.

Horne, Gerald. *Black & Red: W.E.B. Du Bois and the Afro-American Response to the Cold War, 1944–1963.* Albany: State University of New York Press, 1986.

———. *Communist Front? The Civil Rights Congress, 1946–1956.* London: Associated University Presses, 1988.

Houston, Charles H. "Along the Highway." *Baltimore Afro-American,* July 10, 1948.

———. "A Challenge to Negro Youth." *The Crisis* (January 1938): 14.

———. "Cracking Closed University Doors." *The Crisis* 42 (December 1935): 364.

———. "Don't Shout Too Soon." *The Crisis* 43 (March 1935): 79.

———. "Educational Inequalities Must Go!" *The Crisis* 42 (October 1935): 300.

———. "Senator Glass Aided School Inequalities." *The Crisis* (January 1936): 15.

Huff, Archie Vernon, Jr. *Greenville: The History of the City and the County in the South Carolina Piedmont.* Columbia: University of South Carolina Press, 1995.

Huggins, Nathan Irvin. "The Deforming Mirror of Truth." In *Revelations: American History, American Myths,* edited by Brenda Smith Huggins. New York: Oxford University Press, 1995, 252–83.

Hunter, Tera. "Domination and Resistance: The Politics of Wage Household Labor in New South Atlanta." *Labor History* 34 (Spring–Summer, 1993): 205–20.

———. *To 'Joy My Freedom: Southern Black Women's Lives and Labors after the Civil War.* Cambridge: Harvard University Press, 1997.

Hux, Roger K. "The Ku Klux Klan and Collective Violence in Horry County, South Carolina, 1922–1925." *South Carolina Historical Magazine* 85 (July 1984): 211–19.

Ifill, Gwen. "Stars and Bars." *Online NewsHour*, January 17, 2000. <http://www.pbs.org/newshour/bb/politics/jan-june00/flag_1-17.html> Accessed June 14, 2005.

Iriye, Akira. *Global Community: The Role of International Organizations in the Making of the Contemporary World*. Berkeley: University of California Press, 2002.

Isserman, Maurice. *Which Side Were You On? The American Communist Party during the Second World War*. Middletown, CT: Wesleyan University Press, 1982.

Jackson, Augusta V. "A New Deal for Tobacco Workers." *The Crisis* (October 1938): 322-24, 330.

Jackson, Esther Cooper. "This Is My Husband." 1956. Personal Files of Esther Cooper Jackson and James E. Jackson Jr. Brooklyn, NY. Copy in possession of Peter F. Lau.

Jackson, James E., Jr. "Statement before Sentencing." September 17, 1956. Personal Files of Esther Cooper Jackson and James E. Jackson Jr. Brooklyn, NY. Copy in possession of Peter F. Lau.

Jackson, Kenneth T. *Ku Klux Klan in the City, 1915–1930*. New York: Oxford University Press, 1967.

Jackson, Walter. *Gunnar Myrdal and America's Conscience: Social Engineering and Racial Liberalism, 1938–1987*. Chapel Hill: The University of North Carolina Press, 1990.

Jacques-Garvey, Amy, ed. *Philosophy and Opinions of Marcus Garvey*. New York: Atheneum, 1992.

James, Winston. *Holding Aloft the Banner of Ethiopia: Caribbean Radicalism in Early Twentieth-Century America*. New York: Verso, 1998.

Janiewski, Dolores E. "Seeking 'a New Day and a New Way': Black Women and the Unions in the Southern Tobacco Industry." In *"To Toil the Livelong Day": America's Women at Work, 1780–1980*, edited by Carol Groneman and Mary Beth Norton. Ithaca: Cornell University Press, 1987, 161–78.

———. *Sisterhood Denied: Race, Gender, and Class in a New South Community*. Philadelphia: Temple University Press, 1985.

Janken, Kenneth Robert. "From Colonial Liberation to Cold War Liberalism: Walter White, the NAACP, and Foreign Affairs, 1941–1955." *Ethnic and Racial Studies* 21 (November 1998): 1074–95.

———. *Rayford W. Logan and the Dilemma of the African American Intellectual*. Amherst: University of Massachusetts Press, 1993.

———. *White: The Biography of Walter White, Mr. NAACP*. New York: The New Press, 2003.

Johanningsmeier, Edward P. *Forging American Communism: The Life of William Foster*. Princeton: Princeton University Press, 1994.

Johnson, Charles S., Edward R. Embree, and W.W. Alexander. *The Collapse of Cotton Tenancy: Summary of Field Studies and Statistical Surveys, 1933–1935*. Chapel Hill: The University of North Carolina Press, 1935.

Johnson, Elmer D. *South Carolina: A Documentary Profile of the Palmetto State*. Columbia: University of South Carolina Press, 1971.

Johnson, James Weldon. *Along This Way: The Autobiography of James Weldon Johnson*. New York: The Viking Press, 1968.

Johnson, Michael P., and James L. Roark. *Black Masters: A Family of Color in the Old South*. New York: W.W. Norton & Company, 1984.

Jonas, Gilbert. *Freedom's Sword: The NAACP and the Struggle against Racism in America, 1909–1969*. New York: Routledge, 2005.

Jones, Jacqueline. *Labor of Love, Labor of Sorrow: Black Women, Work, and the Family from Slavery to the Present*. New York: Basic Books, 1985.

Jones, William P. "Black Workers and the CIO's Turn toward Racial Radicalism: Operation Dixie and the North Carolina Lumber Industry, 1946–1953." *Labor History* 41 (Summer 2000): 279–306.

———. "Cutting through Jim Crow: African American Lumber Workers in the Jim Crow South, 1919–1960." Ph. D. diss., University of North Carolina, Chapel Hill, 2000.

Joyner, Charles. *Down by the Riverside: A South Carolina Slave Community*. Urbana: University of Illinois Press, 1984.

Kantrowitz, Stephen. *Ben Tillman & the Reconstruction of White Supremacy*. Chapel Hill: The University of North Carolina Press, 2000.

Kazin, Michael J. *The Populist Persuasion: An American History*. New York: Basic Books, 1995.

Kelley, Robin D.G. "'Afric's Sons with Banner Red': African-American Communists and the Politics of Culture, 1919–1934." In *Imagining Home: Class, Culture and Nationalism in the African Diaspora*, edited by Sidney Lemelle and Robin D.G. Kelley. New York: Verso, 1994, 35–54.

———. *Freedom Dreams: The Black Radical Imagination*. Boston: Beacon Press, 2002.

———. *Hammer and Hoe: Alabama Communists during the Great Depression*. Chapel Hill: The University of North Carolina Press, 1990.

———. "Playing for Keeps: Pleasure and Profit on the Postindustrial Playground." In *The House That Race Built*, edited by Wahneema Lubiano. New York: Vintage Books, 1998, 195–231.

———. ed. *Race Rebels: Culture, Politics, and the Black Working-Class*. New York: Free Press, 1994.

———. "'We Are Not What We Seem': Rethinking Black Working-Class Opposition in the Jim Crow South." *Journal of American History* 80 (June 1993): 75–112.

———. *Yo' Mama's Disfunctional!: Fighting the Culture Wars in Urban America*. Boston: Beacon Press, 1997.

Kellogg, Charles Flint. *The NAACP: A History of the National Association for the Advancement of Colored People, Vol. I, 1909–1920*. Baltimore: Johns Hopkins University Press, 1967.

Kennan, George F. *American Diplomacy, 1900–1950*. Chicago: The University of Chicago Press, 1951.

Kennedy, David M. *Freedom from Fear: The American People in Depression and War, 1929–1945*. New York: Oxford University Press, 1999.

Kerber, Linda K. *No Constitutional Right to be Ladies: Women and the Obligations of Citizenship*. New York: Hill and Wang, 1998.

Kessler-Harris, Alice. "Designing Women and Old Fools: The Construction of the Social." In *U.S. History as Women's History: New Feminist Essays*, edited by Linda K. Kerber, Alice Kessler-Harris, and Kathryn Kish Sklar. Chapel Hill: The University of North Carolina Press, 1995, 87–106.

———. "In the Nation's Image: The Gendered Limits of Social Citizenship in the Depression Era." *The Journal of American History* 86 (December 1999): 1251–79.

———. *Out to Work: A History of Wage-Earning Women in the United States*. New York: Oxford University Press, 1982.

Key, V.O. *Southern Politics in State and Nation*. New York: Knopf, 1949.

King, Richard H. *Civil Rights and the Idea of Freedom*. Athens: The University Press of Georgia, 1996.

Kirby, John B. *Black Americans in the Roosevelt Era: Liberalism and Race*. Knoxville: University of Tennessee Press, 1980.

Kiser, Clyde Vernon. *Sea Island to City: A Study of St. Helena Islanders in Harlem and Other Urban Centers*. New York: Columbia University Press, 1932.

Klarman, Michael J. *From Jim Crow to Civil Rights: The Supreme Court and the Struggle for Racial Equality*. New York: Oxford University Press, 2004.

———. "How *Brown* Changed Race Relations: The Backlash Thesis." *Journal of American History* 81 (June 1994): 81–118.

Klehr, Harvey. *The Heyday of American Communism: The Depression Decade*. New York: Basic Books, 1984.

Klehr, Harvey, John Earl Haynes, and Fredrikh Firsov. *The Secret World of American Communism*. New Haven: Yale University Press, 1995.

"The Klu Klux Klan Are Riding Again." *The Crisis* 17 (March 1919): 229–31.

Kluger, Richard. *Simple Justice: The History of Brown v. Board of Education and Black America's Struggle for Equality*. New York: Vintage Books, 1975.

Korstad, Karl. "Black and White Together: Organizing in the South with the Food, Tobacco, Agricultural & Allied Workers Union (FTA-CIO), 1946–1952." In *The CIO's Left-Led Unions*, edited by Steve Rosswurm. New Brunswick: Rutgers University Press, 1992, 69–94.

Korstad, Robert Rodgers. *Civil Rights Unionism: Tobacco Workers and the Struggle for Democracy in the Mid Twentieth-Century South*. Chapel Hill: The University of North Carolina Press, 2003.

———. "Daybreak of Freedom: Tobacco Workers and the CIO, Winston-Salem, North Carolina, 1943–1950." Ph.D. diss., University of North Carolina at Chapel Hill, 1987.

Korstad, Robert, and Nelson Lichtenstein. "Opportunities Found and Lost: Labor, Radicals, and the Early Civil Rights Movement." *Journal of American History* 75 (December 1988): 786–811.

Kousser, J. Morgan. *The Shaping of Southern Politics: Suffrage Restriction and the Establishment of the One-Party South, 1880–1910*. New Haven: Yale University Press, 1974.

Krueger, Thomas. *And Promises to Keep: The Southern Conference for Human Welfare, 1938–1948*. Nashville: Vanderbilt University Press, 1967.

Kuznets, Simon, and Dorothy Swaine Thomas. *Population Redistribution and Economic Growth, United States, 1870–1950*. Philadelphia: The American Philosophical Society, 1957.

Lander, Ernest McPherson, Jr. *A History of South Carolina, 1865–1960*. Chapel Hill: The University of North Carolina Press, 1960.

Lau, Peter F. "Freedom Road Territory: The Politics of Civil Rights Struggle in South Carolina during the Jim Crow Era." Ph.D. diss., Rutgers, The State University of New Jersey, 2002.

———. ed. *From the Grassroots to the Supreme Court: Brown v. Board of Education and American Democracy*. Durham: Duke University Press, 2004.

———. "From the Periphery to the Center: Clarendon County, South Carolina, *Brown*, and the Sruggle for Democracy and Equality in America." In *From the Grassroots to the Supreme Court: Brown v. Board of Education and American Democracy*. Durham: Duke University Press, 2004, 105–26.

Lawson, Steven F. *Black Ballots: Voting Rights in the South, 1944–1969.* New York: Columbia University Press, 1976.

———. *Civil Rights Crossroads: Nation, Community, and the Black Freedom Struggle.* Lexington: University Press of Kentucky, 2003.

———. "Freedom Then, Freedom Now: The Historiography of the Civil Rights Movement." *American Historical Review* 96 (April 1991): 456–71.

———. *In Pursuit of Power: Southern Blacks & Electoral Politics, 1965–1982.* New York: Columbia University Press, 1985.

Lemann, Nicholas. *The Promised Land: The Great Migration and How It Changed America.* New York: Vintage Books, 1992.

Lemelle, Sidney, and Robin D.G. Kelley, eds. *Imagining Home: Class, Culture and Nationalism in the African Diaspora.* New York: Verso, 1994.

Leuchtenburg, William E. *Franklin D. Roosevelt and the New Deal, 1932–1940.* New York: Harper and Row, 1963.

Levy, Eugene. "James Weldon Johnson and the Development of the NAACP." In *Black Leaders of the Twentieth Century,* edited by John Hope Franklin and August Meier. Urbana: The University of Illinois Press, 1982, 85–104.

———. *James Weldon Johnson: Black Leader, Black Voice.* Chicago: University of Chicago Press, 1973.

Lewis, David Levering. *King: A Biography.* Urbana: University of Illinois Press, 1978.

———. "The Origins and Causes of the Civil Rights Movement." In *The Civil Rights Movement in America,* edited by Charles W. Eagles. Jackson: University of Mississippi Press, 1986, 3–17.

———. "Parallels and Divergences: Assimilationist Strategies of Afro-American and Jewish Elites from 1910 to the Early 1930s." *Journal of American History* 73 (December 1984): 543–64.

———. ed. *The Portable Harlem Renaissance Reader.* New York: Viking Penguin, 1994.

———. ed. *W.E.B. Du Bois: A Reader.* New York: Henry Holt, 1995.

———. *W.E.B. Du Bois: Biography of a Race, 1868–1919.* New York: Henry Holt and Company, 1993.

———. *W.E.B. Du Bois: The Fight for Equality and the American Century, 1919–1963.* New York: Henry Holt and Company, 2000.

———. *When Harlem Was in Vogue.* New York: Oxford University Press, 1981.

Lewis, Earl. "Connecting Memory, Self, and the Power of Place in African American Urban History." *Journal of Urban History* 21 (March 1995): 347–71.

———. *In Their Own Interests: Race, Class, and Power in Twentieth-Century Norfolk, Virginia.* Berkeley: University of California Press, 1991.

Lichtenstein, Nelson. *Labor's War at Home: The CIO in World War II.* New York: Cambridge University Press, 1982.

———. *The Most Dangerous Man in Detroit: Walter Reuther and the Fate of American Labor.* New York: Basic Books, 1995.

Ling, Peter. "Local Leadership in the Early Civil Rights Movement: The South Carolina Citizenship Education Program of the Highlander Folk School." *Journal of American Studies* 29 (1995): 399–422.

Lipsitz, George. "'Frantic to Join . . . the Japanese Army': The Asian Pacific War in the Lives of African American Soldiers and Civilians." In *The Politics of Culture in the Shadow of Capital,* edited by Lisa Lowe and David Lloyd. Durham: Duke University Press, 1997, 324–53.

———. *A Life in the Struggle: Ivory Perry and the Culture of Opposition.* Philadelphia: Temple University Press, 1988.

———. *Rainbow at Midnight: Labor and Culture in the 1940s.* Urbana: University of Illinois Press, 1994.

Litwack, Leon. *Trouble in Mind: Black Southerners in the Age of Jim Crow.* New York: Alfred A. Knopf, 1998.

Litwack, Leon, and August Meier, eds. *Black Leaders of the Nineteenth Century.* Urbana: University of Illinois Press, 1988.

Livingston, James. "Hamlet, James, and the Woman Question." *Raritan: A Quarterly Review* (Fall 1997): 49–72.

———. "How to Succeed in Business History without Really Trying: Remarks on Martin J. Sklar's *Corporate Reconstruction of American Capitalism.*" *Business and Economic History* 21(1992): 30–35.

———. *Pragmatism and the Political Economy of Cultural Revolution, 1850–1940.* Chapel Hill: The University of North Carolina Press, 1997.

———. *Pragmatism, Feminism, and Democracy: Rethinking the Politics of American History.* New York: Routledge, 2001.

———. "Why Is There Still Socialism in the United States?" *Reviews in American History* 22 (December 1994): 577–83.

Lochbaum, Julie Magruder. "The World Made Flesh: The Desegregation Leadership of the Rev. J.A. DeLaine." Ph.D. diss., College of Education, University of South Carolina, 1993.

Lofton, Paul Stroman, Jr. "A Social and Economic History of Columbia, South Carolina during the Great Depression, 1929–1940." Ph.D. diss., University of Texas, 1977.

Logan, Rayford E., ed. *What the Negro Wants.* Chapel Hill: The University of North Carolina Press, 1944.

Lott, Eric. *Love and Theft: Blackface Minstrelsy and the American Working Class.* New York: Oxford University Press, 1995.

Love, Richard. "The Cigarette Capital of the World: Labor, Race, and Tobacco in Richmond, Virginia, 1880–1980." Ph.D. diss., University of Virginia, 1998.

———. "In Defiance of Custom and Tradition: Black Tobacco Workers and Labor Unions in Richmond, Virginia, 1937–1941." *Labor History* 35 (Winter 1994): 25–47.

MacDougall, Curtis. *Gideon's Army.* 3 vols. New York: Marzani and Munsell, 1965.

MacLean, Nancy. *Behind the Mask of Chivalry: The Making of the Second Ku Klux Klan.* New York: Oxford University Press, 1994.

———. "The Leo Frank Case Reconsidered: Gender and Sexual Politics in the Making of Reactionary Populism." *Journal of American History* 78 (December 1991): 1917–48.

Martin, Tony. *Race First: The Ideological and Organizational Struggles of Marcus Garvey and the Universal Negro Improvement Association.* Dover, MA: The Majority Press, 1976.

Martin, Waldo E., Jr. *Brown v. Board of Education: A Brief History with Documents.* Boston: Bedford Books, 1998.

———. "'Nation Time!': Black Nationalism, the Third World, and Jews." In *Struggles in the Promised Land: Toward a History of Black-Jewish Relations in the United States,* edited by Jack Salzman and Cornel West. New York: Oxford University Press, 1997, 341–56.

———. *No Coward Soldiers: Black Cultural Politics in Postwar America.* Cambridge: Harvard University Press, 2005.

Martin, Waldo E., Jr., and Patricia Sullivan, eds. *Civil Rights in the United States*. 2 vols. New York: Macmillan Reference USA, 2001.

Matusow, Allen J. *The Unraveling of America: A History of Liberalism in the 1960s*. New York: Harper Torchbooks, 1984.

McAdam, Doug. *Political Process and the Development of Black Insurgency, 1930–1970*. Chicago: University of Chicago Press, 1982.

McCray, John H. "30 Glorious S.C. Years for Civil/Human Rights." Personal Files of Carrie Allen McCray. Columbia, SC. Copy in possession of Peter F. Lau.

———. "Wicked Fleeth in Discord." *Lighthouse and Informer*, April 13, 1947.

McCurry, Stephanie. *Masters of Small Worlds: Yeoman Households, Gender Relations and the Politics of Culture of the Antebellum South Carolina Lowcountry*. New York: Oxford University Press, 1995.

McElderry, Stuart John. "The Problem of the Color Line: Civil Rights and Racial Ideology in Portland Oregon, 1944–1965." Ph.D. diss., University of Oregon, 1998.

McElvaine, Robert S. *The Great Depression: America, 1929–1941*. New York: Times Books, 1984.

McFadden, Grace Jordan. "Septima P. Clark and the Struggle for Human Rights." In *Women in the Civil Rights Movement: Trailblazers and Torchbearers, 1941–1964*, edited by Vicki L. Crawford, Jacqueline Anne Rouse, and Barbara Woods. New York: Carlson Publishing, Inc., 1990, 85–97.

McKaine, Osceola E. "The Palmetto State." *Norfolk Journal and Guide*, November 11, 1945, 11.

———. "The Palmetto State." *Norfolk Journal and Guide*, November 17, 1945, 11.

———. "The Palmetto State." *Norfolk Journal and Guide*, December 8, 1945, 11.

———. "The Palmetto State." *Norfolk Journal and Guide*, February 16, 1946, 9.

———. "The Palmetto State." *Norfolk Journal and Guide*, March 23, 1946, 9.

———. "The Palmetto State." *Norfolk Journal and Guide*, March 30, 1946, 9.

———. "The Palmetto State." *Norfolk Journal and Guide*, April 20, 1946.

———. "The Palmetto State." *Norfolk Journal and Guide*, May 18, 1946.

McKenzie, Edna Chappell. "Daisy Elizabeth Adams Lampkin." In *Black Women in America: An Historical Encyclopedia, Volume I*, edited by Darlene Clark Hine, Elsa Barkley Brown, and Rosalyn Terborg-Penn. Bloomington: Indiana University Press, 1994, 690–93.

McMillen, Neil R. *The Citizens' Council: Organized Resistance to the Second Reconstruction, 1954–1964*. Urbana: University of Illinois Press, 1994.

———. *Dark Journey: Black Mississippians in the Age of Jim Crow*. Urbana: University of Illinois Press, 1990.

McNeil, Genna Rae. *Groundwork: Charles Hamilton Houston and the Struggle for Civil Rights*. Philadelphia: University of Pennsylvania Press, 1983.

McPherson, James M. *The Abolitionist Legacy: From Reconstruction to the NAACP*. Princeton: Princeton University Press, 1975.

McRae, Barry. *Dizzy Gillespie: His Life and Times*. New York: Universe Books, 1988.

Meier, August. *Negro Thought in America, 1880–1915*. Ann Arbor: University of Michigan Press, 1963.

Meier, August, and John H. Bracey Jr. "The NAACP as a Reform Movement, 1909–1965: 'To reach the conscience of America.'" *Journal of Southern History* 59 (February 1993): 3–30.

Meier, August, and David Lewis. "History of the Negro Upper Class in Atlanta, Georgia, 1890–1958." *Journal of Negro Education* 28 (Spring 1959): 128–89.

Meier, August, and Elliott Rudwick, eds. *Along the Color Line: Explorations in the Black Experience.* Urbana: University of Illinois Press, 1976.

———, eds. "Attorneys Black and White: A Case Study of Race Relations within the NAACP." In *Along the Color Line: Explorations in the Black Experience.* Urbana: University of Illinois Press, 1976.

———. *Black Detroit and the Rise of the UAW.* Oxford University Press, 1979.

———. *CORE: A Study in the Civil Rights Movement, 1942–1968.* Urbana: University of Illinois Press, 1975.

———, eds. "The Origins of Nonviolent Direct Action in Afro-American Protest: A Note on Historical Discontinuities." In *Along the Color Line: Explorations in the Black Experience.* Urbana: University of Illinois Press, 1976.

———, eds. "The Rise of the Black Secretariat in the NAACP." In *Along the Color Line: Explorations in the Black Experience.* Urbana: University of Illinois Press, 1976.

Minchin, Timothy J. *What Do We Need a Union For?: The TWUA in the South, 1945–1955.* Chapel Hill: The University of North Carolina Press, 1997.

"Modern Exiles." *The Crisis* 19 (December 1919): 70–72.

Mohanty, Chandra Talpade, Ann Russo, and Lourdes Torres, eds. *Third World Women and the Politics of Feminism.* Bloomington: Indiana University Press, 1991.

Montgomery, David. *The Fall of the House of Labor: The Workplace, the State, and American Labor Activism, 1865–1925.* New York: Cambridge University Press, 1987.

———. "Labor and Political Leadership of New Deal America." *International Review of Social History* 39 (December 1994): 335–60.

Moon, Henry Lee. *Balance of Power: The Negro Vote.* New York: Doubleday & Company, 1949.

Moore, Barrington. *Injustice: The Social Bases of Obedience and Revolt.* White Plains, NY: M.E. Sharpe, 1978.

Moore, John Hammond. *Columbia and Richland County: A South Carolina Community, 1740–1990.* Columbia: University of South Carolina Press, 1993.

Moore, Winfred B., Jr., Joseph F. Tripp, and Lyon G. Tyler Jr. *Developing Dixie: Modernization in a Traditional Society.* New York: Greenwood Press, 1988.

Morgan, Edmund S. *American Slavery, American Freedom: The Ordeal of Colonial Virginia.* New York: W.W. Norton & Company, 1975.

Morgan, Jennifer L. "'Some Could Suckle over Their Shoulder': Male Travelers, Female Bodies, and the Gendering of Racial Ideology, 1500–1770." *William and Mary Quarterly* 54 (January 1997): 167–92.

Morgan, Philip D. *Slave Counterpoint: Black Culture in the Eighteenth-Century Chesapeake and Lowcountry.* Chapel Hill: The University of North Carolina Press, 1998.

Morris, Aldon. *The Origins of the Civil Rights Movement: Black Communities Organizing for Change.* New York: Free Press, 1984.

Moses, Robert P., and Charles Cobb Jr. *Radical Equations: Math Literacy and Civil Rights.* Boston: Beacon Press, 2001.

Moses, Wilson Jeremiah. *The Golden Age of Black Nationalism, 1850–1925.* New York: Oxford University Press, 1978.

Murray, Albert. *Stomping the Blues.* New York: Da Capo Press, 1976.

Murray, Robert K. *Red Scare: A Study of National Hysteria, 1919–1920.* New York: McGraw Hill Book Company, 1964.

Myers, Andrew Herbert. "Black, White, and Olive Drab: Military-Social Relations during the Civil Rights Movement at Fort Jackson and Columbia, South Carolina." Ph.D. diss., University of Virginia, 1998.

Myrdal, Gunnar. *An American Dilemma: The Negro Problem and Modern Democracy.* 2 vols. New York: Harper and Brothers, 1944.

Naison, Mark. *Communists in Harlem during the Great Depression.* New York: Grove Press, 1985.

———. "Paul Robeson and the American Labor Movement." In *Paul Robeson: Artist and Citizen,* edited by Jeffrey C. Stewart. New Brunswick: Rutgers University Press, 1998, 179–94.

Nelson, Bruce. "Class, Race and Democracy in the CIO: The 'New' Labor History Meets the 'Wages of Whiteness.'" *International Review of Social History* 41 (1996): 351–421.

———. *Divided We Stand: American Workers and the Struggle for Black Equality.* Princeton: Princeton University Press, 2001.

Nelson, Jack, and Jack Bass. *The Orangeburg Massacre.* New York: World Publishing Co., 1970.

Newby, I.A. *Black Carolinians: A History of Blacks in South Carolina from 1865–1968.* Columbia: University of South Carolina Press, 1973.

Norrell, Robert J. "Caste in Steel: Jim Crow Careers in Birmingham, Alabama." *Journal of American History* 73 (1986): 669–95.

———. "Labor at the Ballot Box: Alabama Politics from the New Deal to the Dixiecrat Movement." *Journal of Southern History* 57 (May 1991): 201–34.

———. *Reaping the Whirlwind: The Civil Rights Movement in Tuskegee.* New York: Knopf, 1986.

Odum, Howard W. *Race and Rumors of Race: Challenge to American Crisis.* Baltimore: The Johns Hopkins University Press, 1997.

Oshinsky, David M. *Worse Than Slavery: Parchman Farm and the Ordeal of Jim Crow Justice.* New York: Free Press, 1996.

Ovington, Mary White. "The National Association for the Advancement of Colored People," *Journal of Negro History* 9 (April 1924): 107–16.

———. *The Walls Came Tumbling Down.* New York: Harcourt, Brace and Company, 1947.

Painter, Nell I. *Exodusters: Black Migration to Kansas after Reconstruction.* New York: W.W. Norton, 1986.

———. *The Narrative of Hosea Hudson: His Life as a Negro Communist in the South.* Cambridge: Harvard University Press, 1979.

Patterson, James T. *Brown v. Board of Education: A Civil Rights Milestone and Its Troubled Legacy.* New York: Oxford University Press, 2001.

———. *Congressional Conservatism and the New Deal: The Growth of the Conservative Coalition in Congress, 1933–1939.* Lexington: University Press of Kentucky, 1967.

Payne, Charles. *I've Got the Light of Freedom: The Organizing Tradition and the Mississippi Freedom Struggle.* Berkeley: University of California Press, 1995.

Peiss, Kathy L. *Cheap Amusements: Working Women and Leisure in Turn-of-the-Century New York.* Philadelphia: Temple University Press, 1986.

Pickins, William, edited by William L. Andrews. *Bursting Bonds: The Autobiography of a "New Negro."* Bloomington: Indiana University Press, 1991.

———. "The Woman Voter Hits the Color Line." *The Nation* 111 (October 6, 1920): 372–73.

Plotke, David. *Building a Democratic Political Order: Reshaping American Liberalism in the 1930s and 1940s*. New York: Cambridge University Press, 1996.

Plummer, Brenda Gayle. *Rising Wind: Black Americans and U.S. Foreign Affairs, 1935–1960*. Chapel Hill: The University of North Carolina Press, 1997.

Polanyi, Karl. *The Great Transformation: The Political and Economic Origins of Our Time*. Boston: Beacon Press, 1957.

Porter, Lewis. *John Coltrane: His Life and Music*. Ann Arbor: The University of Michigan Press, 1999.

Powers, Bernard E., Jr. *Black Charlestonians: A Social History, 1822–1885*. Fayetteville: The University of Arkansas Press, 1994.

Pranther, H. Leon, Sr. "The Origins of the Phoenix Racial Massacre of 1898." In *Developing Dixie: Modernization in a Traditional Society*, edited by Winfred B. Moore Jr., Joseph F. Tripp, and Lyon G. Tyler Jr. New York: Greenwood Press, 1988, 59–72.

Preston, William, Jr. *Aliens and Dissenters: Federal Suppression of Radicals, 1903–1933*. New York: Harper & Row, 1963.

Quint, Howard H. *Profile in Black and White: A Frank Portrait of South Carolina*. Westport, CT: Greenwood Press, 1958.

Ransby, Barbara. *Ella Baker and the Black Freedom Movement: A Radical, Democratic Vision*. Chapel Hill: The University of North Carolina Press, 2003.

Record, Wilson. *Race and Radicalism: The NAACP and the Communist Party in Conflict*. Ithaca: Cornell University Press, 1964.

Reed, Adolph L., Jr. *W.E.B. Du Bois and American Political Thought*. New York: Oxford University Press, 1997.

Reed, Christopher Robert. *The Chicago NAACP and the Rise of Black Professional Leadership, 1910–1966*. Bloomington: Indiana University Press, 1997.

Reed, Merl E. "Food, Tobacco, Agricultural and Allied Workers Union of America (FTA)." In *Labor Unions*, edited by Gary M. Fink. Westport, CT: Greenwood Press, 1977, 106–9.

———. *Seedtime for the Modern Civil Rights Movement: The President's Committee on Fair Employment Practices, 1941–1946*. Baton Rouge: Louisiana State University Press, 1991.

Reich, Steven A. "Soldiers of Democracy; Black Texans and the Fight for Citizenship, 1917–1921." *Journal of American History* 82 (March 1996): 1478–1504.

Reid, Alfred Sandlin. *Furman University: Towards a New Identity, 1925–1975*. Durham: Duke University Press, 1976.

Richards, Johnetta. "The Southern Negro Youth Congress: A History." Ph.D. diss., University of Cincinnati, 1987.

Richards, Miles Spangler. "Osceola E. McKaine and the Struggle for Black Civil Rights, 1917–1946." Ph.D. diss., Univerisity of South Carolina, 1994.

Rieder, Jonathan. *Canarsie: The Jews and Italians of Brooklyn against Liberalism*. Cambridge: Harvard University Press, 1985.

Robertson, David. *Sly and Able: A Political Biography of James F. Byrnes*. New York: W.W. Norton, 1994.

Robinson, Armstead L., and Patricia Sullivan, eds. *New Directions in Civil Rights Studies*. Charlottesville: University Press of Virginia, 1991.

Robinson, Cedric J. *Black Marxism: The Making of the Black Radical Tradition*. London: Zed Press, 1983.

———. "Richard Wright: Marxism and the petite-bourgeoisie." *Race and Class* 21 (Spring 1980): 352–68.

Robnett, Belinda. *How Long? How Long? African-American Women in the Struggle for Civil Rights*. New York: Oxford University Press, 1997.

Rodgers, Daniel T. *Atlantic Crossings: Social Politics in a Progressive Age*. Cambridge: The Belknap Press of Harvard University Press, 1998.

Roediger, David R. *Wages of Whiteness: Race and the Making of the American Working Class*. New York: Verso, 1991.

———. "White Workers, New Democrats, and Affirmative Action." In *The House That Race Built*, edited by Wahneema Lubiano. New York: Vintage Books, 1998, 48–65.

Rolinson, Mary Gambrell. "The Universal Improvement Association in Georgia: Southern Strongholds of Garveyism." In *Georgia in Black and White: Explorations in the Race Relations of a Southern State, 1865–1950*, edited by John C. Inscoe. Athens: University of Georgia Press, 1994.

Rosengarten, Theodore. *All God's Dangers: The Life of Nate Shaw*. New York: Vintage Books, 1974.

Ross, B. Joyce. *J.E. Spingarn and the Rise of the NAACP, 1911–1939*. New York: Athenaeum, 1972.

Rosswurm, Steve, ed. *The CIO's Left-Led Unions*. New Brunswick: Rutgers University Press, 1992.

Ruiz, Vicki L. *Cannery Women, Cannery Lives: Mexican Women, Unionization, and the California Food Processing Industry, 1930–1950*. Albuquerque: University of New Mexico Press, 1987.

Sarat, Austin, ed. *Race, Law, and Culture: Reflections on Brown v. Board of Education*. New York: Oxford University Press, 1997.

Satter, Beryl. "Marcus Garvey, Father Divine and the Gender Politics of Race Difference and Race Neutrality." *American Quarterly* 48 (March 1996): 43–76.

Savage, Barbara Diane. *Broadcasting Freedom: Radio, War, and the Politics of Race, 1938–1948*. Chapel Hill: The University of North Carolina Press, 1999.

Saville, Julie. *The Work of Reconstruction: From Slave Labor to Wage Labor in South Carolina, 1860–1870*. New York: Cambridge University Press, 1994.

Scales, Junius, with Richard Nickson. *Cause at Heart: A Former Communist Remembers*. Athens: University of Georgia Press, 1987.

Schlesinger, Arthur M., Jr. "The U.S. Communist Party." *Life* 21 (July 29, 1946), 90.

Schmidt, Christopher W. "J. Waties Waring and the Making of Liberal Jurisprudence in Post–World War II America." In *From the Grassroots to the Supreme Court: Brown v. Board of Education and American Democracy*, edited by Peter F. Lau. Durham: Duke University Press, 2004, 173–97.

Schrecker, Ellen W. *Many Are the Crimes: McCarthyism in America*. Boston: Little, Brown, and Company, 1998.

———. *No Ivory Tower: McCarthyism and the Universities*. New York: Oxford University Press, 1986.

Schwalm, Leslie A. *A Hard Fight for We: Women's Transition from Slavery to Freedom in South Carolina*. Urbana: University of Illinois Press, 1997.

Scott, Daryl Michael. *Contempt & Pity: Social Policy and the Image of the Damaged Black Psyche, 1880–1996*. Chapel Hill: The University of North Carolina Press, 1997.

Scott, Emmett J. *Negro Migration during the War*. New York: Oxford University Press, 1920.

Scott, James C. *The Moral Economy of the Peasant: Rebellion and Subsistence in Southeast Asia*. New Haven: Yale University Press, 1976.

———. *Weapons of the Weak: Everyday Forms of Peasant Resistance*. New Haven: Yale University Press, 1985.

Scott, Joan W. "'Experience.'" In *Feminists Theorize the Political*, edited by Judith Butler and Joan W. Scott. New York: Routledge, 1992, 22–40.

———. "Gender: A Useful Category of Historical Analysis." In *Gender and the Politics of History*, by Joan W. Scott. New York: Columbia University Press, 1988, 28–50.

Self, Robert. *American Babylon: Class, Race, and Power in Oakland and the East Bay, 1945–1978*. Princeton: Princeton University Press, 2003.

Sellers, Cleveland, with Robert Terrell. *The River of No Return: The Autobiography of a Black Militant and the Life and Death of SNCC*. Jackson: University Press of Mississippi, 1990.

Shaw, Stephanie J. *What a Woman Ought to Be and Do: Black Professional Women Workers during the Jim Crow Era*. Chicago: University of Chicago Press, 1996.

Sheheen, Fred R., ed. *". . . and Miles to Go before I Sleep."* Columbia: University of South Carolina College of Liberal Arts' Institute for Public Service and Policy Research, 2004. <http://ipspr.sc.edu/brown/AndMilesToGo.pdf> Accessed April 8, 2005.

Shipton, Alyn. *Groovin' High: The Life of Dizzy Gillespie*. New York: Oxford University Press, 1999.

Simkins, Francis Butler, and Robert H. Woody. *South Carolina during Reconstruction*. Chapel Hill: The University of North Carolina Press, 1932.

Simon, Bryant. "The Appeal of Cole Blease of South Carolina: Race, Class, and Sex in the New South." *Journal of Southern History* 62 (February 1996): 57–86.

———. *A Fabric of Defeat: The Politics of South Carolina Millhands, 1910–1948*. Chapel Hill: The University of North Carolina Press, 1998.

Singh, Nikhil Pal. *Black Is a Country: Race and the Unfinished Struggle for Democracy*. Cambridge: Harvard University Press, 2004.

Sinha, Manisha. *The Counter-Revolution of Slavery: Politics and Ideology in Antebellum South Carolina*. Chapel Hill: The University of North Carolina Press, 2000.

Sitkoff, Harvard. *A New Deal for Blacks: The Emergence of Civil Rights as a National Issue*. New York: Oxford University Press, 1978.

———. *The Struggle for Black Equality, 1954–1980*. New York: Hill and Wang, 1981.

Sklar, Martin J. *The Corporate Reconstruction of American Capitalism, 1890–1916*. New York: Cambridge University Press, 1988.

———. *The United States as a Developing Country: Studies in U.S. History in the Progressive Era and the 1920s*. New York: Cambridge University Press, 1992.

Skocpol, Theda, ed. *Bringing the State Back In*. New York: Cambridge University Press, 1985.

Skowronek, Stephen. *Building a New American State: The Expansion of National Administrative Capacities*. New York: Cambridge University Press, 1982.

Smith, Larissa M. "'Where the South Begins': Black Politics and Civil Rights Activism in Virginia, 1930–1954." Ph.D. diss., Emory University, 2001.

Smith, Suzanne E. *Dancing in the Street: Motown and the Cultural Politics of Detroit.* Cambridge: Harvard University Press, 1999.

Spear, Allan H. *Black Chicago: The Making of a Ghetto, 1890–1920.* Chicago: The University of Chicago Press, 1967.

Spero, Sterling D., and Abram L. Harris. *The Black Worker: The Negro and the Labor Movement.* New York: Atheneum, 1974.

Starobin, Joseph R. *American Communism in Crisis, 1943–1957.* Cambridge: Harvard University Press, 1972.

Stein, Judith. *Running Steel, Running America: Economic Policy, and the Decline of Liberalism.* Chapel Hill: The University of North Carolina Press, 1998.

———. *The World of Marcus Garvey: Race and Class in Modern Society.* Baton Rouge: Louisiana State University Press, 1986.

Sternsher, Bernard, ed. *The Negro in Depression and War: Prelude to Revolution, 1930–1945.* Chicago: Quadrangle Books, 1969.

Stolberg, Benjamin. "Black Chauvinism." *The Nation* 140 (May 15, 1935): 570–71.

Street, James H. *The New Revolution in the Cotton Economy: Mechanization and Its Consequences.* Chapel Hill: The University of North Carolina Press, 1957.

Strong, Augusta Jackson. "Southern Youth's Proud Heritage." *Freedomways: A Quarterly Review of the Negro Freedom Movement* 4 (1964): 35–50.

Sugrue, Thomas J. "Crabgrass-Roots Politics: Race, Rights, and the Reaction against Liberalism in the Urban North, 1940–1964." *Journal of American History* 82 (September 1995): 551–86.

———. *The Origins of the Urban Crisis: Race and Inequality in Postwar Detroit.* Princeton: Princeton University Press, 1996.

Sullivan, Patricia. *Days of Hope: Race and Democracy in the New Deal Era.* Chapel Hill: The University of North Carolina Press, 1996.

Swinton, David H. "Economic Research Paper: The Economic Impact on African Americans after *Brown*." In *". . . and Miles to Go before I Sleep,"* edited by Fred R. Sheheen. Columbia: University of South Carolina College of Liberal Arts's Institute for Public Service and Policy Research, 2004. <http://ipspr.sc.edu/brown/AndMilesToGo.pdf> Accessed April 8, 2005.

Terborg-Penn, Rosalyn. *African American Women in the Struggle for the Vote, 1850–1929.* Bloomington: Indiana University Press, 1998.

Theoharis, Jeanne F., and Komozi Woodard, eds., *Freedom North: Black Freedom Struggles outside the South, 1940–1980.* New York: Palgrave Macmillan, 2003.

Thompson, Bruce A. "The Civil Rights Vanguard: The NAACP and the Black Community in Baltimore, 1931–1942." Ph.D. diss., University of Maryland, 1996.

Thompson, E.P. *The Making of the English Working Class.* New York: Vintage Books, 1966.

———. "Time, Work-Discipline, and Industrial Capitalism." *Past and Present* 38 (December 1963): 56–97.

Tindall, George Brown. "The Campaign for Disfranchisement of Negroes in South Carolina." *Journal of Southern History* 15 (May 1949): 212–34.

———. *The Emergence of the New South, 1913–1945.* Baton Rouge: Louisiana State University Press, 1967.

———. *South Carolina Negroes, 1877–1900.* Columbia: University of South Carolina Press, 1952.

Tjerandsen, Carl. *Education for Citizenship: A Foundation's Experience*. Santa Cruz, CA: Emil Schwartzhaupt, 1980.

Trotter, Joe William, Jr. *Coal, Class, and Color: Blacks in Southern West Virginia, 1915–1945*. Urbana: University of Illinois Press, 1990.

———, ed. *The Great Migration in Historical Perspective: New Dimensions of Race, Class, and Gender*. Bloomington: Indiana University Press, 1991.

Tushnet, Mark V. *Making Civil Rights Law: Thurgood Marshall and the Supreme Court, 1936–1961*. New York: Oxford University Press, 1994.

———. *The NAACP Legal Strategy against Segregated Education, 1925–1950*. Chapel Hill: The University of North Carolina Press, 1984.

Tushnet, Mark, and Katya Lezin. "What Really Happened in *Brown v. Board of Education*." *Columbia Law Review* 91 (December 1991): 1867–1930.

Tuttle, William, Jr. *Race Riot: Chicago and the Red Summer of 1919*. New York: Atheneum, 1970.

Tyson, Timothy B. *Radio Free Dixie: Robert F. Williams and the Roots of Black Power*. Chapel Hill: The University of North Carolina Press, 1999.

———. "Robert F. Williams, 'Black Power,' and the Roots of the African American Freedom Struggle." *Journal of American History* 88 (September 1998): 540–70.

Van Onselen, Charles. "Race and Class in the South African Countryside: Cultural Osmosis and Social Relations in the Sharecropping Economy of the South-Western Transvaal, 1900–1950." *American Historical Review* 95 (April 1990): 99–123.

———. *The Seed Is Mine: The Life of Kas Maine, A South African Sharecropper, 1894–1985*. New York: Hill and Wang, 1996.

———. "The Social and Economic Underpinnings of Paternalism and Violence on the Maize Farms of the South-Western Transvaal, 1900–1950." *Journal of Historical Sociology* 5 (June 1992): 127–60.

———. *Studies in the Social and Economic History of the Witwatersrand, 1886–1914, Vol. 2 New Nineveh*. New York: Longman, 1982.

Vance, Rupert B. *Human Factors in Cotton Culture: A Study in the Social Geography of the American South*. Chapel Hill: The University of North Carolina Press, 1929.

Von Eschen, Penny M. *Race against Empire: Black Americans and Anticolonialism, 1937–1957*. Ithaca: Cornell University Press, 1997.

Wallace, David Duncan. *South Carolina: A Short History, 1520–1948*. Columbia: University of South Carolina Press, 1951.

Weaver, Robert C. *Negro Labor: A National Problem*. Port Washington, NY: Kennikat Press, 1969.

Weber, Palmer. "The Negro Vote in the South." *Virginia Spectator* (November 1938): 6.

Weir, Margaret, Ann Shola Orloff, and Theda Skocpol, eds. *The Politics of Social Policy in the United States*. Princeton: Princeton University Press, 1988.

Weiss, Nancy J. *Farewell to the Party of Lincoln: Black Politics in the Age of FDR*. Princeton: Princeton University Press, 1983.

———. "Long-distance Runners of the Civil Rights Movement: The Contributions of Jews to the NAACP and the National Urban League in the Early Twentieth Century." In *Struggles in the Promised Land*, edited by Jack Salzman and Cornel West. New York: Oxford University Press, 1997, 123–52.

———. *The National Urban League, 1910–1940*. New York: Oxford University Press, 1974.

Werner, Craig. *A Change Is Gonna Come: Music, Race & the Soul of America*. New York: Plume, 1999.

West, Cornel ed. *Keeping Faith: Philosophy and Race in America*. New York: Routledge, 1993.

White, Deborah Gray. *Ar'n't I a Woman: Female Slaves in the Plantation South*. New York: W.W. Norton, 1999.

———. "The Cost of Club Work, the Price of Black Feminism." In *Visible Women: New Essays on American Activism*, edited by Nancy A. Hewitt and Suzanne Lebsock. Urbana: University of Illinois Press, 1993, 247–69.

———. *Too Heavy a Load: Black Women in Defense of Themselves, 1894–1994*. W.W. Norton, 1999.

White, Walter. *How Far the Promised Land?* New York: Viking Press, 1955.

———. *Rope and Faggot: A Biography of Judge Lynch*. New York: Arno Press, 1967.

———. "The Shambles of South Carolina." *The Crisis* 33 (December 1926): 72.

Wilkins, Roy, with Tom Mathews. *Standing Fast: The Autobiography of Roy Wilkins*. New York: Da Capo Press, 1994.

Williams, Cecil J. *Freedom & Justice: Four Decades of the Civil Rights Struggle as Seen by a Black Photographer of the Deep South*. Macon, GA: Mercer University Press, 1995.

Williams, Patricia. *The Alchemy of Race and Rights: Diary of a Law Professor*. Cambridge: Harvard University Press, 1991.

Williams, William Appleman. *The Contours of American History*. Chicago: Quadrangle Books, 1966.

———. *The Tragedy of American Diplomacy*. New York: W.W. Norton, 1984, orig. 1959.

Williamson, Joel. *After Slavery: The Negro in South Carolina during Reconstruction, 1861–1877*. Chapel Hill: The University of North Carolina Press, 1965.

———. *Rage for Order: Black-White Relations in the American South since Emancipation*. New York: Oxford University Press, 1986.

Wilson, William Julius. *The Declining Significance of Race*. Chicago: The University of Chicago Press, 1978.

———. *When Work Disappears: The World of the New Urban Poor*. New York: Knopf, 1996.

Wolters, Raymond. *The Burden of Brown: Thirty Years of School Desegregation*. Knoxville: The University of Tennessee Press, 1984.

———. *Negroes and the Great Depression: The Problem of Economic Recovery*. Westport, CT: Greenwood Publishing, 1970.

Wood, Peter. *Black Majority: Negroes in Colonial South Carolina from 1670 through the Stono Rebellion*. New York: Knopf, 1974.

Woodard, Komozi. *A Nation within a Nation: Amiri Baraka (LeRoi Jones) & Black Power Politics*. Chapel Hill: The University of North Carolina Press, 1999.

Woods, Barbara. "Black Woman Activist in Twentieth-Century South Carolina: Modjeska Monteith Simkins." Ph.D. diss., Emory Univeristy, 1978.

———. "Modjeska Simkins and the South Carolina Conference of the NAACP, 1939–1957." In *Women in the Civil Rights Movement: Trailblazers and Torchbearers, 1941–1964*, edited by Vicki L. Crawford, Jacqueline Anne Rouse, and Barbara Woods. Bloomington: Indiana University Press, 1993, 99–120.

Woodward, C. Vann. *Origins of the New South, 1877–1913*. Baton Rouge: Louisiana State University Press, 1951.

———. *The Strange Career of Jim Crow*. New York: Oxford University Press, 1955.

Woofter, T.J., Jr. *Black Yeomanry: Life on St. Helena Island*. New York: Henry Holt and Company, 1930.

Wright, Gavin. *Old South, New South: Revolutions in the Southern Economy since the Civil War*. New York: Basic Books, 1986.

Wright, Richard. "Blueprint for Negro Writing." *Race and Class* 21 (Spring 1980): 403–12.

Yarbrough, Tinsley E. *A Passion for Justice: J. Waties Waring and Civil Rights*. New York: Oxford University Press, 1987.

Young, James O. *Black Writers of the Thirties*. Baton Rouge: Louisiana State University Press, 1973.

Zangrando, Robert L. *The NAACP Crusade against Lynching, 1909–1950*. Philadelphia: Temple University Press, 1980.

Zeiger, Robert H. *The CIO, 1935–1955*. Chapel Hill: The University of North Carolina Press, 1995.

Zinn, Howard. *SNCC: The New Abolitionists*. Boston: Beacon Press, 1965.

Miscellaneous

Hill's Greenville City Directory, 1938. Richmond, VA: Hill Directory Co., Inc., Publishers, 1938.

South Carolina: A Handbook. Columbia: The Department of Agriculture, Commerce, and Industries and Clemson College, 1927.

"South Carolina Agricultural Experiment Station Circular 82." *Cotton Statistics*. Clemson: Clemson College, SC, December 1951.

Thirty-first Annual Report of the South Carolina Experiment Station of Clemson Agricultural College for the Year Ended June 30, 1922. Clemson: Clemson College, SC, December 1922.

Index

Abbeville, S.C., 7, 15, 16, 53
Abernathy, Ralph, 216, 227
Adams, E.A., 133, 195
Addams, Jane, 9
Addie H. Pickens Club, 114
AFL (American Federation of Labor), 77, 91, 95, 122, 138, 145, 148, 152, 174. *See also names of individual labor unions*
African Methodist Episcopal Church, 31, 34, 35, 37, 68, 111, 113, 114, 133, 139, 140, 193, 194, 195, 199, 201, 203. *See also names of individual churches*
Age of Revolution, 3
Agricultural Adjustment Administration (AAA), 75
Aiken, S.C., 47, 56, 57, 58, 59, 61
Aiken NAACP: founding of, 47, 57; decline of, 57
Alabama, 35, 75, 118, 140, 148, 161, 166, 179, 216, 222, 223
Alexander, Will W., 90
Alien Registration Law of 1940, 172
Allen, Richard, 140
Allen University (S.C.), 47, 165, 194
Alston, C. Columbus, 161
Amalgamated Workers of America (ACWA-CIO), 161
Amenia Conference: 1916 (first), 22–23, 49; 1934 (second), 75–78
American Dilemma, 182
American Federation of Labor (AFL). *See* AFL
American Fund for Public Service. *See* Garland Fund
American Missionary Association, 35

American Tobacco Company, 146, 150, 151, 152, 153, 174, 219–20. *See also* FTA
A.M.E. Zion Church, 68, 111, 113
Anderson, A. Maceo, 195, 199, 201, 202
Anderson, Marion, 38
Anderson, S.C., 47–48, 53, 61, 64
Anderson, William H., 101–5
Anderson County, 91
Anderson NAACP: founding of, 47–48, 53; reorganization of, 185; repression of, 53–54, 65
Anderson Tribune, 53–54
Anson County, N.C., 108
Aptheker, Herbert, 165, 189
Athens, Ga., 24
anticommunism, 11, 171–72, 187–91, 208, 211, 223; and labor movement, 174–75. *See also* Alien Registration Law of 1940; Communist Party; Federal Bureau of Investigation; Gressettee Committee; House Committee on Un-American Activities; and Smith Act
Anti-Jim Crow Committee, 157
Anti-Jim Crow Sunday Movement, 157–58, 216
Arkansas, 140, 158, 166, 187
Arlington, Va., 162
Ashford, James, 158
Ashley River, 33
Atlanta, Ga., 24, 54, 90, 91, 194
Atlanta University (Ga.), 23, 34, 183
Augusta, Ga., 5, 24, 118, 186
Avery, Charles, 35.
Avery Normal Institute, 34, 37, 38, 44,

45, 115, 152, 176; founding of, 35; as reflection of black Charleston, 36.

"Baby NAACP," 99–106
Bagnall, Robert, 74.
Bailey, Charles B., 128–29
Bailey, George, Sr., 62
Baltimore, Md., 21, 194, 216
Baltimore Afro-American, 112
Baptist Church, 25, 31, 35, 62, 68, 91, 94, 109, 111, 112, 113, 114, 118, 119, 159, 210, 216. *See also names of individual churches*
Barksdale, W.D., 15.
Bartley, Numan, 11.
Beaufort County, S.C., 43, 124, 179, 218
Beaufort County NAACP, 48; decline of, 66; founding of, 66; membership characteristics of, 66
bebop, 69.
Bell, Louise Purvis, 116
Benedict College (S.C.), 28, 119, 162, 165, 197
Bennette, Isaiah, 227
Bennettsville, S.C., 119, 156
Benson, I.S., 199, 201, 202, 203
Berkeley County, S.C., 139, 185
Betchman, H.B., 203
Bethel African Methodist Episcopal Church, 140
Bethlehem Baptist Church, 31
Bethune, Mary McLeod, 151
Billikopf, Jacob, 73
Birmingham, Ala., 161, 162, 179, 222
black church, 3, 4, 18, 25, 26, 68, 88, 102, 103, 111, 114, 139, 140, 151, 157, 184, 192, 193, 200, 223; burnings of in South Carolina, 229. *See also* South Carolina State Conference of NAACP Branches; *and names of individual churches*
black elected officials: during Reconstruction, 4; since 1965, 219, 228–29. *See also* Tom Briar; R.H. Cain; James E. Clyburn; Thomas E. Miller; and I. DeQuincey Newman.
black landownership, 15, 60, 193, 196, 198, 200
black migration, 7, 8, 21, 69–70, 71,

138, 145, 173; from South Carolina, 26, 34, 39–40, 48, 54, 60–63, 69, 124, 137, 156, 204, 209; within South Carolina, 125–26
black newspapers, 112. *See also names of individual newspapers*
Black Popular Front, 186
Black Power, 2, 222, 224, 225, 226, 231
black schools, 25–26, 41–43, 88, 111–12, 130, 192–93, 197, 201–2. *See also Briggs v. Elliott; Brown v. Board of Education;* NAACP; *and names of individual schools*
black soldiers, 41, 56, 61, 196–97; in France, 53; violence against, 53, 156, 203. *See also* Harry Briggs; James M. Hinton; Osceola E. McKaine; Ferdinand Pearson; and Isaac Woodard.
black teachers, 28, 31, 35–39, 41–47, 49, 53, 66, 88, 97, 111, 114, 129–32, 162, 195, 196, 200, 201, 204, 205, 208, 218. *See also* Avery Normal Institute; Septima Poinsette Clark; J.A. DeLaine; and NAACP
black voting: black understandings of, 30–33, 47–48, 132, 133–34, 164, 165–67, 218–19, 229; dilution of, 228; registration efforts, 30–33, 46–48, 98, 100–105, 114, 117, 175, 176, 179–80, 184–85, 196, 218–19, 220, 227; restrictions of, 6, 17, 18, 20, 21, 24, 34, 100, 119, 153, 161, 173, 176, 178, 193. *See also* black elected officials; *Brown v. Baskin; Elmore v. Rice;* Extraordinary Session; NAACP; NNC; PDP; poll tax; *Smith v. Allwright;* and white primary
Blackwell, Gordon, 92–93
black-white labor alliance, 78–86, 141–42, 148, 151, 152, 154, 158, 161, 167
Blackwood, Ibra, 91.
Black Worker: The Negro and the Labor Movement, 77. *See also* Abram Harris
Blease, Coleman Livingston, 16, 43, 65, 95

Bob Johnson School, 194
boll weevil, 60, 61
Bolsheviks, 57
Booker T. Washington High School,
    130, 131. *See also* Modjeska Monte-
    ith Simkins; and Albert N. Thomp-
    son
Borroughs, E.B., 65
Boston, Mass., 21, 62, 105
Boston Museum of Fine Arts School, 34
Boulware, Harold, 129, 176, 197, 198
Boy Scouts, 89
Bracey, John, 9
Briar, James A., 96–102, 104–5, 114,
    120
Briar, Tom, 97
Bricklayers and Plasterer's Union #5, 30
Brier, James A. *See* James A. Briar
Briggs, Eliza, 203, 204, 209
Briggs, Harry, 201, 203, 204, 209
Briggs v. Elliott (1950), 204–6
Brown, David, 179
Brown, James, 203
Brown, Sterling, 77, 78
Brown and Williamson Tobacco Com-
    pany, 161
Brown v. Baskin (1948), 179–80
Brown v. Board of Education (1954),
    1, 1837, 191, 192, 197, 202, 206,
    207, 208, 211, 212, 213, 215, 222,
    224, 225, 230
Brown v. Board of Education II (1955),
    207
Bruere Board, 91
Brunner, Edmund de S., 91–92
Brussels, Belgium, 129, 174
Bunch, Celestine, 151
Bunche, Ralph J., 76–79, 86, 158
Burke, Kenneth, 149
Burke Industrial School, 41
Burnham, Dorothy Challenor, 161
Burnham, Louis, 161, 163
Butler, A.J., 197
Butler, Matthew, 4
Butler, Susan Dart, 35, 37, 38, 39
Byrd, Alfred D., 108, 110
Byrd, Levi Grant, 108–14, 136; beat-
    ing of, 109–10; role in organization
    of Cheraw NAACP, 108, 110–14,

116; role in organization of South
    Carolina State Conference of
    NAACP Branches, 108, 115, 117–
    21, 124, 127; view of NAACP, 110
Byrd, Mary Ann Love, 109
Byrd, Pinkie Hancock, 108
Byrnes, James F., 56–57, 139, 170–71

Cain, R.H., 139
Calhoun County, S.C., 138; characteris-
    tics of, 66
Calhoun County NAACP, 114; decline
    of, 66–67; founding of, 66; mem-
    bership characteristics of, 66
California, 148
Calloway, Cab, 69
Campbell, Edward, 51
Campbell's Soup Company, 62
Capital Civic League, 21, 26–33
capitalism, 1, 81, 160, 189, 221, 225
Carawan, Guy, 151
Cardozo, Francis L., 35
Carrington and Michaux tobacco com-
    pany, 160
Carroll, Capt. J., 28
Carter, Robert, 176, 205
Catchings, Rose Mae, 161
Centenary Church, 37
Chamberlain, Daniel, 1
Chapman, Cora, 92, 93
Chappelle, W.D., 47, 49, 119
Charleston, S.C., 6, 8, 20, 33, 56 125,
    130; characteristics of black popula-
    tion, 33–34. *See also* Avery Normal
    Institute; Charleston NAACP;
    Charleston Race Riot; FTA; and
    Hospital Workers Union 1199B
Charleston Colored Industrial School,
    41
Charleston County, S.C., 139. *See also*
    Charleston, S.C.
Charleston Lighthouse, 115, 136
Charleston NAACP, 49, 115, 116, 135,
    219, 220; campaign for black teach-
    er employment, 41–47; decline of
    (1920s and 1930s), 64–65, 115–16;
    founding of, 19; membership char-
    acteristics of, 33–47; Navy Yard em-
    ployment campaign, 40; response to

Charleston Race Riot, 52–53; role
in South Carolina State Conference
of NAACP Branches, 117, 119
Charleston Navy Yard, 40, 47, 125, 227
Charleston News and Courier, 52, 116,
136, 211
Charleston Race Riot (1919), 50–53
Charlotte, N.C., 111, 209
Cheraw, S.C., 108; black churches in,
111; black schools in, 111; charac-
teristics of, 67–68, 110–11; racial
violence in, 109–10
Cheraw and Chesterfield County
NAACP, 116; founding of, 113;
membership characteristics of, 113–
14; role in South Carolina State
Conference of NAACP Branches,
119–21. *See also* Levi Grant Byrd
Cheraw Chronicle, 110–11
Cherokee County, S.C., 126
Chesterfield County, S.C., 67. *See also*
Cheraw; and Cheraw and Chester-
field County NAACP
Chicago, Ill., 21, 92, 139, 140, 142,
154, 155, 158, 159, 167, 216, 217
Children's Defense Fund, 119
CIO (Congress of Industrial Organizations), 11, 95, 96, 102, 122, 138,
145, 146, 148, 149, 150, 151, 153,
174, 175, 223. *See also* Operation
Dixie; *and names of individual labor
unions*
CIO-PAC (Congress of Industrial Organizations-Political Action Committee), 142, 151, 153, 154, 155
Citizens Democratic Party (CDP), 180
Civilian Conservation Corps (CCC), 75
civil rights: meanings of, 2, 24–25,
76–87, 133–34, 212, 225, 231;
relationship to economic justice,
76–87, 173, 231, 266n2
Civil Rights Act of 1964, 222, 225, 230
civil rights movement, 151, 177, 212;
origins of, 1, 222; scholarly and
popular views of, 11–13, 187, 222–
25, 231, 233nn1–2, 235n13; South
Carolina's role in, 143, 198, 219
Civil War, 3, 14
Civil Welfare League, 131

Claflin College (S.C.), 28, 89, 183, 215,
226. *See also* Orangeburg Massacre
Clarendon County, S.C., 187, 194, 229;
characteristics of, 191–93; black
voter registration in, 219. *See also*
CORE
Clarendon County NAACP, 198;
founding of, 185, 195; membership characteristics of, 185, 195–96;
relationship to NAACP national
office, 195, 197, 199–200; repression of, 199, 202–4, 208–10; role
in NAACP's campaign for educational equality, 197–206; as underground organization, 195; views of
NAACP's legal campaign, 205. *See
also Briggs v. Elliott*; *Brown v. Board
of Education*; Committee on Action;
and J.A. DeLaine
Clarendon County Teachers Association, 196
Clarendon Hall School, 210
Clark, Septima Poinsette, 36, 219; background, 44, 130; as contributor to
black organizing tradition, 221–22;
experience on Johns Island, 44–46,
130; interracial work, 130, 220;
target of repression, 220; work with
Highlander Folk School, 220; work
with NAACP, 44–46, 130–31, 220;
work with Southern Christian Leadership Conference, 220–21
Clarke, Kenny, 69
Cleveland, Ohio, 49, 50, 54, 89, 216
Clyburn, James E., 229, 230
Coble Dairy, 216
Coca-Cola, 216
Cohen, Jacob, 50, 51
cold war, 11, 12, 146, 171, 172, 173,
174, 184, 186, 187–91, 206, 208,
212, 223, 231
College of Charleston (S.C.), 186
Colleton County NAACP: decline of,
66; founding of, 65–66; member-
ship characteristics of, 66
Colored Citizens Committee, 126–27
Colored Normal, Industrial, Agricul-
tural and Mechanical College. *See*
South Carolina State College

Columbia, S.C., 5, 6, 8, 164; characteristics of, 19–20. *See also* Capital Civic League; Columbia NAACP; SNYC; and University of South Carolina
Columbia NAACP, 43, 49, 115, 131, 176; decline of (1920s and 1930s), 64–65, 115; early program, 29–33; founding of, 19; membership characteristics of, 30; role in South Carolina State Conference of NAACP Branches, 117–21. *See also* Capital Civic League
Columbia Record, 136
Columbia University, 148; teacher's college, 91
Combahee River, 185
Commission on Interracial Cooperation (CIC), 90, 101, 122
Committee on Action, 202
Committee on Future Plan and Program, 78–86
Communist Party, 11, 75, 76, 122, 146, 148, 153, 155, 159, 161, 162, 163, 169, 170, 171, 172, 174, 188, 189, 190, 208, 223. *See also* anticommunism; NAACP; and SNYC
Congaree River, 33, 66
Congress of Industrial Organizations (CIO). *See* CIO
Congress of Industrial Organizations–Political Action Committee (CIO-PAC). *See* CIO-PAC
Congress of Racial Equality (CORE). *See* CORE
Connor, Eugene "Bull," 222
consumer boycotts, 215–17. *See also* Anti-Jim Crow Sunday Movement
Cooperative Independent Club, 159
Cooperative Worker's of America, 97
Cooper River, 33, 146, 147
CORE (Congress of Racial Equality), 221; chapters in South Carolina, 218; founding of, 217; in Greenville, S.C., 219; national convention at Frogmore, St. Helena Island, S.C., 218; organizational activities in South Carolina, 217–19; relationship to NAACP in South Carolina, 218;

in Rock Hill, S.C., 218; in Spartanburg, S.C., 219; voter registration efforts in South Carolina, 219
Cott, Nancy, 29
Cotton Textile Industrial Relations Board. *See* Bruere Board
Coulter Memorial Academy, 111, 113, 114
Cox, Benjamin F., 35, 36, 38, 45
Cox, Jeannette Keeble, 35, 36, 37, 38
Crawford, Anthony, 15–16, 20, 53
Crisis, 21, 24, 26, 31, 41, 49, 55, 56, 71, 72, 73, 81, 85, 96, 105
Crisis of the Negro Intellectual, 122
Crowley, Malcolm, 149
Cruse, Harold, 122
Culbertson, John Bolt, 88, 102
Curtis Company, 216

Daniels, Sarah, 196, 199–99. *See also* Clarendon County NAACP
Darlington County, S.C., 68, 185
Darlington, S.C., 48
Darlington NAACP: founding of, 48. *See also* Hartsville NAACP
Davis, Angela, 162
Davis, Benjamin, 211
Davis, J.E., 112
Davis, John P., 158
Davis, Sallye, 162
Davis Station, S.C., 194
DeLaine, Henry Charles, 193
DeLaine, J.A. (Joseph Armstrong): and armed self-defense, 203, 209; background of, 193–94; efforts to organize Clarendon County NAACP, 195–96; joins NAACP, 195; philosophy of, 194–95; role in *Briggs v. Elliott*, 196–206; as target of repression, 202–3, 208–9. *See also Briggs v. Elliott*; and Clarendon County NAACP
DeLaine, Mattie Belton, 194, 203
DeLaine, Tisbia Gamble, 193
Democratic National Convention: of 1938, 135; of 1944, 139, 140, 142–43, 165; of 1948, 165–66, 178–80
Democratic Party, 4, 5, 6, 47, 49, 95,

107, 115, 137, 138, 139, 142, 143,
    148, 149, 155, 167, 175, 176, 177,
    178, 179, 180
Denmark, S.C., 224
Detroit, Mich., 161, 216
Dewey, John, 23.
Dexter Avenue Baptist Church, 216
Dickson, J.L., 113–14
disfranchisement. *See* black voting
Distributive, Processing, and Office
    Workers of America (DPOW), 174
Dixiecrats, 179–80
Dobbins, Mary, 30
Doctor, Isaac, 50, 51
Dorchester County, S.C., 139
Doster, Lillie Mae, 146, 150, 152, 227
Double V Campaign, 128
Drago, Edmund, 36
Du Bois, Rachel Davis, 78
Du Bois, W.E.B., 9, 15, 21, 22, 23, 24,
    25, 26, 33, 34, 35, 38, 41, 49, 50,
    56, 72, 76, 188, 190, 211; affilia-
    tion with SNYC, 165–71, 189; and
    An Appeal to the World, 189; and
    "Behold the Land" address, 169–
    70; *Black Reconstruction*, 81–82;
    criticism of NAACP, 81; efforts to
    revise Marxism, 81–82; internation-
    alist vision, 83, 169–70; NAACP
    Board of Directors terminates con-
    tract of (1948), 185; relationship
    to Young Turks, 78–84; resignation
    from NAACP (1935), 85; on segre-
    gation, 71, 81–85, 96, 122
Ducket, Hattie Logan, 89–90, 93, 99
Duke, James B., 91
Durham, N.C., 24
Durr, Virginia, 151
Duvall, Viola Louise, 129

Eaddy, Webb, 209
Earl, Willie, 156
Ebaugh, Laura Smith, 92
Edelman, Marion Wright, 119
Edgefield, S.C., 7
Edgefield County, S.C., 56
Edisto River, 185
Eldridge, Roy, 69
Eleanor Roosevelt Society, 126

Elko, S.C., 156
Elks, 25, 89
Elmore, George, 175–78
Elmore v. Rice (1946), 176–77, 179,
    180
Emanuel A.M.E. Church, 34
Emil Schwartzhaupt Foundation, 220
Eschen, Penny von, 188
Ewing, Oscar R., 142
Executive Order 8802, 127
"Exhortation for Solid Voluntary Ac-
    tion," 121–24, 127, 206
Extraordinary Session, 135, 175, 178

Fairfax, Frankie, 69.
fascism, 127, 146, 169, 221
Fast, Howard, 165
Favrot, Leo, 92
Federal Bureau of Information (FBI),
    171, 172
Federal Emergency Relief Administra-
    tion (FERA), 75
Federal Employment Protection Com-
    mittee (FEPC), 178
federal government, 9, 56, 75, 87, 94,
    95, 96, 104, 143, 208
Federation of Jewish Charities, 73
Fels, Samuel, 74
feminism, 9, 29, 32
Fields, Mamie Garvin, 36, 37, 38,
    41–42, 44, 45
Fifteenth Amendment, 2, 3, 9, 134, 177
Fifth Pan African Congress, 170
Fifty-fourth Colored Regiment, 41
Fishman, Sidney, 149, 150, 151
Fisk University (Tenn.), 35, 162
Flint, Mich., 159
Florence, S.C., 48, 58, 198, 209, 218
Florence County, S.C., 185, 203, 229
Florence NAACP: founding of, 48;
    repression of, 58, 65; role in South
    Carolina State Conference of
    NAACP Branches, 117, 119
Florida, 23, 24, 125, 148, 151, 204,
    211. *See also* NAACP
Food, Tobacco, Agricultural & Allied
    Workers Union (FTA). *See* FTA
Foner, Eric, 3
Ford, Edsel, 74

Ford Motor Company, 216
Foreman, Clark, 147, 151, 165, 169
Fort Jackson, 126–27
Fort Sumter, 3
Foster, William, 172
Fountain Inn, S.C., 104
Fourteenth Amendment, 2, 3, 9, 129, 177
France, 49, 53, 129, 174
Frazier, E. Franklin, 77
Frederick, Corrine R., 27–28
Frederick, N.J., 27–28, 30, 58–59, 65, 115, 133
Frederickson, Kari, 180
Fredie's Central Shaving Parlor, 51
Freedom Rides, 218, 222
Freud, Sigmund, 149
Friendship Junior College (S.C.), 218
FTA (Food, Tobacco, Agricultural & Allied Workers Union), 156; expelled from CIO, 170; Local #15 strike of American Tobacco Company cigar plant in Charleston, S.C., 146–53, 174, 227; Local #56 strike in Trenton, N.J., 150; Local # 186 strike in Philadelphia, Pa., 150; organization of, 148. See also Distributive, Processing, and Office Workers of America (DPOW); and "We Shall Overcome"
Furman University (S.C.), 91, 92, 93, 94
Future Plan and Program of the NAACP, 78–85

Gaither, Tom, 218
Gandhi, Mahatma, 217
Garland, Charles, 74
Garland Fund, 74
Garvey, Marcus, 49, 63–64, 83
Gassaway, M.H., 53–54
Gates County, N.C., 118
GCCCD (Greenville County Council for Community Development): creation of, 92; limits of interracial work, 103; Negro Council, 94, 99; opposition to, 94; position on black voting rights, 103; position on segregation, 100–101; program, 92; role in Committee on Interracial

Cooperation, 94; work with black community, 92–101
Geer, Eugene Bennette, 91, 92, 94, 100, 103
General Education Board (GEB), 91, 92
Georgetown NAACP: repression of, 120; role in South Carolina State Conference of NAACP Branches, 117, 119
Georgia, 55, 60, 86, 140, 166, 169, 211. See also Atlanta, Ga.; Augusta, Ga.; and Savanah, Ga.
Georgia, Robert, Jr., 200
Ghana, 170
GI Bill of Rights, 197
Gibson, Annie, 203
Gillespie, James, 68–69
Gillespie, John Birks "Dizzy," 67–70, 108, 109, 111
Gillespie, Lottie, 67
Gilmore, Glenda, 17, 18
Good Samaritans, 28
Gordon, Asa, 37
Grady, Henry W., 91
Graham, Frank Porter, 91, 151
Gray, Wil Lou, 130, 220
Great Depression, 12, 68–69, 72, 82, 87, 108, 109, 146, 223
Green, Ida, 37
Green, Milison, 204
Green, Nathaniel, 37
Greensboro, N.C., 24, 217
Greenville, S.C., 218; characteristics of, 87; Ku Klux Klan in, 88. See also Parker School District
Greenville County, S.C., 86, 90, 180; characteristics of, 87. See also Greenville, S.C.
Greenville County Council for Community Development (GCCCD). See GCCCD
Greenville NAACP: founding of, 97; membership characteristics of, 97; relationship to CORE, 219; repression of, 99–105, 120; role in South Carolina State Conference of NAACP Branches, 117, 119, 120; role of women in, 98–99; voter registration efforts of 1939, 98–105

Greenville News, 102
Greenwood County, S.C., 7, 60, 62
Gressette, L. Marion, 208
Gressette Committee, 208
Grimké, Francis, 40
Grossman, James, 63
Gullah, 45

Haiti, 44, 165
Hall, Jacquelyn Dowd, 90, 223
Hamburg, S.C., 5
Hamburg Massacre, 5, 7, 15
Hamlet, N.C., 108
Hammond, Samuel, Jr., 226
Hampton, Wade, 5, 30
Hampton, W. McLeod, 125
Hancock, Annie, 109
Harlem, N.Y., 61, 69, 157, 211, 216
Harlem Renaissance, 71–72
Harleston, Edwin Gaillard, 34
Harleston, Edwin "Teddy" A., 46, 49,
    52, 119; background of, 34–35
Harleston, Eloise, 35
Harris, Abram L., 76–86, 217
Harris Report. *See* Future Plan and Pro-
    gram of the NAACP
Hartley, William, 58
Hartsville NAACP, 185
Harvard University (Mass.), 9, 76, 92
Hayes, Ruthorford B., 5
Heflin, Tom, 65
Helms, F. Clyde, 90
Henderson, Donald, 148
Highlander Folk School, 46, 150–51,
    220–21. *See also* Johns Island Citi-
    zenship School.
Hinton, James M., 131, 133, 176, 181,
    182, 195, 198, 199; background of,
    118; early opposition to South Car-
    olina State Conference of NAACP
    Branches, 117–21; as leader of PDP,
    140–41; as organizer, 184–86; radi-
    calization of, 126–28; resignation
    from South Carolina State Confer-
    ence of NAACP Branches, 211; as
    target of violence, 186, 211
Hollis, Lawrence Peter, 92, 100
Holloday, George, 50, 51
Holt, Thomas C., 4, 39

Horry County, S.C., 58
Horton, Miles, 220
Horton, Zilphia, 150–51, 220
Hospital Workers Union 1199B, strike
    of University of South Carolina's
    Medical College Hospital (1969),
    226–28
House Committee on Un-American
    Activities, 171
Houston, Charles, 77; as Dean of How-
    ard University Law School, 85;
    relationship to Young Turks, 77,
    85–86, 190; views on NAACP pro-
    gram and structure, 10, 85–86, 190
Howard, H.H., 58
Howard School, 28
Howard University (Washington, D.C.),
    76, 84, 85, 123, 159. *See also* Na-
    tional Conference on the Economic
    Crisis of the Negro
Hudson, Hosea, 165
Hudson, Roy, 87
Hundred Days, 75, 76
Hunter, Jane Edna, 89
Hurst, John, 49

Illinois, 8, 21, 86, 158, 229
India, 165
integration, 82, 177, 187, 205; black
    views of, 123–24, 206–8, 218–19
Interdenominational Ministers' Union
    (IMU), 52
International Workers of the World
    (IWW), 56
interracial alliances, 3, 9, 17–19, 44, 48,
    73, 93–94, 97, 100, 103, 130, 137,
    141–42, 152, 153, 156, 165, 169,
    217–19, 220, 231. *See also* black-
    white labor alliance; Commission on
    Interracial Cooperation; Committee
    on Interracial Cooperation; Cooper-
    ative Independent Club; GCCCD;
    Highlander Folk School; Interracial
    Committees; PDP; SNYC; and
    South Carolina Committee on In-
    terracial Cooperation
Interracial Committees, 37, 38, 103
interracialism. *See* interracial alliances
I.N. Vaugn Company, 161

Irmo, S.C., 163
Irving, Peter, 51

Jackson, Alice, 159
Jackson, Esther Cooper, 189, 190; background of, 162; FBI harassment of, 172; joins Communist Party, 162; and Pan African Congress, 170; philosophy, 162; as SNYC executive secretary, 162; speech to 1946 SNYC Youth Legislature, 166; and Women's Youth Brigade, 170
Jackson, James E., Jr. 189, 190; background, 159–60; joins Communist Party, 160; as leader of SNYC, 160–62; philosophy, 160; resigns from SNYC, 172
Jackson, R.W., 120
Jacksonville, Fla., 23, 24
Jackson Ward, Va., 159, 160
James, Dwight, 230
James, Winston, 63
Jenkins, Daniel J., 35
Jenkins, Esau, 227; and Progressive Club, 220; and voter registration and education efforts on Johns Island, 219–20
Jenkins Orphanage, 35, 37–38
Jennings, Robert H., 216
Jewish Americans, 25, 29, 73
Jim Crow. See segregation
Johns Island, S.C., 44–45, 130, 219–21, 227
Johns Island Citizenship School, 220
Johnson, Charles S., 162
Johnson, James Weldon, 10, 72, 83, 86; background of, 22–23; role as NAACP field secretary, 22–26, 29, 50
Johnson, R.O., 93, 97, 100, 101
Johnson, William H., 35
Johnson C. Smith University (Biddle College, Charlotte, N.C.), 111
Johnston, Olin D., 95, 135, 177
Jones, Charles, 218
Journal and Guide (Norfolk), 112
Journey of Reconciliation, 217

Kantrowitz, Stephen, 5
Kelley, Anna, 220

Kelley, Florence, 9
Kennan, George, 188
Key, V.O., 13
King, Coretta Scott, 227
King, Martin Luther, Jr., 11, 187, 216, 220, 222, 226
Kluger, Richard, 194
Knights of Labor, 97
Knights of the Pythias, 25
Korstad, Frances, 152
Korstad, Karl, 149–53
Korstad, Robert, 224
Ku Klux Klan, 4, 57–58, 87, 88, 91, 95, 103–5, 156, 165, 168, 196, 203

Lake City, S.C., 203, 208
Lake City NAACP, 185
Lampkin, Daisy Elizabeth Adams, 98
Lance Company, 216
Lanham, S.L., 59
Laurens, S.C., 61, 180
Lays Company, 216
LDF (Legal Defense Fund): creation of, 190, 205; split from NAACP, 226. See also Thurgood Marshall
League for Democracy, 129
Leevy, I.S., 27
Legal Defense and Education Fund, Inc. See LDF
Lehman, Herbert H., 74
Lenin, V.I., 76
Lewis, David Levering, 72, 76, 84, 189
Lewis, Lem, 38
Lexington County, S.C., 121
liberalism, 11, 29, 79, 129, 139, 141, 146, 171, 187, 205, 223. See also interracial alliances
Liberty Hill A.M.E. Church, 194
Liberty Hill School, 194
Lighthouse and Informer, 136, 153, 210–11
Little Rock, Ark., 187
Logan, Rayford, 123
Lone Star, S.C., 66.
Long, George Waldo, 111, 113
Louisiana, 55, 172, 211
Lowman, Annie, 58–59
Lowman, Bertha, 58–59
Lowman, Demon, 58–59

Lowman, Sam, 58–59
lynching, 15–16, 20, 56, 61, 72, 87, 116, 156, 182; of Lowman family, 58–59, 65; in South Carolina, 1882–1923, 16–17, 52; in South Carolina, 1919–1923, 57. *See also* antilynching campaign; and NAACP

Mance, Robert W., 176
Manchester, England, 170
Manning, Richard I., 16
Manning, S.C., 193
Manning NAACP, 185. *See also* Clarendon County NAACP
March on Washington: in 1941, 127; in 1963, 222
Marlboro County, S.C., 119, 126
Marshall, Henry L., 113
Marshall, Louis, 73–74
Marshall, Thurgood, 10, 129, 133, 176, 190, 198, 199, 203, 205, 211
Martin, Lillie, 150, 151
Marx, Karl, 76, 81, 82, 149, 159, 160
Marxism, 76, 81–82, 159, 160. *See also* Communist Party; NNC; SNYC; Young Turks,
Masonic Temple, 140
Masons, 28
massive resistance, 186, 211–13, 216, 224. *See also* Clarendon County NAACP; Gressette Committee; South Carolina State Conference of NAACP Branches; and White Citizens' Council
Maybank, Burnet, 134, 142
Mayfield, Henry O., 165
McCain, James T., 217; organizational efforts in South Carolina, 218–19. *See also* CORE
McCarty, Joseph, 189
McCleannan Hospital, 38.
McCormick County, S.C., 61
McCray, John H., 211, 228; and Anti-Jim Crow Committee, 157–58; background of, 136, 139–40; early NAACP activities, 115–16; as founder of the PDP, 135–41; on purposes of PDP, 137–43; relationship with Osceola McKaine, 153–

56, 210; relationship with Modjeska Simkins, 210; role in NAACP expansion, 186; target of repression, 210; on ties between NAACP and PDP, 137; views on CIO-PAC, 153; views on Communist Party, 153–56, 163, 172; views on Southern Conference for Human Welfare, 153; work with SNYC, 162–63, 166–67, 172
McDew, Charles "Chuck," 217
McFall, John, 34
McFall's Pharmacy, 34
McGowan, Celia, 90
McKaine, Osceola E., 132, 157, 195, 210, 217; as advocate of black-white labor alliance, 141–42, 152, 153, 154; background, 129; connection to radical Left, 129, 141–42; death of, 154, 174; as first African American field representative of Southern Conference for Human Welfare, 142, 153; and FTA strike of American Tobacco Company, 151, 152; as leader of PDP, 141–42; relationship with John H. McCray, 136, 153–56; return to Belgium, 174; role in campaign for equalization of teacher salaries, 129, 132; work with SNYC, 162–63
McKee, Don, 101–2
McNeil, Bill, 109
Medical College Hospital (MCH). *See* Hospital Workers Union 1199B
Meier, August, 9, 22, 218
Memphis, Tenn., 226, 227
Mickey, Edward, 34, 35
Mickey, Hannah, 35
Mickey, Richard, 34, 35, 39
Mickey's Funeral Home, 34
Middleton, Delano, 226
migration. *See* black migration
Miller, Thomas, 43, 45–46
Mississippi, 4, 25, 55, 86, 105, 140, 166, 211, 219, 223
Mississippi Flood Control Project, 79
Missouri ex rel, Gaines v. Canada (1938), 176–77
Modern Priscilla club: founding of,

38; membership characteristics of, 38–39; program, 39
Moncks Corner NAACP, 185
Monk, Thelonious, 69
Monteagle, Tenn., 151, 220
Monteith, Henry, 30
Monteith, Rachel Hull, 30
Monteith, Walter, 30
Montgomery, Ala., 216. *See also* Dexter Avenue Baptist Church; and Montgomery Bus Boycott
Montgomery, Eugene A.R., 199–200; background of, 183–84; hired as South Carolina State Conference of NAACP Branches executive secretary, 183–84; as leader of NAACP expansion in South Carolina, 184–86
Montgomery Bus Boycott, 187, 216
Moore, Fred, 217
Morehouse College (Ga.), 128
Morgan, Edmund, 1
Morris Baptist Chapel Church, 62
Moultrie, Mary, 227
Mount Olive Baptist Church, 159
Mt. Zion A.M.E. Church, 37
Myrdal, Gunnar, 182

NAACP (National Association for the Advancement of Colored People), 11, 18, 50, 71, 122, 159, 162; Annual Meeting in Cleveland, Ohio (1919), 49; antilynching campaign, 113, 115, 116; branch decline, 53–56, 59–60, 65–67, 74; branch expansion, 21, 135–36; campaign for educational equality, 129–32, 176–77, 192, 198–207; and cold war, 188–91, 208; creation of Dixie District/Southern Empire, 24; early program of, 9–10, 21–26; financial difficulties of, 73–74, 80; first branches in South Carolina, 19, 47–48; first southern organizing drive, 22–26; in Florida, 105, 211; and foreign policy, 188–91; founding of, 8–9; Future Plan and Program (Harris Report), 78–86; in Georgia, 55, 211; IRS investigation

of, 211; legal program, 10, 72–73, 75, 105, 115, 128, 133, 176; in Louisiana, 55–56, 211; membership as sign of respectability, 113; membership decline, 72, 207; membership expansion, 21–22; in Mississippi, 55, 105, 211; NAACP Youth Councils, 101, 105, 159; opposition to, 56, 75, 76–86, 208–11, 220; organizational structure, 80, 85–86; policy on creation of State Conferences, 116–17; relationship to black church, 114, 184–85, 193, 200; relationship to branches, 10, 21, 48, 85–86, 110, 122–23, 199–200, 205; relationship to Communist Party, 75, 188–91; relationship to Irish Americans, 25; relationship to Jewish Americans, 25, 73–74; relationship to South Carolina, 19, 23, 74, 87, 105, 199–200, 205; role in shaping gender norms, 32–33, 48, 49, 96–98; role of women in, 31–33, 65, 96–98; scholarly views of, 10, 188, 223, 224; as site of conflict and mediation, 20, 36, 48; in Southeast Region, 211; in Texas, 54–56, 105, 133, 211; transition to black-led organization, 19, 21–22, 72; women's auxiliaries, 65, 97. *See also* Amenia Conference (first and second); *Brown v. Baskin*; *Brown v. Board of Education*; Robert Carter; *The Crisis*; W.E.B. Du Bois; *Elmore v. Rice*; Abram Harris; Charles Houston; James Weldon Johnson; LDF; Thurgood Marshall; *Nixon v. Condon*; Mary White Ovington; Joel Spingarn; South Carolina State Conference of NAACP Branches; Walter White; Young Turks; *and names of individual NAACP branches*
NACW (National Association of Colored Women), 9, 17, 36, 37, 89, 98, 114. *See also* SCFCWC; *and names of individual clubs*
Nance, Butler W., 21, 26, 27, 29, 30, 33, 43, 65

Nash, Diane, 218
Nation, 32
National Association for the Advancement of Colored People (NAACP). *See* NAACP
National Association of Colored Women (NACW). *See* NACW
National Conference on the Economic Crisis of the Negro, 84
National Council of Negro Women (NCNW), 151
National Industrial Recovery Act (NIRA), 75
National Labor Relations Act. *See* Wagner Act
National Labor Relations Board (NLRB), 153, 174
National Maritime Union (NMU), 148, 152
National Negro Business League, 25
National Negro Committee. *See* NAACP
National Negro Congress (NNC). *See* NNC
National Recovery Administration (NRA), 76, 90, 91. *See also* Bruere Board
National Urban League, 71, 122
National Youth Administration (NYA), 93, 121, 151. *See also* Negro Division of the National Youth Administration
Nazi-Soviet Pact, 172
NCC (Negro Citizens Committee), 175–76, 178; organization of, 133; philosophy, 133–34; relationship to NAACP, 133, 178
Negro Citizens Committee of South Carolina. *See* NCC
Negro Council of the GCCCD. *See* GCCCD
Negro Division of the National Youth Administration, 93
Negro Women's Franchise League, 98
Nelson, Beulah, 62
Newberry, S.C., 7, 210
New Deal, 74–75, 77, 79, 82, 89, 94, 95, 96, 98, 106, 122, 124, 136, 138, 141, 149, 151, 156, 165, 173, 186, 220; historians views of, 11–12, 96, 223–25, 253n65, 266n2
New Deal Coalition, 141, 146, 148, 173, 266n2. *See also* Popular Front
Newman, I. DeQuincey, 183–84, 228
News and Courier, 52, 116, 136, 211
New York, 22, 76, 86, 209
New York City, 21, 61, 69, 87, 102, 108, 154, 155, 161, 199, 209
New York NAACP, 23
Niagara movement, 31
Nineteenth Amendment, 31, 46–47
Nixon v. Condon (1932), 115
Nkrumah, Kwame, 170
NNC (National Negro Congress), 158, 223
Norfolk, Va., 24
North Carolina, 7, 17, 18, 24, 61, 67, 100, 108, 109, 111, 119, 140, 151, 169, 209, 211, 217
North Charleston, 50, 51
Nullification Crisis, 3, 208

Oberlin College (Ohio), 162
Odum, Howard W., 92, 100
Operation Dixie, 145, 175
Orangeburg, S.C., 27, 43, 48, 177, 181, 183, 194; and student sit-ins, 217. *See also* Claflin College; Orangeburg Massacre; Orangeburg NAACP; and South Carolina State College
Orangeburg County, S.C., 66, 125
Orangeburg Fuel and Ice, 216
Orangeburg Massacre, 226
Orangeburg NAACP: economic boycott of White Citizens Council, 215–17; founding of, 48; petition to integrate public schools, 215; as target of state repression, 217. *See also* South Carolina State College
Ovington, Mary White, 9, 21, 54, 78
Owens, Jerry, 102, 103

Palmetto Bakery, 216
Palmetto Leader, 28
Palmetto State. *See* South Carolina
Palmetto State Teachers Association (PSTA), 132, 218

Parker, Charlie, 69
Parker, John J., 75, 178
Parker School District, 92
Patterson, F.D., 162
PDP (Progressive Democratic Party),
    107, 162, 166, 174, 175, 183, 228;
    and Communist Party, 155; first
    statewide convention, 140; founding
    of, 136, 264n51; internal conflicts,
    143–44, 153–56, 210; on Johns
    Island, S.C., 219–20; program,
    137; relationship to NAACP, 137,
    176–80; as response to conditions of
    1940s, 137–39; as rooted in history
    of independent black political organi-
    zation, 139–41; seating challenge at
    1944 DNC, 142–43, 154–55, 166;
    seating challenge at 1948 DNC,
    166–67, 178–80; ties to other states,
    140; women's auxiliaries of, 196. *See
    also Brown v. Baskin; Elmore v. Rice;*
    John McCray; Osceola McKaine;
    and Modjeska Simkins
Pearson, Ferdinand, 196–97
Pearson, Hammett, 196, 201
Pearson, Jessie, 197
Pearson, Levi, 196–99, 201
Pearson v. County Board of Education
    (1948), 199
Pee Dee River, 48, 67, 109, 119
Pee Dee Union Baptist Church, 68,
    109–14
Pendleton, C.F., 109
People's Informer, 136
Pepper, Claude, 151
Percival, Henry, Sr., 101, 103
Perkins, Thelma Dale, 161
Perry, Matthew, 177
Philadelphia, Pa., 61–62, 69, 73, 107,
    140, 150, 174, 179, 180
Phillis Wheatley Association, 89
Phillis Wheatley Center, 89–90, 92, 93,
    99, 103
Phillis Wheatley Home for Girls, *See*
    Phillis Wheatley Center
Phillis Wheatley Literary and Social
    Club, 36, 39; membership charac-
    teristics, 37–38; organization of,
    37–38; program, 38

Phoenix Race Riot, 7, 15, 87
Pickens, William, 32, 98
Pickens County, S.C., 156, 180
Pilgrim Health and Life Insurance Com-
    pany, 118
Pittsburgh, Pa., 183
Pittsburgh Courier, 112
Plessy v. Ferguson (1896), 6
Poinsette Hotel, 97
poll tax, 6, 101, 142, 182
Popular Front, 141, 148, 153, 161,
    172, 173, 174, 175, 186, 212, 223.
    See also Black Popular Front
populism, 17, 18, 149
postindustrial society, 82
Potts, John H., 151–52
Powell, Adam Clayton, Jr., 166
pragmatism, 9
Presbyterian National Home Mission.
    See Coulter Memorial Academy
President's Committee on Fair Employ-
    ment Practices, 127. *See also* Federal
    Employment Protection Committee
    (FEPC)
Prioleau, D.T., 120
Progressive Democratic Party (PDP).
    See PDP
progressivism, 16

Ragin, William "Mich," 204
Raleigh, N.C., 24
Randolph, Alonzo B., 183
Randolph, A. Philip, 127, 158
Ravenel, Charles J., 125
reconstruction, 1, 2, 3, 4, 5, 27, 28, 34,
    43, 47, 81, 97, 127, 134, 135, 138,
    139, 141, 164, 166, 191, 228
Red Summer of 1919, 52, 90
*Report on the Economic Conditions of the
    South,* 141, 169
Republican Party, 4, 5, 6, 7, 27, 28, 43,
    87, 97, 138, 139, 165, 180
Retail, Wholesale, Department Store
    Union (RWDSU), 227
Reuther, Walter, 227
Richburg, E.E., 194, 195
Richburg, Joseph, Sr., 192–93, 204,
    209
Richland County, S.C., 27, 28, 30, 32,

130, 175, 180. *See also* Columbia, S.C.
Richmond, Va., 24, 72, 116, 158, 159, 160, 161, 216
Rivers, L.B., 195
R.J. Reynolds Tobacco Company, 148
Robert Small Graded and Junior High School, 111–12
Robeson, Paul, 165, 171, 188–89, 190, 211
Robinson, Bernice, 220
Robinson, Maggie B., 120–21
Rockefeller Foundation. *See* General Education Board
Rock Hill, S.C., 64, 218
Roediger, David, 1
Roosevelt, Franklin Delano, 11, 75, 76, 96, 127, 139
Roper Hospital, 51
Rosenwald, Julius, 74
Rosenwald, William, 74
Rudwick, Elliott, 22, 218
Ruffin NAACP, 185
Russia, 57, 171. *See also* Soviet Union

Saluda River, 33
Sanctified Church, 68, 111, 115
Santee River, 66
Saunders, William, 227
Savannah, Ga., 24, 48, 61, 125
Savannah River, 5
Saville, Julie, 3
Savoy Ballroom, 69
Scales, Junius, 169
SCFCWC (South Carolina Federation of Colored Women's Clubs), 36, 37, 114. *See also names of individual clubs*
Schlesinger, Arthur M., 188
Scottsboro, Ala., 75, 190
Scott's Branch School, 192, 193, 194, 195, 196, 197, 199, 203, 204; student protest in, 200–202. *See also* I.S. Benson; *Brown v. Board of Education*; Clarendon County, S.C.; Clarendon County NAACP; and J.A. DeLaine
SCTBA (South Carolina Tuberculosis Association), 92, 131–32

Seals, J.W., 199, 201, 204
Sears, Roebuck Company, 74
Seba, Pauline, 38
Second Cavalry Baptist Church, 31, 118
Second Presbyterian Church, 68, 111
segregation: black views of, 187, 206–7; origins of, 5–6. *See also Brown v. Board of Education*; W.E.B. Du Bois; Integration; NAACP; and South Carolina State Conference of NAACP Branches
Sellers, Cleveland, 224, 226. *See also* Orangeburg Massacre
Shaw, Robert Gould, 41
Shaw Memorial School, 41
Sherrod, Charles, 218
Shillady, John R., 22, 55
Shilo Baptist Church, 119
Shreveport NAACP (La.), 55
Shull, Lynwood, 176
Simkins, Andrew W., 131
Simkins, Modjeska Monteith, 30, 136; background, 131; involvement with NAACP, 131–32, 181, 186; relationship with John McCray, 210–11; resignation from South Carolina State Conference of NAACP Branches, 211; as target of repression, 211; work with SNYC, 162–64
Simmerson, Ralph, 95, 104
Simmons, J. Andrew, 36.
Simmons, Lucille, 150
Simmons, S.B.B., 54
Simpsonville, S.C., 105
Simonton School, 41
Singleton, George, 197
sit-ins, 217, 222, 224; in Columbia, S.C., 218; in Greensboro, N.C., 217; in Orangeburg, S.C., 217; in Rock Hill, S.C., 218. *See also* FTA
slavery, 1, 2, 3, 4, 8, 25, 28, 30, 33, 67, 123, 133, 193, 228, 230
Smith, Abraham, 200
Smith, "Cotton" Ed, 134–35
Smith, Hauleen Green, 187
Smith, Henry, 226
Smith, Ruby Doris, 218
Smith Act, 172

Smith v. Allwright (1944), 134, 143, 175, 177
SNCC (Student Nonviolent Coordinating Committee), 217, 218, 222, 226
SNYC (Southern Negro Youth Congress), 174, 188; charges of Communist influence, 171; Leadership Training School in Irmo, S.C., 163; organizational demise of, 171–73; organization of, 158; philosophy of, 158, 160, 163, 167, 169; relationship to NNC, 158; roles of women in, 161–62; theories on race and class, 168–69; ties to Communist Party, 159, 172; work in South Carolina, 162–71. *See also* James Ashford; W. E. B. Du Bois; Esther Cooper Jackson; James E. Jackson, Jr.; Edward Strong.
Socialist Party, 148, 157
Solomon, Massie, 203
South Carolina, 1; black access to jobs in, 230; black incomes in, 230; black prison population in, 230; distinctiveness of, 7; economic changes, 60, 68, 124–26, 156; population characteristics, 60, 124; shift from majority black to white, 61; spending on black education in, 230. *See also* black migration; black schools; segregation; South Carolina State Conference of NAACP Branches; textile industry; *and names of individual places and regions*
South Carolina Colored Democratic Party. *See* PDP
South Carolina Committee of the Commission on Interracial Cooperation, 90
South Carolina Council on Human Relations, 180
South Carolina Federation of Colored Women's Clubs (SCFCWC). *See* SCFCWC
South Carolina General Assembly, 177, 208, 228. *See also* Extraordinary Session; and Gressette Committee
South Carolina Progressive Democratic Party. *See* PDP

South Carolina State College, 36, 43, 176–77; and student movement, 216–17. *See also* Orangeburg Massacre
South Carolina State Conference of NAACP Branches, 107, 114, 145; battle against white primary, 133–44, 175–82; creation of, 117–21; as cross-class organization, 128; decline of member branches, 210; decline of NAACP membership in South Carolina, 210; expansion of member branches, 136, 184, 191; expansion of NAACP membership in South Carolina, 136, 185; initial composition of, 119–21; philosophy of, 121–24; position on integration, 123, 181–82, 187, 206–7; protests against Confederate battle flag, 229–30; relationship to black church, 181–85; repression of, 208–11; as vehicle for connection to national and international arena, 128; as vehicle for shift from uplift to protest politics, 128, 130. *See also Briggs v. Elliott; Brown v. Baskin; Brown v. Board of Education*; Gressette Committee; *Elmore v. Rice*; James M. Hinton; John H. McCray; Eugene A.R. Montgomery; NAACP; NCC; PDP; Modjeska Monteith Simkins; *and names of individual NAACP branches*
South Carolina State Constitution of 1895, 16
South Carolina State House, 5, 135, 229
South Carolina Supreme Court, 59
South Carolina Tuberculosis Association (SCTBA). *See* SCTBA
Southern Christian Leadership Conference (SCLC), 220; and Hospital Workers Union 1199B, 227–28
Southern Conference for Human Welfare (SCHW), 141–42, 151, 154, 156, 165, 169, 174
Southern Indicator, 28
Southern Negro Youth Congress (SNYC). *See* SNYC

Southern Tenant Farmers Union (STFU), 148
Soviet Union, 187, 188
Spartanburg, S.C., 59, 126, 138, 219
Spearman, Alice, 180
Spero, Sterling, 77. *See also The Black Worker: The Negro and the Labor Movement*
Spingarn, Arthur, 72
Spingarn, Joel E., 22, 76
Springfield Race Riot, 8
Spring Hill A.M.E. Church, 193, 194
Spring Hill School, 193
Stalin, Joseph, 172
Stanfield, Reuel, 148–49, 152
Stark General Hospital, 149
Sterling High School, 92–93
Stukes, William "Bo," 203
Standard Oil, 216
Starks, J.J., 119
States' Rights Democrats. *See* Dixiecrats
St. Helena Island, S.C., 62–63, 218
St. Marks A.M.E. Church, 193, 199, 201
Stover's Chapel A.M.E. Church, 31
strike-wave of 1934, 90, 91, 95
Strong, Edward, 158–59
Stuart, J.G., 65
Student Nonviolent Coordinating Committee (SNCC). *See* SNCC
Sullivan, Patricia, 139
Summerton, S.C., 192, 193, 194, 199, 203, 204, 209
Summerton NAACP, 185. *See also* Clarendon County NAACP
Sumter, S.C., 129, 136, 218
Sumter NAACP, 195, 197, 217; role in South Carolina State Conference of NAACP Branches, 117, 119
Sunbeam Bread, 216
Sweetwater Sabre Club, 5
Syracuse University (N.Y.), 149

Taft-Hartley Act, 174
Talbert, James, 51
Talented Tenth, 76
Talladega College (Ala.), 115
Tampa, Fla., 24
Tappan, Lewis, 35

Tappan School. *See* Avery Normal Institute
Tennessee Valley Authority (TVA), 75
Terrell, Mary Church, 9, 37
Texarcana, Tex., 159
Texas, 54, 55, 106, 115, 133, 134, 166, 211
textile industry, 6, 16, 53, 60, 82, 87, 90, 91, 95, 96, 104
Textile Workers Organizing Committee (TWOC), 95, 101
Textile Workers Union of America (TWUA). *See* TWUA
Thirteenth Amendment, 2, 3
Thomasville NAACP (Ga.), 55
Thompson, Albert N., 130
Thurmond, Strom, 179, 180
Tillman, Benjamin, 5, 15, 56, 57
Tinkham Bill, 32
Tobacco Stemmers and Laborers Union (TSLU), 161
Tobacco Workers International Union (TWIU), 152–53, 174
Tolbert, Joseph, 7, 87, 104, 138
Tolbert, Willie, 210
To Secure These Rights, 182
Township Auditorium, 164
Trade Union Unity League (TUUL), 148
Treaty of Versailles, 50
Trinity Methodist Church, 183
Truman, Harry S., 139, 149, 174, 177–78, 180, 182
Truth, Sojourner, 37
Tubman, Harriet, 37
Turner, Viola, 38
Tuskegee University (Ala.), 161
TWUA (Textile Workers Union of America), 95, 101–4

UNIA (Universal Negro Improvement Organization), 63–64, 70; in Charleston, 64; effectiveness of, 64
Union, S.C., 58
Union Leagues, 4
United Automobile Workers, 227
United Cannery, Agricultural, Packing, and Allied Workers of America (UCAPAWA-CIO), 147, 148, 161. *See also* FTA

United Mine Workers of America (UMWA), 165
United Nations, 189
United Steel Workers of America (USWA), 165, 174
United Textile Workers (UTW), 91, 95. *See also* TWUA
Universal Negro Improvement Organization (UNIA). *See* UNIA
University of Chicago (Ill.), 92
University of Iowa, 93
University of North Carolina, Chapel Hill, 91, 100, 151
University of South Carolina: Medical College Hospital, 226; school of law, 128–29
University of Virginia, 159
Urban League. *See* National Urban League
U.S. Congress, 32, 43, 56, 75, 139, 164, 177, 222; Eightieth session, 165, 173, 174
U.S. Constitution, 2, 3, 9, 13, 134, 182, 183. *See also* Fifteenth Amendment; and Fourteenth Amendment
U.S. Supreme Court, 1, 6, 75, 134, 178, 202, 206. *See also Brown v. Board of Education; Plessy v. Ferguson;* and *Smith v. Allwright*

Valentine, Florence, 167
Veterans of Foreign Wars, 89
Victory Savings Bank, 210
Vietnam War, 226
Villard, Oswald Garrison, 9
violence, 21, 42, 54, 58, 61, 68, 87, 90–91, 103–5, 156; *See also* Charleston Race Riot; Hamburg Massacre; Ku Klux Klan; lynching; Orangeburg Massacre; Phoenix Race Riot; and Wilmington Race Riot
Virginia, 61, 197. *See also* Arlington, Va.; Jackson Ward; Norfolk, Va.; Richmond, Va.; University of Virginia; and Virginia Union
Virginia Union, 159
voting. *See* black voting

Voting Rights Act of 1965, 219, 222, 225, 228

Wagner, Robert F., 71
Wagner Act, 95, 148
Wald, Lillian, 9
Walker, James, Jr., 156
Wallace, Henry, 139, 149, 165
Wallace, Sam, 65
Walling, William English, 9
Walton, Rebecca Hull, 30
Warburg, Felix Schiff, 74
Warburg, Freida Schiff, 74
Waring, J. Waties, 129, 130, 176–79, 180, 204–6. *See also Briggs v. Elliott; Brown v. Baskin;* and *Elmore v. Rice*
Warren, Earl, 206
Washington, Booker T., 9, 15, 19, 20, 25
Washington, D.C., 21, 36, 40, 62, 151, 177, 216
Wells-Barnett, Ida B., 9
"We Shall Overcome," origins of, 150–51
Wesley United Methodist Church, 68, 111, 114, 120
Weston, Annie Belle, 162
What the Negro Wants, 123
White, Deborah Gray, 19, 36
White, Josh, 165
White, Walter, 10, 32, 85, 110, 127, 188, 190, 191; as NAACP assistant secretary, 72; as NAACP secretary, 72–74, 80–81
White Citizens' Council, 207–8, 209, 215–17
white primary, 16, 47, 49, 101, 193; battle against, 10, 101, 105, 115, 128, 133–44, 167, 175–81, 220, 224. *See also Brown v. Baskin;* Democratic National Convention; *Elmore v. Rice;* NCC; PDP; and *Smith v. Allwright*
Wilkerson, Doxey, 189
Wilkins, Roy, 10, 74, 87
Wilkinson, Marion Birnie, 36, 37, 90
Wilkinson, Robert Shaw, 36
Williams, Aubrey, 151
Williams, Hosea, 227

Williams, J.C., 99, 101, 102. *See also* "Baby NAACP"
Williams, Ransome J., 171
Williamson, James, 51
Wilmington Race Riot, 7
Wilson, Woodrow, 50
Winnsboro, S.C., 156
Winston-Salem, N.C., 148, 175
Woodard, Isaac, 156, 176
Woods, Barbara, 132
Woodson, Carter G., 35
Woodward, C. Vann, 17
Workers' Alliance, 99. *See also* "Baby NAACP"
Worker's Defense League, 102, 103
Works Progress Administration (WPA), 95. *See also* "Baby NAACP"; and Workers' Alliance
World War I, 12, 18, 21, 22, 31, 34, 39, 48, 60, 61, 63, 70, 83, 96, 104, 108, 115, 129, 130, 191

World War II, 11, 12, 124, 137, 143, 145, 165, 196, 203, 223
Wright, Alonzo W., 120–21
Wright, Arthur Jerome, 119
Wright, Louis T., 78
Wright, Minnie Ida, 192, 204
Wrighten, John H., 176, 177, 181
Wrighten v. Board of Trustees of the University of South Carolina (1947), 176–77

Yamassee NAACP, 185
Young, Andrew, 227
Young Turks, 78–86, 158, 188, 200, 224. *See also* Ralph J. Bunche; and Abram L. Harris
Young Women's Christian Association (YWCA), 17, 37, 89, 161, 220